SOME OF MY BEST FRIENDS ARE

NAKED

Tim Keefe

BARBARY
COAST
PRESS

SAN FRANCISCO

Published in the United States by Barbary Coast Press, P.O. Box 425367, San Francisco, California 94142-5367.

First Printing, January, 1993

Printed in the United States
Cover art, illustrations & design: Rick Covell
Photo: Bill Turner
Type Setting: Richie Moore
Logo Art: Rick Covell

Cataloging-in-Publication Data

(Prepared by Quality Books Inc.)

Keefe, Timothy P., 1948-
    Some of my best friends are naked : interviews with seven erotic
dancers / Tim Keefe
    p. cm.
    ISBN 0-9634466-0-6
    1. Stripteasers--Interviews. 2. Sex oriented business--United States
I. Title
PN1949.S7K44 1992   306.742
                                           QB192-20051

Library of Congress Catalog Card Number 92-073661
ISBN 0-9634466-0-6

San Francisco

© 1993 by Tim Keefe

SOME OF MY BEST FRIENDS ARE

ACKNOWLEDGMENTS

I t has taken nearly eight years to create this book and many good people have helped along the way. My sincerest apology to those whose names have been lost.

The openess of my co-workers and their commitment to communicating in the interest of creating understanding have made this book possible. Thank you Minx Manx, Ann More, Lilith, Phoenix, Lusty Lipps, Attilla The Honey, Jackie, Angel, Aubergine, Carmen, Celeste, Ebony, Emily, Felicia, Gia, Jorhan, Kat, Lee, Lisa, Little Bit, Lili, Lolly, Mariko, Maya, Myra, Paula, Puff, Raven, Ronalle, Shawna, Silver, Tara, Timitia, Whitney, Zena, Tim, Zoe, Diamond, Honey, Missy, Monique, Passion, Nikki, Penny, Ivy, Juliette, Justine, Mikeh, Dawn, Pauli, Sparkle, Valuez, Sheena, Song-hi, Uvonne, Crystal, Dominque, Barbarella, Yonni, Sugar, Pip, Rhoena, Rene, Bambi, Kenny, Becky, Colette, Athena, Alice, CoCo, Goldie, Jo, Leggs, Nicki, Sissy, Snow, Kisa, Cinnamon, Marilyn, Hot Chocolate, Roxanne, Rebecca, Piers, Zoranna, BamBam, Blondie, Diane, Rose, Sheila, Desi Whitewitch, Aurora, Amber, Angie, Birdie, Christine, Bari, Brigette, Ginger, Jasmine, Mycki, Alan, Storm, Artemis, Jewel, Maria, Eddie, Mercy, Opal, Morgan, Mirage, Pegasus, Manny, Sade, Sasha, Sidney, Tiffany, Tristan, Venus, Zshilda, John, Carole, Vicki, Asia, Britt, Candy, Egypt, Cereage, Luscious, Lydia, Mandy, Noel, Circe, Vampira, Pleasure, Marxie, Suzanne, Slim, Susie, Star, Desiree, Persephone, Dean, Scooter, Angelique, Camron, Benita, Ingrid, Lucy, Paul, Vega, Cassandra, Uschi, David, Bonita, Cat, Brandy, Carrera, Clair, Sugar, Willie, Ginger, Lena, Nicole, Cat, Kitten, Greg, Scotty, Sandi, Tanya, Doug, Ebony, Kristaki, Mirana, Princess, Barbi, Tama, Billie Jean, Darrell, Ivory, Sonja, Tasha, Sonia, Jamie Lee, Savage, Pat, Malissa, Juicy, Lynde Lee, Jenee, Sylvie, Asia, Blue, Jane, Gypsy Rose, Rial, Lolita, Mark, Jack, Meryl, Mercy, Squishy, Red, Shey, Sister Eko Plasma, Tracy, BeBe, Michael, Mimi, Chrissy, Eve, Deborah, Gardenia, Jingles, Glenn, Giselle, Pinky, Scarlett, Brooklyn, Obsession, Dave, Jade, Katie, Tana, Joi, Keri, Lily, D.J., Fass, Avrielle, Chastity, Cherriluv, China Blue, Chloe, Cricket, Eleanor M., Euphrates, Exene, Fiona, Gabrielle, Golden, Brian, Heavenly, Chris, Keisha, La Meme Fromage, Lilla, Lizzabella, Lulu, M'Dena, Samantha, Sasha, Shi, Danny, Silk, Sistar Aqua Divina, Charles, Sly, Sunny, Sybil, Taos, Tawdry, Vallhalla, Wanda, Raggedy Boop, Pandora, Peter, Arp Quazar, Astrid, Babette, Beauty Heart, Belle, Brittney, Cathy, Chicklet, Chizoola, Dizney, Gemini, Gina, Velveeta, Joe, Sandi, Kali, Magdelene, Magenta, Marcel, Max, Nimuelle, Peaches, Persia, Pet, Pixie, Polyester, Rag Doll, Rage, Sabina, Ken, Sacred Amnesia, Seraghina, Serene, Tess, Tralala, Josh, Ursula, Virginia Dentata, Vixen Bliss, ZZ, Wilshe, Sauvage, Seldom, Flavor, Alex, Wayne,

Cherry Koolaide, Jezebel, Johanna, Shakti, Kelli, Kismet, Micah, Stealth, Luna Savant, Cranberry, Wasabi, and Insertia.

The same thanks is extended to the countless number of customers who shared the worker's commitment to communication.

Without Bob hiring me and without the theater owner's openess and unwavering support this book would not exist. Thank you gentlemen.

I extend my gratitude to the management for making my observation post so comfortable during my tenure from January 20, 1985 to January 20, 1991.

The transcription and production of the manuscript were daunting tasks. They were mastered and managed by Anonymous. For the past five years Anonymous has deepened my understanding of our species and provided this project with consistently unerring editorial insight.

The first to transcribe, and under the most primitive conditions, was my oldest friend and supporter Mary Jo Mish. Her support and that of Malcom Shelley and Becky Stone sustained me when little support was forthcoming from people other than my co-workers.

I am grateful to Holly Metz for her help in developing some of the first questions. And to Professors Bertram Gross and F.M. Christensen for their inspiration and encouragement.

Transcribers and typists Mary Uhland, Debbie Platt, Gail Taylor, Christine Nakata, Frances Nakata, Kevin Barrett, Debra Innis, Ellen Carr, Merri Gong, and Maureen Sullivan proved once again the inestimable value of the transcribers art.

My thanks go to Professor D.W., Howard L., Gayle Doss Green, Karla Von Hungen, George Puffett, and Dave, Joe, Andy and Sean from Muther's Recording Studio for their friendship and support in producing the manuscript.

My deep appreciation and many thanks to Rick Covell for his great eye and hand as well as his generous friendship. And to Dr. Richie Moore for mastering *QUARK* right on time.

I am indebted to Kathy Dugle Goodman, Dave Musgrove, and Carol Queen for their many insightful editorial comments and proof reading.

Finally I want to express my deep appreciation for the on-call editorial advice of Robert L. Goodman and Professors Zohreh Emami and John Davis.

For my sons JASON and CHRISTOPHER and for SHELISHA in the hope that they and their generation truly see and hear each other.

And for Eroica, whose support and patience made this book possible.

CONTENTS

A BOOK BY ITS COVER

In the spring of 1972, while employed as a community mental health worker, I was exposed to the tragic consequences of the unthinking, fearful, and bigoted methods that we often use in our attempts to know and judge each other. Particularly when sexuality is involved.

I was leaving the grounds of a 19th century provincial madhouse hidden deep in the Michigan countryside when I came upon a circle of four or five grandmotherly types speaking quietly with each other. The content and feeling of their speech was reminiscent of my ancient aunts gathered and chatting at our yearly farm family reunions. The blue sky overhead and the warm breeze seemed of interest to these gentle creatures in cotton print dresses, along with the aches and pains of age and recent meals.

As I moved slowly past this mid-afternoon coffee klatch my tuned ear waited for the telltale signs of madness advertised as the price of admission to these out-of-sight out-of-mind places. But, if the evidence appeared, it was after I drove off, heading back to the office wondering why these women were locked up and how long it had been.

Appalling answers to these questions awaited me.

My supervisor, who had been one of the institution's clinical psychologists, told me that these women were in for being sexual! He made it clear also that they had many sisters-in-crime similarly confined throughout the land. And that it had been decades for most of them.

Remember Frances Farmer.

In their teens and twenties— for some, fifty plus years ago— these young unmarried women were caught in the act with their lovers. Victorian community standards and law, and the state of understanding of what it is to be human labeled them sick and demanded their removal from proper society.

Outrageous!

It became clear again that day, if all the days of the Vietnam War hadn't been enough, that ignorance, fear, hatred, and the desire for power over others can and does lead to calamity. It was driven home with horror that *you can't always tell a book by its cover.*

Not everyone in the nuthouse is nuts.

Some people are just out of favor and out of luck.

Early in 1985, thirteen years after having these truths underlined and three months before the Meese Commission On Pornography began its work, I spent my first day in the presence of a group of women who the Victorians of our day label in much the same way and if given the chance would surely usher off to the same fate.

It was my first day (of what would be exactly six years) on the job and I was behind the scenes, backstage at a San Francisco peep show. And I was seeing something I hadn't seen before, something that a lot of us in our culture haven't seen, a roomful of the opposite sex — naked, or well on the way. G- strings, cupless bras, garterbelts, scarves on the midriff, or earrings, high heels and nothing else. What an amazing sight! But on this day I was not amazed by what I was listening to.

I knew going in that all too often sex workers are labeled, one dimensionally, as from dysfunctional families (the average family?), as fallen women, and as drug addicts. Victims who are re-victimizing themselves. Losers. The Lost. What other kind of women could possibly be sexual publicly? Well, of course, some think there *might* be a few who are marginally okay, but usually you're not led to expect much in the way of stability, self-esteem, and intelligence, much less your equal or better.

Their conversations immediately betrayed these stereotypes and attempts to mystify and dehumanize them. In spite of their lack of clothes and the job they were doing the women were talking about the weather, food, money, relationships, children, work, sex, art, politics. Anything. Just like you and I. Each came off, for better or worse, as individual as her fingerprints.

That's what this book is about. Our uniqueness/our sameness, the inevitable complexity of life behind the labels we pin on each other, *and ourselves.*

Yes, the women describe, in vivid detail, dancing nude and having intimate contact, through the quarter-operated peep show windows, with customers in darkened booths who may be enjoying themselves sexually. They even tell us about their sex lives. But they tell us so much more.

They tell us that they are real people with real lives. And that their full humanity has to be recognized for there to be any meaningful discussion of their work. They tell us about our shared lives. About ourselves. About the world we inhabit and the struggles that confront all of us.

—Tim Keefe, October 1992

Photo: Bill Turner

MINX MANX

*I DON'T THINK ANY TWO PEOPLE ARE JUST THE
SAME IN THEIR SEXUALITY AND THE IDEA THAT
THEY OUGHT TO BE IS REALLY PERNICIOUS.*

Part of the promotion for your show says, "Live Nude Dancing, Lovely Lusty Ladies, Naked Naughty Nasty." Is this a good description of who you are and how you perform at work? ~ It's a good partial description. Certainly the "Lovely, Lusty, Naughty, Nasty" talk about fantasy and at work I'm working off a fantasy. I guess for some folks it's just a job, but to me it's part of my erotic playtime. And I'm checking out who are the people and what are they doing on the other side of that window. It's my anthropology. There isn't anything on the sign that says "lovely, anthropological nymphette will be watching you as hard as you're watching her," although I suppose some folks know that. It's about a fantasy of women who want to show off for all the guys who walk in. And yeah, part of that's true for me. The role of the place is purveying fantasy.

What were you told was your job? ~ I didn't come in cold, I knew one of the managers. I knew about the stage and the booths and that my job was to erotically dance, tease, and titilate the people watching. And that I was to be pleasant, sexy, lighthearted, sleazy, nasty, whatever fit that day.

By the time I came around, this theater had changed a little bit from the place portrayed by the other interviewees in this book. Besides the stage, there was a talk-booth in which a woman sat behind a glass and lured customers into a booth on the other side of another glass window. Once inside there would be complete privacy for the two of them. I knew that I would be dancing like the rest of the women in the book, but that I would be going into the talk-booth also.

I was taken to the booth and into the red carpeted cubicle, where I would tantalize the customers to come in and be with me and put some dollars through the slot. I would be in this 4 x 4 space for four hours a shift, two hours at a shot. Behind the cubicle there was a private hallway, and a place for a glass of water, my lipstick and things. Inside the cubicle there was room to lean up on pillows. I was shown the in's and out's of seeing how much money a customer put in and clicking in the appropriate number of minutes for his stay, after which time the red light would go on and I would have to say, "Do you want to stay with me a little longer?" The primary difference between the stage and talk-booth is that in the talk-booth the customer can get more ongoing private interaction. The focus of the theater is, in my opinion, voyeurism and masturbation. The talk-booth was much more clearly set up for an interactive mutual jack-off.

Were you told that the men masturbate? ~ I was told, but I knew before I was told. If I was a guy that's what I would do.

Describe your first experience on stage. ~ It was not an audition, I was thrown out there for real the first time. There was a real level of over-whelm – "Oh my God, all these things are happening at once here." I don't have my one-on-one private naughty talk forum any longer. It's mirrors, lights, music, and booths with faces, and other women close by. It's overwhelming, but not in a negative way at all. There's not one person to interact with erotically but several. There are more pussies than mine on view. So my first time on stage was about getting used to all that and figuring out the optimal ways to approach customers and the ways that I could best pose and tease without putting too much strain on my body.

Describe how you dance, display, and touch your body during your stage performance. ~ I start out actually dancing. It warms me up. There's a lot of posing, vogueing, showing off, and sticking my pussy up as close to the window as I can get it. I watch myself in the mirror – it's voyeurism and exhibitionism at the same time. That's fun. I pick customers to interact with and depending on their energy, I'll be somewhat desultory and save my energy. I'll show pussy, pose, and do mostly eye contact interaction, or else get into pretty active masturbation. Partly because it's hot for me to be there and it makes time go more quickly to be actually erotic rather than potentially erotic, or to be an erotic subject rather than an erotic object. Because it turns me on to be an erotic object and an erotic subject, I go, more often than not, to the corner booths where there's a ledge and I can do a lot of body movement. I kneel, lean back on one hand and display my upper torso, arched back. I masturbate with my other hand 'til it gets tired. It's really bad for the spine, so I get up and do something else for awhile.

I've learned how to get my whole body much more involved in my active eroticism and orgasm. I do cum on stage and it can be just from undulating and moving my hips rather than putting my finger there and wiggling it. That's how I was masturbating when I first got there. A lot of times people have to remind me to take my break.

What sexual depictions do you perform? ~ Depictions of reality. I do masturbation. It's fun to spread my legs, bend my knees, and pretend to be on top during a fuck. I do it to the air or place my palm against my ass and fuck my own fingers. I key into the men who are masturbating to make the situation mutual. It turns it into an overtly sexual situation for me. I wanted to be an erotic performer to be erotic, more than to perform. More often than not, the sexual and orgasmic depictions and the actual orgasmic faces are the stuff that I go for, probably because if I was on the other side of the window that's the stuff I would like to watch. "Do unto others what you would have others do unto you."

Does your performance contain elements of dominance and submission? ~
More often submission. That's more natural to me right now. I have used the
talk-booth fruitfully to work on my dominance play but submission is always
easier, since what I do is coming from my sexuality, not my idea of what
someone else thinks my sexuality ought to be. Of course, I'm willing to play
fantasies with people who want me to do something that isn't what I would do
automatically. When I'm in the talk-booth being given directions is more of a
turn-on.

My first day I got a clue that that would be part of my job, part of my adventure. The customer was wonderful, very clear. He put money in the talk-
booth slot and said, "I like to do dominance. Some of the girls don't like it,
do you?" I said, "Yeah, I do." And he said, "Okay, I like to tell you to do
things and use abusive language. Are you willing to hear that?" I said,
"Yeah. Since you're being clear." It's a different matter when someone's
being clear and obviously negotiating, "Are you willing to?" We had quite a
hot little scene. Then he got off his nasty, mean demeanor and said, "Thank
you very much," very sweetly and left.

When I want to eroticize things for myself more, I run fantasies of "Oh, I
have to do this. Ooo, isn't this nasty, someone's thrown me into this mirrored
room and is making me do things." It's fun and the only person I'm playing
with right then is myself. It's an entirely masturbatory fantasy at that point.

Eye contact with customers is very important to some dancers. Is it for you?
~ Yeah, yeah. When I get into an erotic exchange with a customer who is shy
or nervous around eye contact, it's less hot for me because I'm not getting the
feedback I do when somebody's gazing deeply into my eyes and the "window
of the soul" thing is happening. When "the window of the soul" thing happens through a window it's very sexy. When it doesn't, it's like "Well, yeah,
this is kind of fun." That's when I look at myself in the mirror.

Why did you choose the stage name you use? ~ Initially I was going to use
the name I use when I'm writing semi-autobiographical erotic fiction, Kitty.
But there were already a Cat and a Kitten. Minx came to me as a flash on
that. I read some years ago *A Confederacy of Dunces*, in which the hero is
always referring to a woman as "that little minx." I thought "Yeah, I'll be that
little minx." So, I'm Minx Manx. Manx is another cat name. The stage name
adds to the erotic play.

How do you use costuming and makeup? ~ To delineate the erotic and the
peep show person. It's rare that I put on makeup before I get to the theater.
It's a ritual of "Here I am now and I'm going to go out there and do this
thing." I use it to present my most erotic face. The way women are "supposed to" use makeup. I don't use makeup that way ordinarily. In the theater

the eroticism is very much that traditionally made-up female, with a lot of twists like the tattoos, the "rebel girl" energy that so many dancers carry, and I use makeup to enter that world. I use makeup to become the woman I never wanted to be because you're *supposed* to. And now, I can choose to be that kind of woman for my own purposes and my own eroticism.

I use costuming to be playful, to tease with. It seems to be more erotic to have a little something on than nothing most of the time, even if it's only high heels. I wear a wig because management asked me to. It was perceived that my hair was too short, that I was too boyish-looking to lure people in. I didn't have this long hair that men theoretically love. I'd never worn a wig before so that was just playtime. That's the first step into the somewhat altered state that erotic performance is for me. I probably couldn't just stand on a street corner and start doing what I do. Maybe I could, but it wouldn't be the same if I didn't have the face of the erotic dancer. Quarter-a-pop harlot. (Laughs)

Do drugs play a part in your performance? ~ Absolutely not. I don't do a lot of drugs or alcohol outside so I certainly don't do it inside.

On stage music plays almost continuously. Describe the variety and part it plays in your performance. ~ I dance to everything from rap to soul to punk to Patsy Cline to Sonny and Cher, for God's sake. It's hard for me to be erotic to heavy metal. That's more for the biker-slut rebel girls. Music from the sixties gives me flashes of growing into a pubertal sexual person and creaming over The Doors, "Ooo ooo, that's a song about sex, I can tell." I get to go back and talk to that 10 or 11-year-old girl who's beginning to wonder what it might be like to get fucked. Those are my favorites, and the stuff that's been sexy for me over the last ten years or so, Bryan Ferry, Berlin, and Madonna. I get to be as sexy as I ever wanted to be on the dance floor and never quite could 'cause it's not okay to take your clothes off there. I get to play it all the way out when the music comes on. And sometimes if a song has the right beat, I can get off without rubbing my clit and that's pretty profound. I don't know if that makes me a groupie or what. It gives you a whole new appreciation of music. (Laughs)

The stage is covered with mirrors ceiling to floor. What role do they play in your work? ~ Often I dance to and for myself and I use the mirrors to watch others surreptitiously, a lot. Often I'm surrounded by lesbian and bisexual women, so when I want to be lustful, which I am pretty constantly, I do it through the mirrors so that it's not in their face.

Describe the interaction and commentary among the dancers on stage. ~ More often than not the comment is brief and focused on something that's happening with one woman and a customer, or somebody who just left, or something in a song. One way of communicating that's not against the rules is to sing along. If somebody's feeling tired or blue, or not up for being there right then, we'll try to tease her into liking it a little better. There is always a certain amount of bitching like on any job. The comments are much more reflective of the full range of real life than they would be in other places. You really want to be able to talk because the women are interesting and you want to find out more about them. Talk on stage is thought unconducive to the erotic enjoyment of the customers and I'm sure it is, for the most part. A lot more conversation wants to happen than ever does.

Is there competition among the dancers on stage? ~ I'm not aware of any.

Is there humor on stage? ~ Lots and lots. Hey, I don't know if any of us thought we were going to grow up and get naked and have guys jack-off to us for a job. I mean, that's kind of funny, isn't it? (Laughs) Occasionally, humor is shared about a particularly sweet, amusing, strange, or goofy interaction with a customer, or "at a customer's expense" to make us feel better when somebody has been weird, rude, or abusive. This is an edgy place to work, an edgy place to live, an edgy kind of job to do. If somebody disrupts the unspoken rule of "We're all civilized people doing something that the outside world would come down on us for" (and all of us, workers and customers, are nervous about that), if somebody disrupts the "Let's all be nice together and do this fantasy and get you off and get us paid," then we're going to make fun of the bastard when he leaves. Maybe before he leaves, although that's not nice.

Is the myth of the perfect body perpetuated here? ~ It's more like the myth of the perfect range of body. Women who don't come close enough to the middle point of the bell curve, the slim, sexy, pretty, small-titted or busty lusty whatever, if they get too old or too chubby or too this or too that, or let their appearance go beyond a certain point, those women will get feedback and dismissed sometimes. It happens throughout the industry. It would be real nice if customers got a chance to experience a wider range of eroticism, a chance to know how sexy big fat women and older women can be. It would be nice if women were allowed to think of ourselves, the whole range of us, as potentially just as sexy as the pretty 20-year-olds that get the most attention at places like this. It would be real nice if that were true; it's not and the place reflects it.

What can you do on stage that you can't do off stage? ~ It's rare off stage that I get as totally focused on as I am on stage. People go to this place where it's okay to stare. The only situations in real life where I feel as focused on erotically in the same kind of way is when I'm doing private erotic dancing for my lover or putting on a show-off show. I guess the answer is I can be an object in a different way that is very sexy for me.

What won't you do on stage? ~ The things that we're not supposed to do, "live girl-girl tit and pussy action" – more's the pity, I might add. Although in the talk-booth we do occasional girl-girl "cram a couple of hot cookies into a little four by four box and see what happens" shows. There we can pretty much do anything we want. I try to be sensible about possible bugs the other woman and I could be passing to each other and not be messin' in menstrual blood.

There hasn't been anything yet that a talk-booth customer requested that I would not do. It's hard for me to pee in a cup. Some girls are good at that, I'm not. (Laughs) The only time I won't do something in the booth or on stage is when I'm directed in a rude and insensitive manner. When somebody doesn't get it that it's another living breathing smart human being interacting for his pleasure and education, and for her pleasure and a paycheck, and is an asshole and treats me like I'm a piece of hamburger, he is asked to go away. I won't be treated like shit. Doesn't pay enough. (Laughs)

Do you dance for co-workers and friends? ~ A little bit. There is something about safe space in the theater. There's something about contextual behavior, this is what's supposed to be happening, look, it's happening all around me, I'll do it too. There's a flow in the theater that, for me, doesn't exist in other places. When I dance for somebody in another context, it makes me more vulnerable, and therefore, either more likely to feel silly or extremely powerful and hot.

Do you ever do sex education on stage? ~ Absolutely. "This is a dick. Look." The most common piece of sex education I do is communicating with people who are interested in seeing me play with my pussy after I do anal play. "No, no, no, you don't mix pussy and asshole." As far as I can tell, infinitely large numbers of people don't know about asshole bugs getting into the vagina and causing trouble.

When I do overt hand on my pussy masturbation that's always sex education. That's a close-up view for a man of what a woman actually does to do herself. And if he hangs at the theater enough he'll get a chance to see a whole bunch of women doing different things to please themselves.

In the booth often the sex education has to do with G-spot activity because when I masturbate a lot of times I squirt and guys go, "Did you fake that? How did you do that? What did you just do? What? Huh?" I get to do the "Have you ever heard of a G-spot?" routine. "Well, this is what I just did and that's how it happens," and I tell them about

Skene's glands and their cocks fall down. (Laughs) If the person is really interested in finding out, I'm glad to tell him and he can go home and surprise his wife.

How does having your period affect your performance? ~ I just stick my Tampax string up inside me. (Laughs) If I'm having cramps it becomes extremely important to take medication or else it's a big drag. In the booth I need to be careful about putting dildos inside me when I am using a Tampax. It seems important not to be all bloody. It's some people's turn-on and other people's turn-off, so, perpetuating the vision of unreality that the sex industry, at least in part, has us perpetuate, women never have their period in peep shows.

I was quite surprised when I first heard that healing occurs here, women healing themselves, each other, and customers. Describe what you know about this. ~ It's profoundly healing for some women, me included, to take charge of their own eroticism in such a public way. To be able to say to yourself, "Me and my sexiness are going to get in a box and hang out there for all to see for several hours at a stretch" is a profound piece of work and that really is how I have experienced it.

It has done worlds for my performance anxiety. I've learned to be sexually spontaneous in a way that I never was before. I've learned to cum through visual stimulus, talking dirty, and humping the air. It's made me more orgasmic, which is always healing. None of us know what it would be like to have as much sex as we ever wanted because we don't have time, we don't have permission. I get a lot more time and permission in the booth than I get anywhere else. That's been real healing. Good sex is healing.

Any woman who steps across the line to do overt sex industry work has gotten shit from somebody about it. Most probably from herself. We do a lot of "staffing" about that, as therapists would say, we help each other feel good about it. I don't know what we're all going to think twenty years down the line, but right now we can be together and give each other support for being non-traditional women, for being women outlaws truly. This culture has always thought of women who sell it and women who are slutty and women who want it all the time as not really okay. They idolize us and they want to chase our ass but we are not okay.

Often women who come here have never been in a space that's so female before. We're surrounded by hard dicks but we're on stage together and it's about tits and pussies and girl smell and women being erotic. It's funny to watch women who aren't accustomed to female sexuality start to get a clue. (Laughs) There's a lot of lesbian fantasy that gets brought a lot closer to reality cause we are being sexual together, and how could you not notice? (Laughs)

I think men come to places like the theater more than anything else to be in an environment where someone will tell them it's okay to have a hard-on. To want to look at it, and to want it. And there's no place in the world out there, including a lot of marriages and primary relationships, where people get the signal it's okay to want it. It's okay to want it in the middle of the morning when you've got your business suit on, damn it, it's okay to want it when you just got done painting a Victorian and you're taking your lunch break. It's okay to want it when you're wearing your rubber slicker and you just got off a boat down at the Wharf and you stumbled in in your thigh boots. I had this fucking guy come in in his rubber slicker and thigh boots – I'm going, "Whoa, I'm jackin'-off with Captain Ahab. This is amazing!" (Laughs) "Hey, did you catch Moby Dick or what?" And so often what they want is not just orgasm, is not just jackin'-off, it's not just to get their dick hard, it's to talk about eroticism, and sex and feelings. To talk about the fuckin' weather, to just talk to somebody.

What are they in there for, if it's not about some kind of healing? Some kind that I probably can't even put my finger on. Something about just interacting with a woman, a person. A lot of guys come in to do just what the sign says, to talk to a live nude girl. And I think all of that is healing.

This culture doesn't let us have our sexuality, and whether it's because of culture or hormone surges, guys get reminded of theirs a whole lot and feel like they have to get put down and shut down around their sex in order to be productive members of society and good husbands and not pester their wives too much, and damn it, they want a place where they can go and just have it. And more than anything else, that's what the theater and places like it are about. That's what it's about for me. That's especially true of guys who have divergent sexual interests, who want to show off their lacy panties and garter belt to somebody. My favorite guy can stick his dick up his own ass. He wants to show off to somebody. He wears a wedding ring and I bet his wife doesn't know he can do that. Just imagine bursting into the bathroom one morning to get your nylons drying on the towel rack and going, "Honey, uh, what are you doing?" (Laughs) The guys who want you to watch them suck themselves off. The guys who want to play with submission and age play and incest play and want to call me Mommy. And women, too, occasionally we get a woman who is there for the eroticism. Sometimes couples share that. All those people get told by our culture, their partners, by everybody that it's not real okay to be sexy and turned on the way they are and so they've got to find a place where they can have that, where people won't turn them away and shut 'em down and tell them they're wrong and bad and sick and evil. I really think that these people use peep shows for a kind of healing, a kind of affirmation.

And I in turn, because I am obviously a sexually divergent woman, both in my exhibitionism and the fact that I am really turned on to doing this stuff, because I'm a sex worker, because I'm a former overt out lesbian and still am quite queer in the *global* queer sexual sense, because I'm into S&M and dominance and submission, because I'm into watching and being watched, talking and being talked to and finding out all the little byways of sex that women aren't supposed to *know* about, much less practice and see if they can get good at – I'm just as divergent as those guys are. They're coming in to be with me and trust me with their sex, and their desire reaffirms me in mine. I doubt they know that they're doing that for me, but *I* know, and I know that I'm doing it for them. And every once in a while a man will be very clear, like the dominance guy who said, after he got off and stopped being nasty to me and calling me a dirty cunt, "It's so good that you people are here doing this." Just the kind of voice he would tell the waiter to please convey his compliments to the chef, you know? Same thing, same thing. "Please let everybody doing this know that we appreciate you for being here, and giving us something that we can't get other places." I know plenty of people who have well-rounded sexual relationships who started out by understanding that they could get that by visiting peep shows, by seeing prostitutes and getting it that somebody would want to fuck them or talk to them or see them or let them watch. Yeah, there's a lot of healing.

I am very clear that I am like one of the priestesses of the Goddess back in the temples of the Middle East, way before Yahweh showed up and took over, whose spiritual gift was to be there for any man who walked in to see the face of the Goddess. We're showing the face of the Goddess in a culture that doesn't believe in the Goddess anymore.

Have you had any transcendent moments on stage? ~ The first time I went into a real serious "no hands" orgasm was pretty transcendent. My body and my consciousness and the eroticism that unites the two are learning new ways of being from doing what I do here.

My most recent moment of transcendence was at 2:30 a.m. Sunday morning, right before the end of my shift. I had been in the talk-booth off and on for five hours, masturbating the whole time. Seeing many, many cocks, seeing many, many squirts, which is hot for me, all this stuff is real hot for me. Seeing lots of guys from different walks of life, really getting into that priestess, sacred whore energy. I did thirty minutes of tantric sex with my last customer, with "no hands" orgasms for both of us, connecting our breath and our eyes and cumming together. He was obviously a little more adept than the average dude, unless my energy was very special that night. He would see me run my hand along my thigh or my foot and start to cum. I have never cum from the bottom of my foot before, that was a real treat. I tried both feet to see if it worked on both sides and it did. He kept saying, "You have this amazing control over your sexuality," and I said, "What's happening right now is I have no control at all. I'm just *in* the sex."

I do this with my lover occasionally and it's profound then, but when it happens with a stranger in a sex palace, boy oh boy, if it's not transcendent, what is it? It's about being in a river of erotic feeling and sex versus sticking your toe in. When my body has been orgasming for hours and hours it knows something that my conscious mind doesn't. All of us could learn a little something from our bodies if we would just take the leash off and let it show us those things. It's one of the profound things about being in a place where you're just allowed to be about sex.

Do you ever feel caged or wish you could cover up? ~ Occasionally I wish I could cover up. It happens when I get fatigued and I look at my body and go "Uggh." I come from the same great contemporary American tradition of thinking my body is not okay as every other woman.

In the booth (laughs), when I have the curtain to the hallway open I feel like I'm in the Monterey Bay Aquarium, bumping up against the glass waiting for somebody to put a quarter into a machine that gives them a couple of sardines to fling to me, *then* I feel caged. It's probably the least pleasant feeling I've experienced at the theater. It's being unable to interact with the people from *me*, from my truth, from my voice.

Many of the dancers say that they prefer this closed type of stage and see it as safe and fun because of the absence of physical contact with the customers. How do you feel? ~ Part of what is very erotic to me about being in the booth is being in the booth. I like having the glass not so much because it keeps customers away, but because it's a heightened level of kink. It's another piece to erotically play off. Because I have less intimacy with the customers on stage, I don't so much eroticize the windows there. I often feel that it wouldn't make a lot of difference to me if those guys were sitting in chairs around the edge of the stage.

I do know that I have a different level of freedom and different sense of being myself in myself working without physical contact, than I would if I was at one of the theaters where lap-dancing happens. It feels like I have more "personal space" at this theater. Although if I were to work in another kind of theater, I would probably find a way to eroticize it.

Describe your performance at its best and worst. ~ At my best I give the customer total permission to be who he or she is and want what he or she wants. I consent to being a fantasy object in those desires, whatever they are. At my best I become just as erotically involved with the customer as he is with me. So that we really are having sex together. That often results in orgasms for me and almost always results in orgasms for him, although that's not all there is to it. Orgasm is just reminding us that, yeah, we're still connected to our bodies. I communicate total acceptance, joy, and enthusiasm for sex. Which I think is a communication that none of us get enough of. A lot of us haven't really ever gotten it at all.

At my worst, just like in partner sex, I'm too tired to really connect. I'm not with the erotic flow any longer. At my worst it's, "Where's the sex? I can't find it."

Describe the customers. ~ Well, most of them are men. That's about all you can say that's generalizable. They come from a great many walks of life. They are all races. They are from all over the world. Some are travelers and tourists and some live right in the neighborhood. Some of them come from far away to have their sexual fantasy. Some are quite young, probably too young to be there. They are men old enough to be grandpas and you hope they're not going to fall over while they're jackin'-off. And every age in between. Most are in their forties, I would guess. They are packs of boys, Latinos, Asian Pacific, black or white, or combinations thereof; out on the prowl, checking it out, having a little testosterone party amongst themselves. Those are the most likely to misbehave in the hallway and suddenly turn sweet and shy in the booth. That's a little piece of information I never expected to get about the way young men behave. They are from all economic classes. A lot more upstanding citizens than I ever thought. I had some prejudices about "Who would go to those sleazy places anyway?" – well, a little bit of everybody does. The only people that we don't have a good representational sample of are females. I'd love to have more of them visit me. It's a special case when a woman walks in, it's like, "Oh my God, it's a *woman* and she's here to watch!" Sometimes her husband or boyfriend is hauling her in and she's kind of trying to hide her eyes behind her hands and go, "Oh, not this honey," and sometimes she is unabashedly as much a pussy hound as anybody else there. I want to see as many different kinds of women as men feel free to explore sexual entertainment. It's cultural, it's just not okay yet.

Do customers leave their social roles and status behind when they come to see you? ~ Sometimes. In some respects a hard cock is a great leveler. Frequently we cannot guess how a guy is going to behave and speak by what he's wearing or how he looks. I've had some scruffy-looking working-class fellows be extremely courtly and gentlemanly, and I have had some well-dressed gentlemen be creeps, and some people find it easier than others to get off their shyness. I think a lot of people, especially when they first come to places like this, are shy and don't know how to behave. It's about wanting a certain kind of response that nobody teaches you how to behave when you get it. The wanting is the wanting is the wanting. That's the most important part. Then you get it and you have to figure out a whole new set of responses about, "Oh my God, this naked girl is talking to me, what do I do now?" So the differences in behavior don't have so much to do with class and status, I think, as in how the person really feels about women on a scale from misogynist to idealist. What his little trip is about women and himself that he's there to work out; everybody's is different. Also it has to do with how long he's been patronizing peep shows and what his etiquette is around that, because it really is a particular etiquette that some people have yet to learn.

What is your favorite type of customer? ~ The guys who have something special about their sexuality, some kink, some tweak, the show-offs, the talkers, the ones with stories, the ones who want to play games and fantasies. The ones who I know had to really come to terms with their sexuality, in a somewhat different way than the average guy, before they could even get it together to come in. I like those guys because they're interesting and because they overcame those sexually imposed hurdles, and they can ask for what they want.

Do you encounter men who you think hate women? ~ Occasionally. The theater isn't a good place for men like that to go. For one thing, we're empowered by our bosses to not have to perform for anybody we don't like. Nobody's really flip about that, nobody just says, "Oh, I don't like his nose, I'm not going to go over there." It has to do with behavior and energy. People who are truly misogynistic and truly have an axe to grind don't get what they want from the women. They get ignored, or, the worst thing I see happening, it gets reinforced because women get angry with them or mean. They say, "You're a jerk, get away. Go away, you don't belong here." I feel like those people get reinforced in the attitudes that they have, but what do we do? We need to be able to work together and working together is not being demeaned.

Have you ever felt it was dangerous to arouse a customer? ~ No, I never have. There have been a few customers who it was very clear to me were a couple of sandwiches short of a picnic, who were kind of crazy. I don't throw that around easily. I'm very aware that most of the culture calls people like *me* crazy. Just because he wants to put on a pair of silk underwear he's a nutcase. But there were a couple of guys who didn't make a lot of sense. I guess I could have felt afraid but what I felt was that it was really cool that these nutty guys were coming in to get their needs met, like everybody else. If somebody came in whose nuttiness had a hostile part to it, then it might feel dangerous to me. I feel pretty safe in the theater.

Do you ever encounter violent men here? ~ I've refused to work with a couple of people whose level of verbal aggression bordered, to me, on the violent. They were drunk, which exacerbates that energy greatly.

Do you think you've ever danced for a rapist? ~ I don't know. Probably.

There are customers who come here with great regularity. What are they like? ~ They're also extremely diverse. Some come with great regularity because they have enough money to cum with great regularity. Some are the suits-and-ties from downtown who are in close enough proximity that they can whisk by every morning on their break, or on the way to work, or at lunch time. Others seem to be people that don't have a whole lot of outside social contact. But really it's hard to generalize. For me, they become sort of like family. Since, from my perspective I am having sex, they become kind of ongoing lovers and sometimes funny energy intrudes, expectations and desires and "Why don't you come have dinner with me?" questions start getting asked. I'm clearly a fixture in their fantasy lives, they have a relationship with me. I either gasp with pleasure when I see one of them around the corner or I go, "Oh my God, (laughs), it's *him.*"

Describe the variety of sexual behavior customers express. ~ Everything from open lascivious looking, a looking that is so sexual that you just don't see it any place else, except occasionally in the eyes of a lover. To pawing at the glass to pretend to touch your body. Making licking motions, "Oh, that pussy looks so good I could eat it." Kissing through the glass. Guys jerk-off and occasionally sploosh on the window, I try not to let them actually touch the glass with their mouths, but sometimes they do it. I explain that it's not safe. I've seen guys hump the window, hump the wall.

Lots of taking penis in hand and rubbing, stroking, petting, teasing, jerking. I don't know if I've seen every form of masturbation but I've seen lots and lots and lots, and it's a ceaseless delight to see how different guys do it. There's some whole-body self-sexuality too. Some guys will get completely undressed and rub their hands over themselves and play with their nipples and asshole; occasionally guys bring dildos in to use on themselves. Fabric fetishists bring in fabric they like and either wear it or jerk-off into a satin slip or panties or something like that. Occasionally I see coupled partner sexual activity. And I myself, I might add, have come in as a customer with my partner. We call it "entertaining the troops" when we're sexual together. The women tease us a little bit and cluster around to see what we do. It's always a treat for me and a lot of the dancers when somebody is being sexual in the booth with somebody else. It's fun to see what other people do.

Describe some of the more unique encounters you've had with customers.
~ My most unique encounter was with a guy who didn't have both oars in the water and some important part of his psychosexual development had to do with church. He was a minor foot fetishist and wanted me to dangle my high heeled shoe off my toes so he could get into looking at my feet. He wanted me to pretend that we were in church and I had caught him masturbating behind a pew and tell him not to ever come back and do that. He was very into being told not to do what he was doing. And when he came he wanted me to recite a particular verse of scripture. It wasn't verbatim, he had modified it a little bit. All this was very hard to do with a straight face and also the most wonderful trick, because I'm going to be thinking of this man until my dying day, wondering just what happened to him to get him turned on to that particular piece of scripture. I mean, was he under the pew and the preacher said this and then he came and that's what he likes to hear from now on? He's a very furtive, strange little guy. The fact that he could share his interesting variation with somebody else is such a treat to me. I just love it, I just love it. I love also the guy who fucks himself, I adore that guy, I love him. I get at least as much show-offing from him as he gets from me. He's good.

Many customers show a great deal of interest in the dancers' genitalia. Why do you think there is such great interest? ~ It's forbidden, taboo. I think a lot of men, especially older men, started out being sexual with women in the dark, in cars, in bushes, underneath the football stadium, wherever they could cop a feel, and never really got to see except in those strange split beaver pictures that even now, no matter how many pussies you've seen, still look kind of unreal. I had an old man, he must have been seventy-five, one of the real grandpa guys who makes you go, "Is he still pulling it out and doing that? Oh, isn't that wonderful?" He came in and he didn't want to pull it out. He said, "Can I just look at your pussy? My *wife* won't let me look at her pussy." This guy's probably married to this woman for fifty years and she won't let him look at her pussy. He just wants to see what it is, how all the parts look together.

Guys come in and say, "Which part's your clit?" I think part of it is sex education, I really do. An eroticized sort of nasty dirty sex education, like looking at those beaver shots. But it's about, "Now wait a minute, how's this piece of me gonna fit in there exactly, where does it go exactly when I stick it in?" (Laughs) It's that as well as the mystical pussy, and the dirty forbidden pussy, and the pussy that you just want to stare at while you think about a pussy that you miss. It's all of those things.

I love watching them pull their cocks out 'cause it's the part *I* wasn't supposed to look at. So it's like, "Oh good, oooh, this one looks different than the last one did." I can get why they want to look at pussies 'cause I feel the same way about them.

What do the customers want you to do? ~ A little bit of everything. There are gestures that they're not supposed to use. Occasionally women will say, "You can't tell us what to do," but I don't care, personally. I think that's either erotic or neutral. I don't mind doing anything if they're not rude.

They want me to spread my lips, to turn over, bend over, show them my asshole, they want to look at all these little parts close up, often jacking-off furiously while they do. They want me to look at them, talk to them, kiss them, or pretend I'm sucking them off. It's always been just phenomenal to me that the illusion of a blow job was enough to pay money for. I got sophisticated after a while and started sucking on a dildo – without it I felt sort of like the fish in the aquarium, make my mouth into an "o" and bob up and down. (Laughs)

Men in the booth want me to talk about anything and everything. One guy came in three or four times in one night and the first time he wanted me to be his aunt, the second time his catholic school teacher, the third time his mommy, then he went back to auntie again. Another man wants me to pretend to be his sister.

They want me to masturbate with dildos, occasionally use a vibrator. They want me to stick things in my asshole and pee in a cup, and a lot of them want me to tell them how much I like it. And that's easy for me, because by and large I do. I say, "I do, I'm having orgasms, what does it look like?" If they've seen me squirt they want to see me squirt again. They want me to come right up to the glass and watch them squirt, to be unabashedly interested in their cock, or they want me to play along with funny games like telling them that their cock is really big or really small. One guy likes to be told that his cock is extremely short. He holds it into his body cavity a little bit and then at the last minute he pops it out and it really isn't two inches long after all, and Oh, aren't I surprised? I'm supposed to be surprised every single time. (Laughs) I wonder where he eroticized that one too. I wonder about these guys. They're like treats, and enigmas, and puzzles, trying to figure out where things got erotic for them.

They want me to talk to them and do therapy and tell them stories and make up lies and tell them the truth. And tell them about when I first lost my virginity. And how often I like to do it. One guy thought he was going to shock the hell out of me when I asked, "Well, gee, what do you like to talk about? What's hot for you?" He said, "Dogs, doing it with dogs." So I started talking about doing it with dogs and he got out of there really fast. (Laughs) I don't think he thought he was going to get somebody to work with him on that one. Just about anything that you can imagine that's an erotic possibility, somebody wants to see me do or talk about, which is one of the absolute delights of it. I mean, if it was only one thing all the time! Well, I suppose even orgasm would get old, but it's always something different, always something new. I think of those Mummer's parades, where everybody dresses up in outrageous clothes and parades around with their psyches hanging out. Some people come to the theater with their psyches hanging out and it's wonderful.

I think you are possibly the only or preferred sexual outlet for some customers, what do you think? ~ I agree with that. And for some it's because the difficulties and compromises and communications and vicissitudes of a real relationship are just too much for one reason or another. Occasionally I get a customer from whom I have a pretty clear sense that he's got a sexless marriage, that he isn't comfortable going outside in real fleshly life but he's willing to do so in fantasy life. He wants to get that sexual hit back from another person even if it's through a window. Some of the kooky guys, if they have partners and relationships, I would love to see what they're like. The guy with the bible rap, I mean the first time he left I just went, I wonder if he has a wife and he gets *her* to say that when he cums! (Laughs) Sometimes my sense is that people, especially those who feel funny about their kink, use a peep show as an outlet rather than trying to break it to a partner that, "Oh, by the way honey, I'd like you to do this for me." And as we know from the real world, as often as not, honey *doesn't* want to do that for him, and it's not just women who don't want to do for men, either, that's equal across the board. If women could even get it together to *ask*. But, lots of times, I think that people who are sexually variant feel very much alone in it (and some people who are very ordinary feel very much alone in it too), for one reason or another they don't connect with other people as comfortably and as successfully as they connect with somebody in a peep show. And I'm real glad we're there for those guys.

Do you think customers get needs besides sexual needs met here? ~ Absolutely. Emotional, and social sometimes. I've had guys come in and just talk to me. Say, "No, no, don't take your clothes off." On stage, sometimes there is this intense air of curiosity and wonder on the part of the guys. It's not really an eroticized thing, it's, "Look at these creatures doing what they're doing, how amazing this is." Like, "Wow, I've never been to a place like this before," or, "Wow, I come here three times a week and I still want to say wow when I come in the door." It's not so much that their drug is beautiful naked women. It's about, "I can be part of this and this is not like anything I ever thought I would be able to be a part of." It's a different slice of life, and some people really get into it just because it's sort of underground for them, beyond the pale. Guys sometimes talk about feeling kind of beyond the pale themselves, the rebel guys, young guys in their black leather jackets and funny haircuts. Skateboard under the arm, they just say, "Wow, man. What's it like being in there?" (Laughs) It's like anthropology for them to grill those of us who are willing to talk to them about it, about, "Wow, what a thing, how does it feel?"

And they want information about what *do* women feel about whatever. "Oh, hey, I don't know, I'm in a box here in San Francisco, I don't know if we can generalize too well to other women, but I'll be glad to talk to you about what life is like for me."

I work on a sex information hot line, and this is a lot like being with people on the phone. And just where is it appropriate in this culture to say anything about sex? It's not about their hard-on and their sexual need and their desire at that point, it's about, "Wow, how do you cum like that?" It's about, they want to talk about sex. They want sex to be an okay thing to talk about.

Are you ever disturbed by the effect you have on customers? ~ The only thing that disturbs me is the regular customer who wants me to become a part of his real-life reality. I'll do anything for anybody in their brain. I don't mind being used in that way at all. I steal people's souls that way all the time, I don't think there's anything wrong with it. But when the desire gets expressed for me to be part of his life, that's distressing. Sometimes it's distressing because people who get obsessive about women in peep shows might act funny. *Might.* Sometimes this comes from my concern for him and his emotional well-being. That I don't necessarily think it's best for him to be focusing on me to the exclusion of whatever else is going on. Sometimes I talk to him about it a little bit, but it's not my job. He has to make his decisions.

Sometimes a customer will leave angry or disgusted. Do you understand why? ~ Sometimes the customer thinks he's going to get something other than what he reasonably can get in a peep show. Sometimes a customer with a language barrier will think he's going to actually get touched or get a blow job for five dollars or for a quarter. Then I say, "I'm sorry, this is not a third world country, the rate of exchange is a whole lot higher here and besides it's illegal and you're going to have to write your congressman before you can come into a place like this and get that kind of service." Not enough of them have written their congressman yet, obviously. Sometimes he's behaved inappropriately and been told so and you know, "Who's this cunt-whore telling me I can't have it like this?" Well, fine, this cunt-whore just told you you can't act like this. You're going to have to go down the street, bother somebody else now.

Do you ever encourage customers to leave messages? ~ Rarely. Once I solicited this very sexy young man to leave me his phone number. "Oh, I want him for dinner." (Laughs) The natural stasis of the job prevailed, he didn't want to be had for dinner and he didn't leave his number.

Do you ever abuse the customers? ~ I call them worms when they want to be called worms, but my true heart is not in it.

Do you ever feel controlled or possessed by the customer? ~ Only when I am willing to do what they want me to do. I always get to make the choice whether or not I think a guy's request is stated in an appropriate enough way to not make me feel like a piece of meat. Exactly the same request could come in different tones of voice and I'd feel different about each one of them, from neutral to really negative to really positive. It has to do with the kind of energy the customer projects, but the control thing, I always have the last word.

When customers show disrespect the dancers can call security and have them removed. How often do you ask that a customer be removed? ~ I have never asked that a customer be removed. I have occasionally suggested that security watch somebody. In the booth, I'm the one that gets to remove customers by closing the curtain. This has happened a few times. But nobody has ever been sufficiently bad in my eyes to get hauled out by security.

Do you try to get the customers to spend? ~ In the archaic sense of the word. (Laughs) It is a convention in the booth to charge for dildo play, for extras, and I pretty much go along with that. If I did everything for free then the guys would want everybody else to do it for free and that would fuck everything up. Some women really pride themselves in how much they can get customers to give them; I'm primarily having sex and secondarily doing a job. The fact that I'm getting dollar bills and fives and tens and twenties, and occasionally a really nice big one, is enough for me without having to solicit for more. I don't want to step on the sexual energy by starting to wheedle somebody about money.

How do you feel about dancing for customers in the three booths with one-way glass? ~ I don't like it as much at all. As you've already gathered, one of the reasons that I like this job is because of the sexual energy exchange that happens. I like knowing that I'm being watched and being able to interact.

As the desired do you have power? ~ Yeah, in the good power sense as opposed to the power-over sense. I guess it could also be power-over. I don't see it that way, or use it that way. And conversely, if I'm in a good mutual masturbation thing with a customer, he's got the same kind of power over me that I would have over him. It's flowing pretty equally at that point and it's my favorite situation – not that equality is always real important to me. Sometimes I like a distinct differential of power in my eroticism. It's especially exciting to have caught somebody, and to have him catch me with the energy we're exchanging.

Has doing this job affected your consciousness of your body? ~ Yeah, it's made me more turned on to myself most of the time. It's made me more *aware* of what I look like and that's basically a positive, good-feeling awareness. Although I have the sense that as I get older and my body starts to change, I've instilled in myself such a hyper-awareness of what I look like that I'm not sure how that's going to be. I mentioned before my orgasmic pattern has really changed due to the job. I've become more thoroughly aware of my arousal patterns, probably more thoroughly than I would have gotten any other way. Unless, for some reason, I decided on my own to spend four hours at a shot masturbating several times a week. (Laughs)

Have you experienced burnout in this job? ~ Yeah, and thankfully the job is something I can put on hold until I feel like coming back. I miss it when I'm not there. If I have more than three shifts a week, by the end of the week, it's like, "What else have I done this week?" It becomes very overwhelming in that way when I'm doing it a lot. It takes a certain kind of energy that nothing else really takes and I seem only to have so much of it.

How do you spend the ten minute breaks you take every forty minutes? ~ Mostly talking to whoever else is back stage. I find my co-workers alluring and fascinating. I want to know more about who they are, what else they're doing in their lives, what their history is, how they got here, and what it's like for them to be at the theater. Most of the women are so much younger than me and I want to know how do twenty-one year olds get to this place? When I was twenty-one I never would have come here. And I eat and pee and freshen my makeup. I put my feet up and if there's nobody else around sometimes I read.

Off stage it is not uncommon to hear dancers referring to each other as slut, whore, or bitch. What do these remarks mean? ~ It's rebel talk, the sort of thing that sometimes makes blacks call each other nigger and gay men call each other faggot. It's not fighting words, rather, "This is what they call us, we'll take it over. We'll take this word now, thank you very much, and it's going to mean something different when we use it than when you all use it."

Is there a difference between the male support staff and the male cus-

tomers?* ~ Oh, yeah. The male support staff tend to be rebel boys just as surely as we are rebel girls; most are fairly young, iconoclastic fellows. While we certainly do have our share of iconoclastic customers, they're rarely of the same ilk.

The owner and management of this theater say they want to create a safe, nurturing, fun, and profitable business. Have they succeeded? ~ I *guess* it's profitable. (Laughs) It usually feels safe to me. Sometimes the nurturance flows easier than at other times. Sometimes I see in guys' faces that they don't think jacking-off is fun. It's often fun for the dancers – "Oh, let's go and dance around naked with a bunch of other cute girls" *that's* fun. Dispensing sex for money in this culture is not ever going to be *simply* fun and nurturing; it should be like going to a restaurant, but it isn't. Everybody brings their own baggage and it sometimes gets in the way of the fun and nurturance.

The owner and management also express the desire to empower people. Have you been empowered here? ~ I have. The fact that we don't have to take bad behavior and bad attitude from customers, like in some other sex-purveying places, is empowering. It's empowering to be able to explore my sexuality and the sexuality of other people. We have to do a lot in this culture to set up a situation where we get to find out as much about sex and wallow in it as much as we want. I want to speak in favor of overdoing it, it's tremendously empowering. I've learned things at the theater that I never could have learned anywhere else, certainly not with as much ease, or as fast or with as many people a day. (Laughs) And the level of trust that I feel like I can acquire with a stranger around intimate, charged topics, topics of sex and fantasy and kink and diversity, all that private stuff, feels really empowering to me. It makes me more socially at ease in the world outside. It gives me a leg up in my interactions with other people, a little piece of my ego that I never had before in quite that way. This is a pretty miraculous place, really, these things that go on between us here are pretty miraculous, given that they're not supposed to be going on between people at all. That's all tremendously empowering. I hope it feels the same way to the customers.

Describe worker/management relations. ~ Ummmmmm, very friendly and sweet on a surface level. A little undercurrent of what is always present in worker/management relations – they're watching you, you better not fuck up. (Laughs) When the level of implicit control becomes explicit, it doesn't feel very good. One thing that I don't particularly like in this little circus of empowerment and amazement and storytelling that I'm living in is knowing that I'm doing it with a boss. There's a dynamic of social rebel about us that I think bleeds into worker/management relations, but things are great considering we'd really rather not have people telling us what to do at all.

Describe the periodically scheduled dancer meetings. ~ They have been mostly for the purpose of management telling workers how they want them to behave. Occasionally to address more theoretical issues. One meeting recently was partly devoted to time for the women to talk about how it was to be there and when they did have trouble with customers how did that feel and what did they need when that happened. There's time for dancers to give feedback and criticism to management. There are opportunities for the dancers to make decisions, for example, what they want to do with the common kitty of tips that accumulate. What do we want to order this year, "Vogue" or "Spy?"

They're fairly typical worker/management meetings on one level, except that they have a veneer of "We're all friends here, we're all on the same side." There is a certain management/worker bond that doesn't happen in other jobs, maybe because we are all in this off-the-beaten-path profession together. Management probably gets as many ascant looks as the workers for choosing to do this for a living. So the facade of "We're all buddies in the same boat talking about common concerns" seems to be maintained okay, although *it is* a facade.

Do you have job security? ~ As long as I continue to bring in a certain amount of money and don't make trouble, I have some job security. I feel much more secure that I can go back after an absence than I ever did, say, working in a restaurant. I have pretty good feelings about my connections with the place and the management.

In response to the question "Are you exploited?", a well known dancer and erotic film star replied, "Yes and no. We don't have a union, but I like what I do." How do you answer that question? ~ Everybody who works a job to put money in somebody else's pocket is exploited on one level or another. It's not the owner's pussy out there, it's mine, and I don't get all the money I bring in. The place is not a cooperative, or a collective. So in an economic sense, yeah, I am exploited. Although I feel fifteen dollars an hour ain't bad for getting sore knees and flashing my pussy at people for four hours at a shot. That's okay. I have somewhat stronger feelings about the ratio of my tips that I get to keep when I'm in the booth.

Another level of the question is sexual exploitation. I imagine a lot of people hearing a question about exploitation of sex workers would assume that it was around that erotic objectification thing. I don't feel exploited on that level, I have choice. I'm there to learn things, to do what I naturally do happily and erotically, which is being an exhibitionist. If people want to pay me to be an exhibitionist that's swell. Occasionally I feel treated in a non-comradely way by customers but I don't ever feel *exploited*, not any more than I felt exploited by people for whom I was opening the expensive bottles of wine as a waiter and they didn't offer me a glass.

Do you ever consider unionizing? ~ If union talk came to me I would support it. I have a history of talking union in other jobs and the experience of not having enough of the workers support me, and I was one of the mouthiest ones. Amazingly, I didn't lose my job, but I got a relatively severe amount of shit for fronting the concerns of everybody. Without a sense that a whole bunch of people want to do it, I ain't sticking my neck out, it's too much grief.

Is sexism promoted or resisted in any way here? ~ Well, sexism is promoted in that all of the dancers are women, most of the customers are men, that's not very fair, is it? If the city and the country were dotted with places where every gender and sexual preference could watch the kind of show they wanted, I would feel pretty okay and just call this a heterosexual place. But the fact is that this is pretty much the only kind there is. The only other place like this has men dancing and stripping for men. There really isn't much of a sex industry for the benefit of or for the entertainment of women. And yeah, that's sexist, right there.

The theater encourages the quality or the stereotype of women being nurturing and sweet and pretty and erotic and there for men and there's something a little sexist in that, although that's part of the range of who women are to men. We're just not there to provide the rest of the range. The guys can go home to their wives for that.

It certainly is a variety of sexism that the women who keep their jobs are the women who fit into a fairly narrow category of what is attractive for a woman in this culture. It's partly the policy of management, and partly customer feedback about who they want to see and what they don't want to see, that makes that happen.

The thing that's *not* sexist is that for at least some of us, we're also there for our *own* sexual gratification. We're there because we like the kind of exhibitionism that we're there to engage in. We are able to take our power as sexual women into our interactions with customers.

That I'm allowed to have my sexuality to the degree that I can at the theater is actually a very anti-sexist thing. This culture doesn't want women to be as sexual as we are in that theater. It might want us to look pretty and sexy to sell cars, but it doesn't want women with true erotic power. And what I'm learning there, and what I think other women learn as well, is it takes true erotic power to express, enjoy, and wield our sexuality. I don't find that sexist at all. Except maybe that some of the guys are probably not experiencing their erotic power in quite the same way. And I don't think all of the women who do the job have that perspective. I wish we all did.

The fact that we're empowered in our limit setting, in our "No, mister, you're not appropriate, you're going to have to either shape up or go someplace else," that's another piece of power around our sexuality. A lot of women out in the world don't experience that much control over their sexual situations. We're encouraged to know that we have that control and to use it. I consider that an antidote to sexism.

What I think is sexist is that in this culture only certain people, mostly men, get a chance to look at and play with other people. That's an overarching thing. The theater welcomes women as customers. Most women don't want to see my sexual entertainment yet. Catch up! Well, first we want to make a dollar on the dollar; when we have a few more cents to piss away on erotic entertainment, then we'll see what happens. That economic thing *is* there, and yet it's a lot more complicated than that. The place of sexuality and the question of sexism is a really big one and there are lots of different versions of what sexist is and how sex impacts on it.

Women are struggling very hard to be sexual beings in a way that feels good to them and are fighting just to say no, and just to say yes. They're trying to figure out, "Okay, who am I? What do I want? Who can I do it with that will make me feel good? What kind of limits can I set? With whom do I need to set the fewest limits? Let me see what these people are doing here fucking on film. Can I learn anything? Does it make me hot?" A lot of different things are going on out there.

When you walk into a place that's dark, and smells vaguely of semen, you've got to be a brave woman, not the thing that an average gal, even if she wanted to see some pussy and tits, would go and do. That's why women are creating erotic strip shows for each other and why the Chippendales do so well with an all-women audience where people can scream and squeal and stick dollars in g-strings. Women want this kind of stuff, it just hasn't been marketed in a way that a lot of women respond to. If lots of things were different, if censorship weren't rife, if we had a little more encouragement from each other and the men in our lives, we'd be spending more on sexual entertainment; we increasingly are.

Do you ever feel in danger coming to or leaving work? ~ Not really. I carry my attitude of "I'm having a good time walking after dark and I've got some place to go, you're not going to fuck with me, are you?" It doesn't feel any more dangerous to me than walking on any street in any other part of the city, especially after dark. This area is more populous after dark. In some parts of town I'd feel a lot more nervous.

What do you feel passing customers in the hallway whom you have just danced for? ~ Usually I feel them as a little bit awestruck. Like, "Oh wow, it's *her*." Sometimes, because I have my wig off they don't recognize me. I pass customers who recognize me most often when I'm on my way to and from the booth. It's the only case in which a woman is in the hall wearing very little, where she's in her sexy persona. I'm always escorted by a male support staff member, but it's not a fearsome feeling or anything. I either get, "Oh wow, that's Minx," or "Hey baby," the dopier forms of sexual chit-chat devised by humankind. "Hey baby, what's going on?" The guys are trying to be outgoing and get noticed, so it's okay.

Do you have anger about this job? ~ When I have dealt with somebody who's a creep. But it's not so much about the job, it's about the creep. I have anger globally that men who are creeps about women and sex think it's okay to come into a space like the theater and be creeps there, or that they do it any time. The only people who ever try to intercede with a creepy person are the support staff. I want people to be willing to intercede when they see misbehavior and I don't see that. I see other guys turning away. I get angry about that. I would get angry if I saw a bunch of people on the street turn away from somebody who is knocking somebody around. It's, "Why don't people just come together and be a *society* like we're supposed to be," that kind of feeling.

I could get angry that this is a job, somebody else is getting some of this money that I'm supposed to get, you know. By and large, I feel that's anger that I can't do too much about.

How does this job compare with others you've had? ~ Very well. I've never had another job where I was so encouraged to set my limits and knew that management would stick by me when I did. And never had another job where I learned so much except possibly a job that I had in AIDS-related social services. And I've never had another job where I got to masturbate all the time.

Describe your earliest memories. ~ I have very early memories of the house I grew up in out in the sticks. We got to our house via a rugged dirt road that was several miles from the nearest paved one, past pastures with cows. I remember driving along these bumpy roads and having some kind of baby conversation with my mother about the cows. I was about two and I remember people being in the house when my brother was about to be born. I remember being in the crib also, that is probably a pre-two memory. I remember looking through bars. That's probably the very earliest memory I have. (Laughs)

Describe your family and its circumstances as you remember them during your childhood. ~ I had a nuclear family, two big ones, two little ones. My father was a schoolteacher out in the coast range of Oregon. My mom was a mom, barely. The housewife type. She took a job when I was eleven or twelve as a bookkeeper, which is what she had been before kids came along. We didn't have a whole lot of money. It was a little better when there were two incomes but there was a lot of paranoia about money. We had summers to kick around and travel because Dad didn't work summers, but we had to be frugal. One summer Dad built a playhouse for me and my brother from trees he cut. Once we traveled most of the summer around the West Coast and Midwest.

There were museums and a kiddie library card and lots of books to read. There were a lot of trees, a little bit of meadow, and fantasy games. We filled a lot of hours with our brains, our toys, and Mom. She drank too much and didn't like where she had wound up. She wanted to be a concert pianist and got sidetracked. She got married, had kids, and just wasn't up to the challenge. She didn't really want to be doing those things. It was the fifties, when a lot of women who didn't want to be doing those things did 'em anyway.

Dad *wanted* to be doing all those things but wasn't much help. He was real big on, "Oh, boy, I'm a dad, there's kids, oh this is so cool, I'll take them to museums, I'll take them around, I'll teach them things, why's my wife so fucking unhappy, what's the problem here?" He didn't get a clue until she had, between alcohol and stress, ulcered herself into nearly dying one night and then this confession happened: "I never wanted to live in the country, I never wanted to be doing all of this." By that time I was nearly ten and the shit hit the fan. We moved to a different place, but she was just as isolated. It was about Dad not wanting to live in the city and Mom not wanting to live in the country and who gets to pick where we live? Well, Dad does 'cause he brings home the paycheck. I hung out watching that shit for the first ten to twelve years of my life.

What kind of child were you? ~ I was slightly rambunctious, very smart, very cute. I had a seven or eight-year-old nerdy phase and then a pubertal nerdy phase that lasted for quite a while. The rest of the time I was cute as a button and what my midwestern forebears used to describe as "a pistol." I was curious, verbal, and very popular with adults, liked adults better than kids almost the whole time I was growing up. I liked to hang out with my parents and their friends and be part of the conversation.

I started reading in first grade, and by second grade I was real good at it. I got to choose all sixteen books per week that we were allowed on our family library card. I went through fairy tales and mythology most ravenously, biographies next most ravenously.

Describe your relationship with your brother. ~ We were real important to each other, each others' only support system a lot of the time. Even after we went to school that was true because of the summers, when our relating with other kids was brief. We played together a lot. He was not as outgoing and adventurous as I was so I kind of big-sistered him. I got him doing stuff that he probably wouldn't have done himself. "Let's go jump off the roof of the barn today and land in the hay." We did a little bit of sexual exploration with each other, not a lot. When we started to move towards puberty, when I was ten, eleven, twelve and he was eight, nine, ten, we started fighting like cats and dogs and were real adversarial for a little while. Partly, I think now, because of the tension in the house about us becoming pubertal at all. Mom wasn't real comfortable with us in any case and Dad was really uncomfortable as we grew out of being kids.

Describe your relationship with your parents. ~ I took care of my mom from a really young age, especially just preceding the time that she got sick with her ulcer and precipitated the move. At that point she had basically blown a gasket around the wife and mom routine. And she never really got back to it either. She went into heavier alcohol abuse after that. As I got older, I could take on more of her responsibilities so at the age of nine I was doing the family shopping every week. I was never very into these adult responsibilities. When I was a little, little girl, I thought Mom was the most beautiful, wonderful mom in the world and then she started looking kind of not there. It was around the alcohol abuse and her antipathy about being a mom at all.

My relationship with my dad was quite different. He was my buddy. I was very into him when I was a little girl, more so than my mom. I was like a parent's kid, the kind they like to show off. My dad and I hung ,ut together a lot. He was into me being his little sidekick and I liked that. Dad didn't do girl stuff so I couldn't do girl stuff with him. We were quite close until puberty.

We fought off and on, mostly on, from the time I was eleven or twelve to the time that he died. What was going on there was some inappropriate intimacy, not anything that I would label as incestuous *behavior* ever, but what I might label as incestuous *feeling*. Always, always the fighting was about putting distance between us that on both our parts evidently needed to be there. For me it really needed to be there, there was a lot of boundary-crossing that he did with me emotionally that was weird. All of a sudden he wasn't my cool dad anymore, he wouldn't take me to do things and show me museums so I could learn more interesting stuff. He was way too focused on how short my skirt was when I walked out the door. He was way too into my sexuality and he would be uppity about it. And it pissed me off, so there were big fights, and it kept us separate. I can't imagine what it would have been like if he did things differently.

About the time I hit puberty and junior high school I started to turn into a "smart kid," the kind other kids have problems with 'cause she's the smart one, and it became real evident to me that I was also the smart one at home. My brother also was real real intelligent but he kept a lid on it a lot. So I was parenting my mom, sparring with my dad and attempting not to be in an adult emotional relationship with him, and getting smarter than both of them by leaps and bounds. That was hard, to look at the people who were supposed to be my parents and go, "I don't think I can even explain to these people what's going on with me 'cause I don't think they'll get it." There was a lot of "I don't think they'll get it" about my relationship with my parents.

Were you raised under a particular religious tradition? ~ Not really. We went to church for two or three years when I was about seven, to a little Fundamentalist community church. Not because we were trying to be religious but because Dad was a teacher in that community and it seemed politic to him to be a member of this church. I was already reading a lot of mythology and I wasn't into the church's mythology. (Laughs) I was very bewildered and weirded out by the level of enthusiasm around this Christian schtick. It wasn't what I wanted to be doing, so I would take books and hang out in the back row of church. They busted me for that, so I hung out in the car and read until they got out of church. If they were having cookies and punch in there I'd hang out with them for a while before we went home, but I didn't want to hear that sermon shit. They allowed me to do that.

I was consciously pagan at a fairly young age, around eleven. I was identifying as a witch, though I thoroughly forgot that all through my high school years. It was this embarassing kid thing and I forgot about it until I re-emerged as an adult pagan at about the age of nineteen or twenty. I started to re-identify as a witch and then I remembered this baby-witchness. As an adult, I knew the whole history of it, the goddess-worship and matriarchal culture remnants which are patchworked together in the present and form an alternative to the Judeo-Christian tradition. I hadn't known any of that stuff when I was eleven, I just wanted to have another measure of control over my world and a spiritual context, which the early witchcraft never really gave me. The second time around I got my creed. I think going to church made me want to connect with something the way all these people around me were obviously connecting to this Christian hoo-ha.

Describe your childhood play and friendships. ~ I had my first friend, besides my brother, when I was five and I didn't meet her until I was six. She was a picture pal, kind of like a pen pal and she was going to be in my first grade class. My dad knew her and her mom. We were kind of friends in first grade but we didn't have a lot in common, except that we both liked to draw pictures.

When I was five or six I got a new babysitter, a woman on welfare with four daughters, and her daughter who was a year older than me became my best friend all the way through junior high. She was another kid who was different. Thinking back, there were a lot of kids around me who were different, it just wasn't acknowledged much. She was also brighter than average and we read the same books and talked about them. We hung out in the woods and looked for fossils in the shale cliff and had, in retrospect, androgynous girl adventures with each other. We didn't do too much doll-house stuff.

I had my first boyfriend when I was nine; *that* didn't last too long. I corrected his love letters and sent them back to him. (Laughs) My dad had let me help him grade papers for spelling errors so I did it with my boyfriend's letters. Some of my friendships and crushes started to have explicitly erotic overtones when I was about nine.

Into high school my friends were the weird kids mostly. The mainstream kids came from good Christian families. The weird kids were the kids whose parents had gotten divorced or kids who were gay, although not necessarily out yet, who were too into sex, or drugs. Anybody who was divergent was in the pool of people who were my friends.

Describe your childhood school experience. ~ I was good in school, I liked school a lot. It introduced me to reading, which is probably what saved my life when I was young. I always liked my teachers and I was always teacher's pet in grade school. My teachers could talk to me about what was going on in the world when I was a real little kid. They were the most important people in my life when I was young.

Describe your teachers and classmates. ~ My teachers were mostly middle-aged ladies who thought I was a wunderkind. In sixth grade I had a male teacher who I had a real uncomfortable feeling around; when I met him as an adult I realized that he was inappropriately cruisy and flirtatious to a bunch of eleven-year-olds. Never had anything happen though. It wasn't that he was completely pedophilic, but rather a hick small town version of a suave guy.

In junior high I started finding teachers, this was in the late sixties, who had some sense of what was happening in the world. They had been influenced by the sixties, whereas most of the people around me didn't have a clue, like "Where's San Francisco? What's a hippie? What's Vietnam?" I was starting to get with younger, more progressive teachers who had a real important influence on me. I was becoming, basically, a political person and they could give me support. One of them a couple of years later became my lover.

Classmates were a lot of ordinary little kids. I was aware very early that there was a sort of person who was regular, and a sort of person who was not regular. I knew I was one of the latter and most everybody else was the former, that I could do my best to interact with them but it wasn't going to be very smooth-going and I wasn't going to get what I wanted emotionally.

For the first half of my eleventh year I was hanging out with the girls who were going out for cheerleading the next year. They all became cheerleaders and popular. I attached myself to them, I think, because I was coming into my sexuality and it was clear that those were the girls the boys were paying attention to, and I wanted to get some of the attention. It didn't work very well at all.

There was one other girl in our gang who was nerdy. I was nerdy but she was *really* nerdy. So I helped the popular girls exclude her from the group. I colluded in being mean and chasing her away. The popular girls loved me 'cause I helped them with their school work, but a couple of weeks later I got them all together and crying I said, "I'm not going to hang out with you guys anymore. I don't like what we did to that girl and you're really not the kind of people that should be friends with me. I don't know if you really like me so we're just not hanging out together any more." Looking back, it was a really weird thing for me to have done, and centered and painful. I can still get in touch with how hard it was for me to identify that I was different from the mainstream. It was about being true to myself.

In high school I got involved in theater so I could be out-there with other people who were out-there. It felt like nobody knew the same kinds of out-there stuff that I knew, especially when I started being sexual—then I felt *really* isolated from my peers. Of course some of them were also being sexual but we didn't talk about who was doing it and who wasn't. It was a process of herding myself away from everybody else, more than everybody else herding me out. Always I was looking for a community that I could feel right in and I set myself up as a rebel in various ways.

At an early age humans exhibit a wide range of erotic behaviors. Describe what you were up to as a child. ~ A little peepee-touching between me and my brother. It felt fine at the time and has always felt fine in retrospect. At age seven I got my first hit of pre-pubertal sexuality. I was rubbing up against a bunched-up satin comforter that was supposed to be my boyfriend. I was trying to figure out, if it was really Randy, what would we be doing exactly? This rubbing felt good. I remember getting pretty wild with the old red satin. The fooling-around play with my brother was "show me this, show me that." I wasn't sure what fucking was yet, so I didn't try any of that stuff but I was conscious of feeling real turned on a lot of the time and being real frustrated because I didn't know what to do with it. My masturbation was pre-orgasmic so I wasn't getting all the way through to the Thing Itself. One of the things that did for me was get me very accustomed to being really turned on all the time. Which actually is something that I draw on today. (Laughs)

What were you taught about human sexuality by your parents? ~ Well, I'm one of those kids whose parents never had sex. My brother used to say, "Yeah, Dad must have tossed and turned in his sleep, or else where would we have come from?" I think my parents' sexual relationship was real problematic, full of miscommunication or a complete lack of communication. They didn't tell me much of anything. I'm sure I got the "Where did babies come from?" thing when I asked. I don't remember not knowing. They were liberal parents in that regard. I got the "Honey, in the next year or two you will start to bleed. It's perfectly natural, don't let anybody know it" lecture. And the little stupid book that tells you "You're a woman now, you're flowering, don't let anybody know about it." That wasn't exactly sex but it was the closest thing that they were direct with me about. I got sent to be in on the lecture that my dad was giving my brother and walked in on the part about wet dreams, which was news to me and acutely embarassing to me and my brother. If we had been a family that talked about that stuff, it would have been no big deal.

When I was eleven my mother asked me if I knew what masturbation was. I was pretty sure I had a relatively clear idea, I was doing some things like that and so I could've said yes, but I wasn't sure if I knew the full details and I wouldn't want to get embarassed being asked, "Well, what is it, then?" So I said, "Uh, no." And she said, "Good." And left the room! Many years later I reminded her of that incident which she had of course forgotten totally, and asked her if she'd ever stopped me from masturbating when I was a little kid, and she said, "Oh, I don't think so, honey." To me that means she did. (Laughs)

They were not real good when I went away to college. My mother had a great conversation with me, she said, "Uh, honey, uh, you're going away to college now, um, I, uh, uh, well, uh, but..." I said, "Mom, are you asking me if I know about birth control?" and she said, "Yes." (Laughs) And I said, "I do." And she said, "Okay, good." When I got to be an adolescent my dad and I talked about sex a little bit but his energy was funny so I didn't much like talking to him about it. I talked to other adults.

Did you receive information about human sexuality in grade school? ~ No. We got the "girls are different than boys" lecture in junior high school. There was a little bit of sex education in high school, not much. Nothing that I have very distinct or fond memories about. Nothing very sex-positive.

Was there nudity in your home? ~ There was some, that was the way my parents were the most liberal. There was never any "squeal and cover up" when we kids walked in on Mom and Dad. They didn't parade around naked but they were pretty natural about it, so we got to look at bodies from when we were really little. In spite of that openness, and probably partly having to do with the rest of the sexual silence, from the time I was fairly young I became pretty embarassed and pretty private. I didn't want to see Mom or Dad walking naked through the house. It was weird for me and I still don't know why. It took until I was older to get over that privacy and nervousness about showing my body. That's one of the things I like about being at the theater, truly.

Were you ever punished due to sexual expression? ~ No.

Were you ever sexually abused as a child? ~ Sloppy, horrible kisses from old relatives, which is a mild but yukky form of sexual abuse. The grabby grandpa syndrome, there was a little of that. No fingers in pussies or any of that stuff. Nothing went far. Probably all innocent as far as they were concerned, just yukky as far I was.

What were you taught about human relationships in your family? ~ It was sort of assumed that since I was a girl I'd grow up, get married, and have kids. That wasn't taught but it was put out. I, being the smart kid, looked around and went, "Fuck that noise, look at these people, Mom hangs out on the back porch and cries in the daytime while Dad's gone, something's fucked up, I don't want to do this," and in fact, I was very adamant about that up until very recently. No kids, no husband, no nothing. That was part of the emotional background that sent me into a lesbian identity for a while – "Look, men and women just can't communicate with each other. Look what my experience has been, and I've never seen *anybody* that liked it." That whole set of assumptions came from a real early place for me. What I learned from observation was quite different from the lesson they had planned and hoped to teach me.

Were you taught to look good to attract and be chosen by a man? ~ Real schizophrenic around that, from a very early age. I have pictures of myself at three, four, five, six, that period when all those images that you see are getting consolidated into your self, some of which were just as frilly and posed and as baby "Marilyn Monroe" as could be. I apparently chose to present myself, most of the time, as real tomboyish, dungarees and sneaks and a t-shirt. Both of those things were going on at the same time and I got permission and strokes for both, so I never thought that I would have to be one way. I think in a way my mom purposely didn't teach me to attract a man. I didn't get much in the way of "This is how to dress, this is how to make up." If anything they wanted to put a lid on my expression of young sexuality and attractiveness and I was teased or tormented when I went out in a dress that they thought was too short. Even in early adolescence, when it was important to meet or attract guys, I didn't get support for that at home. Consequently, for a long time I didn't learn how to do it very well.

Were you taught to value truth? ~ Ostensibly. I got a lot of individual attention from my dad and part of the independence, "be smart" rap, included some "value of honesty" stuff. Unfortunately, neither of my parents, I think to the day that he died and to this day for her, had a clue about how non-honest their lives together were. Honesty's real important to me 'cause I saw how lack of it fucked up my family.

Did your parents teach you that you could have power, choice? ~ Yeah. They also taught me that if I wasn't a smart girl and a Little Miss Perfect, that I was not as lovable. So while the function of getting encouraged to be Miss Perfect is to take a certain amount of power in the world and to be proud of your initiative and your intelligence and all that stuff, and that's all empowering, on some levels it doesn't give you very much room to just be who you are. So in a way their focus on that was *dis*empowering at the same time as it was empowering. It left me with a lot of loose ends about the things that I was scared of and didn't think it was okay to get taken care of around, because I was supposed to be a smart, cool, strong little girl.

What effect did your body changing have on you? ~ Well, a pretty pronounced hormone surge hit and I started thinking about sex all the time. I sublimated the sexual energy for two or three years into that pubertal girl crush syndrome and wouldn't have read it, most of the time, as sexual energy, although that's exactly what it was. It was the time of my greatest and most frenzied attempts to learn how to have orgasms, which I didn't learn how to do 'til several years later when I got hold of a vibrator. But, boy, I'd get myself right up there and be panting like a little animal. So there was definitely a lot of sex happening in my body. And this worked at total cross-purposes with the changing of my body, starting to menstruate, and starting to get breasts. I was worried about every little part of myself. Anybody teasing me about my body, which of course, pre-adolescent boys do constantly (and my dad did as well), made me acutely self-conscious and convinced, like every other twelve-year-old girl is, that I would never get laid and nobody would ever love me because my body looked weird and yadada, yadada. It was a very uncomfortable period. At that point, anything that had any mention of sex was very interesting to me, whether it was crap or gold. I wanted to know how fucking was described, body parts, I went to the library to deal with all that.

Describe your adolescent sexuality. ~ I started to calm down about what my body looked like, a little bit, by the time I was fourteen or so. I had gone to the library and found out what fucking was, and decided I wanted to do it. I was up against the dilemma of the unusual kid: "I'm weird, who's going to want to fuck me?" The boys I hung out with were the oddball boys who were less in control of, less proactive with their sexuality than the boys on the football team, who had discovered that they could fuck pretty much anybody they wanted. *They* didn't want to fuck me. I was getting extraordinarily horny and I wanted to do something about this stupid virginity. I would try masturbating and I would get up to "T-1 and counting" and my hand would freeze. There was so much physical tension in me that I could not make my hand move the last four strokes that it would take to get me over to orgasm. So I was a maniac, like a monkey on a string.

And what I did was have an affair with one of my former teachers. That helped take care of matters. It took me out of the social fishbowl of high school, where I wasn't fitting in very well, and put me into another realm altogether, an adult sexual realm, essentially. I don't suppose it was an adult sexual realm the first couple of times, but after that, I was having a relationship, the way I have relationships now. And it made a great deal of difference. I still wasn't orgasmic, but at least I was getting all the other things I wanted from sexuality, the touching, the attention, the "Yes, you're desirable" stuff, all of that. And then I got the vibrator and that fixed the rest of it.

After a while it got around that I fucked – that took care of a multitude of sins, as far as all the boys were concerned. (Laughs) But having sex with guys my own age was always perfectly weird. The level of communication and body knowledge that I shared with my older lover never got replicated with people my age, not 'til I got to college.

How did you first discover and use the ability to arouse? ~ I think the first time that I ever really felt attractive, like my presence, my body, what I did, how I was, could arouse somebody, was with my older lover. It's completely possible that I was arousing boys my own age all the time, but they never acknowledged it to me, I never saw it. Even later when I was fucking them I didn't really get it that I was arousing to them, except they showed up and they had a hard-on. My older lover, on the other hand, clearly found me sexy and was willing to tell me and show me.

There was nothing like the feeling of dressing up, going out, and turning heads. That's been a brand new revelation for me, in the last handful of years. By the time I was in my late teens, I was no longer trying to dress to attract because my early teen experience of that had failed so miserably.

How did the discovery of pregnancy affect you? ~ Well, it made me afraid to get pregnant, it made me afraid to fuck, though it didn't affect the desire to. Getting the clearer description of what fucking was was great because I had been so very curious about it and hadn't been around anybody I felt I could ask. Because I didn't use any birth control throughout my first three years of being sexually active, except withdrawal, there was a lot to be afraid of. I was lucky.

Describe your first exposure to sexually explicit media and its impact on you. ~ I had seen maybe a picture or two by the time I was in junior high. In high school I had gotten hold of my lover's magazines. He let me know where they were so I could look at them if I wanted to. Of course I wanted to! It was stuff like Playboy and Penthouse and a few hard core things. I was fascinated with it. I remember beaver shots were just as weird as they could possibly be, partly because it was a way of looking at female anatomy that I had never seen before. Subsequently I dragged a mirror out and sure enough, mine looked like that too, kind of. Mostly it was enormously intriguing and kind of titilating. I liked reading the Penthouse Forum stories that went with the pictures. That was all a real big turn-on for me. I don't remember finding anything shocking except in that sort of titilating, "Oh, my God, look at that, I'm not supposed to see that," kind of way.

Did you date in high school? ~ I fucked. (Laughs) I didn't really date. I was asked out on probably three real dates in high school. Opportunities to fuck happened when my parents were not home in the summertime days. People would come over or I would go to parties and we would go off in the bushes or in somebody else's room, that kind of teenage thing. But partly because I lived in the country, there wasn't anything to do on dates per se, and so there was much less of an excuse to go out with somebody. My parents would say, "Well, what do you want to do that for?" If there wasn't a movie to go to, or something as a destination point, they were very suspicious about it. So there was some restriction by my parents, but mostly, kids either didn't date or they didn't date people like me. I was not good date material. But calling me up and saying, "Hey, you want to go out for a ride?", that was another matter. That started my last year of school. Occasionally, guys that I had never talked to in school called me up. Go up the logging road and hump in the car, go home and not talk to him in school again. Very strange. It was the way our sex and our sexuality and our social interactions were structured, they didn't overlap very much for a lot of us. It was a little like growing up in the forties and fifties, off in the sticks.

Describe your relationship with your family during those years. -- Really tense. My dad and I were having fights and my mother was drunk a lot, a lot. My brother was a mess. He fit in less well than I did, if you can imagine that, and our whole family was just kind of on the skids, probably like a lot of other families. Although I never thought of it that way then. I just thought, "Oh my God, I live in a nightmare here. I'm really from Mars and they adopted me and I can't get home." Wished I was adopted a lot in those days, just so there wouldn't be a genetic link to all this awfulness. There was a lot of pain because I wanted to be able to count on them and felt like I couldn't. Felt like I needed to keep my private life, including my sex, but also just my feelings, very separate from them. Didn't feel like they would honor it or help me with it at all. We probably could have communicated a lot better if we had known how, things would have been better, but we didn't know how.

What was your first job? ~ I graduated from high school at sixteen and went away to college immediately. My parents supported me my first year. When I had just turned eighteen, I followed my college roommate to Texas to work in her brother's bar, which was frequented by bikers. That was my first job. It was a very interesting splash on the work world and a much better place for having sex than anyplace I had ever found. (Laughs) I was a bar maid there for about three months. I was getting a buck and a half an hour and if I was really lucky I could make three to five dollars in tips a night. Every cent I made was going into paying my rent and it was absurd, but bar maid's not a bad job for getting laid. My next job was waitressing, for many years after that, never went back to bars.

Did you have heroines or heroes during those same years? ~ Well, I certainly had famous people that I wanted to fuck. Would have given my right arm to fuck Jim Morrison. My first hit of truly adult sexuality was listening to Jim Morrison sing. I was eleven or so, and I *got* it, I went, "Oh, *that's* what this is all about. Light my fire." My heroes and heroines were Abby Hoffman, Jack Kerouac, the "feminists," didn't have one picked out, but I was strongly feminist identified from the time I was thirteen. More than anyone, interestingly, beat writers. As I got a little older I was very sensitive to lefty politics. I was a little too rural to idolize Che Guevara or anybody like that but I listened to a lot of Woody Guthrie. I idolized Woody Guthrie.

Describe work you've done prior to dancing. ~ The bar maid thing bears some serious resemblance to dancing, although dancing is much more pleasant in that you don't have to deliver beers while you're being flirted with. Waitressing included a stint of restaurant management, which I just hated. I didn't like being a person responsible for giving shit to the workers. I've had jobs doing AIDS education and I was a teaching fellow in graduate school.

Have you had other jobs in the sex industry? ~ Yes, I've been a working prostitute. I began doing prostitution before dancing. One of the things that brought me into the theater was the post-Christmas downturn in yuppies spending their discretionary income. A prostitute's income goes down after Christmas just like a waitress's does. My career as a prostitute at that point was about a year old and for the most part I liked it very much, although I'd had a handful of the kinds of experiences that if you have too many of them give you a bad attitude. Mostly, customers being weird about money. One customer just wanting to cop a feel and then vanish without paying, one of the little rapes that nobody gives a shit about when they happen, and certainly not when they happen to prostitutes. When I have a connection with a client that feels non-problematic, direct contact feels fine. When it's problematic, it's stressful. So while the pay is good, the stress is higher. I was real happy to come to the theater and have those two things balance out a little bit. My work life since then has been mostly a combination of the two things, more at the theater than seeing clients, with some writing thrown in, which of course doesn't pay anybody's rent. Most of my writing has to do with sexuality. It's the thing that interests me most in the world. And it's also the place where I think my contribution is most valuable, since so many of us are afraid to put it all out there. Anybody can write about, "Oh, I went down to Fisherman's Wharf and went to a restaurant." Not everybody is willing to or can write about sex from an insider's place.

Describe living situations you've been in since you left home. ~ I first lived with roommates at college and in the hiatus times when I wasn't in college. It took me ten years to get my bachelor's because I was in and out of college. Once a roommate turned into a lover, which was a nightmare. (Laughs) A couple of times I lived with lovers. When I have roommates I usually have only one, although once I lived in a houseful of people, which was fun, but unworkable. And I've lived alone a lot which is my preference. If I'm not living with a lover with whom I'm getting along seriously well, alone is my lifestyle of preference. Partnered but not living together works really well for me.

Describe significant friendships and love relationships you've had since leaving home. ~ A lot of my significant friendships have also been significant love relationships. I think partly because I'm bisexual I don't have a lot of limits on who I like versus love versus lust for. A friendly fuck is as good to me in certain respects as a romantic one. I place a high premium on romance but that doesn't mean that I don't place a high premium on the other kinds of connections that I have. My close friends with whom I haven't been sexual are few and far between. My closest old friends now are my ex-lovers, two in particular. Another close friend is a woman who's primarily heterosexual with whom I had a three-way, so even there, where the bounds of sexual orientation were in the way, we fucked anyhow. That tends to be how I like to be with people if I like them. Most of my closest friendships have been with women, although that's changing now, rather profoundly. Even when I was lesbian-identified there were always significant men in my life balancing that energy out, who occasionally I was sexual with. One of the reasons that my closest friends are starting to be men as well as women is because I've started to understand that men and women are not separate species; it took me a long time to figure that out. With a little bit of openness and willingness to learn each other's language we can communicate as closely and intimately as women can together. Why not have men friends and men lovers? Who attracts me are smart, witty people, who are good-hearted, open, and accepting, although I've had friends who were as judgmental as the day is long. Mostly I have to feel like they challenge me and interest me.

Describe your current living arrangements. ~ I live in this cool little studio apartment in San Francisco and I'm happy as a clam to be here. I have my little lair, I work here, I write here. I entertain my lover here and just hang out and veg here. It's the center of my universe. I manage to do just enough lucrative work to pay the bills, since living alone in San Francisco is a luxury in itself. I anticipate living like this for at least the next year or two. My partner and I might, at some point, live together, we'll cross that bridge when we get to it. Right now it's just me and my cheesecake pictures on the walls.

Describe your interests outside of work. ~ Sex. (Laughs) I guess a lot of people find something that is microcosmic of the rest of creation. Sex is my microcosm which helps me look at questions of diversity and acceptance and communication and relationship and secrecy and honesty and all kinds of things. It's not just sex, it's metaphoric, so that, like Shakespeare said, I can "unite my vocation and my avocation in two eyes that share one sight." I love to read and occasionally I write something that *doesn't* have to do with sex. I was a poet as a teenager and a young adult and occasionally I spit something like that out —that rarely has to do with sexuality. Poetry is more about a spiritual relation to the cosmos for me.

I love to sport dine, I like good food. All my years in the restaurant business gave me an appreciation for a well-designed restaurant, a well-set table, and a really good meal. I like watching good movies. I like to think about things. At other times I've been much more politically voracious than I am now. Right now, my main politics are around sexual issues. All the shit that's going on out in the world scares me, saddens me, makes me sick and I try not to pay very much attention to it. I feel kind of bad about that, but that's where I am right now.

Describe your social life and your current friendships. ~ Most of my current friends are people for whom sexuality is also important or at least happily neutral. It's like, "Oh yeah, sex, uh, big deal, so you're into that stuff? Oh, that's cool. Oh, what'd you think of that book?" Not people who will be liable to struggle with me around what I believe, although a couple of my old friends who still are important current friends are not happy about the way my life is. There are little cat fights from time to time, and then we talk about something else. Most of the people who are close to me now are gay, lesbian, bisexual, transsexual, transvestite, sex workers or some version of the sexually stigmatized. I like it fine that way. Being around difference makes it more okay that I'm different. It is fascinating. Occasionally people will say, "What's so interesting about sex?" It's like, what's *not*? Some of my friends are activists and educators. Some just like to do it. Or talk about it. It's more important that they like to talk about it than they like to do it as far as I'm concerned because talking about it is a great joy. Most of them also like to eat and can be engaged in other sorts of conversation. They're bright, they're caring, they're accepting.

Do you use drugs? ~ A little bit, not much. Having had an alcoholic mother has I think pre-disposed me to a low tolerance for people getting stupid around me. I have low tolerance for stupid energy anyway, which is not to say that I didn't drink a good deal too much when I was younger and get stupid myself, which was kind of fun then, but I don't like that any more. Maybe I smoke pot once a year. Maybe I share coke with my partner or friends three times a year, maybe I have two glasses of wine when I go out, rarely. I'm open to doing other kinds of drugs but they don't cross my path. Psychedelics have always tended to be sacremental for me, but I'm not doing any vision quests right now, that just isn't where I am. There's no reason to pop anything.

Have you suffered any traumas as an adult? ~ Yeah, I'm in the middle of the AIDS epidemic. And I've lost people who are dear to me who I'll always miss. I have incredible, brilliant friends who are HIV-infected and whom I might not get to grow old with. I live in a world that is probably not going to deal *me* that card because I'm careful, but I can't predict the future, and that tragedy is so far from over that it's hard even to think about. One of the reasons I moved to San Francisco was because I was doing AIDS work in Eugene where nobody thought it existed. One of the reasons I came here was to be among people with whom I didn't have to feel crazy and from whom I could get support.

Describe your fears and insecurities as an adult. ~ My fears and insecurities were so much more profound when I was younger that sometimes I don't even feel like I have any, although I do. I guess they're grown-up versions of the ones I had when I was younger. I'm acutely aware that I am a rebel whose main call seems to be to communicate to people who are more "normal" than I am, to try to maybe expand their range of normalcy or to talk to people who don't live the kind of life I do and try to help them understand it. On some level, I do that to make myself okay with those people. On another level I do it to make them okay with me because for a long time I hated them and I don't want to hate them anymore. I want to have some sense of who they are and why they are the way they are and why I always haven't fit in and how we can all share a community together. So, one of my biggest fears and insecurities as an adult is that I won't be able to communicate with them, that I am, in fact, cut off from the greater community by virtue of how I see the world and what I choose to do with my life. Can I make this connection? Can I make myself understood? Can I help the community edge towards a better acceptance of diversity? Am I equal to that? Are people going to listen? Sometimes I feel insecure around the amount of work, the amount of projects I take on, real overwhelmed sometimes. I live life in a non-linear enough way that it's easy to feel like I take on the whole world and I have to figure out which part of the world I want to put on hold while I tend to all the rest of it. That's probably my worst habit and the most anxiety-provoking thing in my life.

Do you have any male inspired fears? ~ I can't say that I'm not afraid of being jumped and raped. I used to be rather obsessively afraid of that, I no longer am. And yet when I'm out by myself on the streets, especially at night, I'm very careful around male energy. I understand that one of the ways of being male, and I think there are a lot of ways of being male, doesn't lend itself very much to me being able to communicate and get through. What's more fearful than something like that happening is how it would affect my world and my worldview and the balance I've been able to establish around kind, loving, trusting men. I would hate to lose that. I know how it feels not to trust men and I don't ever want anybody to get in my face and take that away from me. I want to be able to live with as little fear as possible.

What media do you consume? ~ I read about sex and anti-censorship, questions of sexual civil liberties. I subscribe to *Penthouse Forum*, *Writer's Digest*, *Utne Reader*, and *Metropolitan Home*, which is my *true* pornography. (Laughs) With starving children all around the world, it's really irresponsible of me to look at kitchen makeovers that cost twenty grand, but I do. (Laughs) Tom Wolfe called that kind of stuff "yuppie porn," and I think he was quite right. That's exactly how I use it. I read *Wigwag* for something completely amusing and different. *Wigwag* is a new quirky little writing magazine, it's pretty delightful. I read local alternative media, *The Bay Guardian*, *SF Weekly*, and *Spectator*, for which I also write. I avoid major media, I don't want to know. I'm one of those people that the anti-nuke, peace movement, and Green folks talk about feeling helpless. I feel pretty helpless about the big world, it's one reason why I have made a smaller piece of it my purview, so I don't have to just read *The Chronicle* every day and weep.

Do you have a favorite book? Author? Movie? ~ One of my favorite books in the whole world is *The Art of Eating*, by M.F.K. Fisher, which eroticizes food without meaning to; it's a wonderful book. It saved me from going crazy after a messy divorce so I'm very fond of it. My favorites shift all the time. I still love Kerouac. And I go back and read him every year or so, very happily. The best thing I've read lately is *Geek Love*, which is the story of a bunch of circus freaks dealing with the non-freaks of the outside world, which speaks fairly directly to my emotional experience. There's a little sex in it. I love the part where the Siamese twins get laid. (Laughs)

It's a hard question. I read all over the map. And I appreciate all over the map. If there's one book that's been extraordinarily important to me in the last few years it's been *Sex Work*, 'cause it was the book that allowed me to get off my old uneducated feminist hoo-ha about how awful all of that stuff was, all those women catering to the needs of men, yadada, yadada, and look at what else might be there. It allowed me to go into sex work, which has been a profoundly meaningful piece of my life's path. I think I'll love *this* book. I can't wait to read it. I want very much to know what everybody else has to say.

"Wings of Desire," my favorite movie, is about angels that hang out and take notes about the people going about their business down below. They meet at night and compare notes so they're sure they know what's happening on earth. They're completely cut off from earth and one of them decides he wants to go down to earth and become a real person because he falls in love. A profound movie, I love it.

Do you read romance novels? ~ I really don't read romance novels. I like mushy love stuff when it intrudes, but I like rawer stuff. I haven't found one that's not kind of syrupy.

Do you use sexually explicit media? ~ Absolutely. I read those little novels that you're supposed to turn the pages with one hand while you jack-off. (Laughs) The nastier the better. I actually like stuff that completely supercedes my snobby criticism of good writing/bad writing. The stuff that's not supposed to be good writing in the first place is great because I can just get off on it.

More than anything I watch porn. I have seen at least some of most every genre of porn and I like the lush romantic stuff, the nasty-kinky stuff, I pretty much like all of it. If it doesn't get my panties wet at least it makes me think and as you've probably noticed, one thing is as important as the other to me. (Laughs) If I had to give one up I'd have to let somebody else decide 'cause I wouldn't be able to choose. I watch porn to masturbate; aside from being in the booth and going on marathons in there, the most intensive masturbation I do is watching porn. It keeps me at it, keeps me up, it keeps me interested and it keeps me aroused more than I would be if I was just noodling around with my finger or a vibrator. It takes over the fantasy for me and I can concentrate on what my body is doing. And I use it a lot with my partner. We masturbate together or we have it in the background while we're making love, or we just sit down and watch it together, especially the stuff that doesn't immediately turn us on but is interesting. It's a very important part of my sexuality. Hasn't always been true, at one point I didn't like porn, I thought it insulted my intelligence. I finally got it that I wasn't supposed to be deconstructing it, I was supposed to be getting wet. And once I got off my high horse, it does for me just exactly what the people who make it intend it to do.

Had you been a customer in a peep show or other sex show prior to dancing? ~ Once or twice. I had been to an erotic dance place in Hawaii and I had been to the Market Street Cinema for a long amusing afternoon of staring right up the girls' legs from my perch next to the stage. And I loved it both times. I had feelings about seeing women come on stage who were obviously not altogether happy about being there. That's hard to watch, but it's more than made up for by the ones who love it. That level of vitality and expressed sexuality is profoundly exciting to me – and affirming. Not just sexually exciting, *affirming*. I look at women happy in their sexuality and being so proud of it that they want to strut it out onto a stage in front of a bunch of strangers and it's a gift. I certainly respond to it spiritually in a way. It's Goddess energy, when it's good. When a woman is strong and hot and in her sexual energy it's a little bit more than just an ordinary human figure. It's a big deal and we don't get to see enough of it. And the fact that when we do get to see it, it's trivialized, makes me furious.

Which of society's values have you rejected? ~ (Laughs) The one that says that we're all essentially supposed to be one certain way. That's stupid, fucked up, and just plain wrong. And it'll never work 'cause we're not.

Sort of the middle-class, heterosexual values around success, money, and marrying up. I don't get it. How could you possibly marry for *up* instead of marrying for love and lust? I don't get it. Clueless. Happy to be clueless.

The one that says that power is best utilized in a non-consensual one-up, one-down way, which is sunk so far into the fiber of our society that I don't know if we're ever going to get it out. I reject it. I don't want power to be anything in my life other than either a life source, the thing within me that lets me go out into the world and be the best that I can be, or a toy. Who gets tied up in bed? (Laughs) Those are the only kinds of power I want anything to do with.

The attitudes that make us hesitant to communicate with people who are different than we are, I reject that out of hand and struggle with it because it's hard for me to communicate with people that are different from me but I want to do it. I think that's the way we will save the world, if we can. I like it that we're not hissing at the Soviet Union anymore but I hate it that we found somebody else to hiss at right away.

And I reject that men and women are, or have to be, a certain way, either in and of themselves or with each other. I reject the assumptions of heterosexuality and sex roles. I want those to be toys also, I don't want them to run my life. There are a lot more ways we can be together than me-Tarzan, you-Jane and if I play that game, I want it to be a *game*, and I want that to be clear.

I don't much like that we're destroying the earth, either.

Has the media ideal of beauty affected you? ~ The media ideal of beauty turns me on. I spent a lot of time in my politically correct lesbian twenties trying not to have that happen at all. Fuck it, either I am brainwashed, or beauty is beauty, and that slice of beauty that the media likes right now is part of the spectrum of beauty that I respond to. I feel just as pornographic about MTV and the Levi's ads as I do about hardcore, I mean it's all there to titilate me, to sexify my world. It leads me still, to some degree, to compare myself to who's in mainstream movies, commercials, and porn movies. Fortunately I've come to a place where I feel pretty A-okay about my body. I feel attractive and sexy enough to live the kind of life I want to live, which is all that really matters. Don't feel like I need to get a 38-DD or anything, wouldn't improve my sex life. But I also find a lot of people, a lot of images attractive that aren't the ones that the media picks, so I feel like I haven't been totally poisoned. I haven't been set to bark after one particular deer in the forest, forsaking all others.

Occasionally, the fact that sex is used to advertise products that don't have anything to do with sex pisses me off. Why don't these fuckers stop it? Why don't they let their godddamn products sell themselves, why do we have to get confused? Why do our hormones have to get tied to our pocketbooks? Things might be easier if that wasn't a social norm.

What is your self-image? ~ A smart rebel and a bridge person. Articulate, adventurous, majorly romantic. Nasty enough to offset that. (Laughs) And curious, a scholar. Part of what I'm doing all this for is scholarly, but it's not the kind of scholarly that academic journals are made of, it's Socratic, it's "know thyself and know thine environment."

Are you a tolerant person? ~ Yes and no. I have tolerated a lot of shit in my time and am both more tolerant of other people's shit and other people's quirks than most and also really intolerant of bullshit. I'm intolerant of people who are too chickenshit to communicate their own truth. I've got a certain amount of compassion around that but I also have a real high level of intolerance. Because I think those are the people who are allowing the people of whom I am *really* intolerant, the religious right and the forces of conservatism who are scared of our diversity, to run roughshod over us.

I am tolerant of people's individual stories, everybody's separate quirks that make them do the things they do. I'm extremely tolerant of guys wanting to come into a booth and jack-off. I'm extremely tolerant of somebody wanting to try different things erotically until they get to their limit, see if they know themselves better and get a clearer idea of what their true turn-on is. I'm just not very tolerant of dishonesty and bullshit.

Do you trust people? ~ Mostly. I tend to trust people to do right and good in one-on-one interactions with them. Most of the time my trust seems well founded. Occasionally I wind up wishing that I hadn't trusted so immediately, but I think I'd rather take it on the chin a few times than not trust. I don't trust my government. I don't trust the intolerant ones, the ones I haven't ever had a chance to tell my truth to and who I'm not sure would listen even if I did. I don't trust them at all.

Do you exploit people? ~ No, I don't think I do. It's hard for me to think that way. In a way, what I wish would happen with the sex industry is that it would help facilitate everybody's needs getting taken care of to the degree that it would just disappear, like "the withering away of the sex industry." I want everybody to get what they want and ideally it would be nice if they didn't have to pay for it. But right now, since I can't put out everything for *free* for heaven's sake, I don't feel it's exploitive to do what I do. I'm on guard against it becoming that way. I tend not to cadge for tips as much as some people do because I think everybody should have the opportunity to see and get what they want and have the kind of fantasy development they want to have. I don't think kinky people should have to pay more.

Have you ever been violent with people? ~ The most violent I have gotten is yelling, and I broke something once. A knick-knack. If I were being attacked I imagine I would fight. But I wouldn't go out of my way to have violent energy with another person.

Define love. ~ (Laughs) Well, I recognize two kinds. One is the general global blissed-out kind that those of us who came of age anywhere near the late sixties were encouraged to feel all the time. That's about acceptance and compassion and fellow-feeling. And I think I'm fairly good at that. And the other kind, for me, is a more romantic sense of profound connectedness with another, usually including some component of lust, at least for me. Love is where you pick people to be your family.

Describe the variety and frequency of your current sexual activity. ~ I have a variety of sex with clients. I see clients usually one to three times a week. My connection with them ranges from the old suck-and-fuck, with plenty of rubbers, to masturbation and fantasy play. One of my clients is into being fisted. And, of course, I have between one and four shifts per week in the talk-booth.

I have occasional "lesbian sex," more often than not with other sex workers. A lot of my sex with women these days is happening in the context of sex with men, either with clients or with my partner. I'm so into my partner right now that I would be perfectly happy to include him in anything that I do sexually. We are together anywhere from a couple of times a week to all week long. Most of our time together we spend being sexual, we suck and fuck and kiss and cuddle and pet and hug and watch porn and masturbate and dress up and cross dress and he's a girl and I'm the boy, and sometimes we're both guys and sometimes we're both girls. We do anal play, we do a lot of fantasy, including some S&M, more dominance and submission kinds of stuff than pain or intense sensation, but some of that too. We have, separately and together, a lively sex party life, including S&M parties.

There aren't many kinds of sex that I haven't tried and there aren't many kinds of sex that I haven't liked at least to some degree, if I was doing them with somebody that knew what sexual energy was all about. The only kinds of sex I haven't enjoyed happened before I knew how to say what my needs were, and with people who didn't know how to ask what was going on for me. A true exchange of sexual energy can happen with me just as easily through a glass window at the peep show as it can in the arms of my lover. It's not qualitatively the same, but it's the same juice.

Describe your sexual fantasies. ~ Wow. I spend so much time living so many of them I don't (laughs) have a real active fantasy life right now. Actually I do. My partner and I play family sex games, brother-sister and other kinds of taboo sex. I've got some strong fantasy charge on that stuff. Maybe I'm taking my funny business with my dad into a place that's entirely safe to have the parts that did get under my skin erotically. I have a strong fantasy charge on dominant-submissive energy. I've been a bottom for as long as I've been in touch with that, which is ten, twelve years now. I'm just starting to, in my fantasy life most of all, move into a place where I can be on top, and that's a real exciting change for me. I always knew it would happen but I never knew when. When I fantasize I stop at *some* humans; I'm not willing to imagine having sex with either Jesse Helms or Andrea Dworkin. Currently, my favorite non-human fantasy has to do with going to Marine World and getting a job as an underwater mermaid and having the dolphins try to get me when I go in to feed them after the place closes. I majorly want to have sex with a dolphin and I don't know if I will ever get the chance. That's my big quirk fantasy for the moment. They're so smart, they must be good lovers, you know.

When do you get sexually involved? ~ It has to do with the quality of energy. I am *willing* to be sexual with most anybody under different circumstances. I am *interested* in being sexual with people who interest me and whose sexual energy is right out there. I get involved when the energy exchange is good and when my sexuality, my agency, can also be part of the scene. Most of the time, as a prostitute, my involvement is fairly minimal because it's not a simple, "I find you attractive-you find me attractive" exchange: "Let's take this to bed and see what's there." I'm performing a service. Sometimes, though, greater depth is present and I can't always predict when that's going to be. So it's profoundly energetic. It's just not tangible. It's not even very defineable. I will add that the more complex a person's sexuality is the more attractive it is to me. The more little quirks, the greater the fantasy life, the more complexity is there. The more little sub-personas in me and my sexuality are called out to play.

Prior to becoming a dancer had you publicly exposed your body? ~
I had made one movie. Not a porn movie, a sex educational erotic movie, featuring safe sex options for women with each other. I had also been with groups of people, in a hot tub, being sexual or just being naked.

What is sexually degrading for you? ~ Being with a partner who doesn't give a shit what's going on for me. And that is only truly degrading when there isn't some kind of equal exchange. It doesn't feel degrading to be in that situation as a prostitute because it's my job. It's better, it's fun if I'm with somebody who's responsive as a lover, but if I'm not taken into account in a sexual situation and there are a couple hundred dollar bills left on my bedside table, I don't feel that I've been used. My sexuality is such that I'm willing to perform that service, that's what prostitution is, it's a service profession.

The other experience that has felt degrading is when I do a mercy fuck, when I fuck somebody that I really don't want to because I want to be nice. It's been quite a long time since I've done that, but there I can feel degraded whether my partner's a man or a woman. And it's not about them degrading me, it's about me not being honest with my energy. It's not about, "Ooh, I'm in bed with this person that's not attractive," it's about, "Ooh, I'm lying and I shouldn't be lying, this really isn't okay."

Is sex a power for you? ~ Absolutely. It's one of *the* powers. It's the place where I can reach deep into my body and reach out to somebody else and that's profound.

Do you ever use sex as a weapon? ~ No. It doesn't work for me to do that.

Has living in a male dominated society played a role in shaping your sexuality? ~ Oh, yeah. First it taught me that men and women were different, that sexuality was basically the purview of men. That women's proper role in the context of sexuality was to be responsive and that made me hang around and wait to find somebody to be responsive to, which, as I already talked about, in my adolescent years majorly affected my self-image. If sex was something that anybody could prowl around and try to find, whether they were male or female, then maybe I would have been a little more proactive. And done something else besides just frustrate myself masturbating. Now, I feel very strongly that my interest in gender play and my sense of myself as a gendered person ties in with the fact that as my last boyfriend before my current lover put it, I basically have the sexuality of a gay man. He was saying that any woman who was willing to be as out there with their sexuality and enjoying of their sexuality as I was must be a faggot in a woman's body. Sometimes I feel like that. Sometimes I feel that there's a "male streak" about my sexual adventuring. On the other hand, that's totally bullshit. I'm not male, I'm a woman. And what it means that I am this way is that women are more ways than they say we can be. *Men*, in fact, are more ways than they say they can be. One of the reasons I came to be this way was that my very first response to feminism, when I was about thirteen, was a really visceral, "Oh, *yeah*," when I read the stuff about women controlling their own bodies and being in charge of their own sexuality. That played in really well to what my hormones were telling me right then. And it has continued to be the fundament of what's left of my feminism.

In some ways it's hard for me to identify as a feminist because of what some feminists have said and done around sexuality. I call myself a pro-sex feminist to distinguish myself from those women who are anti-sexual in some way. But how I got to be this sexual was with the help of feminism telling me that, yes, I would be supported for trying to live a different kind of life than my mother lived. If there wasn't that gender imbalance in the first place, who knows what I might have done with my life? Probably would have had plenty of sex, but whether I would have made it a crusade is another matter. It's affected me a great deal. That gender thing was the very first part of all this. Then the hormones hit and the rest is history.

How would your sexuality be different in an egalitarian or female dominated society? – I would hope that more women's sexuality would be more like mine. But it's really hard for me to think about what that might look like. The closest thing to a female dominated society that I've encountered is the lesbian community, and of course all those women grew up in a male dominated society so how do we know how we really are? What I found in that context was a lot of thinking that women's sexuality was fundamentally different from men's, that we needed different things out of sex. That was the big theoretic that helped us explain why we didn't want to sleep with men, men weren't as good with us as we were with ourselves.

Men and women learn different languages, for the most part, and we've got to attempt to learn each other's enough to be able to communicate well when we come together. But I think it's a whole lot more important that we see that "women's sexuality as an aggregate is different" and "men's sexuality as an aggregate is different" than "men's and women's are different". I have a lot more in common erotically with a lot of men than I do with a lot of women.

If the result of a woman-dominated society would be reductionism of a different kind, I say we don't need it. Maybe in an egalitarian society that reductionism wouldn't be there; that's my hope. Once we understand that we're all a lot more alike than we are different, then maybe we won't be so simplistic about who we are. We won't take gender and turn it into a prescription for how we have to be. It affects our society in its sexuality as well as in other ways profoundly, in ways we don't know, we don't have any idea.

Have birth control and medical technology affected your sexuality? ~ Yes, although I have never taken advantage of some of the more technological technologies available. The most technological I ever got was using a diaphragm. Now I use condoms and spermicide. Getting the diaphragm meant that I didn't have to worry about communicating with partners about pulling out in time, which was the old technology of choice. Frankly I'm a lot more comfortable around condoms, less paranoid than I ever was about diaphragms. It probably has to do with being more comfortable with my sexuality too. I think young women especially are encouraged to subsume some of their worries about sex itself into worries about pregnancy and vice versa. In a heterosexual context pregnancy and sex can't be separated until a workable technology for that comes along.

Tell us more about how the women's movement affected your sexuality? ~ The women's movement encouraged me to think of my sexuality as different from men's. It encouraged me to buy a pre-ordained set of rules about what my sexuality was, in fact. The same way that male-dominated society decided what female sexuality was long before I was born. It fucked my mother up and she helped fuck me up. Almost all of my life up 'til now has been a process of intellectually and emotionally warring with those two different and somewhat opposed essential ideas, and what I *really* wanted to do was find out what my sexuality was like by myself and with the help of like-minded others, which is what I'm doing now. I know it makes a whole lot more sense for me to lay out my sexuality, my beliefs, opinions, emotions, and experiences about it now than when I was waiting for somebody to come along and *give* me sex. Or feeling angry and resistant because so many were out there wanting my sex. I wanted more than anything to be able to lighten up about all of this. I wanted to let the sex speak for itself in my body and in my heart, and I'm getting there.

Describe your current love relationship. ~ We have been non-monogamously partnered for a little less than two years. We are family-of-choice for each other in a way that I haven't ever experienced before. I finally get it why people want to get married. It's to ritualize this feeling. Whether we'll ever do that is another question. I don't think of it as a heterosexual relationship, just as I don't think of myself as a heterosexual person, although he's a guy and there's no two ways about that. We were introduced by a mutual friend and our introduction moved into connection, eroticism, and play at a sex party. That's a non-traditional way to meet a partner! It was a good start to encourage us to stay as open as we were when we met. That's been real important for both of us.

I had not started dancing yet and I was just beginning my work in prostitution. He was extremely open and supportive about me doing sex work in both contexts. The only thing of concern for him is that I be careful and stay safe. The relationship is real intense and it's the first time in my life I've felt successful being very coupled and being very free at the same time. We work on it, but it's really part of who we are together and that's a good sort of relationship to have as a sex industry worker.

In your experience are dancers more deprived, abused, and battered than other women? ~ Not in my experience.

Do you recognize any characteristics common to those who dance? ~ Only one, really – that we are all somewhat rebellious. Some are pierced full of holes and tattooed and are obviously wild children who, when they take their wigs off, have shaved heads and are little biker maniac girls and punks and wild dykes and things. Others are moonlighting secretaries with a secret, but there's a little rebellion in all of us; something's got to make a woman willing to step across the line to do this job. I was going to say that we're all exhibitionists but I don't completely think that's true. I occasionally see a woman who's more acting out rebel than she's acting out, "I like being there and I like turning on guys." I don't trust a clean level of exhibitionism for somebody who doesn't really appreciate that it's okay for the guys to be there watching her. To me, that's not exhibitionism, but some other kind of power thing that's happening. But it's always about being willing to be a rebel in some way.

When you started dancing did you fear being separated from other women? ~ Yeah, not just dancing, sex work in general. It is always more difficult for me to disclose to a non-sex working woman that I'm a sex worker than it is for me to disclose to a male, *always*. I fear judgment and I frequently get judgment. How I deal with that is by trying to let them in on, through my experience, things that they might not have already known. Usually my speaking for myself lets people who judge me know that maybe there's more to it than they had assumed. Occasionally, I meet somebody that I'm frankly afraid to disclose to. I want or need her support and I'm pretty sure that I'm not going to get it if I tell her, so I don't. But that's rare.

Have people treated you as a bad woman since you started dancing? ~ For the most part, no. I talked earlier about being a bridge person. I can articulate things about this life that a person who had never experienced it wouldn't think of by themselves. And so more often than not, the response I get is, "Oh, that's really interesting. I never thought of that before." What they're thinking in their heart of hearts about what kind of a human being I am is known only to them. I do know people and I do have friends who obviously have a hard time with it. They don't label me "bad," I don't think, but I think they label what I'm *doing* "bad." Think I'm, you know, just one step away from white slavery or something. They think I'm messing myself up doing this so I'm just going to have to show up when I'm sixty and say, "Am I a mess or not?" (Laughs) You know, it's not over 'til it's over.

Have you lost self-esteem due to dancing? ~ No, no. I've gained it. In no way have I lost self-esteem. The only thing that even remotely brushes on my self-esteem in a negative way is the fact that I have to punch a time clock. No, I'm getting more comfortable with my sexuality and other people's. What's disempowering or bad for self-esteem about that?

Does your family know you dance? ~ My mother doesn't know I dance; she still thinks in terms of nympho-maniacs and good women. She was very supportive of me coming out as a lesbian. She was a little more nervous about me coming out as a bisexual and showing up with men again. So the more out there I am with regard to sharing my sexuality with a variety of men, my reading of her and her world view is, the harder it's going to get for her. I cop out on her, I'm chickenshit on her. She's an old lady, she's not going to get it. She doesn't get why I like having sex with my partner, she didn't like having sex with my dad. She's not going to get why I want to show my pussy to strangers. It won't compute.

My brother, his wife, and their two kids, adolescent boys – talk about me being a good role model for the young! – do know that I'm dancing. They don't know a lot about it, partly because the conversation occurred when the kids were there and I wanted to respect my family's level of disclosure around sex to their kids.

Has dancing affected your politics? ~ It's certainly emphasized the shift in my politics that becoming a sex worker represented. It's all around my love-hate relationship with feminism and remembering that "You told me I could do what I wanted with my body and now you're telling me that I'm a brainless victim. Cut it out!" This is very emotional for me. I respond to this one like when my mom said the flu shot wouldn't hurt and then it hurt. I was so furious I screamed, "But you said it wouldn't hurt, you *lied* to me!" Just how I feel about feminism. "You said I could, now you say I can't. You lied to me!" I need Mom to hear that I'm disappointed in this mixed message and feminism really is my other mom. My live mom was a dysfunctional human being, especially as a mother; feminism was going to pick up that slack for me emotionally, and now come to find out I'm too queer for it. It pisses me off. My own birth mother was much cooler about me being a lesbian than my ideological mother of choice is about me being a sex worker and *it's not okay*.

Do you identify and feel solidarity with other sex workers? ~ Absolutely. I feel extremely in pain and confused about those sex workers who don't want to be doing what they're doing. The ones that anti-porn feminists talk about. I know they're out there, and I wonder if there's anything I can say that will communicate the things that I like about this life. Given that there are so many things that they obviously don't like about this life. It's a lot easier for me to relate to the women who, like me, are excitable rebels, going, "Oh great, this is cool! You mean I can touch my pussy on the job?!" I don't quite know how to address the situation of the women who don't feel good about it, or the men, 'cause the sex work spectrum is not all female. I think more men feel okay than women. That's just my take. What I do feel is, this is not a job that just anyone is cut out for. Bottom line. I'll say the same thing that I would say to somebody who works at McDonald's. I really appreciate that you hate your job. Can you find another kind of job to do? And I hope I'm not completely ignoring all kinds of social forces that make that impossible. I want us all to feel empowered, especially around this kind of thing. If somebody doesn't, they need to not be here. It's important. This is a sensitive line of work and it can be emotionally difficult for people who are predisposed to it being emotionally difficult, and those people need to take care of themselves.

Have you been discriminated against because you are a woman? ~ I certainly, up until finding the sex industry, have had jobs that would pay me less than a guy with comparable skills doing some kind of job that a guy can get more easily than a woman can get. So there's *that* little thing. For me, "discriminated against" feels almost reductionist because there's so much about this culture that makes it rough for everybody around sex and gender roles, but it really makes it rough for women around, especially, issues of self-esteem and getting out there. Being more brave and adventurous than scared and self-protective is one of the reasons that I treasure sex work and the way that it feels to do this. The fact that I am doing it at all tells me that I was brave to do this. It's a piece of my self-esteem in a non-sexual way that I didn't take the low road around this "I'm scared to go out into the world" thing. If I can do this, I can probably write great books and be an articulate spokesperson for whatever I want to do. If I can take this energy, that I'm not supposed to be able to even *feel*, feel empowered in it and take what I learn into other endeavors, it's going to assist me in being successful my whole life through. It's *not* turning me into a loser.

Are you politically active? ~ I am politically active in sex-radical sex education, and anti-censorship forums. I am gearing up to do some political organizing around those kinds of issues in a fairly major way with other like-minded folks. And I do things like vote and recycle which are little pieces of the political thing. I used to be more out there than I am now. Again, my purview has kind of narrowed into sexuality and sexual politics and censorship issues, but I really feel like all of creation is political and it's just too much for me to swallow all of it right now.

Tell us more about your feminism. ~ I'm a post-feminist, a sex-radical feminist, an anti-censorship feminist. I'm not the born-again version of the suffragist whose biggest thing was to do away with the white slave traders. I'm not the kind of feminist who thinks that women's sexuality is more delicate and genteel and emotionally attached than a man's. I'm not a separatist. Although I once had more sympathy for separatism than I do now and I actually think that it's a real good thing for women to do, to step off the merry-go-round and learn a different way of being empowered, but I don't think it works as dogma. "I'm the kind of feminist that I thought feminism was when I was thirteen years old that says, You're a woman, you can do what you want, being male or female is not going to restrict you from living the kind of life you want."

I think a lot of women and men feminists have started playing "let's figure out who we can blame for this state of affairs" and that is not productive. That's not the kind of feminist I am.

I'm not sure that most feminists know what we're trying to get in terms of our goal. I'm not sure what patriarchy is, either, although I know it when I see it. I know its fallout when I see it. I don't think that most feminists have thought all the way through what this revolution that we/they are trying to foment is going to mean to us in the way that we deal with each other. I think there's a lot of blaming men for being wrong, a lack of analysis of how so many women are completely complicit in the sex-gender system. Either questions of compulsory heterosexuality are ignored or they're turned into the whole banana. We don't have agreement on the basics. It's easier to focus on what's wrong than to look at what's right, to dovetail those two things and get somewhere. Too many have seemed too enmeshed in anger and our process. I think anger and process are fine, I *don't* think they're a politic. I want permission to move away from my anger and into a different way of relating to men and I haven't always felt that feminism gives it to me.

Historically some feminists have tried to exclude some women from the women's movement based on their sexual behavior and preferences. Do you experience this exclusion? ~ Absolutely. Absolutely. That I have been a lesbian has made me not the right kind of feminist or the right kind of woman to some. That I am bisexual has made me not the right kind to a whole slew more. That I'm a sex worker and pro-pornography has made me a demon on earth to a whole bunch more. What I'm more angry about than anything is the tendency of this mainstream feminism, that fears and dislikes pornography and sex work, to try to turn me into somebody with a problem because I have different politics and a different comfort level around sexually explicit material and behavior. If I have a problem, vis-a-vis them, then they *certainly* have a problem vis-a-vis me and that's not a useful way to think and it's hard not to get enmeshed in that anger. It's back to "Mommy rejected me," and it pisses me off. I'm not willing to let that be the end of the conversation but I'm certainly not feeling very warm and cuddly about anti-porn feminists even though I know that their politics come from a real serious emotional place for them. Maybe sometimes our politics are a little too emotional. Maybe we need to take two steps back from "the personal is political" and look at all the cat-fights we've let ourselves get into around that. The most empowering thing about "the personal is political" to me has been the understanding that I could move from a place of hating pornography and feeling like it disempowered me sexually. I don't even know where I got that idea. Nothing in my experience led me to that, somebody else's experience got privileged within a politic and it got taught to me. I am more than happy to let her have her experience, I am more than supportive of her doing whatever process she needs to do around that, but let me have my life. Let me have my experience and let me teach from my perspective, just as surely as she teaches from hers. They're both valid perspectives. Neither one of us is wrong, we're both right and I'm real tired of being told that I'm wrong.

What have been the most damaging and the most constructive influences in your life? ~ Being a child was damaging. (Laughs) Being a kid in a dysfunctional family, being a kid of an alcoholic mom and a dad whose capacity for emotional communication was way down there, and who was never happy, and who took it out on other people, was all damaging. I grew up feeling that I would never be quite perfect enough, that I was plainly from another planet. And that I would never find out whether there were any other people from that planet on this world with me. That I would never really be able to relate to people intimately. I did feel *that* isolated and alone.

That has been as well one of the most constructive bits of my history. That's empowered me to value, appreciate, and treasure friendship. It's made it feel real important to me to be able to communicate my otherness in whatever form that takes *du jour*. I finally got it when I was part of a community that I wasn't simply from another planet, doomed to be alone. I got it that even people who weren't just the same as me were people that I could communicate with and find places of commonality with, and that turned me into a real homo sapien again and gave me a lot of insight about the way we cleave away from each other. The majority, whoever *that* is, separates all the rest of us out into little categories. The fact that I don't know who they are has given me a whole other sense of empowerment, because if I can't identify who that amorphous majority is that I'm different from, then maybe I'm not so different from them after all, and that gives me trust in my own experience that I can teach from. It has literally led me to be everything from a peep show worker to a writer to a teacher.

What person or people have had the greatest influence on your life? ~ My dad and my mom, probably in that order. Again, not all good but certainly they gave me a framework. Between the extra necessities of learning to communicate and learning to juggle weirdness that were required to grow up in that household, I got taught very early that sexuality was an important issue, if only by default. Obviously the way that I deal with it is *not* by default and for me, that's a big step. It would have been a big step for the kind of people they were to think about sex as an important thing that they needed to get clear about, but they never did. They just got all fucked up around it. I would like to put a bug in everybody's ear who struggles with it the way they did, and they weren't all that unusual, that you can be *pro*active, not *re*active, around sex. That's a big part of how I succeeded personally in the world vis-a-vis them, and a big part of my missionary zeal around all of this.

My first lover, the high school teacher, had a profound impact on my sense of my own sexuality, my sense of being different, and my sense of being not so different that somebody couldn't want me.

My high school theater teacher let me put on the masks of other people for a while so I wouldn't have to suffer so behind my own. She broke every rule in the book to tell me exactly how smart I was, even gave me my IQ test results. She helped me understand one of the problems that I was having vis-a-vis everybody else: "I hate to break it to you, kid, but you're up there in that one percent, everybody's always going to treat you like this." Her attention helped me put things in perspective, helped keep me from killing myself when I was an adolescent, so she let one more peep show worker survive to entertain the world. (Laughs)

Other big influences have been people who have stood up for their politics and their sexuality, either or both, especially when it was both at once. People who didn't knuckle under, didn't become white-bread middle-of-the-road passive people whose most active act ever was to vote. People like that let me know, and there have been a slew of them, from lots of historical periods, places, politics, and kinds of sex, that you can make a difference at least with yourself and people around you, and if more people did that I think we'd make a bigger difference out in the world.

And, finally, my lover, who showed me once and for all that there wasn't anything to be afraid of about any kind of sex and that if I was from Mars, somebody else was too. Please alert the dolphins!

What are your greatest gifts and limitations? ~ My greatest gifts are my intelligence, my sense of humor, my sense of myself as different, my desire to get clear about that difference with people who are different from me. My desire to find people who are different too to bond with. And probably my courage, 'cause a lot of this has been scary, sounds kind of like it's been easy but it hasn't, it's scary. Exploring up to the edge and trying to dig around in the muck of who you are is a scary thing no matter whether you're from Mars or not, I think. The fact that I'm not just like everybody else and unrepentent about it is experienced as scary and threatening by some people, if not a lot of people, especially when they haven't met me. Perhaps it's a limitation for me that I really am going to say the things that I feel need to be said and not everybody's going to be able to grasp that. That limits, to some degree, whom I can address and how I can address them. It does keep me separate from a lot of people. On the other hand, how do I want to live? With people who feed me or people that I have to tow some kind of imaginary line to fit in with? That choice seems really clear for me.

What would you like to be doing in 10 to 15 years? ~ I'd like to be living a sexually wild and emotionally quite secure lifestyle with my honey-of-choice, who I think will be my current honey-of-choice, and who knows how many dancing girls. (Laughs) I want to be doing some form of sexuality education. I'd like to be able to look up at the shelves and see a couple of books with my name on the spine. I want to be, probably, in San Francisco, doing a lot of the things I'm doing now and a lot of things that I haven't discovered yet. I want the process I'm on to continue and be as enriching and interesting and as growthful as it is now.

Recently in San Francisco we witnessed the appearance of women dancing for women. Why do you think this is happening? ~ I think women are finally getting a clue that erotic entertainment is for them also. Everyone from fundamentalist Christians to psychologists to feminists have for so many years said women just don't like that kind of stuff. Well, it's learned. It's *learned.* Maybe there's some biology to it but a whole lot more of it is learned and when women don't have permission to enjoy sexually explicit material, or have any explicit material that speaks to them to enjoy, of course they're not going to enjoy it. (Laughs) That seems kind of simple. The fact that women are beginning to say, "Oh, let's explore this kind of sexuality, our right to sexual entertainment and what kind of entertainment we would appreciate and produce on our own," it's a little revolution. My dream is that in twenty years or so, all women in this culture, not just a certain brave lusty cadre of lesbian and bi women, are going to have access to that kind of stuff. It's already happening. You see women going into paroxysms, howling, and throwing their underwear at the Chippendales, it's out there. More and more women will know about this stuff as time goes on, unless the big "they" manage to quash all of it and I don't think they will.

Have you danced for women only? ~ No. I've danced for an audience that included women. It's a scary and very alluring idea to dance for women only and at some point I'm sure I will.

If social and economic equality for women became a reality, would some women still dance? Would you? ~ (Laughs) Sure. It happens that this pays better than a lot of other "traditionally female jobs," but it also happens that I do it 'cause I like it. I certainly can't see wanting to join the ranks in a field where, up until the day before yesterday, women didn't get as much credit and pay as men. What would I want to do that for? That would be weird. (Laughs) If social and economic equality became a reality maybe the diversity of women's and men's choices in occupation would become a little wider, and maybe *more* women would dance. Maybe more men would start dancing for women. (Laughs) I'm curious. I will stay tuned.

Would commercial sex work exist in your ideal society? ~ I go both ways on that. I think yes, and it would be a good deal more acceptable to everyone than it is now. It wouldn't be stigmatized, it wouldn't involve that people go into a red light district. People from all economic ranges would have access to it. Maybe it would be socialized. The no side is, in my ideal society everybody would have what they want with each other already and would never have to pay for it. And really both sides are about everybody having fully what it is they want.

For many people it is impossible to conceive of anyone choosing to dance as you do. Why do you think that is? ~ I think many people have a profound sense of shyness and even shame about their bodies. They couldn't conceive of doing it themselves and so they can't conceive of anyone else choosing to do it of their own volition. I think probably just as important as that is the fact that in this culture erotic entertainment and service is stigmatized. In some places it's not legal and most people in this culture get raised thinking that they're not going to do things that are overtly illegal, that will get them stigmatized by their peers and so – I don't want to be offensive about this but I will – it's the good sheep mentality again. It's, "Even if in my little deep, dark erotic heart of hearts I'd love to do something like that I keep it on the fantasy level because really nice girls/nice boys don't do this, and I want to stay nice."

Many people paint female sex workers as among the most obvious victims of male domination and declare that if you don't see yourself as such you are suffering from "false consciousness" and "delusions of the oppressed". What is your response to that? ~ Well, (laughs) first, I want to remind them that my delusions pay me much better than theirs, for the most part. And that as a female sex worker in this culture, I experience what, in fact, male sex workers in this culture also experience – a relatively high ratio of free time, to do with what I wish. In my case that includes write, fuck, and do political work. It don't feel like oppression to me from a purely material standpoint, and I can certainly discuss materialism with the best of 'em.

Additionally, you can *label* anybody anything. Most people label other people *something*, whether it's victim, pervert, bad, wrong, stupid, what have you, to distance themselves from the experience and the reality of the person, very often to justify a level of oppression that if they didn't label them, they would feel uncomfortable putting out to somebody who is essentially like them. The feminists who label me a victim are trying to do just that to me. They are also projecting their fear of their own sexuality and especially of men's sexuality onto me. If they want to feel afraid of, victimized by, hurt by, fucked up over the expressions of somebody's desire for them, whether it comes in the context of a one-on-one relationship or whether it comes in the context of, "Hey she looks pretty good walking down the street," that's okay. It's not how I want to live, but if that's how they choose to live okay, fine, but don't tell *me* I have to live like that. I could, well, in fact, I will, I'll get set off here for a minute and name call right back. I think those women are victim to a sense of their own inability to negotiate sexually for what they want. I think they are the victims of poor communication. They are the victims in the worst way of misogyny because they believe women can't stand up for who they are and what they want. And I feel real sorry for them, profoundly sorry. I understand that feeling, I was there once, I'm not in my teens anymore, I grew up, I want them to grow up too. You know, women, get strong. If you hate men, be clear about it, be ultimately clear about where the source of these projections on me are coming from. Because then other people can listen to what you say and know exactly where you're coming from. Right now a lot of people don't.

Has the sexually explicit media you've seen accurately portrayed humans and their sexual relations? ~ My experience viewing sexually explicit material extends from the explicit films made for college sexuality classes and therapists to crass loops, made for coin-op machines, to a good deal of the new wave of amateur stuff. My reading extends from antique Victoriana to hard core S&M porn and I went through a lot of scientificized explicit reading on the way. I was masturbating to Wilhelm Stekel's *Patterns of Psycho-Sexual Infantalism*. I've seen a wide range of what's out there to be seen. Some of it is absolutely accurate, right on. The amateur stuff tends to be what real people do. The educational stuff absolutely is meant to be what real people do. Much of the commercial stuff that's available shows the sexual athletes who are trained to do what they're doing and are following somebody else's script. The majority of the media out there, especially film and video, show people who look a certain way, performing, in some cases, a wider range of activities than the people viewing it do in their own lives. It tends to be formulaic, the men tend to have bigger dicks than average, the women tend to be shaped and look different than average, perhaps. It is both permission-giving for people, and also tends, I think, to make people think, "Oh, *that's* the way you do this." I would like to see "a thousand flowers bloom, a hundred schools of thought contend" and everybody out there making some kind of explicit media. If it were as okay to do that as it is to enter a cake in the bake-off contest at the county fair, well then you would get some sense of what people *really* do. That ain't going to happen until a few folks in this culture change their attitudes about whether or not this stuff is okay in the first place.

At what age do you think people should be allowed to view pictures of human genitalia? ~ Well, they got to be out of the womb because they can't see in there. I'm serious. Maybe on the way out. There should be decorations on the walls of the obstetrics ward. People should be able to view pictures of human genitalia at every age. People should be able to view live human genitalia walking past, in the persons of the brothers, sisters, mommies and daddies, and when they go out on weekends to the nude beach. Genitalia should be not more outrageous to view than ears and until we get over that one, we will have certain problems associated with shame and guilt. And probably a higher level of adrenaline attached to our titilation around nudity.

Do you think any sexually explicit media should be banned? ~ Well, much has been made of the violent genre of porn and the snuff film. From my graduate work at the Institute for Advanced Study of Human Sexuality I have been given to believe that that was a whole lot of talk. Certainly if it existed it ought to be banned. Just like killing people, period. Already existing laws should take care of that.

It's important for people who talk about banning any material to understand that what they think is right and proper to do and to think about sexually is not what everyone thinks is right and proper to do and think about sexually. That we live in a pluralistic society sexually, as well as in every other cultural way, and when they start talking about banning things, they're talking about messing with other people's realities. They need to be very clear that, yes, we want to mess with other people's realities. I personally think the dangers in doing that far outstrip the dangers in watching *anything*.

The things that are the most controversial are also the most difficult to get. They really are not being made. A lot in that controversial realm, the under-age stuff, the so-called violent stuff, was made twenty years ago, it wasn't made this year. There's not as much of that being produced as fundamentalists, feminists, and government leaders believe. That's extraordinarily important for people to know. People are being sold a bill of goods.

At the outset, the Meese Commission declared that it intended to contain the spread of pornography. At its conclusion, the Commission, like most others, could not define pornography. Yet it recommended the prosecution, fining, and jailing of people who produce, distribute, and consume it. What do you think of the Commission and its recommendations? ~ I think the Commission is a self-serving bunch of conservative bureaucrats and politicians attempting to write itself a blank check to conduct sting operations, to nose around in the private affairs of citizens and to make names and careers for the people involved in it. It's as stellar an example of what's wrong with the political system in this country today as you could possibly get. And they wouldn't have gotten away with it, except it's not okay in this culture for people to stand up for their own and other people's sexual rights. And until it is, folks like that are going to be able to run roughshod over the politics of this country. We're going to see it for a long time to come, I fear.

I think the recommendations are totally specious. When people want access to something like sexually explicit material, it's going to do more harm than good to try to restrict and criminalize it. Certainly to try to set people up around it. Those folks want to make a name and they want to make a buck. They incidentally want to make a point and I think they're a tremendous danger, more dangerous than any purveyors of any kind of pornography ever will be, because you have to seek out pornography. Since the Meese Commission, the Justice Department will send it to you in the mail and then come by and bust you.

Why do you think the government shows virtually no concern with violence in the mainstream media? ~ They want to train us to be violent. They need people to know what violence is, and to glorify it to some degree, or else they'd have a really hard time getting kids to go fight stupid, stupid battles about oil and other things in countries where we really don't have any business fucking around. As Wilhelm Reich mentioned, when you control a culture's sexuality, you control them ultimately. So they have every reason to want people to feel more comfortable with violence, force, and killing than with sex and pleasure.

How are sex work and sex workers portrayed in the mainstream media? ~
They're portayed either as hapless victims, or as gratuitous teasers. There's a
little gratuitous hooker action in the cop drama, oh good, you can trot by a
woman in a mini skirt and spike heels. What was this last little bit of ridiculous fluff? *Pretty Woman*, which is like the Pygmalion story of somebody
being rescued. Folks love to rescue us in the media. Show us the error of our
ways and take us away, marry us, make us honest women. Occasionally we're
portrayed as extremely powerful temptresses. We're almost never portrayed
as real people doing real work, partly because this culture can't conceive of
sexuality as real work, they can hardly conceive of sexuality as real *play*.
There's almost always some tinge of "poor thing," or "evil thing." We are not
normalized.

***Some people argue that humans are born with a sex drive and after that our
sexuality is socially constructed. How do you think human sexuality is
shaped?*** ~ Human sexuality is shaped, perhaps, through some ineffable biological influences that nobody's been able to really test and determine. I *certainly* think human sexuality is shaped through family interactions, most profoundly, through cultural images that filter down to kids even when they are in
nursery school, having more to do with gender images and gender roles than
anything else at that age. But gender and sexuality are very intimately connected, especially in this culture. So that, the more you tow a gender line, the
more likely it's going to be later on that you're going to tow a sexual behavior
line. Schools, peers, the kinds of toys we get, the age at which we get access
to sexually explicit material and what kind it is – boys seem to get and go for
explicit images much more readily and girls seem to get and go for images of
love, fantasy, and romance much more readily – all that stuff affects our experiences and what we think is possible and right for us. I still think the
sex/gender control system has more affect on our sexual behavior than probably any other: men do this, women do this.

Are there a wide variety of sexualities produced? ~ Probably as many as
there are individual people. I don't think that any two people are just the
same in their sexuality and the idea that they ought to be is really pernicious.
It makes us feel not okay with each other. It creates problems in finding compatible partners. It requires that in order to have good sexual relationships we
have to have good communication skills. In those senses it makes it a little
more difficult that there are so many sexualities out there, even within gener-
alized groupings of sexual interest and focus, like heterosexual male, heterosexual female, gay male, lesbian, bisexual male, bisexual female, beastialist,
trans-gendered person, person who eroticizes power, S&M, dominance and
submission, and person who eroticizes infantilism and age – to name only a
very few of the many different sexualities available to people. Even within

those general sub-groupings there are a phenomenally wide range of different kinds of people pursuing different fantasies. And what it means is that there are so many influences on us that just like the kind of food you like, each and every person gets to have their favorite thing. Gets to have the thing that makes their heart beat the fastest, gets the juices going the quickest. If we honored that, we would have more ease in finding compatible partners, 'cause it would be committed to not everybody is going to be just so for everybody else. It would make us feel more comfortable about who we are and we would feel a higher sense of self-esteem because, "Oh, well, I'm like this, Jane's like that, Joe's like that. Oh, that's cool."

Do you think the State tries to manage sexuality? ~ The Meese Commission certainly did, didn't it? Yeah, the State attempts to manage sexuality and it's able to do its job with not a great deal of effort because the cultural-religious complex does most of its work to begin with. The State shores that up. It allows for a religiously influenced morality and set of standards that means the State itself rarely has to step in. But when it does, it's stepping in on behalf of those standards, most of the time.

What do men and women have in common sexually? ~ Nerve endings, blood-engorged places, more of them than most of us ever know about, orgasmic contractions. (Laughs) Many men and women share an ejaculatory process. We share the biology. All the parts on you and all the parts on me were the same tissue for the first few weeks of gestation. It's all the same stuff. It's shaped different now. Our hormonal levels apparently, and our cultural upbringing potentially, help men and women get aroused by somewhat different processes. But I think that, again, there's more diversity *within* genders than there is *between* us. Men and women have a great deal in common and we would have more in common if we would let ourselves. My sexuality is more "male" than it used to be. And that doesn't mean that my sexuality *is* male, it means that I'm learning to allow my sexuality to expand into places that have been *culturally defined* as male. I think anybody could do that if they would. Male sexuality could look more "female." The fact that we've categorized anything as male and female got us off to a lot of trouble to begin with.

Is there any sexual expression that society should ban? ~ Yeah, killing other people for fun. Non-consensual pain and abuse. From those people who are sociopathic and who have not perhaps been given permission to explore fantasies of pain and domination and control consensually with other people, we get some folks who are dangerous. I think that should be banned, but then it already is.

What part does sexual pleasure play in life? ~ I guess it differs for different people. For me it plays an enormously important part. It's one of the most strongly empowering things in my life, the pleasure itself and my discourse around it, my emotional relationships, thinking about it, fantasizing, determining what I might want to do and try, determining what I've done that I like better than other things. All of those things together make me a strongly sexually empowered person.

I probably think about sex more than the average person although I don't know that, because we don't really share that kind of information with each other. I know I think about it openly more than the average person and I also know people for whom sexual pleasure doesn't seem to play a part at all. The breath of the wind across their faces may be as good for them as a good fuck is for me – I certainly hope that's true.

But it also seems to be true that a lot of people don't get what they want sexually because they haven't been able to believe that they could. In fact, some people haven't even been given permission to start to think about what they would want *if* they thought they could get it. I think those people tend to be the ones who believe that I'm most disempowered in what I do. They can't imagine a sexuality that's fully empowered. Whether it's from religious and social upbringing or whether it's from a certain politic, I think that many people are encouraged to see sexuality as a one-up one-down situation. Most traditionally, at least most traditionally the way I learned about it as a female, and as a female who was early influenced by feminism, it's man's up, woman's down. I'm beginning to talk to men now whose one-up one-down is the woman has all the power, she can withhold it if she wants to. That was a whole new perspective for me to think about, that men could really, really feel disempowered sexually.

Some people seem to think that sexual pleasure without procreation is a threat to society. Is it? ~ Well gosh, if we were all fucking all the time and not having any babies, what would happen? (Laughs) I guess there has to be a little procreation eventually. I think if we had a lot less than we have now that we'd still do just fine, thank you very much, especially if all the other countries in the world would join us. I can't help but believe that many of those folks also see sexual pleasure *with* procreation as a threat but procreation is sufficiently important that they're willing to face the threat to have a kid. I think that's a difficult and painful set of concerns for people who believe that. For the rest of us it's difficult and painful that there are people who are trying to impose that on us.

You believe it is okay to be a sex object, tell us more. ~ It's okay as long as that's not all you are. And, in fact, if that's all I am to somebody that I see for two seconds walking down the street, sorry, my old feminist allies, I don't get hurt by that. There's just simply nothing painful or disempowering or wrong around that. And as somebody whose eroticism has strong components of the show-off and the exhibitionist, I, in fact, often get something from a situation like that. I get my own charge. It doesn't have to do with any kind of disempowerment. That's not what it is. This is the best way I can explain it, because I'm a voyeur too, because I get turned on by other people's sexuality, sexual images, dicks and pussies, because I like to view a video, see a cock in tight jeans or a glimpse of panty when somebody goes over a subway transom, if somebody seeing me gets the same kind of charge that I get out of seeing somebody else, that feels perfectly okay with me.

My suggestion to people who are concerned over the sex object questions, start to make other people sex objects for yourself. See if there are ways that you can make that feel good for yourself, ways to do that where you don't feel like you're taking their humanity away from them. If you do feel like you're taking their humanity away from them, what seems to be the problem? There must be a way to do it where it's okay. I would say the same to men whose looking tends to disempower and dehumanize the women they look at. If there's something about that that's not a positive life-affirming look, change the look, change your heart, look at your attitudes. There should be no reason why us being sexually pleasant to each other is a bad thing.

Do you think gratification of sexual needs diminishes anti-social impulses? ~ Yes, I do. I think that gratification of sexual needs, especially when combined with gratification of emotional needs, probably drains anti-social impulses out of most people. I think when you are happy about the way you're having your orgasms, you tend not to want to fuck with other people. Now, a few people seem to have crossed wires around that question so I won't say that every single person in the universe will have that experience but I think more often than not. It's the emotional stuff that makes people feel bent. And when sex and emotion become entirely separated, and one gets gratified and the other doesn't, then people feel an imbalance sometimes. But I want to caution that we don't know enough about any of this. Social-scientific research is suspect almost all the time anyway and there haven't been enough people who have felt comfortable about doing value-neutral, sex-positive research about this stuff.

Feminism as it emerged in the early 1970's had as basic tenets sexual exploration and sexual self-determination. Subsequent exploration has led to intense debate over female sexual identity and behavior. How do you define female sexuality? ~ I define female sexuality on a micro-level, to borrow one of my old sociological phrases, as "the sexuality of any female." I define it on a macro-level as little as possible. I think there has been a great attempt on the part of one important strain of cultural feminism to reify female sexuality. To say that there's an essentialism that exists, that in fact doesn't. There are way more women out there than ever get looked at and asked questions. There is way too narrow an amount of theorizing going on that embraces the experience of all women. And feminist theorizing about female sexuality tends to take mostly into account feminist women and their sexuality, and not even all of *them*. So I try not to say what female sexuality is.

There do seem to be some social tendencies around females and their sexuality. We do seem to be pretty tactile. The visual-tactile differential is something that we don't know enough about. We seem to have a greater tendency to connect our erotic and emotional realms. I don't think there's anything innate in any of that, or if there is, we don't know it yet. There are certainly plenty of women who can, far from requiring soft tactile touch, watch somebody in a porno movie, breathe, and wiggle their hips in a certain way and have an orgasm. And there are certainly women who stalk alleys like alley cats or like *men*, heaven forbid (laughs), to try to find somebody to get off with.

So I don't think that there's any *one* real kind of female sexuality. I think female sexuality is the sexuality of females and it is under studied and under acknowledged. And as long as it's under acknowledged, little girls growing up will have fewer ideas about what it's okay to be and how it's okay to be than we might otherwise.

A recent Kinsey Institute survey of western nations concluded that people in the U.S. feel the worst about their bodies. Have you seen evidence of this problem? ~ All over the place. I have a perfectly okay body but I gave myself shit about it for a good twenty years. I think that is endemic among women *and* men, although we don't hear so much that men should look a certain way, or what men's concerns are about how their bodies look. There seems to be less body modification on the part of men but that also may be changing. I heard recently that you can now get a silicone washboard stomach and pecs. Hey guys, save your money, you too can look like Roger Craig, for a price. (Laughs) Way too many of us don't feel attractive and worthy around our bodies.

In the late 1940's American writer Philip Wylie saw equally strong tendencies to excite and constrain the erotic drive as pervasive in this society. He observed that they continuously reinforce each other and declared, "The United States is technically insane on the matter of sex." Is his diagnosis good for today? ~ More than technically insane. While we are in an era in which sexually explicit X-rated material is being sold more than at any other point in history, and is the object of bans and even sting operations, sexually explicit advertising is totally on the rise. Watch MTV if you want soft-core porn. Everybody gets to see that stuff. And yet we're supposed to worry about Mapplethorpe's nude images and the fact that when Jock

Sturges goes to France, he can take pictures of unclothed underage girls running around on a beach with everybody else unclothed and then that's pornography and dangerous. We are a cultural nutcase around this issue. Some of us are trying to go to the edges of what we see as sexually feasible to see what good, exciting, informative stuff we can find there while other people are too terrified about stringing words into a sentence to ask their partners to wear a condom, so they don't have sex at all. We're a mess. We're a big mess.

In a recent decision the Supreme Court ruled that the State does have a role in regulating bedroom behavior. Do you agree? ~ No. No. Short of lust murder. No. No. In bedrooms, in living rooms, in kitchens, in bathrooms, in every place where non-consenting people don't have to watch it, people should be able to do exactly what they want erotically and there are far more impediments to that in our cultural upbringing than the State will *ever* be able to impose. They should just get the fuck out of the way and let us get healthy so we can have a good time.

People in the U.S. are spending billions of dollars each year on sexual needs. What does this say to you? ~ It says that we want to have good, healthy, honest, sexy, satisfying sex. That we think we can do it if we get a new dildo, the most recent porno movie, if we go X number of times to a peep show, if we see a sexual surrogate, if we see a shrink. We can do it if we buy the right self-help books or magazines, but we all want it. And the only ones of us who don't want it think that the aforementioned citation is just absolutely scandalous and satanistic. More evidence of the schizophrenia that you alluded to a couple of questions ago.

Can sexual needs be met commercially in a non-sexist way? ~ Yes, I think so. It helps if both people in the exchange are not particularly sexist. I mean, when one or two sexist people come together the result is usually some kind of sexist encounter. (Laughs) Although I guess if their sexism runs parallel they could both be quite happy with it.

I think the attempt by feminists to make commodified sex, by its very nature, sexist, is doing infinitely more harm than good. And it's doing more harm, I think, to the men who buy sex than it is to the women who sell it. Because the women who sell it already have to confront X amount of shit in their lives to get to the place where they sell it. They either have to say, "No, I want to do this, and to hell with everybody who thinks I shouldn't" or "I need money so bad I gotta," or whatever the reason is. But men don't so much have to step across a real clearly defined threshold. It's a male thing, a male rite of passage. I would guess that most guys in this culture have purchased some form of commodified sex at some point, whether it was walking in and looking at some hootchie girls, buying a blow job, a magazine or a movie. So it's much more clearly the average guy who is the purchaser, it's *not* the average woman who's the purveyor. She's got one up on him. She already had to confront the fact that she's not average around this and he doesn't have to.

Do you think the schools should teach about human sexuality? ~ Yep, and I think they should do a damn better job than they're doing now. They should teach everything. They should teach people that there is no one way to be sexual. There's a range of behavior. They should teach safe sex and responsible contraception, anatomy, physiology, fantasy and everything else. They should teach reality. And they don't. I don't think they're going to any time soon, either.

How is sexuality portrayed in the mainstream media? ~ Sometimes the mainstream media does a relatively good job portraying sex as it is. The rest of the time it's gratuitous, it's "exploitive." I mean that it's there in a way that we're supposed to distance ourselves from it somehow. We're supposed to go "tee-hee, snigger, snigger, I'm not like that." The queer jokes that they're always telling on "Three's Company." Or almost pornographic titilation like they use it on the soaps. You know, that's women's common pornography and all that's missing is the monster shots. (Laughs) It's just as formulaic sex as it is in XXX. I think sex in the media is over-hyped and under-talked-about. We see scads of it and we don't get to learn very much about it.

Some people argue that there is a sexual hierarchy in the United States with heterosexuals at the top and everyone else treated as second class citizens. Do you agree? ~ Yeah, I think that's true. But I also think that *heterosexuals* are treated as second class citizens. (Laughs) I truly don't believe that outside of the people who have managed, from whatever sexual subculture, to come to real clear good terms with themselves and their sex, that there is a sexual uppercrust in this culture. I used to believe there was. I used to believe that heterosexuals had it together and had privilege. Now I will remind anybody that a lot of behaviors that heterosexuals can and want to do together aren't legal in a whole lot of states in this nation either. Of course, homosexual and other behaviors are still illegal. Adultery is still illegal in many states. You can get thrown in jail for getting a little from somebody that you're not legally wed to. Heterosexual kids don't get any more sexual rights than gay or lesbian or any other kind of kids. Nobody gets much permission and information to be the kind of sexual person they are or could be. At least in sexual subcultures, the real stigmatized subcultures have the opportunity to come together around their difference to find out what in fact their sexuality really means to them. I don't think most heterosexual people are able to do that in the same way. In some ways, I think those who think they're normal are a couple steps behind everybody else in terms of their own sexual self-awareness. You can change that, however. Just start to talk about it. (Laughs)

Some people also think that non-heterosexuals should not have the same rights as heterosexuals. What do you think? ~ Well, that's perfectly absurd, of course they should. Everybody should have a lot more rights than we have now. Just because non-heterosexuals are non-heterosexuals, what? What's the problem?

Do you think heterosexism is a serious problem in the United States? ~ Absolutely. Absolutely. And I'll take one step further. Lesbian theorist Adrienne Rich talks about compulsory heterosexuality, which I think is the next step or maybe the parent quality out of which heterosexism spreads. Heterosexism is of course the privileging of heterosexual people but I think that on top of the privileging and how painful it is for everybody else to feel silenced around that, heterosexual people themselves don't get enough information about the ranges of behavior that are possible for them. While on the surface it seems that hets have it more together because they get all this privilege and they get to get married and yadada yadada, in fact, true information about heterosexual behavior, you know, depictions of it, or down and dirty hot descriptions, or real helpful clinical descriptions are just as hard for folks to get access to as it is for beastialists to find their beast books and gay and lesbian people to find each other and overcome the problems that heterosexism has given them around *their* sexuality. I think we really are profoundly in the same boat.

How does society respond to the outspoken sensuous person? ~ With nervous laughter, discomfort, and intense fascination.

What have you learned about people through sexuality? ~ I've learned how much more the average person wants and what he or she really has around sex and relating. I've learned how debilitating fear is, especially fear of difference. There's a phrase that I heard a storyteller use once that I just love: "Follow what fascinates you." I've learned about people's fear of following what fascinates them. And that so many people manage to do it anyway. They don't feel too good about it all the time, but they manage to get something in their lives that resembles or points the way to what they really want. That's what I think my work in the peep show is all about, people finding a door that they can close and lock and have somebody to talk to and deal with around what their fantasies are. Some of them make the mistake of thinking that because I'm willing to talk to them at all that I must be a logical partner for them. I've learned that we are so starved for people we can tell our truth to that a man or woman in a Greyhound station that we tell our life history to must be somebody we should go home with. I've learned that people, out of fear and ignorance, or maybe just out of plain old human viciousness, want very much to make other people different and wrong. And that when that tendency is overcome, most folks have essentially the same needs. And there's a lot more uniting us than there is pulling us apart. If we let that be seen and acknowledged.

What would a sexually positive society look like? ~ One in which kids weren't stigmatized and punished for their sexual feelings and explorations. It would be one in which gender roles were not strict and behavior by gender category was unknown. It would be one in which everybody was encouraged to make sexual pleasure a priority in their lives. It wouldn't be assumed that just because you found a partner that everything would fall into place easily, that sexual pleasure would have to be something that real compatibility was found around, and that would be honored. When you bring your potential spouse home to your mom, Mom wouldn't say, "Oh, how nice, dear, how much money does he make?" but, "Oh, how nice, dear, are you having multiple orgasms together?" (Laughs) That would be healthy. I think more people would try more kinds of sexual behavior so there wouldn't be so clearly defined sexualized groups of people. Maybe some people would settle in one particular kind of behavior but maybe other people would just zoom up and down the range of things that they could do for their whole lives. I think there would be less heterosexual monogamous partnering, perhaps less monogamous partnering altogether, that jealously would be much less a problem than it is now. And for good measure we might eradicate all sexually transmitted diseases.

How can we achieve that society? ~ Talk about sex a hell of a lot more and a hell of a lot more honestly and openly than we do now. Start to look at the fact that strict gender role differentiation hurts people, doesn't help people, doesn't allow for men or women to achieve their best qualities and makes us feel like we're separate species, which we're not, even though we're trained to act like it. Start providing kids with space to be sexual and good sex education. Throw a lot more money at sexually transmitted disease eradication research than is being thrown now. In the meantime make free condoms available everywhere. Make sex okay, make it a cultural priority.

Do women play a part in the creation of male sexuality? ~ I'm quite convinced that the male-Freudian, feminist-Freudian analysis that says a lot of men's sexuality and emotional reality vis-a-vis women is formed in response to their relationship with their mothers is completely true. I know that because a lot of my sexuality was formed in response to my relationship with my mother, so why should it be any different for guys? And a lot of the rest of it was born from my relationship with my father. The mother-son and mother-child bond stays important in people's sexuality throughout their lives. Probably the more it's examined and looked at, the less important it is, and the less it's looked at the more it's the hidden secret that really carries the power.

The traditionally feminine standpoint that we have to get a man, have kids, have a family, and keep the man around to provide exerts a civilizing influence on men, perhaps, but also tends to make men, at least in a traditionally heterosexual context, often ashamed about and certainly dishonest about the lengths to which they go to get the kind of sexuality they're not getting at home.

I don't think enough women, heterosexual and otherwise, put a high priority on sexual pleasure with their partner or partners throughout the course of their lives. I think mothering gets in the way of that a lot, but I also think that women just aren't encouraged to make sex as much of a priority as men culturally are. So there's always a dearth/abundance dichotomy in the way that men and women relate to each other. That at least is what I've seen around me. And I haven't seen a lot that tells me that our society is changing, although I see pockets of change. I know older women who have always found sex important. But for the most part, the way women are encouraged to let sex as a priority slide in their lives means that men and women are going to have a weird time together in perpetuity. I suppose you could say that men should let their sexual priorities slide too but you know, then what would we do? Invade more third world countries? (Laughs)

How do you think batterers and rapists are created? ~ In families that often have battery and non-consensual sex as part of their structure. In families which don't allow for other forms of empowerment, self-esteem, and ways to work out anger and resentment. Families that are characterized by emotional dearth or poor communication. I think there are people who have been led to believe that they're never going to be able to get what they want except by force.

Do you have any suggestions on how to create a peaceful male? ~ Encourage them to masturbate all they want. (Laughs) Ensure that he gets laid as much as he wants. (Laughs) End the cultural insistence on competitive games for males, little males, the culturally implicit directive that men are going to be the ones who are going to defend. I don't think that's *just* cultural; certainly it gets expressed in cultural ways. Little boys playing all kinds of war and competition games are able to achieve a lot of their self-esteem as kids, vis-a-vis their families and peers, by how they do in those games. Those things don't teach men to be peaceful, they teach men to be war-like and competitive.

The strict insistence on men getting their touch and sexual and emotional needs met from women, rather than from each other as well, tends to subsume feelings that men feel about other men in competition and homophobia. The encouragement of men to hold in their feelings tends to make men's feelings pop out at the funniest times and sometimes in violent ways, or less than peaceable ways. The young male pack rituals that often include things like drugs, alcohol, knives and guns – not that every man goes through something like that, but most males have at least some semblance of the late adolescent drinking buddy syndrome, I don't think that promotes peacefulness in males for whom all those other things have already happened. That kind of gang or group behavior tends to kick guys into competitive ritual and sometimes the ritual goes past ritual. I don't think our culture values peaceful males and until it does, males ain't going to be peaceful.

Are there feminist men? ~ Yes, and I think feminist men respect women more. That's about all you can say across the board. They tend to be more peaceful, less war-like, less competitive, etc., etc., than the more average male, whoever *he* is. I think some feminist men would prefer not to sully their consciousness with objectifying women sexually at all or being troubled with that desire. And I think some feminist men think that women are the Goddess, and I think some feminist men think women are just folks. But all have a level of respect that's not pedestal respect, it's women as necessary co-creatures in the world.

What is their relationship to sexually explicit media? ~ I think the anti-pornography strains of the feminist movement have had a great effect on at least those feminist men who *identify* as feminist men. The group-affiliated feminist men have been talked to a lot more by the anti-porn feminists than by the pro-porn feminists. The pro-porn are too busy feeling reactive and having cat fights and going down to the corner newsstand and buying smut and enjoying it (laughs), to go down and start klatching with the feminist men.

In my experience of talking to feminist men about sexually explicit material, porn, and commodified sex, what I get is a lot of men feel funny about it because it's not emotionally fulfilling like a relationship, it tends to remind them of what's absent in their lives, and they don't feel like they can share it with the women in their lives. That's not true of everybody, but even guys who feel basically good about what they're doing and what they're watching, even those folks are struggling around the difference between, is a picture of a hamburger a hamburger? If I eat the picture of the hamburger, am I still going to be hungry afterwards? They're looking at that hunger and looking at the way pornography does or doesn't encourage that hunger.

Describe the impact male dominance has had on women. ~ I think male dominance has made women look for their power in circumscribed little spaces. The right-wing woman, "glorify the wife-mother," springs to mind. Although they're getting pretty good with direct mail too, so maybe their power is not as circumscribed as I think it is.

I think male domination has encouraged women to think of ourselves as different from men. For some reason, and male dominance is clearly a part of this, nobody has wanted to encourage us all to think of ourselves as the same. Granted we're not, exactly, but if we start to bring ourselves to an equal place conceptually, that will be the first step to bringing ourselves to a equitable place in the material world, and emotionally in relationships.

I think it's made women, as a whole, though not always individually, take the family and relationships as their purview, and they kind of batten down the hatches and then, especially over the last several decades, see that that purview hasn't been given equal status. To feel disempowered having battened down the hatches, feeling like the hatches need to be opened up and the separate but equal realms thing has got to be changed. I can't even speak to all the impact, it's like the forest for the trees. I think it's made women think small or really pissed-off around our tendency to think small. So that we can't even see what's real in front of us for a while.

Do you see men working at changing themselves? ~ Yeah, a lot. And I see a lot of men really confused about what that means. Often I see women's demands being made in a context and a language that the men can't quite understand. I see guys trying up to a point and then feeling helpless and mad that they tried and didn't get it fixed. And I see some men who have been able to transform themselves into the kinds of men that I didn't think existed when I was younger. Who I feel like I'm not speaking a foreign language with. Who seem to be just as concerned about me and my issues and the way my life is as they are about their own. Who don't seem to feel any need to dominate me in any way except if we both decide maybe it would be fun to do in bed. And who more often than not are willing to let me flip them over and do the same thing back. I think some changes are being made, or maybe there were always some men like that and I just didn't know it. But I know that there are some men with whom I can relate on as equal a level as I ever could with a woman, and that's enough to keep me going.

How can women help men change? ~ Women can understand that sometimes the communication that they're making isn't heard the way they think it's being heard. We've got responsibilities to learn how to communicate our requests and our demands in a way that men can understand. It's important to acknowledge that when people are interacting they need to communicate and compromise all the time, in relationships especially, remembering that men are bringing as much stuff to relationships as women are. Women can give positive feedback to men who are the way women think men ought to be and be clearer about their negative feedback to guys who aren't. I think some guys are not hearing specific criticism and feedback, they're just hearing a barrage of anger and rejection. Most of all I think women need to be honest with themselves and the men in their lives around setting limits and not just fall into helpless fury which then makes them completely inarticulate and unable to be dealt with. Anybody in helpless fury is impossible to deal with. Be clear and communicate before you lose yourself in pissed-offed-ness, slam the door and not communicate.

What do you think the future holds for relations between men and women?
~ Some men and women are going to get a lot better at relating with each other. There's an undercurrent of strong desire to start communicating effectively and make things work. A bit of a backlash against the sub-category that has told us that was impossible, a backlash against old-fashioned "men are this way, women are this way, and you shouldn't bother to understand each others concerns." Instead of just women thinking in terms of overthrowing their imposed sex role, women and men thinking together, "Okay, let's see if we can make this thing work out in a way that lets us communicate and understand each other."

For the folks that don't fit that profile, I predict ongoing confusion. I think there has been, at least since the advent of this most recent wave of feminism, a profound number of really confused people. And a bunch of people who think that all of that is bullshit, dangerous and divisive, and whose lots are going to stay as bad as they've ever been and get worse 'cause I don't think that enforced gender separation serves any longer at all. About the only thing one gender can do that the other one can't is impregnate the other one or have a baby. It's down to just a couple of little bitty pieces of technology here, it ain't much. And they're going to have machines to do all that shit pretty soon anyway.

Unless we have to get back to being hunters and gatherers, it doesn't make sense that we emphasize sex differences. Trying to behave as though there aren't any doesn't seem to get anybody as far as fast as they want to go, but emphasizing them really fucks us up. I predict that more and more people are going to learn not to do that, whether they know it or not. Yuppies don't think in terms of minimizing sex differences when they get married and have their 1.1 baby and get an expensive stroller, but if it's a two income family they're acting like that anyway. All kinds of folks are acting like it whether or not they have the analysis around it because, in fact, feminism has made gains and, in fact women, are behaving differently vis-a-vis men and vice versa than was happening twenty or thirty years ago.

If rape and sexual assault ended today how would your life change? ~ I probably wouldn't think so seriously about arming myself when I go out at night. Not my most intimate friends, not most gay-identified men, but most of those ordinary fellas that I pass on the street in the course of my daily goings-on, I would have a sense of relaxation around them that I don't now. I've gotten so much more relaxed than I was formerly around dealing with men. I've stopped thinking primarily in terms of a new strange man, "Oh, is he an agent of violence against women or isn't he?" That was always an important question and it became really clear that living my life around wondering it made me profoundly upset all the time. It didn't allow me to like very many men very much and made me paranoid and exacerbated my anger and that didn't make my life more liveable. So at some point I started to let that serious paranoia that I carried recede, but there's residual paranoia that's there for a reason. I can't just go, "Oh, well, rape and violence against women have vanished!" like, "I trust the President now!" No thank you. Nothing that magical has happened yet and probably won't.

The difference between me relating to men now and ten years ago would probably be at least as pronounced as me relating to men now and in post-rape culture. I mean really well, and a lot of men mean really well, and it makes it difficult for us to trust and connect when this shit goes on that we haven't been able to put down.

What is the source of inequality between men and women? ~ It's based on a gender class system that for most of our history on the planet has emphasized differences between men and women and assigned valuations. Those assigned to men seem to have been more positive than those assigned to women, at least if you look at indicators like money paid for jobs done, and whether or not somebody could have the vote. Of course, a lot of men haven't been treated very well either, but there do seem to be these inequalities that have been broad and in our current generation we're trying to figure out what to do with that. We're struggling with a really profound amount of historical backwash.

I don't think that the sex-gender class system, caste system, whatever you want to call it, is functional. Now we have physical and potential social technology that make the fact that women have babies and men don't pretty irrelevant. The fact that, you know, mommies need to stay home and daddies don't is completely irrelevant. The fact that we're not taking more advantage of those social and technological tools is because we're mired in history, the fact that Mom and Dad did it this way, the fact Grandma and Grandpa did it that way. Historical change is slow because people don't all agree at the same time to go, "Oh, okay, let's change."

Right now I think the inequality is exacerbated by the fact that men and women have been trained to think and relate very differently around sex and intimacy. And so, just like Mom was supposed to deal with the baby and Dad was supposed to deal with the Boss, the woman is supposed to be the caretaker of relationship and commitment and the man is supposed to be the one who pokes his wife with his hard dick in the morning and makes her all annoyed because he's being too pushy. That's a caricature of course, but as long as it continues to be somewhat true, men and women are going to have a lot of reasons, even beyond financial, to blame each other and to stay angry and divisive and divided around things that we probably could put our heads together on and fix if we just drop a little bit of the piss-off and go, "Okay, now, let's see if we can figure this thing out here."

Feminist people have long observed the system of male domination in the United States and exerted considerable effort to overturn it. What strategies do you think have been effective? What strategies do you recommend now?
~ I think the advent of the Pill and the "sexual revolution" was at least a partially effective strategy. It had ramifications beyond the sexual in that a whole generation of men who've kind of been convinced that women didn't really want to, were faced with at least some women who, in fact, *did* want to, and wanted to on often roughly the same terms as they themselves did. And that helped crack a deep belief that women and men were quite different, and had some ramifications even in the workplace.

Before feminism developed as accusatory a tone as it did a few years into the development of feminist rhetoric, there was an emphasis on consciousness-raising and on telling the truth of our lives to each other. That was an extremely effective technique. For people not only to begin to get that they weren't alone in the way they were feeling about the relationships between sexes, but also that telling that truth could start to change things, helped people understand each other a whole lot better. I think a lot more of that needs to be done. I think it needs to not be done in same-sex groups only, but across gender lines. How can the truth and the culture of one sex and the truth and the culture of another sex be explained to each other? It's like two countries, there's diplomacy and acknowledgement that they have two separate cultures and languages. Some people will learn the customs and language of the other culture and will be the diplomats. If they're close together and they decide that they want to be friendly countries forever and ever, then most of the people will learn the other's language and cultural exchange will happen. Men and women could do that. I mean, we *are* neighboring countries, we could do that, a lot of us already are. The other option is to say, "Well, you're wrong about that," and go to war. A lot of men and women are that kind of neighboring country, they're the warring kind. That's sort of a heavy-handed metaphor, but I really think it's true.

There needs to be a willingness on the part of men and women to be diplomats with each other and to realize that for the most part, we see each others' customs from the outside, unless we take the time to find out what the inner reality is. We need to tell each other our inner realities a whole lot more. My prescription for the future is, communicate a whole lot better and a lot more.

What do you consider to be the failures of the women's movement in the United States? ~ Its tendency to polarize people. I think that's its only failure. It pisses off not only men and other women, but women who want very much to affiliate with it. The women's movement isn't monolithic, but certain segments have attempted to behave as though they're monolithic and name rights and wrongs from everything from what kind of food they eat, what kind of surname they should be using to who you should have sex with at all times. It's a facistic tendency that has made something of a mockery of a lot of good goals. It needs to stop. Right now. Yesterday. Cause we need to get back to the good goals. Quit being caught up in this bullshit.

Anti-censorship feminists have emerged who believe that some sexually explicit media reflects and reinforces the oppression of women, but disagree with the pro-censorship feminists' view that sexually explicit media is the cause of women's oppression. They argue that the causes of women's oppression are much deeper and precede the mass production and distribution of sexually explicit media by centuries. What is your point of view? ~ I'm absolutely anti-censorship. I think that people who are so reductionist as to assume that something that was going on 1,000 and 2,000 years ago comes from pornography are obsessing on something and what they're obsessing on is not historical reality. (Laughs) In fact, they're not even taking historical reality into account.

Again, it's back to the language of the other gender and back to different languages. People who don't understand the iconography of sexual fantasy and who don't want to understand it, who don't bother to understand it, who assume that they understand what they see, tend to be pretty imperialistic about what they see. They make assumptions, they obsess about the assumptions that they're making and they pay no attention to a whole lot of other stuff that's going on. For me the proof that the kind of sexually explicit material that they point to as causing the oppression of women doesn't do that is the fact that plenty of women engage in those kinds of sexualities without a sense of themselves as oppressed or functioning as though they're oppressed. It's like, so how did they escape this fate then?

I can't figure out how it works for them, I really can't. It puzzles me. It makes me twitch but it puzzles me even more deeply than it makes me twitch. How could you possibly think that way?

I understand the visceral power of explicit sexual images and that not everybody is comfortable with them, that's fine. Not everybody needs to be comfortable with them. But turning visceral discomfort into political analysis, that's not a movement that I want to be associated with.

Where do you think sexually explicit media should be placed on the movement agenda? ~ Well, I don't think it should be placed in the fore-front necessarily, but I think it should be right up there with the demands that proponents of gender equality are making. Well, actually it *is* close to right up there because it's part of my right to do what I want to with my body and my mind and there isn't much that's in the forefront of that in terms of feminism or gender equality.

If sexually explicit media enhance even a few people's sexuality in this culture, and there's evidence that they enhance way more than a few people's sexuality, then they ought to be celebrated, not denigrated. If they confuse anybody around their sexuality and there's evidence that that happens too, then we ought to be trying to analyze *why* instead of getting rid it. I don't think the slogan should be "a porn movie in every bed-room," but it certainly should be the right to choose whether or not it's going to be there, just like my right to choose whether or not I'm going to have a baby, my right to choose what kind of birth control I am going to use, my right to choose what gender, and whom amongst all the different examples of each and every gender there are, I want to have sex with. It's how my sexuality and how my body and how my mind are going to be run by me or run by somebody else.

Do you think our constitutional guarantee of free speech includes sexual speech? ~ I think what the government of this country meant all along by free speech was what was expedient. If we're going to go down to the hallowed kernel of the Constitution, then, yeah, sexual speech just like every other single kind of speech including treasonous speech is pro-tected. I think this government is still in the hands of zealots whose agenda is very different from the agenda of the liberals who have been telling us that free speech was enshrined in this country. (Laughs)

In my opinion you've got to deal with the cultural and sexual plurality in this country by allowing everybody to say what they need to say. Not everybody at the top thinks it's okay that we *have* a cultural and sexual plural-ity in this country. And a lot of them would like to see it gone. Theoretically, there's freedom of sexual speech, in reality, no, I don't think there is. I'm willing to struggle for it, that struggle is profoundly important but it never sur-prises me when it's chipped away.

How would you advise courts ruling on sexually explicit media? ~ I would recommend that the first thing they do when they wake up in the morning is put their hands on their genitals and stroke them, not hurried and furtively, but lovingly, and think about anything they want to while they are lovingly stroking themselves. They should bring themselves to as many orgasms as they feel capable of right then, or that they have time for, 'cause I know those folks are busy, and then I would ask them to go into court and do the right thing because when they can love themselves and love and cherish and honor sexual energy like it was meant to be, they won't be having a problem with what other people want to do with their sexual thought.

Tell us what you know about AIDS and describe the impact it is having on your life and society. ~ AIDS is a constellation of medical conditions caused by a sexually and blood-transmitted virus. It can and frequently does lead to death. It's costing the government a lot of money and should be costing it a lot more because they should be giving a lot more attention to figuring out a way to put a fence around this whole fucking epidemic and they're not. One of the things that I do is teach safe sex. I've directed an AIDS education program for a small community-based organization that deals with AIDS education for the public. I know about T-cell counts and P24 antigen tests and viral receptors and all that shit, though I will spare you. (Laughs)

It's affected my life profoundly. I've lost far fewer people than most San Franciscans because I haven't been here as long, but I've lost more people than I can count on one hand to AIDS and may lose more. There are people in my life now who are living with AIDS. That in my twenties and thirties I had to look around and see members in my peer group dying in front of me has had an incredible impact on the way I look at the world, at the way I look at intimacy, probably that more than anything. What honesty and communication mean to me. What the importance of honesty and openness about sexual matters means to me. What let AIDS spread was a lack of honesty on the part of our culture about sexual speech and sexual choices. I think that each and every one of us who are willing to say who we are, and to say no to the fact that our culture wants us to shut up about sex, is striking a blow against the cultural conditions that made AIDS possible.

Do you think it is possible that this society will confine those who test HIV positive in spite of the medical evidence that it is not casually transmitted? ~ Absolutely. Sure I think it's possible but before they do that, they're probably, these days, going to start rounding up Arab Americans. I think that if they stop being xenophobic and hysterical about people with AIDS it will be because there is an easier pick of the population. But that's only a historical moment that we're talking about.

The people who run this country are not following any other call but political expedience and some of them, an outdated morality that they seem to feel very close to, at least on the surface. It's entirely possible. I don't, for an instant, think that we've seen the last of the kind of xenophobic stupidity that sees people get set aside and shunned and attacked because of who they are; we're not out of those woods yet.

What future do you see for erotic theater and erotic dancers? ~ Whether the erotic theaters of the future are going to look like the erotic theaters of the present and past, I don't know; I doubt it. I think as long as there are people who aren't getting all the erotic theater they want at home, there will be a market for erotic theater, even if it's commodified. The future will also be determined by how successful the censors are at telling people that it's not okay and not honorable and not healthy to watch people who are proud of their bodies and their sexuality perform for them. It seems like a simple thing, but we've got some folks up there who are disturbed around this and I quite frankly don't know if we're going to be able to overcome them and their disturbances, put them out of office and get on with our lives.

ANN MORE

*IT'S BEEN NO GREAT
ENLIGHTENMENT FOR ME,
I ALWAYS KNEW MEN WERE DOGS.*

Part of the promotion for your show says, "Live Nude Dancing, Lovely Lusty Ladies, Naked Naughty Nasty" Is this a good description of who you are and how you perform at work? ~ No, that's not correct. It's not a description of what I do at all. Actually it's pretty ridiculous. Not everybody is naughty, no, nothing naughty at all. (Laughs) Absolutely not. I make believe I'm on a stage in Vegas or somewhere. Nasty? Yes, but not in a sexual way by any means. I'm nasty toward them because I think they're dogs, and ignorant.

What were you told was your job? ~ I was told that I was there to entertain men and to do what I wanted to do.

Were you told that the men masturbate? ~ I was not told. I must have figured it out as soon as I got on stage. (Laughs) As a matter of fact, as I watch other people get hired it seems to me like it's something that's totally avoided. Women seem to be really shocked. (Laughs) Management is kind of ignorant, so I think they just assume you know, or it's just part of the game now. Personally I had no idea. People beat-off, that's what happens.

Describe your first experience on this stage. ~ It was great. I remember thinking I was like a Playboy bunny. It was fun because I don't do the whole sex trip when I dress. I don't wear dresses, just pants, and I'm really uptight about showing. This job has probably made me that way but, I always wanted to be one of the guys. I had bandanas all over me. I thought, "Wow." I looked pretty cool, I liked what I saw, and (laughs) the guys were stupid enough to be paying for it. It was a real thrill for me, real good for my ego.

When you were hired were you asked to work on certain aspects of your performance? ~ No, Sally loved me. Everything I did was perfect. I was cute, sexy, and playful. You have to understand this is four years ago, before I was jaded. I came off stage, and she was like, "You're perfect. When do you want to start working?"

Describe how you dance, display, and touch your body during your performance? ~ All I really do is fondle my breasts and play with my hair. I seem to go out of my way now to touch everything but my genitals, because it's so old. I try to portray something more statuesque, (laughs) more of a dance theater presentation, as opposed to, "Hi, I'm here to let you look into my ovaries."

What sexual depictions do you perform? ~ (Laughs) None! God, I don't do anything now. I dance. I'll bend over. I play with my breasts, over and over and over again. I just move around. I'm more concerned about how far I can stretch my leg, how much I can suck my stomach in, where my cellulite is. I'm not worried about the customers, or showing them anything. They might catch a glimpse of my labia, since I have a gold ring there. I'll play with that, but it's not for them, I'm looking at it. To bend over, to me, is basically an insult. But (laughs) they love it.

Does your performance contain elements of dominance and submission? ~ (Laughs) I don't give them that much thought or training. Basically I don't look at them anymore. If I catch a glimpse of something young with long hair I look. That's not often. I guess I don't give them the time of day. I just move for them because it's my job. I very rarely have any kind of real contact with them, now. They think that I'm looking at them, and most of the time what I'm doing is trying to find an excuse to leave. I'm waiting for them to do something wrong. (Laughs) Basically, everything they do irritates me, and I'm such a bitch about it now that I will pick the littlest thing.

When you say dominance, I'm thinking about when Phoenix gets her little whip out. We have slaves who want to be dominated. I don't bother with them, I think they're pathetic. I watch people humiliate them, that really gets me off, but I don't engage in it at all. As far as me being submissive...(Laughs) Please. (Laughs) I wait for them to tell me to do something, it's like, "Fuck you!" and I leave.

Do you test your power to arouse? ~ Not any longer. I did the first year and a half. It was a trip. You want to see what you can do, and now it's been proven to me that anything with tits and a cunt can do anything to a man. (Laughs) I know they're desperate to get attention from me because I have no pants on. So there's no test. They walked in the door, I won. (Laughs)

How much of your performance is you and your sexuality and how much is persona? ~ Basically, it is me. I am basically a negative, cold, non-sexual person. I think the world has been overloaded with all of it. I wish there were somewhere else to go, but unfortunately, there's no other world. Well, as far as my sexuality goes, the relationship I'm in now is wonderful. I'm very sexual with this person. That is very important to me because (laughs) my last relationship was very asexual. Nothing was happening. I saw cock all day and then went home to another ignorant cock.

What persona do you project and where does it come from? ~ I have a reputation for being a bitch with the customers and staff. It probably comes from this job. When I first started working here it was a totally different trip. I think I've gotten really hardened to the whole sex thing through this job. It disgusts me now. To me, it's a cop-out, I should just go for it and be a goddamn hooker, and suck these men. (Laughs) But I don't. I wimp out and do it this way. It's a contradiction I'm going through all the time. There are other places in the city where I could make more money. But one side of me says, "Fuck it, I don't care." But that's why I'm here, because of the money, but I don't go all the way.

The world's a cold place. I guess it's not that negative, but I pick up all the negative aspects of it. Through this job it just hits you in the face all the time. (Laughs) And I don't repel it very well. (Laughs) I take it all in and throw it back at them.

Why did you choose the stage name you use? ~ That's not my stage name. I'm using it so the people who read this book don't know who I am.

How do you use costuming and makeup? ~ (Laughs) Oh God! I use very little of anything, it's just something I do to get my paycheck. I don't even own high heels. (Laughs) I use the makeup that I use in the streets, lipstick, eyeliner. I go nude, or I'll throw on a few belts, but nothing extravagant. I used to wear sunglasses quite a bit, but now everyone's doing it, so I don't. It was kind of hard for me, because I hid behind them. Now I have to see their faces, see them oscillating, I have to see that pathetic stuff. (Laughs)

Do drugs play a part in your performance? ~ Absolutely not. (Laughs) I think I should start!

On stage music plays almost continuously. Describe the variety and part it plays in your performance. ~ If the music isn't happening to your taste, it can definitely drag you down, make your show absolutely suck. The variety is soul, rock, they also try to throw in some creative stuff, or some off the wall rock or jazz. They definitely mix it up a lot, but there are always women who make it all soul, or rock. If I wanted to change it I could. I just really don't care that much.

The stage is covered with mirrors ceiling to floor. What role do they play in your work? ~ For me, they're everything. If I couldn't look at myself I'd be in a lot of trouble. I look at my body all the time and try to keep in shape. I'm there (laughs) to dance for me, or to look at the other dancers. I don't have any mirrors in my house (laughs) I need to see how it all looks. Everyone should have a job like this, just for that reason. How many people know what they look like from behind when they walk? I mean, seriously? Who looks at their big toe? Who really looks at their body, ever? Everyone should. We were discussing that the other day as we were looking at our assholes, actually.

Describe the interaction and commentary among the dancers on stage. ~ It's basically all the same, "Look at the idiots!" It's always a shock how men in a certain age bracket or profession can be acting so...ignorant is the only word I can use, over and over again. We engage in putting down the customers, and talking about us. Putting down is the wrong word. Questioning their behavior (laughs) over and over again. Why they're here, on this earth, not in the theater.

Is there competition among the dancers on stage? ~ No, not at all.

Is there humor on stage? ~ (Laughs) The job can really get you down if you can't laugh at it. There's lots of humor, but we get in trouble and get paid less for humor.

Most erotic dancers I've talked with say that they like to dance. Is this important for you in this job? ~ Yes! I love to dance. I've danced all my life, classically, ballet, the whole scam. Can you believe this? Clumsy as I am? You definitely have to like to move around. For me, it's the reason I went there. I was a dancer and it was like, "I should just take my clothes off and make some money." (Laughs)

Is the myth of the perfect body perpetuated here? ~ (Laughs) No, not in this theater. (Laughs) It's funny because I give myself a little credit or pride for trying to take care of myself, and having one of the better in-shape bodies there, and it doesn't matter. What matters is who has their legs open, who is sticking their asshole in some man's nose. (Laughs) Who has tits hanging to their knees, who has the biggest is what it's all about. Whoever's giving a man attention is what it's all about. If you're anorexic, and you're looking at him, spreading your cheeks, then you're it to him. You're like a wallflower unless you are showing him your pussy, which is what he came to see. (Laughs) I mean, please! (Laughs)

Do you ever become aroused by what you are doing and what is happening around you on stage? ~ I remember three times, in the first year, when I was in heat right before my period, where I actually did get horny being with a pathetic man, using my power (laughs) and watching how he could just gawk and be so desperate. I just beat-off and forgot about it. But it had nothing to do with them, you know what I mean? But now, nothing. (Laughs)

Do you ever have sexual fantasies during your performance? ~ I have murder fantasies. Nothing sexual ever goes through my mind. Except maybe that I can't wait to go home and make love with my man, because this is so disgusting to me. I feel bad for the men with wedding bands. They're jacking-off to strange women. That's kind of wrong. (Laughs) It makes me think, what's my man doing?

What can you do on stage that you can't do off stage? ~ (Laughs) That's where I am Marilyn Chambers. That's where I am a hooker. I read it all the time and it's true: every woman wants to be a hooker. For me it's a power trip. Every woman knows what we can do with our bodies, and it's kind of fun, and it's revolting, and it's power. That is where I live it. That is where I am a sex kitten, which I am not, in real life. That's where I make believe I'm a showgirl, a prostitute.

What won't you do on stage? ~ Give them what they want to see. I won't spread, I won't do any of that stuff. When I see the little desperate interaction going on, I just go the other way. I'm actually boring, unless someone is there to watch me fly around like a butterfly.

What are you prohibited from doing on stage? ~ We can't masturbate, we can't insert, we can't use sexual props, we can't have sexual contact with anyone. You have to play it up. You can't really be a whore, you can just say, "I'm a whore, but not here." (Laughs)

Do you dance for co-workers and friends? ~ Yes. I'll dance for them before I'll dance for a customer. I guess I'm showing off. I get a kick out of it. Why not? When there's a boss in there with a dancer I'll go right up to them. It's because the co-workers and friends have some worth to me. I know they aren't these pathetic men who come in off the street with a hard-on.

Do you ever do sex education on stage? ~ Absolutely not. I don't give them that kind of attention.

How does having your period affect your performance? ~ (Laughs) Well, I'm on the pill, so my period isn't anything it's a trickle. It happens maybe for three hours, so there's no effect at all.

I was quite surprised when I first heard that healing occurs here, women healing themselves, each other, and customers. Describe what you know about this. ~ I don't know what you're talking about. This is news to me. (Laughs) Healing? What are we talking, sexual, mental, physical healing, what are we talking about?

Have you had any transcendent moments on stage? ~ Absolutely not. Nothing like that ever occurs here.

Do you ever feel caged or wish you could cover up? ~ I wish I could cover them up, not me. (Laughs) I have to be here. It bothers me when I don't like something and I can't change it. I probably could, but right now I'm not going to find anything like this where I can come and go and make this kind of money. I just can't live my lifestyle doing any other kind of job. I do feel caged, because I have to be here a certain amount of time out of the year. Many times, I just want to walk off, or kick the window in.

Many of the dancers who work here say they prefer this closed type of stage and see it as safe and fun because of the absence of physical contact with the customers. How do you feel? ~ That's the only way I could do it. Or else I would be out hooking. That's too threatening to me, to have to speak, let alone have someone, a stranger, touch you on that level of, "Hi, I'm a sex object, and you're the dog."

Some topless dancers I've talked with are appalled at the thought of going bottomless as well. Is this difficult for you? ~ It's not difficult for me, because it's the only thing I've ever known. But I can definitely understand what they mean. The breasts are no big deal, but as soon as the pants come off, it's all of a sudden, a real threatening personal thing. I can see that when I wear a G-string for a period of hours. The womb. (Laughs) You wanted to close the door to the womb. (Laughs) They came out of it, and they keep trying to get back in. That's the philosophy. They spend their whole lives trying to get back up in there.

Describe your performance at its best and worst. ~ (Laughs) At its best, I'm like a butterfly in the springtime, no, like a bumblebee, going from flower to flower, just flying through the air. (Laughs) At my worst, I'm sitting on the jukebox, picking my toenails. I will look at them, and say, "Hi, how you doing?" and then walk away. That's sad. That proves right there that I shouldn't be working here. Boredom.

Describe the customers. ~ I have to find vocabulary, pathetic is getting old. They're like strays. It reminds me of being at the Humane Society and seeing a bunch of dogs in the kennel. But these you don't want to take home. These are the ones that you want to send away to be destroyed. Which is not fair to say, because you don't know them. But they're all so desperate and they come there expecting so much. For a quarter, they expect a fucking prostitute. (Laughs)

In our job there's nothing that you have to do. You're supposed to entertain the men, but you are not there to cash in on their whims. They think it's Burger King. They expect you to wait on them hand and foot. They're classless, they're just something that you want to be removed. With the exception of a handful of men who take the time to talk to you. They respect you, they're looking at you in admiration. They know that you're human and that you have intelligence, that you do other things.

But, basically, the men there are wrong. They're wrong, they're lost, they're lonesome, but they don't know how to deal with it. They're also afraid. I think there's a great fear that's going on. A window goes up, "Hello!" you think you're Mr. Tough Guy? Here's five nude women; what are you going to do now? They freak out, and I think out of fear, nervousness makes them act stupid. They say the wrong things, they do the wrong things. Should I be macho? Should I be sensitive? They don't know, so they do everything wrong.

I'm very intimidating. I go out of my way to intimidate them, which makes them slip even more (laughs) into the revulsion level, so...they acquire a lot of training. But that's what the whole theater's about I guess, training, and I'm at a point right now where I don't even do that. They sicken me, and I go somewhere else mentally until they leave. Those are the male customers.

There are two kinds of female customers. The women who have never been here before, who don't know what to expect, women who have taken showers and never looked at themselves. They're out for the night, either with their boyfriends or other girls and they don't know how to handle it, so they giggle. They come off very silly. Then there are the women who totally know what to expect. They're wonderful. They're full of admiration, they look at everyone in a very respectful way, watching how they move, like they're watching a ballet. They're very interested. They'll say hello. They're obviously in touch with themselves. Women are definitely cooler. There are no demands, no expectations.

There are lesbian and straight women. Straight women come in with their partners. Some of the couples are wonderful. The women are totally into their partners looking at these other women, and they're getting off on it. I can't imagine how it can be such an experience for them, they really enjoy it. (Laughs)

Do the customers leave their social roles and status behind when they come to see you? ~ I think they are in those booths as they are in real life. There's the macho men, the men who have money and seem very anxious to flash it. Then there are the bums (laughs) who scam off the corners. That black crazy guy came in today, that guy with a radio hanging from his wrist. (Laughs) He puts a cigarette in his mouth to light it, and then he starts looking at me, and he breaks it. He's too funny. I believe they don't hide anything. Except their faces. (Laughs) A lot of men hide their faces.

What is your favorite type of customer? ~ The non-customer! (Laughs) The one who stays outside. No, I do have a favorite kind of customer, the guys who are really cute. They're not afraid to let you know that it's a little uncomfortable for them, but they aren't dicks. They're just themselves. They'll laugh, they'll smile, they'll be shy, it's just an aura that men have. Some are totally cool.

I figure that if I were all of a sudden exposed to a roomful of nude men, or nude women, which ever I was into at the time, the first thing I would do is have a pleasant fucking look on my face, whether I was embarrassed or not. So many have fucking stone faces. There's no smile, there's no emotion, and they expect you to perform to that. It's like, being with a corpse. (Laughs) They expect you to put out all your energy to interact, and they're just beating-off, or whatever they're doing. That's wrong.

Do you encounter men who you think hate women? ~ I've never thought about that before. Maybe that's why they're so abusive. I don't know. Men who hate women are everywhere, I'm sure they come in here. It's nothing that's really hit me on the head in that way.

Have you ever felt it was dangerous to arouse a customer? ~ No. I can't turn anyone on to the obsessive point, where you're worried about him waiting for you, or following you. It never worries me.

Do you encounter violent men here? ~ Those are the kind of men that I attract, violent men. They'll be loud and I've even had a couple of them threaten me, "I'll kick your ass." It can happen if you provoke them in the way that they don't want to be provoked. Look, the men in there have hard-ons, they think with their hard-ons, their hard-ons aren't getting satisfied, they go off.

Do you think you've ever danced for a rapist? ~ I hope that I have. (Laughs) That's cool. It wouldn't shock me in the least if one of those customers had indeed raped a woman. But again, it's nothing that's ever hit me on the head.

Are there any customers who come to see you on a regular basis? ~ (Laughs) I really don't think so. I would bet there are none. I have no affect, because I don't go for it. I'm not like, "Hey man, I'm going to make you feel good."

Describe the variety of sexual behavior customers express. ~ (Laughs) There is no variety to me. They beat-off. I guess there's variety in how they beat-off. Some are exhibitionists, others cringe in the corner.

From stage you see a lot of tongues. Describe this. ~ (Laughs) Well, I will tell you, there are tongues that I wouldn't sit on if you paid me all the money in the world. They're dead tongues. I say to many of them, "Gee, that totally turns me on, Dude." They just stick it out and lay it there, it's like, you want that on your crotch, right?

Describe some of the more unique encounters you've had with customers. ~ One I will probably remember until I die is the boy who came in and sucked himself off. I think that's wonderful. He rolls over, brings his hips up, and sucks himself off. Then he spits it out, which is a beautiful finish.

The businessmen with the lingerie totally kill me. They're the ones doing the "right thing," and then they strip down, and they're in women's lingerie and garter belts. That's just wonderful. I love the businessmen who get their dicks sucked by other men. (Laughs) That's a real turn-on, actually! Because it's like they're allowing their power to be demoted in front of us. I love it.

Many customers show a great deal of interest in the dancers' genitalia. Why do you think there is such great interest? ~ I don't know. Could you tell me? I guess they've had sex in the dark all these years. Kind of makes me think of when I was a whore in college. The first thing you did was turn off the light.

Women's bodies are great to look at and we aren't their wives. They don't have to talk to us, there are no threats here. It's like, there she is, like a fucking bear at the zoo and they look.

What do the customers want you to do? ~ They want you to make them feel that they are the man of your dreams, I think. They want you to make them feel that they are actually arousing you, that their cock is the biggest and best and hardest cock in the world! (Laughs) They want to feel macho. That's disgusting, because they're all so wimpish. They want to be your fantasy, and you to just perform, perform, perform, for me, me, me. To make them cum is what they want.

I think you are possibly the only or preferred sexual outlet for some customers. What do you think? ~ I agree with that one hundred percent. It's obvious in the way they act. I find that very sad, and the sadness turns to revulsion, one more time. I think it's sad that society can allow a place like this to be open, and that there's a need for it! (Laughs) That people have to look at something like *me*, and I'm not even interested in their well-being! I don't know why they don't buy a magazine and just beat-off in their room. It's very sad. (Laughs) It really is.

Is there a difference in the customers' behavior when they're alone or in a group? ~ Yeah. When they're in a group they tend to be more embarrassed and that's when they really don't know how to act. They're with their peers, it's like, "Oh my God!" They don't really feel O.K. about it, so they act strange, rude, dumb, stupid, (laughs) ignorant male. When they're by themselves, the threat's gone, so they tend to be quieter, better.

What do the customers say when they speak? ~ (Laughs) Ruff! They come up with a lot of unique lines, like, "Oh, baby, I could make you so happy," "Can we have dinner?" Useless things, the typical pick-up line. Like you would actually be interested. Since I have a ring in my labia, it's a little different, like, "Who the hell did that?" (laughs) or, "What's that?"

What do you say when you speak? ~ (Laughs) "Fuck off!" I don't speak to them at all.

Some customers experience ecstatic surprise when they first encounter the stage show. What do you think surprises them? ~ I think for a lot of them, it's going to be very private and they're not prepared for more than one woman or the positions they're in. I don't think too many men have ever really been in a room with a lot of nude women, have you?

Are you ever disturbed by the affect you have on customers? ~ (Laughs) No, I enjoy it. I like to piss them off, I like to make them feel something else besides their fucking dicks. I want them to be in for a banger. It's like, you think you're here for a quarter, getting a fucking hooker? Hell no, you're getting a woman who's intelligent, a woman who thinks you're fucking pathetic, who can't understand why you have to do it. I've masturbated my whole life, and the idea of going to a place like that and putting myself on display... there's just something wrong about it. It's not wrong, it's just...it's pathetic. It's just pathetic that they have to pay a quarter and beat-off. It's pathetic.

Sometimes a customer will leave angry or disgusted. Do you understand why? ~ Yes, I've angered or disgusted them. (Laughs) They don't get what they want. They're just spoiled babies. We have dancers here who fulfill every whim. If your first encounter is with a woman who's willing and going for it, and then you come back, and don't get it, it's upsetting. They don't get what they want, and they cry.

Do you ever abuse the customers? ~ (Laughs) Yes! Yes, I abuse them. I find myself going out of my way to make them feel intimidated and insecure, and make it hard for them to achieve an orgasm. (Laughs) I enjoy that, because it's not supposed to happen. You're supposed to make it easy, so I think they should be in for a little treat. (Laughs) I'm so rude to them. I'm going to have to start being aware that when I laugh at people and they have sexual problems they may go kill themselves.

Do you ever feel controlled or possessed by the customers? ~ Absolutely not. Absolutely not.

When customers show disrespect the dancers can call security and have them removed. How often do you ask that a customer be removed? ~ Once a shift. The day crowd and night crowd are definitely different. I usually work nights.

How do you respond when a customer orgasms? ~ If it's early in the morning, it makes me a little putrid. (Laughs) I look away. Sometimes I'll say a wise remark, but basically, when a customer cums, I do what they do: I get up and walk away.

Do you feel good when the customer feels good? ~ (Laughs) I guess when they cum they feel good, then I do feel good, because then I know they'll leave. It's over. (Laughs) The game is over.

How long do you stay with a customer? ~ (Laughs) Not very long. It's up to your discretion and I very, very rarely stay with a customer from start to finish. Very rarely. I don't feel that I am there...to have sex with the man.

How do you feel about dancing for customers in the three booths with one-way glass? ~ I enjoy that, I don't have to look at them. I can perfect what I'm doing and I don't have to deal with their shit. You will always find me in front of the one-ways.

As the desired do you have power? ~ Of course! That's what it's all about for me. They're there to see you, it's like my music thing, they're there to see me. With my music it's a good feeling because I'm trying to inspire people. This way it's kind of derogatory because the whole sex thing is revolting to me, so I tend to abuse it, I abuse my power at the theater. I try to demean them, it's rude, it's terrible. This is a terrible thing you're making me realize here. I don't like them. It's like go out and at least be real, at least get a hooker, spend money, take her out to dinner, have to think, have to come up with conversation, this is just a wimp way. You have all the power in the world if you have no clothes on, come on!

Does this job suit you? ~ (Laughs) Does it sound like it? (Laughs) It's good for me personally. It makes me take care of myself, makes me stay monogamous. It has its good points, definitely. Allows me to do what I really want to do.

Have you experienced burnout in this job? ~ Oh, most definitely. (Laughs) It's called going on stage and just standing there. You get tired, you work many hours, you need a break from that whole sex goddess scene. The theater tries to make you create this illusion that you are perfect, flawless, and just such a wonderful fuck. It gets old and tiring. I am permanently burned out. (Laughs) Permanent. I need a break. You need to have interaction with men as friends to realize that men are people too.

How do you spend the ten minute breaks you take every forty minutes? ~ I usually read. I do whatever I can to escape. I'll call a friend.

Off stage you encounter other dancers, support staff, and management. Describe the interaction and conversation that occurs. ~ (Laughs) Everybody talks about each other. There really are no cliques. Everybody basically likes each other, obviously there are a few people everybody talks about. It's like any other job where people get together and put down authority.

Many of the workers say they can be themselves here. Can you? ~ Definitely, there's no pressure about that at all. Everyone is accepted and dealt with.

The owner and management of this theater say they want to create a safe, nurturing, fun, and profitable business. Have they succeeded? ~ Not in my eyes. I see everything they do as really half-assed. Profitable should be in the beginning, by the way, (laughs) caring and nurturing at the end. They create this whole facáde of this beautiful little Garden of Eden palace. It should be, but it just doesn't work. They only put out a limited amount for us and expect us to put out a massive amount. I've been there for four years and there's only so much money you can make. Yet they go out and spend money putting a stupid cow sticker on my check every week. (Laughs) Their priorities are a little weird. I can't make fifteen dollars an hour, but when someone has a stomach ache or something they go out and spend $60 on a balloon bouquet.

The owner and management also express a desire to empower people. Have you been empowered here? ~ Absolutely not. What they've done for me is made me realize how useless routines and systems are, I mean their whole EST bullshit. They use twenty words, pay money, and hang out in groups and think that their lives are together. They can't practice what they preach. They go to these seminars and get their heads filled with someone telling them how to make their life better, because they have no clue of what life is anyway, and then they pass it on to us and think that they've done their job. It hasn't worked. Making someone get to work on time does not get their life together.

Is there a difference between the male support staff and the male customers? ~ Definitely. The male support staff works with us, they know what it's about. Usually they are people like yourself who are doing research, or they have education and goals in life. They're human, they have lovers, they don't have to go into little fucking wooden booths to beat-off. They're real different, they're on your side, they know what it's like, they're a part of us. With the customers, they either set you up or put you down, and know you are there to do a service for them.

Describe worker/management relations. ~ (Laughs) Well, they try to keep it real cool. They hang out in the dressing room and consider themselves one of us. They just annoy me. They try to keep it less as boss and worker, more as friends. There are a lot of power games going on, and favoritism has always been a big part of what happens here. It's typical, just like any other job I've ever had, and they're trying to create something different, having atmosphere, and there's nothing different about it at all. You work for them, they make the rules, you follow them, you get paid.

Describe the periodically scheduled dancers meetings. ~ (Laughs) They haven't changed for four years. They talk about the show, what needs to be done to make more money, dadadadadada. People bitch and complain, everyone always has new ideas that are going to make the theater more fun, it's the same old shit. People bitch about the jukebox. They don't accomplish anything. Except, everyone gets together at once, and you get free breakfast.

In response to the question "Are you exploited?" a well known dancer and erotic film star replied, "Yes and no. We don't have a union, but I like what I do." How do you answer that question? ~ I don't think I can say I'm exploited because I choose to do it. You are exploiting yourself to make this money, but exploiting the audience. Who's exploiting who?

Do you ever think about unionizing? ~ It's something we talked about and a couple of women who talked about it, they're no longer here, so...

Is sexism promoted or resisted in any way here? ~ It's definitely not promoted, it's not even an issue here. I guess they fight it. We're trying to make the customers feel okay and we're okay doing it. They're trying to alleviate the whole feeling of sexism, trying to make sex acceptable, make this a place where it's all okay.

What do you feel passing customers in the hallway whom you have just danced for? ~ I don't really feel anything. I zoom by because I can see that they're all looking. I feel that they expect me to maybe proposition them. (Laughs) They're thinking okay, here she is, she's off work, so, she's got to hook. I think they're watching, hoping that I will say, "Hey, Babe, got any money?" Which could be totally wrong. They're curious, they look at you because now you have clothes on.

Do you ever feel in danger coming to or leaving work? ~ No, I also don't put myself in that situation. I'm realistic about it. At 3:00 in the morning you don't go walking through Chinatown by yourself, you take cabs.

Do you change your appearance when you leave work? ~ I put clothes on.

How does this job compare with others you've had? ~ It's just another job, but I don't have to worry about what I'm going to wear. Despite the way I'm sounding, it really doesn't have that much of an affect on me. I do my job, I get my money, and leave. It's been no great enlightenment for me, I always knew men were dogs. It's actually been kind of disappointing, but it's the real world. I will never marry because of this job. (Laughs)

Describe your earliest memories? ~ My earliest memory is when my parents adopted me, and picked me up at the kennel. (Laughs) I was at the court-house sitting on the judge's lap, behind a big desk. It always freaked out my mom that I could remember exactly what I was wearing.

Describe your family and its circumstances as you remember them during childhood. ~ My family was the perfect, All-American family. Mom and Dad were married, happy, and there was no abuse. They both worked and I went to Catholic school and had the bike and the dog. I have an older brother, adopted also. Everything was just fine.

I remember things from my childhood that Mom tells me did not happen. My parents did not believe in slapping or spanking, or any physical contact with children, but I seem to remember times that my mother slapped me that she says never happened. I guess I have a vivid imagination. I seem to remember my parents having an argument, Dad was downstairs crying and talking to her about another woman or something. My mother doesn't know where these things came from. I think I've watched tv and created a little drama. I'm very melodramatic, and my family was just too normal.

My family is middle class. My dad was always a truck dispatcher for major supermarket chains. My mom has been the secretary, computer analyst lady. I went to Catholic school so, I was always sheltered, in regard to sex education. It's still taught in a sheltered way. We always did what we wanted, the piano lessons, the ballet, everything. We always got what we wanted, but had to work for it. They instilled that.

What kind of child were you? ~ I was a show-off, I was loud, always needed attention, loved my brother to death, cute – I'll throw that in (laughs) – fat. I was hyper, I would never sleep, I always wanted to eat. I would always make my mother bargain with me, "Eat all your dinner and then you can eat as much Halloween candy as you want." I would continue to eat candy to the point where she would need to tell me to stop, and I would pin her on it. Like, "Hey, fuck you, you told me I could eat *all the candy*, if I ate dinner." She said that I was constantly holding her to her word. During the typical rebellious stage I'd push her to the limit, see how much I could swear etc., I needed attention.

Describe your relationship with your brother. ~ My mom tells me I was always totally into him. I never wanted the dolls, I always wanted his trucks, his bikes. I always hung out with him and his friends. When we reached puberty he asked me things about my body. By seventh, eighth, or ninth grade, we didn't have to go with my parents to see Grandma and Grandpa if we chose not to. My brother would ask me to take off my shirt. (Laughs) He'd look at me and touch me. I'd allow him to, it was a totally cool thing. I'd take off my pants, and he'd just look at me, and ask me questions about my friends. (Laughs) It was wild. He would show me himself, and ask me, "Have you ever done this with a boy?" He would explain what certain terms meant.

When we went to high school he was always the straight A, jock student, I had to live up to that, and I did. But my brother was really straight, and I've always liked a lot of different people. I liked the druggies, the jocks, everybody. We started splitting up because my brother would get repulsed at the people I spent time with. I would go off drinking and doing the drug scene, and he never did. He always thought that was horrible and he used to lay this trip on me, "How can you do this to Mom and Dad?" It was that whole religion bullshit thing going on there.

After he left high school, I was 2 years behind him, it was real strange. Then I went away to school and continued to do drugs, and it was still the same old trip, "How can you do this to Mom and Dad?" I would return to town and not let my parents know I was there. I would do sneaky things like that, typical college shit. My brother was always real aware of it, and so this dislike started building up. Then, I moved and never really went home again.

My brother and I see each other once a year at Christmas and say hi. To this day we don't really talk. He definitely went the straight route. He's got a wife and a child, the garage, and the job. I left home, I don't have any material things, and I'm doing music. He has no idea about this job, nobody does. I don't really have a relationship with my brother, it's kind of sad.

Describe your relationship with your parents. ~ Well, my dad is a lot like my brother. I don't really have a relationship with him. God, I don't even remember my dad being there. I was always with my mother. My mother was the disciplinarian, everything, because dad worked at night, and I was at school all day. I remember in my junior year my brother came home and ratted on me because I had been out drinking with friends, and we'd gotten busted by the cops. It was one of the times that Dad hit me. I remember angry times, times that I got caught doing things like that. For birthdays, or Father's Day, I bought him socks, nothing ever really thrilled him. I'm still, to this day, trying to find something that would thrill him.

It's always my mother, I just relate to my mom. Dad will even answer the phone, and it's "Hey Dad what's up?", and he'll say, "Oh, well, here's your mother." It's a relationship like that. (Laughs) It's weird. A couple of times in the past year I've written him personal letters, and he's written back. It's been touching, because it's been a "God bless you, I love you" type of thing. I think he has this fear about it, it's really strange.

Mom has been everything to me. She's done it all. Mom, (laughs) she's too funny. Mom always took me to horse riding, to ballet, shopping, and gave me my allowance. Mom was always the one I'd have to ask to do things and she'd always say, we'll have to ask your father, but she was the authority figure. My mother was the one I would hide stuff from. I never *really* talked to her either, but... she's the one I talk to. I call her, I write, I address mail to her, she's the Jesus Christ in my family. (Laughs) When I was in college and went through the whole suicidal phase, my mother was the one who got all the letters, oh God! (Laughs)

Describe being raised under the Catholic religious tradition? ~ Catholic school, Catholic church. They put me in Catholic school up until eighth grade. All the bullshit fucking church and ceremonies, and the Blessing of the Throat, and the fucking yin-yanging that they do. I don't even remember what it meant, the ashes that they put on your forehead. I was so young, I guess it formed a lot of my morals but my parents weren't particularly strict. We went to church every Sunday and said grace before meals. In eighth grade they let me make the choice to go to Catholic school or public school. After that it all changed. I still went to church because I sang in the choir, church was a social event. But there was no pressure to go to church after entering high school.

Describe your childhood play and friendships. ~ It was me, my brother, and Jimmy, my brother's friend. It was my cousins, it was me trying to be a part of my brother's life. There are no childhood friends I can tell you of. There were neighbors, but they weren't like friends. I was by myself, really independent, I've always been independent. I was involved in the neighborhood kickball scene. I was always masturbating on the field, it was great. (Laughs) I started masturbating, God, as long ago as I can remember. I would be on home plate ready to kick the ball, and I would have my hands down my pants, playing with it because it felt good. (Laughs) And my brother would say, "Mom, she's doing it again." I used to do it to go to sleep. That was my childhood play, I used to beat-off. Also, I would have my dolls do sexual things to me. I still have a doll at home that I used to masturbate. His name is Tom. (Laughs) When I found out through sex education that people actually did this, actually put their mouths to that part of the body, I died. (Laughs) I thought it was my secret. The church, during religious ed, taught that there were things in our lives that could be abused, there were wrong ways to use them. I remember having that in my head, and thinking, "Oh my God, I'm doing this thing, and it's wrong, and I'm going to go to Hell." So every night I would talk to God and make a bargain, "Look, just one more time, I'm going to do it one more time, and then I'll stop." But I could never stop.

I never liked to go to bed, so I would always do something drastic. Once I wrapped my body inside the rungs so bad that they had to break it to get me out. I would do anything to get attention. I used to, God, I haven't thought about this in so long, be in a crib having these fantasies that I was an animal. It's how I would masturbate, now that I think about it. I used to make believe that I was a beautiful animal, and the crib was a cage, I was in the zoo. (Laughs) How appropriate. I was a lion or something, and all these people were coming to see me, and I'd be showing off. But then, someone would start throwing things at me, start victimizing me. I'm always victimized, I'm still doing it. And that's what I would beat-off to, people trying to hurt me, and then people coming and feeling sorry for me. Throughout my childhood I did that. As I got older, seventh, eighth, and ninth grade, I started masturbating to being on a street, hitchhiking, my shorts up my ass, and having all these truckers take me out in the woods and rape me. (Laughs) And then people find me and go, "Oh my God." (Laughs)

And the dolls. When I did play with dolls it was a sexual thing. My Barbie dolls. I never had a G.I. Joe, so if I couldn't find my brother's men dolls, I had Jane West, and I used her for the male doll. My mother would spend all this money on these Barbie dolls, and I would totally slut them out. I would cut their hair, put all this makeup on them, and have them out in the horse barn fucking. (Laughs)

I don't remember ever not masturbating. When my mother caught me, I had to be in second grade or first. She caught me, man, right in the bathroom. I was sitting on the floor, up against the bathtub, and she was knocking on the door, "What are you doing, what are you doing?" She came in and caught me, and I said, "I have an itch." I just freaked out. She said, "I want you to take a bath, and I never want to see you touching yourself again." I tell her now that she handled that wrong, because I was terrified. For the rest of my life I thought I was going to Hell. I thought there was something wrong with me. It was the wrong way to handle it.

Describe your childhood school experience. ~ I remember the first day my mom brought me to school, everyone was crying, not wanting to leave their mothers, and I was, "See you later." I have the same personality now. I was fine. I started getting to know everybody, and I tried to run the whole place from then on. I tried to get all the attention, always tried to look the best and strut around. School was a great experience for me, I loved it, but I always had trouble with teachers. Mom said it was because I was always a little too aggressive, and a little too ahead. She had problems with a couple of nuns because they were actually abusing me, verbally abusing me, and trying to cut down my personality. My mother still talks about it. She went to the Board and she's like, "How can you try to take away a child's personality?" It was a big thing. One nun used to go out of her way to humiliate and embarrass me. I had a teacher in third grade who used to pull my ponytail and rip me out of the chair. I've always been a little intimidating to adult women. I don't remember going out of my way to upset them. I was just doing my thing.

My parents found me one day hiding behind a tree, afraid to go to school. As obnoxious and aggressive as I've always been, I think they should have handled it a little differently. My parents were always on my side, like, "Fuck you, this is a child, and... you can't da da da da dum." But I just loved school, so I was on top of it, real good marks, everybody liked me and I liked everybody. My classmates were just normal kids. They were always following me, I could make them do anything.

What were you taught about human sexuality by your parents? ~ That it was this wonderful, glorious, miracle thing, that you did only if you got married. Since I was always so disinterested in boys, I was like, "Oh."

Did you receive information about human sexuality in grade school? ~ Yes, starting in fourth grade. We'd have an hour in class and then they'd send pamphlets home to your mother. They taught us all the parts of the body and the whole bleeding thing, and what it meant. I remember Mickey Mouse, Minnie Mouse, and the little tampon. Actually, it was third grade, because it was the year Mom told me that I was adopted.

The adoption trip for my brother was real traumatic, but I thought it was great. I was telling everyone in the schoolyard, "This is great! We're adopted! We don't belong to them!" My brother got really upset. He said, "Ann's out there, fucking telling everyone that we aren't your kids." (Laughs) We're free! We don't belong to anyone! It was great!

Was there nudity in your home? ~ No, no. My mother was always very modest. As a matter of fact, she looks at me now and says, "I thought I instilled modesty in you." No, no, no. They would only kiss hello and good-bye in front of us. My dad never hung out in the underwear scene. I walked in on my dad in his underwear once and he freaked.

Were you ever punished due to sexual expression? ~ That one time I got caught in the bathroom. I thought that I was sick anyway, so that kind of rein-forced it. I'm sick and now Mom knows, so I have to be careful, (laughs) but I'm going to keep it up. I wasn't the girl who fucked in high school. I had one boyfriend in my senior year, and I had sex with him three times, after I graduated.

Were you ever sexually abused as a child? ~ No. Not at all.

Did incest occur in your family? ~ No, but you know what my brother did to me once? It was great. One of the times when my parents weren't home, and we were showing each other our bodies, he said, "Look, I'm going to go out with this girl, so you should let me stick it in so I know. I have to know what to do." By this time, I was in eighth grade and knew about pregnancy, but I let him talk me into it. I remember lying down on the bed, but he didn't penetrate me all the way. I remember allowing him to lie on top of me and saying, "Well, I think this is it, okay, that's enough." I had dreams for months that I was pregnant, and had to tell my mother that Paul and I did it.

What were you taught about human relationships in your family? ~ Nothing, there wasn't a lot of emotion in my family, now that I think about it. You just lived your life, went to school, got the job, said grace, had dinner, went to bed, and did your chores. There was no "Let's talk," or, "Well, how do you feel about this?" I don't remember ever feeling, like, "God, I wish I could talk to my mother." I watch soap operas, we never talked like that.

I remember talking to her once when I wanted to break up with my first boyfriend. I said, "I want to break up with him, because I want to do whatev-er", she was like, "Oh, well, make sure that's what you want to do." There was nothing personal going on in our family at all. Just real...hm, strange...well, Catholic, everything was kept behind closed doors. You just have to follow the Ten Commandments, and go to Heaven.

Were you taught to look good to attract and be chosen by a man? ~ (Laughs) No, no, it never came across that way. When I was 15 years old I said to my mother, "I can't wait until I'm old enough to get a hysterectomy so I don't bleed anymore." She slapped me across the room, and said, "Don't ever talk like that." I said, "What, I'm here to have kids?" From that day on, the whole Catholicism thing came out, "Oh, I'm a woman, I'm supposed to reproduce, dammit."

Now I'm 28, and my mother still says things like, "Oh, my God, you've been with your boyfriend a year and you still like him he must be so special." When she met him and saw that I really liked him, she said, "I still live for the day that you'll get married. That will be the happiest day of my life." So I think it's something that they definitely feel, but it's nothing that they've ever pushed on me. My mother's disappointed that I'm 28 and single, but I think it's more or less that she wants to feel that I'm taken care of. My mother never hassled me about not going out on dates, because I wasn't into it.

Were you taught to value truth? ~ Oh, totally, because I was the massive liar. Always punished for it. When my mother caught me I'd say,"I'm sorry," just to get out of being punished. Yeah, truth was a big, big thing in my family.

Did your parents teach you that you could have power, choice? ~ No, no. (Laughs) I'm from a Catholic family. (Laughs) No, never. I think it surprises them, too, that I have the aura I do. My mother doesn't know where it came from. My mother's real powerful too, she just doesn't know it. She has no concept that she runs the whole fucking family, you know what I mean? My mother runs my dad's life, but she has no concept of what a power figure she is. My Grandmother was like that also.

What effect did your body changing have on you? ~ Ohhh, I thought it was great! I went shopping with Mom and got my first bra. But she only let me wear it on Sundays, when I went to Church. I wore undershirts the rest of the week. (Laughs) I remember standing in front of the mirror going, "Oh, yeah, wow, these are cool." And then, going out in front of my brother and his friends in this tight shirt, knowing that they were looking at me and liking it. After the change began, my brother would say things like, "So and so likes you." The whole sex thing happened. It was real exciting for me. But not in the aspect of, like, fucking, it never came across like that. (Laughs) It was just attention. "Someone's looking at me? Oh, cool!" (Laughs)

Describe your adolescent sexuality. ~ I used to fantasize about Donny Osmond, big time. Donny Osmond made such an impact on my life, I have to tell him that, sometime. He's the only reason I started singing. I started getting into musicians really early, these rock type guys, going, "Yeah!" And not for any other reason than I was attracted to them. The Donny Osmond thing started around fifth grade, and I used to go to bed at night crying. I cried for years that I wasn't with this Donny Osmond guy. I was going to start singing and doing music, and I was going to marry him. He was going to be a fan. Even my daydreams about him were only about kissing on the cheek, that was sex to me. I never thought of anything else. What a boring person! What a boring child!

There was never any Playboy or Penthouse or anything around the house. I don't think my Dad even has a dick. (Laughs) I wasn't exposed to anything, any nudity, anything sex at all. There were cows and horses, that was it.

Have you ever been pregnant? ~ Yes. I ended it with vacuum sucking.

Describe your first exposure to sexually explicit media and its impact on you. ~ I started buying Playboy back in New York. Me and my girlfriend used to buy them because we liked looking at the women. I thought it was great. I used to beat-off to them. I saw a porn flick at a bachelorette party in college. They showed *The Devil In Miss Jones*, or something. I thought it was wonderful, because it seemed... female dominated, it was all the men being subservient, and I was like, "Yeah!" (Laughs)

Describe your high school years. ~ I was the homecoming queen, (laughs) I was in the prom court, I was real popular. I was the president, and a cheer-leader, and I was this and I was that, and so I was very happy. I went to a small school and I was one of the hundred people who did everything. I was singing and it was great. I loved going to school.

My mother used to buy me really hip clothes, it was great, it was like, L.A., it was a party. That was the problem with my grades, it wasn't that I wasn't intelligent. I was there to play volleyball and softball and be a gymnast and cheerlead. I was into being a performer all the time. Having my hair up, and stuff. I loved it. No sex at all. Not interested in having a boyfriend, just wanted to play with them, sports. Wanted to be with them, wanted to be accepted. I stopped wearing dresses then because I heard, "Ooh, nice legs." I never wanted it to be like that. It was like, "So what, let's go play basketball or something." It's something I've always fought. Maybe I was a whore in a previous life.

Describe your relationship with your family during those years. ~ My freshman and sophomore years started out great, I made all the teams. The summer between my freshman and sophomore years, I started straying a little, hanging out with people who got high, I didn't get high. In my junior year I had to crack down, because it was regents. You either took non-regents or regents classes and you have to take all these intense state tests at the end of the year, or else, you wouldn't get your diploma. That's the one year in high school I did work. I passed everything just fine, I figured, fuck it. So my senior year, I start-ed drinking and getting high a little bit, and getting in trouble. My parents start-ed getting a little tense then, my brother too. It was a little sticky, but I graduat-ed, and everything was fine. I was out of there at eighteen.

I remember being in high school and starting to see that things like lectures and seminars were being held, and saying to my mother, "I want to go to this." She'd say, "What do you want to go to that for?" She made me feel inhibited. I'd say, "I don't know, I just want to check it out." I would ask her to take me to these things and it would never happen.

In my first year of college I knew that I wanted to do music. I wasn't sure about the band trip at that time, I was doing it theater-wise, the Broadway stage dream. I saw all these ads for "singer wanted," I thought, "Wow, this is what I should try doing." I told my mother, and she was real lackadaisical about it, like, "Oh, well, I don't know..." So I thought, "Oh, man, that must be wrong." I wasn't daring enough at the time. (Laughs) I had no one to encourage me, or feel the same way. So, it just kind of passed along.

What was your first job? ~ Working as a cashier at a drugstore. I made $80.00/week, my junior year. Actually, my first job I babysat for a couple of kids and made ten bucks a week. Children, my calling. (Laughs)

Did you suffer any traumas as a teen? ~ No, I haven't been through anything.

Describe your fears and insecurities as a teen. ~ I don't remember having any. Now, they're all catching up to me. I thought I was the hottest thing, I knew I could do anything. I wasn't competitive though, in any way, shape, or form. It was like I accepted everyone, and there was room in the world for everyone. There were no insecurities, nothing. There was no embarrassment about it, it was just massive self-confidence about everything.

Did you have any heroines or heroes during those years? ~ I started getting into Marilyn Monroe pretty deeply, and all the classical dead people, Jimi Hendrix, etc. And I started reading about the Nazi trip, really diving into the War. That's about it. And, of course, Donny Osmond. (Laughs)

What did you plan to do after graduation from school? ~ I knew that I was going to college to study theater. It was just a matter of where I was going to be accepted, and the money situation. I'd been prepped for years, and I was ready to leave. I did.

Describe other work you've done prior to dancing. ~ I trained horses at a dude ranch in New York. All through college I worked as a waitress, hostess, bartender, and in the kitchen. I worked in a couple of offices doing general clerical, can you imagine, me? And drug dealing, the usual.

Have you had other jobs in the sex industry? ~ When I first moved out here, I was nude modelling for a little old man who had been a Navy psychiatrist. He was wonderful. He is now senile, in his late seventies. I posed nude, made fifty bucks a half hour, so that was cool.

Describe living situations you've been in since you left home. ~ College dorm. It was great. Six wild women out on the run, with their own beds. (Laughs) Then I had an apartment with three of those same women. A little, average type apartment, with donut furniture and a dog, who pissed and shit all over. I lived with a couple of boyfriends. I immediately moved into their places, they had houses. I came out here and lived with another woman, and lived by myself for a while.

Describe significant friendships and love relationships you've had since leaving home. ~ (Laughs) I had my first *real* boyfriend in college. I still think about him all the time. It was a great thing. I'll never forget him, probably because we were both really growing up at that point. We had all these dreams and goals and we were really into each other. He was just out of high school, I was 19, he was 16. Oh God, mmm. We used to do all these sexual things together, it was so open, it was just like, "Hey, let's do this!" We did a lot of drugs and talked about what we wanted to do, but never about us in future terms.

Later I had this woman...the second woman I had sex with. She was my best friend, to this day, the only best friend I've ever had. I've lost touch with her also. We would whore together, do drugs together, dye our hair together, hitchhike across the state together, cry together, laugh together, we did everything. It was another situation where everything was cool, there was nothing hidden. I don't think too many people have that in their lives.

Describe your current living arrangements. ~ (Laughs) I live with a pig, a woman, in Marin County. We don't see each other much, so I feel like I live by myself. It's really a bland lifestyle. The only thing we do together is eat or do coke. (Laughs) I often stay at my boyfriend's place. Life is not so much of a party, anymore. It's not a party anymore at all, actually. I pay my bills, and go to either place, and go to bed.

Do you still practice the religion you were raised with? ~ No, I'm totally out of touch with it. It's not like it did anything terrible to me, it wasn't the life that I chose. I don't believe that you have to praise statues and eat wafers to be a good person. I don't worry about being a good person. (Laughs)

Describe your interests outside of work. ~ It's really only music, and nature. I have a lot of animals, and my boyfriend lives in the redwoods, so a lot of my time is spent outside. I don't watch too much television, I like to read. When

I do watch television, it's educational. Basically I'm the homebody type, I like going for walks with the dogs, eating Chinese food, and having sex.

I'm a vocalist in a band that only recently has started playing out, to expose ourselves. We've made records since 1985. It started out as a project to get on vinyl, because in this business it's much easier to get attention that way. After two records we got some attention, then we ran into some money and decided to go for it. Lots of great things are happening.

My musical interests are really starting to stray. I'm interested in Top 40 music, but I don't do it. I've been into the heavy metal scene, nothing really hardcore and punk, but enough to not really sell-out and make money. I'm doing someone else's music, which I do really enjoy, but I find myself coming to a dead end a lot of times. I look at it as a means to an end. I'm going to try doing other things because I do like commercial music. I'm going to try to find the in between for the little aggression I like as a woman, which isn't that easily accepted. It's becoming acceptable now, because of me and others. Everything about the music business interests me, the people, the money, the scams, the lies. It's just another dirty business that I would like to be involved in. (Laughs)

Do you use drugs? ~ Definitely. The people that I talk to from the sixties, the Airplane, and those type of people, everything they fought for is now acceptable, it's no big deal any longer. Everybody smokes pot, snorts coke, does heroin, so who cares? After I'm high, I don't enjoy it, it's like, "Great, I'm not going to be able to go to sleep, I'll look like shit." But it's the whole religion of getting it, and paying for it, and chopping it up, or rolling it, or whatever you do. And after you do it, it's over, then you're broke and you look like shit. (Laughs)

I guess we do it to escape, but I like to do amphetamines, and there is no escape from anything when you do those. Everything is intensified. All my insecurities pop up. It's like, "Oh my God, I'm getting old, I'm not doing anything, I don't have any friends, no one wants to marry me, I don't have a car," and it just builds up. Who has fun doing that? That's no escape, that's just reality in the face.

I never do drugs when I'm on the road and the music thing is happening, but that's only part of the year. When we make the record, that's a couple of months, when we go out and play, it's a few more months. In the in between times, I do it once a week, twice a week, whenever it's there. (Laughs)

Have you suffered any traumas as an adult? ~ My last boyfriend and I were very heavily into the coke scene, and because I was so whacked on it, I lost a couple of good gigs. I had an opportunity to work in L.A. twice, and I blew it, because I was just so out of it. My relationship broke up, which, at the time, seemed pretty drastic, to me. I stopped doing coke, it was like, "Fuck it, this drug is controlling me. I've had enough." Now I think it all happened for the best, because none of that stuff turned out to be that wonderful for me. Now, I'm pretty traumaless.

Describe your current fears and insecurities. ~ The same old shit as everyone. I'm 28 years old, I'm not married, I have no children, I don't own a home, I don't own a car. I don't even own any furniture. I haven't done any of the societal things. I don't even vote, I don't have any credit cards. I don't go out on dates. (Laughs) FUCK!

Sometimes it really wracks your brain, but if I wanted these things bad enough, I would obviously have them. It's just not important to me. It's more important for me to have a band, and make a record, and be able to go out to dinner and do coke when I feel like it. That's what I do with my money.

I'm kind of insecure about my boyfriend. I do relate that to drugs a lot. Maybe I need something to blame. I'm also very caught up in the whole societal thing that's done to women. Cosmopolitan, Playboy. These women are the hottest things in the world. In this business, you want to look like that. It's the typical, catty woman shit. You don't know if you look as good as you can. Women worry about what they're going to look like when they grow up, when they should be worrying about, who's shooting who in some other country, or putting their energy into something deeper. They should be looking inside of themselves, and not into the mirror.

Do you have any male inspired fears? ~ No.

Do you use sexually explicit media? ~ I read Playboy a lot. It's amazing that I buy and read it as regular as anything else.

Had you been a customer at a peep show or other sex show prior to dancing? ~ I experienced it twice in New York, only because I had a friend who was a stripper. That was my only exposure to it.

Which of society's values have you rejected? ~ Everything! I guess I've rejected the whole heterosexual thing, though I do it. It sickens me, I'm 28 and still running around. I used to tell my parents that I didn't want to be like them. I'm not, I don't have anything they have. I rejected the whole societal thing of what a woman from upstate New York should do. I just got up and left, and everyone else stayed back and raised families. They work at Kodak and they're financially set and secure, and I'm not. (Laughs) I own nothing!

What is your self-image? ~ (Laughs) A fucked up person. I'm searching. I never thought about anything until I was, like, 25. I remember saying to my mother, "You never asked me to think." Our way of life never demanded that

I look inside myself or think about what I really wanted to do, besides a fucking job to support myself. So, now I'm in this struggle, and I think that's why my attitude is so bad, I don't like what I see in myself. I've been really sheltered, *and* I've lead this party life of... nothing. Life seems really empty to me. There's something missing. It's no big fucking deal. It's boring, a drag, nothing it's hyped up to be. Life sucks, so you have to deal with it. That's negative, but that's just the way I feel.

Are you a tolerant person? ~ No. (Laughs) How can I be? It's something I'm working on actually. It was one of my New Year's resolutions. My boyfriend is teaching me a lot about that, he's very tolerant.

Do you trust people? ~ No. They've given me no reason to trust them, and I have been untrustworthy in my life. It's survival, people are not trustworthy. We're in a jungle. It's like you and I are friends, and we hang out and da da da, and when it came down to you and me, man, it's going to be me, you know. That's the way it is! Survival of the fittest.

Do you exploit people? ~ No. I don't even hang out. I've been told I need to learn to exploit myself, but I don't even do that.

Have you ever been violent with people? ~ Oh, sure. I've had my fighting days. I used to be very violent. (Laughs) Got my ass kicked by three Puerto Rican women. I used to get drunk and be the tough bitch at the bar. Anyone who looked at me wrong, or looked at my boyfriend, I would start shit. I would try to pick up men or women who were with their mates, to cause trouble. Girls in dresses, I liked to push them over. I used to try to be a biker-type woman, with no bike.

Define love. ~ Love to me is when you put someone or something in front of yourself. There are a lot of people in your life that you value, but how many will you put before yourself? My boyfriend will always come first to him. My life was always like that, too.

Define power. ~ I'm losing touch with that. I used to think that I had so much of it. I'm reacting to life differently now, I'm letting it get the best of me, it's having the power over me. Power is... it's just a feeling of confidence, a feeling of control, knowing what you want and being confident, you make the decisions. I don't feel very powerful. I feel powerful when I'm performing, but that's a different type thing.

Describe the variety and frequency of your current sexual activity. ~ Well, I only have sex with one person and that's been for a year and a half. I'm very monogamous and we do a lot of things. When I first met him we were both coming out of relationships that had been burdens. I didn't think I had a sex drive any longer. But we would do a lot of things, the whole handcuff, ice cream trip. (Laughs) That was fun. I always wanted to screw in the mud, on the gravel, on the hood of the car, the elevators, we did that whole scene. But now it's mellowed out, and (laughs) I just want to be in bed. It used to be more of an exhibition when we had sex. It was in front of people, at the parties. Now it's definitely more of a private and personal thing. It's more of a mind, spiritual thing, as opposed to props and gadgets. (Laughs)

Are you orgasmic? ~ Actually, not very. (Laughs) Which bothers my boyfriend. Doctors have told me it has a lot to do with masturbating all my life. I've never had an orgasm through intercourse. I can't believe that it exists. I didn't know that you had sex to cum, actually. I didn't cum, the guys came. I discovered what it was about with my first boyfriend in California. I started having orgasms when he'd give me head. Once a night.

These women who say that they keep cumming, I have no concept of what they're talking about. I've cum twice in one night in my whole life, with the guy I'm with now. Primarily I cum by myself. I'll go to bed and beat-off four times and cum. I don't have sex to orgasm, it never has been about that for me.

Describe your sexual fantasies. ~ My sexual fantasies are other women having sex with my boyfriend. I did it with my last boyfriend. With Stan I envision things I almost did the first year I knew him. I was going to buy him two whores. I picture them seducing him, and of course, he doesn't fight it because he knows they're for me. Or else, I have women, he's such a looker, pick him up and he just has to go for it, because he's just so weak. (Laughs) Yeah, that gets me off.

Do you ever act out your fantasies? ~ No, I'm actually boring. Once though, in college, four or five men had sex with me.

Are dominance and submission part of your sexuality? ~ Not with my new boyfriend. It used to be a real power thing for me. I used to see what I could do to these men, and then walk away, or I would give them head and then spit their sperm out in their face. I would abuse them. Nothing really major, though, it was more a head trip for me. I would just verbally abuse them, make them feel like shit, make them realize that they were begging me, which they were. I don't do it any longer, now, I would beg him. (Laughs)

When do you get sexually involved? ~ It would always be when everything was real positive in my life. When I was feeling down and dirty about myself, or getting into a real drug thing, it never happened.

What sexual taboos besides dancing have you broken? ~ Sleeping with the same sex. Taking it up the ass. That's not a taboo is it? Are anal and oral sex illegal in this state? They are in New York. There aren't any sexual taboos any longer, really. I mean, what is there? What can't you do? Have sex with farm animals? I've never done that, or electronic equipment. (Laughs)

What is sexually degrading for you? ~ (Laughs) Men who have no reaction. It makes me think of work when the windows go up and there's no emotion, there's nothing. There's no negative, there's no positive, there's just, "Hi, I'm a void." That's real degrading to me. The command...when they demand things from me, that's degrading, too.

Do you ever experience guilt or shame about your sexuality? ~ Absolutely not. No matter what I did, whatever phase I was in, I always wanted to do it, so I felt great about it.

Has living in a male-dominated society played a role in shaping your sexuality? ~ Of course it has. I want a dick, you know. I want a dick to show them what it's like. I want a dick and I want to drive it up their ass and stick it down their throat, and show them why I am cold and what I am feeling, to show them what they're like. Of course, it's made me very angry when I look at the world, dominated by guys. Yeah! That's why I'm cold and bitter and angry, I don't like them. Fucked up.

Do you think your sexuality would be different if you lived in an egalitarian or a female dominated society? ~ I think I would have reached the point that I'm at now much earlier. You would know that it's okay to be sensitive, there's no one way that you have to be, that you're supposed to be. Yeah, it would be wonderful!

Has birth control and medical technology affected your sexuality? ~ Yeah, it let me fuck like a pig when I wanted to.

Has the women's movement affected your sexuality? ~ I don't really think so. The women's movement, I imagine, is about being what you're about. I was always the one who picked up men; maybe it did have some kind of effect on me.

Describe your current love relationship. ~ I had been dancing for two years when I met him. We knew each other well enough to say hello, he was a friend of the guy my roommate was seeing. He needed a ride to a concert one night and we ended up in the backseat together, I put the move on him. We slept together that night and it's been love ever since! We like to fuck! And we're friends, which is wonderful for me. We actually have conversations about world affairs or the way we're feeling. He's a very sensitive guy. There're no hang-ups about anything. It's just great! It's the best thing I've had. It's more like having a female friend. It's really rounded and we're both really independent. We both have our own things going, definitely. And it's an accepted thing that what we do in our lives may bring us somewhere else, apart. It's a realistic relationship. Very much so on his side, which kind of pisses me off, he kicks reality in my face all the time.

Is your partner supportive of your decision to continue dancing? ~ Yes. He goes through the little insecurity trips about it, but he knows what it's about. He knows why I'm there.

How do you think your relationship will evolve? ~ I think we will fulfill our contract, which is to be together for, what, fifty-eight and a half more years. We will continue to grow and prosper, and we will go to the moon and raise huskies.

How did you feel about your body prior to becoming a dancer? ~ I didn't really pay that much attention to it, unfortunately. Now I feel great about it or I wouldn't be taking my clothes off, like some people shouldn't.

How did you get this job? ~ I walked in and auditioned. I saw the ad in the paper and fell for the warm, caring, and honest.

In your experience are dancers more deprived, abused, and battered than other women? ~ Absolutely not. As a matter of fact, I find it quite the opposite. They're usually very goal oriented and very professional, or they have families and their lives are together. They aren't just drifting. It's usually a means to an end, definitely.

Do you recognize any characteristics common to those who dance? ~ Yes! We all don't like it! (Laughs) We're all there to make a living. We all have the same poor attitude about men. We all feel that they need to be trained. We're all disappointed in them, in the whole thing.

When you started dancing did you fear being separated from other women? ~ I don't think like that. I could care less! It never entered my mind. In fact, I thought it was kind of cool. I thought everyone else would think that, too, which they did.

Have people treated you as a "bad woman" since you started dancing? ~ No, the only people that know what I do are people who are involved in it also.

Have you lost self-esteem due to dancing? ~ I think that I have. Through this interview, I've seen it. It goes up and down. But nothing is really due to dancing, it's just me personally. I don't want to be here, it's really not for me.

What have you learned due to dancing? ~ I've learned that society is in a lot of trouble. People don't know how to communicate with each other. We don't take the time to, we're very judgmental, we don't take the time to look into a person to see why they're acting a certain way. People are very selfish. It's all me-me-me-me-me. If you don't like what you see you put it down, it's very sad. I think I've always had that in me because I've always been such a hot shot. My opinion of other people has been low, but it's really fried me. Now it's basically a joke, my whole attitude. All the prejudiced jokes that I've made are becoming very real for me. (Laughs) So now I'm reversing it.

Has dancing affected your politics? ~ Politics? I don't have any politics.

Do you fear becoming a prostitute? ~ Absolutely not. I wish I had the balls to do it! I'm just going about it the wrong way. I'm already taking my clothes off, I'm already a window whore. If there wasn't the fear of disease and...but I hate men, so I'd probably be very good at it. Suck them dry for all their money...

Do you identify and feel solidarity with other sex workers? ~ Most definitely. It's a real camaraderie. It's a very good feeling, it's a real strength.

Have you been discriminated against because you are a woman? ~ Musically I have been many times. I was very insulted, but it just shows where the world's at.

Are you a feminist? ~ That is the way I feel, but I don't really live my life in that fashion where I go around...I think in what I do I promote it in my own way.

Historically some feminists have tried to exclude some women from the women's movement based on their sexual behavior and preferences. Do you experience this exclusion? ~ No. But, they haven't been too much help really.

What is your relationship to the women's movement? ~ I'm a woman, and I believe in everything that they're trying to do and everything they're saying. I'm just not involved in it. I have to worry about me. I should become involved in it, after this book is finished. I think every woman has a sense of it.

What have been the most damaging and the most constructive influences in your life? ~ The most damaging have been men, the relationships that I've had. The better thing has been working with men in the music industry and succeeding. I'm getting out there and accomplishing what I want to accomplish *with* them.

What person or people have had the greatest influence on your life? ~ All the dead ones. Dead musicians, actors, actresses. All the people that have passed out of...the whole sixties thing. I feel so close to that and I wasn't even there. I'm so jealous. People were together and into peace and love.

What are your greatest gifts and limitations? ~ My greatest gifts are my tits! My music, my voice. Limitations are that I'm very... I don't want to say shallow...uninformed. I don't care enough about a lot of things to do anything about them. I don't have a lot of drive.

Do you feel that you are growing? ~ Yes, I'm becoming more aware. But it's all so disappointing, so I just shut myself off from it. Life is a drag, it's just all depression and people hurting each other. Everybody wants the same things, but the way we go about it...I don't even involve myself in it. I'll read a book about whatever happened, it's safer than getting involved.

What would you like to be doing in ten to fifteen years? ~ I would like to be living in Beverly Hills and doing everything that I'm doing now, but on a major label. I'd like to have a major deal, major tour, major money, and major dancing. And when I do all that, then I will read the paper, maybe. I'll have someone to bring it to me! And I want to be fully clothed.

I *will* be doing music no matter what level it's on. And I will be with the same boy, but I will have a better attitude.

Recently in San Francisco we witnessed the appearance of women dancing for women. Why do you think this is happening? ~ Women can relate to each other. Society has allowed us to be sensitive and feeling, something that men haven't been able to be. We haven't been big macho studs, we've been relating to each other forever. We appreciate each other. We're always on each other's side. We see the beauty of it when we watch women dance. It's not this jack-off type thing, it's not a dog-cat thing. It's horse and chicken! (Laughs)

Have you danced for women only? ~ No, I haven't! I would like that.

If social and economic equality for women became a reality would some women still dance? Would you? ~ Oh sure, women enjoy it. Sure! People are exhibitionists. Your body, you want to show it...yeah, I know a lot of women who enjoy it, very, very much. I wouldn't dance.

Would commercial sex work exist in your ideal society? ~ No, there would be no genders. We would be like amoebas. There would be no sex, nothing. Or else it would be like in *Sex World*, where you have sex by thinking about it. "Can we try it without sex... please?"

For many people it's impossible to conceive of anyone choosing to dance as you do. Why do you think that is? ~ Well, they're older. People are inhibited, I don't know. It's always been a taboo, although it's always been happening. It probably comes from jealousy, at least from the women's point of view. I think every woman has that secret fantasy of being adored by all these strangers. People are just sticks-in-the-mud, old fashioned.

Many people paint female sex workers as among the most obvious victims of male domination and declare that if you don't see yourself as such you are suffering from "false consciousness" and "delusions of the oppressed". What is your response to that? ~ (Laughs) I'm sick! I don't look at it like that at all. I see how you can, but it's like, come on ladies. No, no. We dominate that whole fucking thing. We have no clothes on. We run the show. Oh, God, no!

Why do you think people use sexually explicit media? ~ Because it works. Because people like to see things they aren't used to seeing. Everyone probably wondered what Mom and Dad were doing in the bedroom, and now finally society has allowed you to see it. Everyone wants to know what Billy looks like without his clothes. You always want what's covered, you want what you can't have. I'm so bored by it now, after seeing it all the time. But the idea of people having sex with each other is very interesting to me. I would look immediately. I would watch. I wouldn't take my eyes off it. Everyone wants to fuck.

Has the sexually explicit media you've seen accurately portrayed human sexual relations? ~ I would hope not! For me personally, what I've seen doesn't. I don't think anything really exists like what I've seen. There is no Linda Lovelace with flocks of men in her house. I haven't experienced it. No, it's just another story, another fantasy.

At what age do you think people should be allowed to view pictures of human genitalia? ~ From day one. If they found out early that it wasn't such a big thing, there would be no need for what I'm doing, probably. I think everyone would be more adjusted. It would be accepted. It's just life. There would be more respect about it. Yeah! Put it all over his room as he's growing up.

Do you think any sexually explicit media should be banned? ~ No. It's a free country. Except there is one magazine called *Big Fat Mamas*...Eeek! "Everyone should be allowed to make a buck, eh, girls?" Have you seen that? They're huge.

At the outset the Meese Commission declared that it intended to contain the spread of pornography. At its conclusion, the Commission, like most others, could not define pornography. Yet it recommended the prosecution, fining, and jailing of people who produce, distribute, and consume it. What do you think of the Commission and its recommendations? ~ Is this really going to happen? Does this mean that Hugh Hefner would be put away, is that what they mean by stuff like that? That's ridiculous! How can you say that one is okay and one is not? What's the difference? That's totally ridiculous. They probably have a stack of them in the garage. They should worry about people dying. It's out of control. We need to clear the planet and start again! (Laughs)

Why do you think the government shows virtually no concern about violence in the mainstream media? ~ They're trying to take sex away, they're trying to take the music away. They've got to leave violence, there's got to be something to write and read and do. Something to talk about in the news.

How are sex work and sex workers portrayed in the mainstream media? ~ As bad women, bad people. They're always trying to ridicule or make us look like we're all junked up hookers. It's not on our side right now, but I think as time goes on, because of books like this, people will become more aware and informed. They'll realize that it's really no big deal, two sides of the coin like anything else.

Some people argue that humans are born with a sex drive and after that our sexuality is socially constructed, produced through our experiences. How do you think human sexuality is shaped? ~ It starts from day one, when you get a pink dress and he gets blue shoes. He gets the trucks and you get the dolls. From day one. He's the macho, the stronger one, the more active one, she's the little submissive thing. And in school, or watching tv, it's Charlie's Angels or Dan August. Then there's the church, which doesn't want you to have sex, period.

Are there a wide variety of sexualities produced? ~ I suppose, as opposed to when I was growing up. But it hasn't changed much. It just depends on where you are, I guess. For me there was just men and women. Married.

What do men and women have in common sexually. ~ They both like to orgasm. They like it. They're dogs! When you're into sex and your partner is, too, then you're both dogs. It happens once all the barriers are gone. (Laughs)

Is there any sexual expression that society should ban? ~ Absolutely not. Everything should be okay. I don't believe in discrimination of any kind. Whether people agree with it or not, it's just – fuck off! Close your door, you don't have to deal with it. If everyone is exposed to EVERYTHING – then it will be understood. The authorities, the law makers, the government, the fuckin' liars, cheaters, people with money, who run this country should stay the fuck out of it.

What part does sexual pleasure play in life? ~ It plays a big part in mine! It should be a large part of everyone's life. It should be something that is done every hour!

Some people seem to think that sexual pleasure without procreation is a threat to society. Is it? ~ Fuck no! There are enough children in this world! No. I was raised that way and it was wrong. Sex is not just for reproduction. If you reproduced every time you looked at someone and had a sexual twinge, you'd be in trouble.

Is it ever okay to be a sex object? ~ If you so choose, sure. It's always okay if that's what you want, if that's what you're about. Isn't it what I'm doing now? (Laughs)

Do you think gratification of sexual needs diminishes anti-social impulses? Yes, they're much more relaxed. It makes them happy, of course, they're much more social.

Feminism as it emerged in the early 1970's had as basic tenets sexual explo-ration and sexual self-determination. Subsequent exploration has led to intense debate over female sexual identity and behavior. How do you define female sexuality? ~ Women want to have sex like a man, they get horny too, and they like to orgasm. I think we want to feel that it's a little deeper, though. We aren't so hip on just the sex act and thank you very much, see you later. We'd like to carry on in some way, shape, or form, whether it's just friendship or whether it's your lover. We tend to get a little carried away with the deepness.

Are there any sexual behaviors you think women should not engage in?
~ Absolutely not. Anything you feel like doing, go outside, find somebody, go for it.

A recent Kinsey Institute survey of western nations concluded that people in the United States feel the worst about their bodies. Have you seen evidence of this problem? ~ Well, you see a lot of overweight people here, that's evidence. It really has an effect on me that people don't take care of themselves. It's really important to me, not for anyone else, but for me, to get up in the morning and like what I see, you know?

In the late 1940's American writer Philip Wylie saw equally strong tendencies to excite and constrain the erotic drive as pervasive in this society. He observed that they continuously reinforce each other and declared, "The United States is technically insane on the matter of sex." Is his diagnosis good for today? ~ He's absolutely right. It definitely applies now, probably even more so, because now It's much more open than in the '40s. No one 28 years old would have been doing this. Now it's wide open, both sides are wide open. We're nuts! Yes. It's basically what I've been saying in this interview, how I don't like any of this shit, but I'm doing it. Right?

In a recent decision the Supreme Court ruled that the State does have a role in regulating bedroom behavior. Do you agree? ~ That's ridiculous! They're going to put a little guard outside everybody's door? I think it's ridiculous! You can do drugs in the privacy of your own house but you can't have sex. That is preposterous. I can't believe it. I can't. I can't. I couldn't believe that anal or oral sex are actually illegal in New York. This is ridiculous! But how could they regulate what goes on in the bedroom?

People in the United States are spending billions of dollars each year on sexual needs. What does this say to you? ~ It says to me that people are pretty lonesome. Pathetically lonesome. Everyone's looking for friends, for warmth, for caring, for someone to look at them and smile. So they get dildos and smile at them. Searching for love. L-O-V-E, love.

Do you think the schools should teach about human sexuality? ~ Yes, I do. The more aware of something you are, the better. They should teach that we are sexual beings and how to relate to those feelings. I don't know how you can teach someone to make the right judgment about something, but they should be made aware of it. No one should tell them what to do. It's just a matter of information, from day one.

How is sexuality portrayed in the mainstream media? ~ There's no feeling really involved. It's just to cum, to orgasm.

Some people argue that there is a sexual hierarchy in the United States with heterosexuals at the top and everyone else treated as second class citizens? Do you agree? ~ That's what I see. It will probably be like that forever because of the Bible. I believe that. When I was gay I thought it was like that.

Some people also think that non-heterosexuals should not have the same rights as heterosexuals. What do you think? ~ I think they should be shot! No. Of course they should. Any sexual preference that anyone has is fine, as long as they don't push it on anyone else. They can fuck my dog if they want. But not my chinchillas!

Do you think heterosexism is a serious problem in the United States? ~ It's hard to say. I live in the San Francisco area and I didn't become aware of all this sexuality stuff until I came here. I was brought into it in this atmosphere where everything is okay. In San Francisco there's a large gay population of men and women and everything is accepted. I am heterosexual myself, but me and people I hang out with feel everything's okay. I would imagine yes, it's a serious problem, but I don't live in that environment.

How does society respond to the outspoken sensuous person? ~ Do you mean like Marilyn Chambers? I think they all want to fuck her. I think women dislike her because she's got the balls to exploit herself and she is intelligent. Men just want to fuck her. They probably treat her as a lower class citizen because her clothes are off. Right now she's a celebrity. I think she's my real mother!

What have you learned about people through sexuality? ~ That they're all pathetically hung up! Men are dogs but in a shy way. They want to cum all over women's breasts and faces.

Do women play a part in the creation of male sexuality? ~ We run the whole show. We run this whole fuckin' world. The world is based on pussy. Face it. Obviously we've made them dogs at this point. We have created that. We've made men really pathetic and desperate for women, for sex, for naughty sex, for infidelity. Yeah, we've made them macho. We have made you like you are, and now, I think we're trying to reverse it all. We've lured them on to make money, to survive, so we've gone to our bodies. It started in the age of slavery when we were getting banged, but that was no choice, and we've just reversed it. We're basically making you the suckers. We've made you the dogs. Because we know that you want it and we've played on it.

How do you think batterers and rapists are created? ~ Any research I've done on it, or seen, it's usually something in their childhood. It's usually the relationship with their mother. It's not sexual, usually. It's either a loss of a mother or emotional neglect from their mother. It's aggression that's been built up over lack of something.

Do you have any suggestions on how to create a peaceful male? ~ Cut off their balls! (Laughs) I am with a very peaceful male now, and how is he peaceful? He's involved with a lot of people. There are a lot of women in his life. I think men who have been surrounded by women, have a lot of female friends, and I'm not talking sexually, are peaceful. Let them be around women, and just be themselves. Help them to be funny and not really serious about sex. Anything that's said or done...make it like a game, like a party, I guess that would help a little.

Are there feminist men? ~ I'm sure I have no idea. You're kind of a feminist, aren't you? No, I'm sure there are.

Describe the impact male dominance has had on women. ~ We're the reason for everything, so who's ruled who? Men have had the titles, but women...

Do you see men working at changing themselves? ~ In my life I don't. You have to understand, I'm not very social. But, I don't believe men can do it alone, we have to work on it with you. I'm sure it's happening. Something's going to happen.

What do you think the future holds for relations between men and women? ~ Well, the bomb is going to fall probably before the century is over. Meantime, it can only get better. I think men and women, women especially, are becoming okay with their sexuality and it's finally okay to say, "Look, do it this way." It's going to improve. There's going to be more openness, more honesty, and I think people are really getting into monogamy. They're going to realize that to live together they're going to have to really work at it. Also, women are becoming career minded. It's definitely going to evolve into this big, wonderful balloon of bubbling happiness. (Laughs)

If rape and sexual assault ended today how would your life change? ~ I guess that I would have a sense of warmth. Nothing drastic. I don't read the paper that much or see the news too much. When I hear about somebody getting raped it twinges me a bit, but it doesn't have a close connection to me. I'm very apathetic.

What do you consider to be the failures of the women's movement in the United States? ~ I don't even know what they do.

Anti-censorship feminists have emerged who believe some sexually explicit media reflects and reinforces the oppression of women, but disagree with the pro-censorship feminists' view that sexually explicit media is the cause of women's oppression. They argue that the causes of women's oppression are much deeper and precede the mass production and distribution of sexually explicit media by centuries. What is your point of view? ~ It's in the way it's been done, in the way it's been presented. I'm right in the middle of it and we're presenting sex in an okay way. We're trying to clean it up a little. We're in a very powerful, humane position doing that.

Where do you think sexually explicit media should be placed on the movement agenda? ~ I'm so engulfed by this world now that I can't see anything else. So to me that would be the number one place to start. And with all the religious bullshit that's happening now, too, that's where I would start.

Do you think our constitutional guarantee of free speech includes sexual speech? ~ Sure, it's speech.

How would you advise courts ruling on sexually explicit media? ~ Sex is a part of human nature. Simply walking into a theater like this can make somebody's day or week. It definitely can serve the purpose of helping people continue on their day.

Tell us what you know about AIDS and describe the impact it is having on your life and society. ~ I have read a lot of pamphlets about how it can be spread, so I am aware of it that way. I'm not promiscuous in any way, shape, or form any more. It doesn't even enter my mind. There's that fear of even touching someone. In the music thing I do, fans will come and kiss me and I find myself being unnecessarily cold because I'm freaked out about this stuff. It really touches me when I see something on the news. It's one of those things that really hits home. And in a way, it's also kind of exciting because I feel that I'm living through a Black Plague or something.

Do you think it is possible that this society will confine those who test HIV positive in spite of the medical evidence that it is not casually transmitted? ~ Yes, we're going to see another leprosy thing happening here. People are afraid, and there's the uptight, rich heterosexual pigs that run the country and they want to put it away. It's like the Nazi thing. They just want to put it away and close their eyes, like it's not going to happen or it didn't happen. It very well could happen. People are afraid and uninformed, or still afraid, they don't want it to mess up all their bourgeois shit. I've read some stuff where they say this is a government plot to get rid of the gays and now it's gotten out of hand. They do actually have something that's trying to get rid of all of us. It's all so dirty! I mean, they put coke on the streets, so why wouldn't they put people somewhere else?

What future do you see for erotic theater and erotic dancers? ~ The future is pretty gloomy. In the short time that I have worked in this industry, in this city, I've seen it decrease and become more commercial. It hasn't improved. The owners of these theaters just want to make money. They see it as a tourist thing where they don't rely on regular customers. The average looks and intelligence of the women has gone down. A lot of the bullshit things you hear about are unfortunately becoming true, like the prostitution and drugs. It's become more of a party scene, as opposed to professionalism. That show girl image, that untouchable, intangible image is gone, and now it's just like the slut off the street. It's going nowhere...its peak is over.

LILITH

RECLAIMING THE BAD GIRL, THAT'S LILITH,
MAKES A WOMAN WHOLE.

Part of the promotion for your show says, "Live Nude Dancing, Lovely Lusty Ladies, Naked Naughty Nasty." Is this a good description of who you are and how you perform at work? ~ It's a mediocre description, but "Naked Naughty Nasty" is not a misrepresentation. The marketing of sexuality to sell sexuality is, at least, clear. We're not under any pretensions about what's going on here. Sexuality is a consumer product in a capitalist culture. Doing this kind of work confronts you with the question, if you sell a look at your pussy for a quarter, how can you object to somebody in a bikini selling breakfast cereal or cars? Selling women's bodies in the sex industry is less insidious than using women's bodies to advertise and market other products besides sexuality. This on the one hand is a liberated place, because people are more open. But...as soon as people are liberated, we have to make money from it, it's twisted and turned towards profit rather than liberation. That's what I object to, not that we advertise that women are being open and erotic.

What were you told was your job? ~ I was told to be my erotic self, to be relaxed and to have eye contact with customers. To have a good relationship with my body. The first time I auditioned I was stiff and the show director advised me to go home, put on bath oil and caress myself in front of a mirror as an exercise in achieving this relationship with my body. I did and the second audition I was fine.

Were you told that the men masturbate? ~ No, I wasn't.

Describe your first experience on stage. ~ My first audition I was paralyzed with nerves, somewhat hyper with adrenaline, stiff, and awed by the other dancers. I was challenged by the experience, and aware of my own limits, in regard to how in my body I was able to be under those circumstances. The first five minutes were particulary scary, but after that, I attuned to it. Becoming totally relaxed took a few days. I had a lot of respect for the dancers being able to do it so naturally and to be so in control of the situation.

When you were hired were you asked to work on certain aspects of your performance? ~ Yes, I was told that I needed to smile more, that I looked too severe. I was to engage in more eye contact with the customers, and loosen up, but not to push myself to anything I wasn't able to deal with. Go with your own flow. Get in touch with your own eroticism. And power. I got some advice on how to do that and support around the fact that that's possible for every woman, no matter how uptight she may feel. I found the show directors to be very supportive of the idea that every woman can come into her own erotic power given time. I believed them.

Describe how you dance, display, and touch your body during your perfor-

mance. ~ Displaying and touching are considerably different after months of work than they are in the beginning. I didn't engage in the more graphic, up-front stuff until I was working for a while. What I mean by graphic and up-front is coming up backwards to a window and spreading. I am more into body caresses than just attention to my pussy. There are times during a show when I lay down and do a more wide-legged pose, including an opening of the labia and caressing my clit. That feature is dependant on mood, energy level, and dynamic with the customer. There is never any coercion. We develop a maximum of ease in being able to touch ourselves anywhere, and display our-selves...in a provocative and comfortable way.

What sexual depictions do you perform on stage? ~ I depict myself as erot-ic, sensuous, and solo. I have depicted myself as being turned on when I wasn't and when I was. I depict myself as being very interested in the cus-tomer and his sexuality. At times it's genuine flowing behavior and other times it's an act. I've touched my breasts and genitals, and masturbated to a minor excitation. I've shown and touched all parts of my pussy. I give a lot more rear view to the one-way booths.

Part of the routine I've developed is to dance toward the customers back-wards, look over my shoulder, and touch myself while I have eye contact. I've done fellatio portrayals, licked my fingers, and feigned intercourse at the corner windows. I bump and grind in unison with the person on the other side of the glass, with eye contact. Anal intercourse I didn't do often, seeing as it's not a practice of mine, and under those conditions it has more of a submissive connotation.

Does your performance contain elements of dominance and submission? ~ I only like to portray elements of dominance. The submissive position is not something that comes naturally to me or that I choose. I am mostly in control of the dynamic direction. My reaction to potentially dominating behavior from customers is negative. I'm an anti-authoritarian and that applies to every aspect of this job. I have experimented, in a more playful way, where it's very clearly not psychologically imperative on the part of the person who may want you to submit.

I carried a whip on stage a few times and quite enjoyed flicking it. (Laughs) For a while it was common stage practice, and a playful experience to have that as an aid to loosening up certain situations. For certain men it was very intimidating, despite the playful context. Dominance and submission out of the dog-collar and whip scene context is real different because it's not a direct, one-over-one situation. It's more subliminal. I react against men who aren't admitting that this is what they're trying to do. The one that's out is very dif-ferent than the one that's covert.

Do you test your power to arouse? ~ Yes. Being aware of your power to arouse, testing it, feeling comfortable with it is a constant part of the work. What eventually become the characteristics of your show are known gestures, depictions, glances, and behaviors that are deliberately destined to arouse.

Eye contact with the customers is very important to some dancers. Is it for you? ~ A certain amount of eye contact is necessary for the job, otherwise you appear cold and hard. It depends on my mood. Most of the time I try to do the necessary amount of eye contact to be "professional". There are off-days when I don't want to look at anybody and I work the one-way windows all the time. There are times when the eye contact is what makes it real. The amount of genuine relating that can go on even under these supposedly strange conditions makes it worth doing. When you want to go deeper with the experience, it's not through looking at someone's foot or cock, to get to any depth, to who the person is, or why they're there, or to relate to them in a different way, it's through the eyes.

How much of your performance is you and your sexuality and how much is persona? ~ This is an interesting point because performance develops persona, brings out hidden aspects of persona, can be the only place where the real persona can live. In my case, aspects of my persona which I hadn't lived out before came alive on stage, and that was something that I consciously went there to create for myself. I notice when I stop dancing that an edge of the persona isn't available to me.

Everything you do here is part of you and your sexuality even if it's feigned. The feigned is a part of you that you are living out and exploring. Sometimes the feigning can detract from the amount of energy for the real sexual you. When you get to bed with your lover at 3:30 a.m. it can be difficult to produce the real sexual you if you've been feigning for five hours. Lastly, the actress on stage, is she real or not?

What persona do you project? ~ What this type of work brings out of the women is an aspect of persona that they might not have lived before, and that's the free acting out of the high powered, erotic woman. It comes from the self, the soul, the psyche and the body, it comes from deep within. It comes from the movies, from magazines, everything that goes to make up a person in this culture.

We're quite aware of the blaming of women, the Eve complex, the seductress being blamed for the fall from the state of grace, plus the seductress being blamed for her own rape on the street. This is a very safe place to play the vamp, in the rest of society it is not necessarily safe. You can project pretty much any part of your sexuality in this context and know that it may arouse excitation from the man or jokes from the girlfriends on stage, but it's a safe, secure place to do it. Because of that, a lot of women project aspects of themselves that they never had before. That's a point for victims of abuse, to find that part of themselves again. It was put down at a very early age. That's a second reason people dance, to find parts of themselves, live them and project them into reality. Parts of themselves that were killed earlier on.

Why did you choose the stage name you use? ~ Lilith is a famous, dreaded mythological character from the early Hebrew folk tales that got left out of the bible. Lilith was the first woman in the Genesis scenario created by God as a wife for Adam. When they came to copulate she refused to lie under him, finding that demeaning, she uttered the name of God and flew away. She turned into a screech owl and forever afterwards haunted the night as a demoness. She reappeared throughout Hebrew mythology and right up to the Middle Ages as a demon succubus who haunted medieval monks. When they had wet dreams they blamed Lilith because they had intercourse with her.

I chose Lilith because of the obvious connotation of a seductress that's implied in the name. Conscious autonomy also, the reclaiming of that power of women to say no, which was denied in the writing of the Genesis myth.

Afterwards Eve was created because she would lie underneath Adam. Lilith was a woman who refused to lie down, to be the second. She insisted on not being subordinate to men and that's very important for women to reclaim in the latter stages of patriarchal society. The seductress is not a role women are encouraged to play on their own terms. It gives them, potentially, too much power.

How do you use costuming and makeup? ~ I started to use makeup to produce a face to hide behind, or to become a different personality. It's the same as in any theater, it's an aid to change your persona, the same with the costume. Makeup and costume are essential to making the transition from the street persona, to the stage persona. If I am late I have to do it on my first break, because it affects my show. The makeup, the nail varnish, the high heels, and other stuff is putting on the seductress role.

A lot of the costuming is traditional burlesque costuming. It's mostly to enhance, titilate, and increase the possibilities of behavior. It brings us into better contact with our sexual selves. There's a charge associated with particular items of lingerie. Just wearing them, standing there without moving a muscle, can turn the customers on. Costuming is a big part of trying to arouse people.

Do drugs play a part in your performance? ~ Very little. I've been high on stage maybe five times in all. I was a lot more able to project and be imaginative and turned-on. I was able to trance out on the possibilities of this work being different, as it has been in other places, at other times. That's the insight that the occasional use of drugs on stage gave me. There are pretty strict rules about the use of drugs in the theater and I didn't violate those rules. The few times that I was on stage high, I had gotten high outside on cannabis. One time I danced the day after an ecstasy trip. That was pretty intense, but I'd rather keep that for my private life.

On stage music plays almost continuously. Describe the variety and part it plays in your performance. ~ At one point there was a lot of really bad music. That was a big distraction from my performance. I'm not that much into moronic heavy metal, which some of the women are. I like songs that have a good beat. The lyrics of the more mainstream pop songs can be incredibly boring to listen to ten times. The music's much better right now. Dance music that I like is a positive pleasure, where the rest of it is like an endurance test that robs a lot of my energy. I never offered my services to the jukebox committee because they don't get paid. I think they do now.

Rock and roll has very stereotypical sexist attitudes and some of the songs seem to be particularly ill chosen in terms of perpetuating stereotypes that women working in the sex industry would suffer from a lot more than others. Songs where women are passive onlookers to be dated, courted, and fucked. There hasn't been that much reggae or commercial stuff like Prince that's popular, but still good.

The stage is covered with mirrors ceiling to floor. What role do they play in your work? ~ I've always been narcissistic, always liked to look at myself in mirrors. I'm very into the other person, the alter ego, through a glass darkly, Alice in Wonderland, the voyeur of the self, the whole trip. Mirrors play a large role in coordinating movement, dance, how you come across, and they enable you to check out everything at once, your gesture, every shake and rattle. They play a vital role in being able to change your image, that has a very strong affect on your psychology, whether you're into it or not, but I am into it in a big way.

On the negative side it promotes pure nitpicking vanity. Mirror, mirror, on the wall, who's the fairest of them all?

Describe the interaction and commentary among the dancers on stage. ~ It depends on who's on stage, how you get along with them, if they have the same musical taste as you, if you have things in common or not. I find I have different perceptions than a lot of the people because I'm not American. I'm not quite sure to what extent the Americans are aware of that.

There is a genuine level of warmth and support that's deeper than what's required for the job. Most of the women are very caring and empathic towards each other, even when they're being bitchy. There's a certain base level of support that doesn't disappear. I have been on stage very few times when there were incidents or bad feelings. It's one of the best work environments I've ever worked in.

Incredible levels of intimacy are reached because we're being sexual with people. Up-front sexual with four other people. There's a lot more sharing about where people are at with their sexuality. There's advice, commentary, exchange of anecdotes, flirtation, right down to enactment of real life sexual stuff. You hear about couples in the theater, plus, crushes, fancies, and admiration.

I feel a very strong admiration for several of the women. For the warmth and compassion of their natures and how they deal with different situations on stage. These are traits not necessarily cultivated by the job, but traits that the women have themselves. It was very much an eye opener for me to see some typically female qualities stronger here than they would be allowed to be in many other environments. Here we're dealing with the connection between female power and female eroticism, the forbidden, repressed secret not to be allowed connection, it's being forged, and that obviously empowers the women.

This is an excellent observatory of human nature and behavior. Very few people have self defenses, fronts, or attitudes when they're naked. People are a lot more open and honest with each other here than they are in other fields. That's something that people want, partly this is what's on sale, the vibe between the women. It's pretty dead with four girls on stage who don't relate particulary well. When you are on stage with women who are possessed of high amounts of physical and erotic energy, it's a very strong, power experience, very interesting. It definitely is a big part of the growth experience for me having the opportunity to learn from some of the women. People make very sexual comments to each other, about each other, about their bodies, about how big or little their breasts have gotten, did it hurt when you pierced your clitoris and your nipples, oh, you've put on weight, oh, that looks nice on you, that doesn't, if you don't get along well with men you should try it with women, everything.

Is there competition among the dancers on stage? ~ There's more a recognition of someone being so much of an energy emitter. It's a, "Can you come up to that level?" It's more evocative than pushy, not a race to see who can dance the fastest, or shake the most, or turn the most men on. Several of the star dancers seem to have a better relationship to their own eroticism. I have felt twinges of envy on a few occasions. There is no top to get to here. Of course, there's a cult of being beautiful and wanting to be beautiful, and who's the fairest of them all, that's definitely there.

Is there humor on stage? ~ Yes, a lot. Often it's the saving grace that helps anyone get through a six hour show. It's a great gift, an asset, and a lot of the women are endowed with a great sense of humor. It's a very up-front, raunchy, erotic blend of humor. You have the freedom to make jokes about people's behavior, and, of course, the idiosyncrasies of male behavior are most often the subject of the humor. Humor is often a way of dealing with negative and potentially negative energy that men project, a way of diffusing potentially strange situations where the nasty can be real rather than pretend.

Most erotic dancers I've talked with say they like to dance. Is this important for you in this job? ~ Yes, I like to dance. Unfortunately, when you are dancing for five hours a day you do a lot less social dancing. The last thing you want to do that night is go out dancing. Here you get to dance a lot more erotically, or own your body in a very different way than you can at a public dance club. Dancing gets the life force and erotic energy flowing, and that flow has been, up to now, very strictly curtailed. Being an erotic dancer has affected my general style of dancing. I notice this when I have to draw back from doing certain things in a situation where people are more uptight.

Is the myth of the perfect body perpetuated here? ~ There are one or two women who have classically perfect bodies. I think this is a place, more than anywhere else, where true beauty is recognized. It seems that beauty does not depend on how big or small you are or whether you're white, black, or brown, but how much you can be in your body and let your spirit shine through. The women are really aware of what men want to see as a particularly beautiful body, but there's a lot of support if your body is different. It's really clear that a woman who doesn't look like a centerfold can have a provocative affect upon a man. A lot of women realize that what they have is fine, it's how they use it and live in it that matters. That's how they come in contact with their eroticism. Management definitely validates a woman's sense of her own sensuality. The myth is more exploded, than perpetuated.

Do you ever become aroused by what you are doing and what is happening around you on stage? ~ Sure. I don't come from a society where lesbianism exists openly and I had never seen a woman to woman love act. Some of what I find most arousing on stage is intimate behavior between women. Watching male-female interaction can be very arousing too, where there's some real stuff going on. When you're aware of that subtle change in everybody's aura or in the energy emanation, that can be erotic because it touches the body. You can be on the other side of the stage and realize there's something going on, even if you've got your back turned, and you can become aroused. It's very intense. You're presented with visually beautiful cunts all the time, and its hard not to be aroused. I think that women, irrespective of their lived out sexual preference, are very attracted to and appreciative of each other's beauty.

Do you ever have sexual fantasies during your performance? ~ I do a lot of fantasizing on stage. My fantasies are how it could be when I get a good interaction, a healthy, warm, human, sensual, sexual flow with the customer. Where they respected me and I respected them, and it was very up-front, very sexual, but clean. I use "clean" in a "no one tried to put anything over on anyone else" kind of meaning.

I have fantasized a lot on how the sex industry could be, basing that upon what I know has happened in the past, the ways of sexual healing. It's an erotic fantasy, but it's also about the broader use of sexual energy to heal instead of just to titilate. One of my biggest fantasies is a reconstitution of the temple. I see the need from the deprivations of the customers, their kinks. There is obvious, necessary healing that needs to be done on human sexuality. Pluto in Scorpio, transform or die.

Humanity's sexual attitudes are leading us towards the AIDS epidemic. Heterosexuals are getting AIDS. People's attitudes toward their sexuality influences whether they get AIDS or not, influences their immune system, their bodies. At no other point have we been so repressed or so in need of healing in the sexual sphere.

I have fantasies of doing stuff with the other women, or with some of the good looking men who come in. But the main fantasy is how I would change the sex industry to cater to human needs instead of commercial exploitation. It's a fantasy that I don't consider utopian, but very real and necessary.

What can you do on stage that you can't do off stage? ~ Obviously having done stuff on stage means that you can do it off stage, but the energy level might not be there. There is a lot of touching of yourself that you grow to regard as natural that you can't do on the street. You can't touch your breasts or genitals in public without evoking a prudish reaction, or else people see it as a sign of a turn-on. A lot of the stage behaviors will lead to harassment in places other than there or in your own bedroom.

Theoretically, everything you do on stage you can do in your own bedroom, but you can't, because there is a power that's created with the flow of eroticism between the women that's greater than the sum of its parts. It's directly tapping into the mystery of orgone energy, life force energy, and how that augments itself when it's flowing. The energy to counteract the bomb – that's not contactable by yourself in front of a mirror in your bedroom.

What won't you do on stage? ~ I am less inclined to stretch my labia and genitals than some women. I've become more considerate of the eventual side effects on my body. I won't come up to people's windows just because I'm told to. I know that for some men the doggie position is seeing you in a degrading position and I won't do it for them. For other men it's not and I've done it a few times.

You can pick up misogyny, you can see it. When they ask you to do things, you are very aware of whether you're cooperating in your own lowering in their eyes. There are very few things I won't do for moral reasons. Anything that has to do with natural touching of the human body is fine, whatever the context.

Do you dance for co-workers and friends? ~ Two women friends came to the theater to see what it was like and I danced for them. That was difficult because of potential judgment, them protecting their own good girl images. Sometimes dancing for co-workers is exciting, but I was wary of being judged "less of a turn-on" than the newest girl.

Do you ever do sex education on stage? ~ There's a way of encouraging by showing how you touch yourself, how you are with your own eroticism. There's definitely a way of gently leading men into observing women's erotic worth, and this hopefully affects their behavior. I've made men aware that the clitoris is the primary focus of stimulation and pleasure for women, not the vagina.

When very young guys come in to see a woman for the first time how you deal with that experience can affect their whole impression of women. Pride in ourselves and our beauty and a "clean" attitude can affect men. The main surprise for men, that women can be this sexy, can portray so much eroticism and sexuality, without having to be so graphic. It makes a big difference to understand where eroticism lies.

How does having your period affect your performance? ~ I am not prone to cramps or pains. Occasionally it makes me more inward, low energy, contemplative, and I want to keep my energy for myself. It makes me withdraw. With any other job I'd take an off day. Blood is a very, very powerful erotic stimulant, but there is a strong conditioning to consider it our weak time of the month.

In my background, there were major prohibitions around it which I broke through. It's a high power point for me now in several areas of my life. A lot of times, I like peace and quiet on the first or second day of my period. The third day, the major power point, I have a lot more erotic energy, general body energy, greater power to be extroverted, a very strong physical charge, high vitality carrying over into the rest of my life. It depends on how you deal with your period as an experience. I am often sad in the theater about traditional women's attitudes that it is a curse. Some of the women haven't transformed it into the power time.

I was quite surprised when I first heard that healing occurs here, women healing themselves, each other, and customers. Describe what you know about this. ~ I feel that I healed myself by deprogramming a lot of basic Catholic attitudes toward my sexuality, guilt, and the last vestiges of being unable to touch my own body. I've learned to feel proud about my vagina, feel that this is a good part of me. A lot of the final stages of my break-through went on in the theater, by reprogramming out of patriarchal attitudes. Healing is happening on a physical, spiritual, and psychological level.

For a lot of women, it's a healing experience if it's the first time they come in touch with their erotic power. To feel their flow is definitely empowering and strengthening. It heals the whole space that women have between the nice girl and the bad girl. Reclaiming the bad girl, that's Lilith, makes a woman whole. It's healing finding and healing menstrual wounds, realizing that it's not a wound, it's sacred drops, the wonderful elixir of life. It took the healing process to realize that, and that I could dance and be so strong on my period.

I'm firmly convinced that what we have here is women healing men of the wounds that patriarchy has dealt men in relation to their own sexuality, and the general burden of sexual repression on all of us. The blocked orgone ener-gy, the crossed neural pathways. The circuits where we should have pleasure and love and free sexual flow have been imprinted with violence, hatred, and freakouts. There is a major chance here to uncross, reprogram. This can occur on a very unconscious level. A man can jack-off and receive a healing experience, as well as an erotic one. In spite of the semi-sleazy environment, genuine, warm, human interchange occurs with compassion and a basic level of caring. For a lot of the men downtown, it's the only place in the city where they get to relate, at all. We are dealing with the most severely alienated soci-ety in the world.

In ancient Sumeria Lilith went out into the streets and brought men into the temple where priestesses of the goddess made love with them, and showed them how to love women, and showed them the power of love. San Francisco is a long way in place and time from that culture, but certain elements of that experience continue to carry over. It has been a repressed part of the female psyche and some of the women are living it out now. And even if they aren't conscious of it, healing is occurring. It's a general releasing of the blocks, you can see it with a guilty customer.

How the dancer handles the guilty type of customer has a major impact on them slowly coming to terms with their guilt and how they received it. A lot of them may go out just as furtively as they come in, but there is a great potential for healing. One of the big wounds to the collective psyche is Christian sexual guilt. There are a lot of energies interchanged through the window. If you have a good orgasm with someone who remains human with you to the end of it, it cannot help but be good.

Have you had any transcendent moments on stage? ~ This may seem illusion to the cynical, but a lot of times I was in a light state of trance, and felt my mind open to direct experiential contact with a part of that female collective unconscious. There is the point of view that time is circular, that past, present, and future are all coexistent, this is an insight of modern physics. I've felt direct contact with gynocentric cultures and with the women's experience of that time. I've drawn power from it and realized that somehow my doing this has a role to play in drawing this out of the darkness, out of repression, out from under the crushing heel of patriarchy. Transcendent!

My mind definitely transcended (and my spirit as well) the constraints of the theater, to get to a place of human experience, where I was experiencing something far above and beyond the maybe obvious level of outer reality. I don't use drugs much, but certainly when I am into the dancing, I am high. I am always in contact with being able to change my perception, I have a lot of flashes. I use the word "flashes" for intuitive insight into how it was, and again, how it could be.

Do you ever feel caged or wish you could cover up? ~ Not so much wish I could cover up, I have felt caged. I've felt, "God, I don't want to be here today. Let me out of here." There are times when I feel shut up and shut off and it becomes just a very mundane job, but free will is operating here all the time. You can't leave in the middle of your shift, but you can leave if you don't want to do the work. So it's not caged in a totally oppressive sense.

Describe the customers. ~ All the men in downtown San Francisco. From 14-year-old Chinese boys (they just look fourteen) to 90-year-old Chinese men, to rude white college students, incredibly rude, crude under twenty WASP men. Lunch time businessmen and sad, lonely men. Men in for fun and games or a party. Men who want to get rid of their work related tension by jerking-off. Some friendly, some aggressive, some gentle and shy and furtive and worried about their sexuality. Some adoring and admiring, "Wow", and some, "Spread it, girl!", and some normal, conversational. All looking for something.

Probably a lot of them are suffering from birth trauma. I think birth trauma is a big thing here, it's what draws people to vaginas. Something that went wrong on the way out, hopes to be cured by re-entry. (Laughs) I've had friendly, warm, human, loving, erotic, exchanges with people, plus some downright nasty, yucky, aggressive, horrible exchanges.

Women who dance in the theater come in to see a girlfriend's show or their favorite dancer. That's somewhat regular. There are women who are coupled. Some hover shyly behind their boyfriends and he's urging them to look, and maybe follow our example. Others are there to get off on the situation and make love with their boyfriends, or indulge in foreplay. There are definitely women who come in to feel superior.

There's a small number of lesbian women who come in. One memorable night I had a really good exchange with four lesbian women in a corner booth. They were all loud and raunchy and really in to "see", very into explicit display, like show me cunt and masturbate for me. They were very appreciative and getting really turned on, starting to do stuff with each other, not at all putting any attitude over about, you girls shouldn't be here. A lot of women point, and don't engage in eye contact with the girls. They're sort of embarrassed, sometimes a mutual embarrassment scene goes on woman to woman. There's mutual condescension sometimes, too.

Do customers leave their social roles and status behind when they come to see you? ~ Some do. Students definitely don't leave their boisterous, nonsensical roles behind and businessmen tend to remain businessmen. But, I think a lot of people evolve a new role for themselves in the theater, one they can't express on the outside. Maybe it's a composite. Mostly they're there to let some kind of mask down.

At first I was amazed by the passivity of Asian men. I don't know if they are having Zen orgasms or what, but, no matter what you do, or what fun and games the girls go through, they have the same passive expression. It's fascinating. It is definitely possible to get a guy with a rigid, tight face, and warm him up, make him more human. The healing is going on when you see someone come in with a real stressed demeanor and go out more open and loose. People look better after an orgasm.

What is your favorite type of customer? ~ A customer who likes me, smiles at me, and recognizes that I'm a person as well as a body. I like customers in their 20's who are into the fun aspect of sex and don't have attitudes. Also people who turn you on, who give something back. After they leave you feel more erotic, good about your eroticism, and about what has just gone down. You've shared an experience in "this kind of place", it's been definitely not demeaning, it's been good for both.

There are a few older men I am fond of because I think they need sympathy and are lonely. I *like* to talk to them, just to be supportive. They are usually pretty adoring with certain girls. There's a lot of worship that goes on. Customers who worship the women are obviously pretty popular. (Laughs)

Do you encounter men who you think hate women? ~ Yep. There are men looking for sexual satisfaction who resent the fact that they want a woman and that they can get satisfaction from women, and they project that hate onto the women. They're just as involved in the interaction as the woman is, but they'll follow along this Christian mute thing and after they've cum, they've absolved themselves of their guilt, by blaming the woman. Before they've cum, you can tell in their faces that they want you to be sexual, but they're going to hate you for it. That's a direct result of Christian values toward sexuality.

Among the guilty ones, when their guilt is too much, they hate women rather than deal with their own guilt. It's the most common projection that we have in this society, why women are scapegoated. It's the "Eve" syndrome, original sin and sexuality. We offer the apple, they take it and bite it and then they want to spit it back at you, and say, "You offered me an apple Eve!" "...Bitch!"

There's a very high level of overt misogyny in this country that I perceive everywhere. It's pervasive, the internal war against women that goes on in this country. Terrorizing women by crime and always a threat of violence. The desire to dominate, male power, patriarchy, it's all based on hating women. At times, if you don't perform like they want you to, you'll quickly feel the hate because they can't control you. Sometimes it's really intense.

Have you ever felt it was dangerous to arouse a customer? ~ No *physical* danger can happen, but dangerous sometimes in terms of the kind of vibes that are injurious to my mental health and well-being. On an ongoing basis, there's a certain amount of psychic damage incurred in being the brunt of intense misogyny.

One time I danced for somebody and when I left the theater, he was waiting for me. He got very turned-on, fantasized, and obviously wanted to connect with me on a real life-level. I was getting into a cab and he touched me. He begged me to unlock the taxi door.

Do you encounter violent men here? ~ The possibility of being violent is limited. I consider men who persistently bang on the glass for attention as coercive. Psychological coercion is a form of violence that we have to deal with.

Do you think you have ever danced for a rapist? ~ Probably. That is something I worry about. Am I perpetuating the image of "women as objects" in a pornographic mind or women as something to be dominated? We know that rape is primarily a desire to dominate as much as a sexual crime. Perhaps dancing for a rapist in a lighter atmosphere alleviates the chances of them raping, by reducing the sexual tension. If they receive no satisfaction, then that perpetuates it. It's a very fine line.

I believe there are statistics from the year this theater and some others opened, indicating the rape figures went down in the city. However, multiple rapists are not going to *not* do it because they go to a theater to alleviate their sexual tension. We have to remember that most rape is family members and date rape.

There are customers who come here with great regularity. What are they like? ~ Str-r-r-r-range! (Laughs) Saturday morning five-past-ten and they're here. We joke, "Gee, haven't you guys had any breakfast yet?" People come in as soon as they're up in the morning. I've been weirded out by the regularity of some people. I attribute it to loneliness and alienation and that this is the only human contact some of these guys have. I think *most* of the regulars have more of the human rather than sexual need. They just want to talk, they look at your body, but they don't jerk-off. It's so pathetic. It's sad watching guys sit there for five or six hours – just hoping for any crumb of friendliness, wanting human attention. Those kind of people unquestionably, are where women heal in the theater. They're there because they have nobody else in the world. It's testament to the men who suffer tragically under patriarchy, the silent male sufferers. No outlet for human feelings. It's easy to cut them down and say they're perverts and dirty old men, but I feel a strong compassion for them sometimes. Other times I'm annoyed and wish they'd leave.

I've had discussions with feminists where they argue that men being able to use porn theaters as outlets means that they never have to tackle their weird attitudes; if sex establishments didn't exist they would have to do without sex or learn to relate to women. Well, maybe there is some truth in that, there are also men who are irreparably damaged by their life in this country where so many people are irreparably damaged, neurotic. Compassionate women would say, "Hey, maybe it keeps them more human." And that's a contribution to humanity.

I propose a return to the temple. "All the lonely people, where do they all come from?" Lilith took the lonely men off the street. There is still a path of priestess training where an older woman educates young boys. But that's very different than dropping quarters in a slot. In the Yoruba West African tradition that's still a path of priestesses training, whereas, sex worker is a "low" road. A return to the temple is a return to the roots of gynocentric pre-patriarchal civilization.

Describe the variety of sexual behavior customers express. ~ Voyeuristic behavior, mimicking fellatio. Guys want you to masturbate so they can masturbate. There's the guy who sticks cucumbers up himself, the guy who puts the tube up his penis, the guy who measures his prick with a ruler. (Laughs) Gay men come in together, guys with their girlfriends, guys who want you to mimic kissing them through the glass, who want to engage in cunnilingus with you through the glass, licking their lips while imagining they're either of your lips. They mimic intercourse through the glass. Then there's the odd guy who goes into the corner booth takes off his clothes and dances for the women. They're into reciprocal performance, into fun and shaking their asses around, exhibitionists basically.

From stage you see a lot of tongues. Describe this. ~ It's a common come on gesture, sticking out, licking lips in anticipation, an invitation, a provocation, and also as aggression, depending on the context. It can be off-putting or enticing. With depictions that involve cunnilingus or fellatio you see a lot of tongues. It's quite common for dancers to use the tongue to pretend to lick the hand, foot, or cock of the customer. It's common for the women to feign tonguing each other, and to lick whichever parts of their anatomy they're into at the time. Generally it's provocative, enticing, alluring behavior.

Describe some of the more unique encounters you've had with customers. ~ One guy filled his mouth with some substance and spit it all over himself and wanted to spit at me through the glass. It was weird, but it wasn't hostile behavior. One guy was really into licking your foot. Older Chinese guys like to lick feet, which is a foot fetish from the time they used to bind women's feet in China, maybe a generational carryover. I've seen it even in younger Chinese guys, and that's a bit eerie. I don't mean to be picking on older Chinese men – they're *really* into feet.

I read about foot binding in *Gyn-Ecology* by Mary Daly and the first few times it definitely felt weird. I felt the patriarchal mutilation of women's bodies and felt that they were trying to project that on to me. It was very different than somebody who wants to look at your cunt, that's normal. I see men who obsessively want to see inside of your vagina, who are obsessed with the "vagina dentata."

Many customers do show a great deal of interest in the dancers' genitalia. Why do you think there is such great interest? ~ There is an unconscious desire to return to the womb, as well as the need to dispel the primitive fear of the "vagina dentata"; the strong muscles of the vagina wall that can suck the penis and give rise to fear of castration. Also, hospital birth has given rise to a high level of birth trauma which can distort sexual expression. Maybe it's the "jewel in the lotus" or the mystery of the unfolding lips of a pink and beautiful flower that is the gateway to life and ecstasy. Who can resist?

I would obviously like to say that all people see all other people as humans, but I know that's not true. Unfortunately, a high percentage of men would easily reduce you to your genitalia, you're just a cunt, a pussy, and they just want to see pussy, they want to divorce pussy from woman. That's the split. It's a functional split between mind, body, and spirit that began in Western civilization long ago. It ties into cutting up women's power into little pieces. If you can cut off a woman's genitalia from the rest of her body, and her being from her body, and her soul from her being, you can justify domination. The challenge is to not become part of it, to not become dismembered. That's a power some people don't recognize exists: to be so wholly human that you defy dismemberment. I don't attest that I could produce that power all the time, or that I could defy the process all the time, but I think that women rise above this attempt to dismember them a lot more often than people will give credit for. It's a key question in terms of this being exploitive work or not.

If all the men who come in here with that mind frame, succeeded in dismembering women, they would be totally exploited and couldn't dance. If every single interchange left you burnt out, you could be cut into seven different pieces. But, focus on one part of the body and dismemberment are different processes and we should be aware of that. Just focusing doesn't mean that you don't see the rest, just that that's the part that gets all the attention, so to speak.

Is there a difference in the customers' behavior when they are alone or in a group? ~ Younger guys are easier to deal with individually. There's all this peer pressure to be rude to women, to point fingers and stare. You see that men encourage each other to be patriarchal, whereas the man by himself when confronted with the woman by herself, often has a harder time being obnoxious if that's his inclination. Some guys are really shy about their sexuality, afraid to be sexual in front of their male friends, but, when they're by themselves they can be sexual. With younger guys, you can see that how you deal with them can have an influence. It's very different than a centerfold, a centerfold can't speak and say, "Oh, don't cum all over me."

What do the customers say when they speak? ~ It can be as mundane as "what's your name", to asking, or telling you to perform for them, or asking if they can see you outside. They make comments if they like your body, your costume, or the way you dance, or they want you to turn around so they can see your ass.

What do you say when you speak? ~ Depends on the man, and if I'm feeling good about dancing tonight or not. I keep a lot of my real personality hidden. I ask about what they are doing sexually, if they like it, if they enjoyed cumming. I maintain a human level of contact and have fun.

Some customers experience ecstatic surprise when they first encounter the stage show. What do you think surprises them? ~ I've experienced this with men from cultures where sexuality is more repressed. They're surprised and delighted at the beauty of the naked female (laughs), beauty they really didn't know existed. It has much more an air of mystery if you're from a culture that doesn't allow it, where you've never seen. Ever, ever, ever. Total mystery. What a revelation. But, there are also American men who have never seen pussy in real life. Looking at a real woman is greatly different than looking at a picture, she moves, and you can relate to her, it can be a transcendent experience.

Are you ever disturbed by the affect you have on customers? ~ Not often. If I walk away and they bang on the window, that really disturbs me, if they do it aggressively. In the beginning it's disturbing if you're not aware of women's power to arouse. But, it's not a bad kind of disturbing to realize, once you become strong enough to defy dismemberment, that the reason they have to dismember this power is because it's a great power. A power that should be revered instead of dragged into the under belly of the beast. When you feel that power, and realize that you can disturb, it is a realization that women who are connected to their erotic powers are strong women. Ivory tower feminists won't accept that the woman who knows how to allow energy to flow from her cunt, to her heart, to her mind is stronger than a woman who's a "good girl". That's one of the major things I've learned here, that I could have that big an affect on men by being so in my erotic power, and realizing that I had been separated from it before. My culture had deprived me of it. You can blow men out, you can give them such alarming detail that they'll freak. (Laughs)

Sometimes a customer will leave angry or disgusted. Do you understand why? ~ Sometimes customers want you to obey and when you don't, they'll leave angry and disgusted. Sometimes customers don't get a good show, meaning somebody's bored or listless or refuses to cooperate in their sexual fantasy. If they're told by the dancer that she won't tolerate their bad behavior they get angry and they leave.

Do you ever abuse the customers? ~ I've retaliated a few times when I was the object of verbal abuse or insulting gestures from customers.

Do you ever feel controlled or possessed by the customers? ~ You're there to entertain the customers and you have to, but you're not possessed. Nobody can possess you unless you want them to.

When customers show disrespect the dancers can call security and have them removed. How often do you ask that a customer be removed? ~ I did that a lot when photographing was going on, that really burns me.

How do you respond when a customer orgasms? ~ (Laughs) If I've been involved in them getting there it can be nice to see them cumming, getting pleasure. Sometimes I get yukied out seeing men cum all the time. When the men cum and then don't smile at you, and don't say thanks, or don't give you a nod or a wink, that often turns into revulsion. What you're aware of then is that it's very empty sexuality. I've never been adverse if someone's been human. (Laughs)

Do you try to get the customers to spend? ~ If more of the profits would be diverted my way, maybe. (Laughs)

How long do you stay with a customer? ~ Sometimes I stay quite a long time if they are okay and everybody else isn't. I stay with the nicest one.

How do you feel about dancing for customers in the three booths with one-way glass? ~ I prefer dancing for the one-ways. I had occasional paranoia about being recognized by someone I wasn't out to, about being a dancer, but often it's more interesting, a real anonymity mystique.

Does this job suit you? ~ Yeah, I do a lot of other things and it's flexible. You can make your own schedule. And not work at all. But, the money I can earn for evoking desire isn't loads.

Have you experienced burnout on this job? ~ Surrrrre. (Laughs) Burnout is bad. You may be scheduled to work, but not want to, can't face the negative aspects of the job. It's the same with any job, but this is more intense. When the first half hour is terrible and you have to stay four more hours, it's real hard. Of course, we're responsible for what we volunteer for. The physical fatigue aspect is probably easiest to deal with because with sleep it goes away. The psychological burnout can have repercussions on your sexuality, your self-esteem, your position in your community, your inability to visualize doing something more fulfilling, or just that you can't face looking a man in the face or at his cock again.

I've seen dancers not be able to work for months because they just couldn't face it. It encourages drugs, for sure. The potentially healing aspects are equalled by the destructive aspects. The Goddess is creator and destroyer. You can create a stronger erotic woman with her contact, you can end up like a crumpled, burned out woman.

How do you spend the ten minute breaks you take every forty minutes? ~ I take a pee, fix my lipstick, talk to people, read, stimulate my mind a little. Or sometimes I just close my eyes and think, just lie there and recuperate. Often I read theoretical material relating to the sex industry and sexuality. Look at some theory, go out there, do some practice. I've gleaned a lot by combining those two things. I've read erotica as well and thought about how I might write that someday.

Off stage you encounter other dancers, support staff, and management. Describe the interaction and conversation that occur. ~ I quite enjoy the vibe in the dressing room. It's a different world than the stage. I've gotten a lot of insight into the women there. I came to respect and admire a lot of the women because of the intense conversations we've had. You get to see what's going on in their lives. People give each other advice, and because it's such an intimate work environment, people don't have any qualms about talking about their intimate stuff. I've heard insightful and up front discussions about what goes on in the human sexual realm, while people are fixing their makeup or screaming "Who took my G-string?" The women are compassionate and supportive of each other about their outside shit and their stuff with men.

Management hangs out on the couch cultivating people and being nice to their protegee's. I've had some good conversations with one show director, but I had a certain distance. I watch support staff and how they relate to the women more than I interact with them. I have to commend them for their non-sexist demeanors and attitudes, they do a really good job. It really shows you what could go on if nudity were not such a heavy thing in our society. It opens up interactions and shows how much clothes are a front that divide people.

Off stage it is not uncommon to hear dancers referring to each other as slut, whore, or bitch. What do these remarks mean? ~ These are playful allusions to the roles that are projected onto us by straight society. It's a recognition of owning that energy in our own way.

Many of the workers say they can be themselves here. Can you? ~ Yeah, another aspect of myself, that I don't necessarily live on the outside and didn't even necessarily know was part of me before I started working here. Then there are aspects that I live on the outside that I didn't find expression for in the theater. We're all multi-faceted people. Lilith who works here, that's me too, she's an interesting aspect who has added to my overall character development.

The owner and management of this theater say they want to create a safe, nurturing, fun, and profitable business. Have they succeeded? ~ Certainly they've created themselves a profitable business. Workers get their wages and that's it. It's fun though and a lot of times in spite of the best efforts of people to tone it down. I've had fun there a lot, in spite of the hard work.

Nurturing? It is a lot more nurturing for the profits of the owners than for the workers. There is an attempt to look after people, but I disagree that it is very nurturing. More attention is paid to nurturing the customers than the dancers. There is a lot of hype around nurturing and a lot of use of EST terminology to mask a lot of shrewd manipulation that goes on under the guise of nurturing. A lot of people see through it, but don't necessarily call them on it. I've seen a lot of cases where people who made human mistakes got balled out really abusively. I've also seen people getting support around personal crisis in their life outside the theater. So, both nurturing and not nurturing occur.

The real nurturing comes from woman to woman, the dancers nurture each other, that energy is definitely there. It is part of the employment agreement to nurture each other, but, that's a human thing that grows between people or not. I resent when management tries to tap that force and pretend they are creating it, when in fact they are trying to use EST to bend it to their own needs, to create profit from the nurtured. There is a lot of "grin and bear it" encouraged but it's really hard to always keep a smile on your face.

Customers are encouraged to persist at the expense of the women. It is safe from obvious physical harm, but a minor amount of harassment can occur, on the way to the lobby or out of sight of the cameras. There are definitely things that can destabilize you mentally. There is just no way you can be protected, mostly because all of your chakras are open if you're somewhat aroused sexually, you can take on heavy, aggressive vibes. When these guys cum that energy gets released and is usually taken up by the women and transformed, but, not always.

The owner and management also express the desire to empower people. Have you been empowered here? ~ I've empowered myself with the help of the other women, by breaking through the blocks *for* myself, at my own speed.

I was empowered to be punctual by management. The employment agreements are limiting, there are compulsory meetings with management talking down to people, using ESTian jargon, a hierarchal approach. They use slick psychological manipulative techniques to try to put stuff over on people, there is a lot of condescension towards people. A lot of it is empowering people to be cogs, to know your place and stay there. That's what EST is used for within capitalism. That's the viewpoint of an alien European.

People should have their own union and not these little meetings where things are supposed to be taken care of. The main forum for the worker/management relationship is the compulsory monthly meeting where the managers sit on chairs two feet above the dancers who sit on the floor. The dancers are talked down to, told the rules over and over again. It is intensely authoritarian and punctuated with very carefully manufactured laughs and jokes...transparent, really transparent.

But, on a level of being able to be up front and erotic and break through society's barriers around women being strong with eroticism, obviously it is a very empowering experience.

Do you have job security? ~ If you keep all of your agreements and are the perfect person – which no one is – you have job security. I've seen people lose their jobs for taking sick or for doing a no-show and not getting a replacement for their shift. People have lost their jobs quickly with no apparent reason. I have job security because I am "good and conscientious."

Is sexism promoted or resisted in any way here? ~ There is care about choosing male support staff who don't have overtly sexist attitudes. But, I had the experience of a manager making an extremely sexist comment, and when I called him on it, he was supported by both of the women managers. They felt that it wasn't a sexist comment. That's one time I felt in danger of losing my job. To me, that showed that EST had turned their minds as to what sexism is, or that they had an ambiguous, somewhat hypocritical attitude towards the sexist monologue. But, this is a hip world and everybody tries not to be sexist by keeping their real attitudes hidden. When men are hanging around women and they know they won't get away with stuff, they don't say it overtly, but think it.

Within this context, you have greater freedom, because you're naked and open and honest before the world. You're also, a lot of times, charged with erotic power and you have a really clear opportunity to reverse sexism, and show them however narrow their concept of you, you are above and beyond. That happens a lot.

Sexism is endemic in this society, totally. America is an advanced patriarchal society.

What do you feel passing customers in the hallway whom you have just danced for? ~ Strange sometimes. An exchange of secret smiles, sometimes you don't want to have any exchange. I feel fine dressed at the desk, talking to a few guys who come past. In the hallway there is a certain, lurking, potentially sinister, menacing energy because there are all these uptight guys, waiting to get in and cum. They've got all that tension and you're cutting through their space. They're carrying the whole weight of whatever drew them there in the first place, and, of course, it isn't just a hard-on, that would be easy to deal with.

Do you ever feel in danger coming to or leaving work? ~ I always get a cab late at night.

Describe your earliest memories. ~ Throwing-up in my crib, my first snow storm, and watching my kid sister learn to walk.

Describe your family as you remember them during childhood. ~ I come from a large Catholic family, three boys, four girls. We lived in an agricultural community. My family has traditional values, is conservative and lives according to Christian codes of conduct and morality. My family is middle class, but not high income middle class. We're a pretty harmonious family. My father had a bad temper and he reprimanded us frequently, especially the boys. Heavy handed, but not severe. Strong mother, but, strength through quiet manipulation, rather than overt confrontation. My mother worked when I was a child and the women neighbors provided childcare.

There were always lots of people around and a lot of space for play. I hung out a lot with my brothers and one of my sisters. I'm different than my siblings, I'm *real* different. And that was apparent. I also hung out a lot with my extended family.

We had a farm and there was a lot of work looking after the animals, including our pets, and tending the fields. Our relationships were part of a larger community. There's nobody in my family that I don't relate to, with everyone there's some basis for rapport. I have good memories of childhood, somewhat idyllic, I guess we all have, and I'm not sure how much of that is road nostalgia.

Describe your relationship with your parents. ~ I have a good relationship with my mother. I'm quite like her in appearance and personality. My mother always encouraged my education and was supportive of my maturation process. She's very strong and loving, but a little detached in some ways. She's not directly, physically affectionate, but shows a lot of caring for your physical and material needs, more so than emotional needs. My mother was the head of the family. We lived in her house, that had a strong influence on my perception of women.

My father is a quite strong figure, he had a good relationship with my mother. They didn't fight in front of us anyway, they seemed to have things worked out. I had a good relationship with him until I was about five and went through that being dropped by your father phase. He used to hit my brothers and I didn't respect that or his temper. He didn't drink a lot so it wasn't bad. He never hit my mother or anything like that.

After puberty he freaked out at my psycho-sexual development. I guess he was always astounded because I was impertinent. When I became politically aware I had contrary political opinions and expressed them. It was challenging for him to be attacked by his daughter, who wasn't supposed to have an opinion at all. There were traditional roles, but from my mother, there was an appreciation and support of my being able to transcend them.

Feminism was just breaking in the early 70's when I was growing up and I was into it. I saw out of my little, quiet back water soul that there were other places to go and that I could. My family encouraged me.

I was bold, my parents had trouble with me at parties. I was strong willed, not into being told what to do. In later years, I've gotten in touch with that resentment against my father. My childhood was good times in comparison to what I can gauge goes on in the American family. The more negative patterns were sexual repression and my mother's maneuvering to deal with a husband who had a bad temper.

Describe your childhood play and friendships. ~ I spent a lot of time alone as a child, I wandered in the fields and developed a deep contact with nature. I broke the taboos of what girls were supposed to do. I was boisterous, tomboyish, took physical risks, and encouraged my peer group to do so. I was bossy. (Laughs) It was hard for me to have close friends because of all the stuff going on in my head. I played a little football and with dolls. I lived a lot in a fantasy world as kids do. My two best friends were trees.

Describe your childhood school experience. ~ I was a reasonably bright and precocious kid. I teased the other kids a lot.

Describe your teachers and classmates. ~ One of my teachers had an uncontrolled sadistic streak and she was cruel to slow learners.

At an early age humans exhibit a wide range of erotic behavior. Describe what were you up to as a child? ~ I had a girlfriend when I was 5 and we would take off our clothes and play games of examining each other's genitalia. It was a big thrill because it was forbidden nature. We used to do this every couple of months. At 7, I got embarrassed about it and we quit. I remember this in terms of it being my childhood sexual orientation, even though I have been primarily heterosexual since.

On one occasion a crowd of kids were playing in a water hole and I had everyone take their clothes off and run around. This is in a society where nudity is taboo, from a very young age you are not supposed to show yourself. The body is dirty and there is body hatred. There we were putting strings of long grass into the cheeks of people's asses, and having fun. I remember somebody catching us and my fear of being caught naked. It was a really big thing that I did it. My natural orientation was to break out of these things and defy shame.

I had an early experience with bestiality, oral sex with this dog, when I was a child. I knew that was wrong and forbidden, but did it twice with this newly born puppy.

I used to play with another bunch of children and we would try to get the games around to having nudity because of the reaction against it, the whole blanket of body terror we were growing up under.

What were you taught about human sexuality by your parents? ~ Very little. My parents were part of the old school, Catholics, sex for procreation. I think my father probably enjoyed his sexuality, I don't think my mother did. I asked, when I was about 9, how babies were born and Mom told me. At thirteen I menstruated without her knowing and then I was given a little booklet. We never sat down and had a talk. She was too embarrassed. She passed on to me the sex as a duty kind of thing. My father never mentioned it.

During puberty my father exhibited this very classic fear of the emerging female sexuality as I represented it. He didn't like bikinis or short skirts. I pushed against all those things. My parents grew up with very proper clothing and I got from them, cover your body, behave like a "proper" woman.

In a lot of the country areas in Europe, only our generation has emerged into the light of modern values. The past weighs heavy in Catholic communities and there is an incredible amount of misogyny which girls pick up. They are guilty, Eve is projected onto them and they feel guilty.

Was there nudity in your home? ~ When I was 13 my brother gave me a lot of sex researchers material. He was aware of the nudity taboo and made me realize that I could break through it. I've wondered if he was breaking me through these taboos for his own ends, but I broke out of the nudity taboo shortly after puberty. I was a lot more open about it than the other members of my family and still am. I realized around puberty that this nudity taboo was ridiculous, that there was nothing wrong with the body.

Were you ever punished due to sexual expression? ~ Once I stood on my head in my dress and exposed my legs and underwear and I was asked to leave this children's group I was in. I was about 10 and I really didn't understand why. It was all weird adult shit to me. I thought it was for general boisterousness, but it was for not being a "good little girl."

Were you sexually abused as a child? ~ I remember being locked in a room with an old hobo kind of figure when I was about 7, and him putting his hand up my skirt. I was totally terrified. When I finally got away, I expressed my fear and was laughed at. Human sexuality remained mysterious until I was about ten. My brother locked me up as a joke because he knew I was afraid of him. This is my first imprint on the bogey man that's used to program women into fear of the night. I was afraid of this guy afterwards.

At age 8 an older trusted male friend of the family encouraged me and my sister to expose ourselves to him. He liked to look at us and asked us not to tell. He did molest us and I asked my mother if this was wrong and she said, "Who did that?" I said I imagined it, I just made it up and she said, "No, you didn't, tell us." I guess she confronted him on it. I used to sit on his knee with a lot of other adults present and he used to try to touch me. He got me into it by, "Pretend they don't see, pretend they don't see." This furtive aspect appealed to my childhood imagination and I don't think I was unduly traumatized. He never did insertion or any painful stuff, but he was obviously getting kicks out of it as a dirty old man. I would characterize it as minor abuse, not as a major level trauma. Later on, the initial explorations of the peer group boys into my budding sexuality quickly became them pulling me into sexual awareness before I emerged into it myself.

Later I had an incestuous relationship, which was abusive. From age 11 to 13 an older brother came into my room at night and touched me as I slept with my sister. I worry about the effect that had on her observing this going on while I tried to fight him off. I told my mother, she didn't stop it and I got into trouble with him for having told her. I'm sure my mother was afraid that my father would massacre my brother if he knew. There was no intervention except for chastisement. Penetration never occurred. From 13 until 16 it focused on oral sex, then I summoned the power to stop it.

It was a strange interplay because I was sexually active those early years, in a society where women weren't sexually active, and became aware of sexual pleasure, but in this context of breaking incest taboo. By 16 the social significance of incest taboos dawned on me, and I knew this couldn't go on. I was freaked, but it was a very hard pattern to break.

Incest, in my culture, is a totally closet subject. I'm becoming aware of it's implications and affect on my life, in terms of powerlessness, exercise of will power, my self-esteem, and my ability to set goals. There is an amount of ambivalence in my self-image that I trace back to this experience. These are revelations which have come up since I have been working in the sex industry. They have come up in terms of my examination of the common feminist concern about people being drawn into the sex industry because of a pattern of re-victimization of people who were abused in childhood. I have examined that dynamic in myself and I am still in that process. Sibling incest is considered by psychologists to be less traumatic than father/daughter incest. I am still good friends with my brother, but I have a lot of unexpressed hatred and anger towards him.

What were you taught about human relationships in your family? ~ I was taught to look after people, to be nice to them and to have a very strong sense of community. I was never taught theoretical things. I was taught the idea of harmony and keeping on good terms with people, that people are more important than property. That's all primary programming for me. I learned that men are in charge. I was taught hierarchy in human relationships and that I was uppity for questioning this. Basically, I was taught to love and care for people as much as I could, and to be compassionate.

Were you taught to look good to attract and be chosen by a man? ~ To a certain extent. For a while, when I was a child, I was really into makeup and clothes and looking good. I stopped wearing makeup when I was 14 or 15. My family was more into looking nice than looking sexy. I knew about attracting men, but I never got it as a main program in life. My mother never gave us marriage is the main vocation in life. The family and society lay incredible trips about beauty and appearance on teenage girls. I picked up from my peer group how important it was to be attractive.

Did your parents teach you that you could have power, choice? ~
Somewhat. My country has suffered war and its effects in this century. The
national self-esteem and sense of power and powerlessness has gone through
incredible upheaval. So, I'm not sure my parents experienced that much
choice and power that they could pass on to me. During the economic boom
of the sixties and seventies, people all over Europe sensed opportunity they
hadn't before and I was encouraged to become educated and have more
choice than my parents had. They were very aware of more choices opening
up and wanting their children to take advantage of it. They wanted me to
achieve a better material basis in life than they had, because they'd both been
poor when they were younger. They wanted me to get a good job. My father
would have been happy for me to take a bureaucratic position in banking or
insurance. They wanted me to have a profession that would reflect well on
the family and to maintain Catholic standards and ethics in relationships.
They didn't want me to stray too far beyond the bounds. They had no idea of
who I was becoming. I appreciate what they wanted for me, and realize that
they have always wanted the best for me and I love them for that.

I decided early on that education was the key to getting out of powerlessness, and my mother encouraged me to go to university. I grew up under the
shadow of feminism in a Catholic dominated society and into expanding
choices for women and more than just career choices. The career opportunity
was the area that I picked up on first. After I travelled to other countries I saw
that choice means social choices about the kind of roles you play in relation to
men also.

At home, I was taught that choice is in relation to the community, that you
don't do something for yourself that's going to damage other people. The
sense of self, of power, that I have now is more to do with my later development. I always knew that I was going to get out, that I did have some choice
and abilities to change my situation. I've done that and gained awareness of
power and choice.

What effect did your body changing have on you? ~ I was proud when my
breasts started growing. It drew all this reaction from people around me.
Having to deal with being an object of desire, having overtures from men, was
confusing, but I was proud. I was pretty and I was proud. I developed, from
12 to 14, into this power that comes with being precocious and attractive.
But, it produced that whole trauma of being plunged into sexuality before I
had any awareness or choice. I resent, now, being approached sexually as
soon as I developed.

My body changing was a miracle. I felt pride in becoming a woman, even
though the mystery of menarche was not marked as an honorable passage
from girlhood to womanhood with any ritual and ceremony. It gave me a
sense of the potential power of woman and the limited power of woman. I

developed a detachment from my body after the first flush of puberty was over. At 15, I went into my head.

Describe your adolescent sexuality? ~ My first hot tingling feelings came from reading romantic novels. That was all very innocent, but it moved very quickly into older teenage boys asking me about masturbation. They wanted to know if I did it, and I didn't. I had to pretend that I didn't know what they were talking about. Knowledge was offered to me before I became curious myself, that really affected my emerging sexuality. I feel I was primed to exploration by prior knowledge to a great extent.

In this relationship with my brother I was having orgasms a lot when I was 14. I related to it as a positive, so I had a double value here, I didn't want to be in a relationship with my brother. Being involved with an older person, I didn't have patience with boys my own age. I did have a kissy thing some, but I wasn't into having boyfriends. I felt superior because I had a broader view of the world than they did. Incest though is a very strong taboo and it had an inhibitory effect on me later. I was 17 when I lost my virginity, which is a bit younger than most. It's not like here, where people are sexually active from the time they're 13.

The high value placed on chastity in a Catholic culture attempts to make you feel bad about people who express their sexuality and good about your own purity. That was a really strong dynamic, and it has a very strong affect on the class position of the family. The behavior of the women in the family is one of the main indications of class background that you become aware of, subliminally, very early on. So that was another thing that formed my emerging sexuality, I wasn't to make any mistakes. Like going with, or being with boys from the wrong background. I had definite codes of not having boys touch my breasts or my genitals. That was what a good girl didn't do, and I didn't. Until I got out of my Catholic education. I broke out when I was away from home.

How did you first discover and use the ability to arouse? ~ Men made me aware that I was having an affect on them. My father freaked around it, my brother was interested...people told me all the time that I looked good. Men are incredibly attracted by pubescent girls, there's the sexy school girl syndrome. So, I discovered early the ability to arouse. I wasn't necessarily into using it, I was often disdainful of people who were into me. I would just laugh it off.

At 14 in school they told us that it was dangerous to arouse men's passions because bad things could happen. I realized that I had a certain power over my brother and it was mostly in that relationship that I discovered the power to arouse and what that was. That wasn't very good, it was a loaded environment. But I was really into the power of being able to arouse and seeing a man totally aroused by my sexuality. It was definitely a kick.

Describe your discovery of how pregnancy occurs. ~ An aunt had a child. I asked my mother and she told me. I was afraid to ask because I knew stuff like this wasn't talked about. I knew about animals already. I was fascinated. I didn't know anything about reincarnation, but I actually thought, my grandmother died, my aunt had a baby, this was my grandmother coming back. A child was born after an old person died to let the person come back.

There was a certain amount of unmarried pregnancy in our area and that was always a severe loss of reputation for the girl and the family, because of the loss of opportunities and a lifetime of pariahdom. That affected my relationship with men. I had very clear limits about how far I was going to go. The possibility of getting pregnant was just not one that I could ever consider. And, of course, that had a very inhibitory affect on my sexual expression.

Did you receive sex education in school? ~ A very minimal amount throughout. We received strong indoctrination against contraception, abortion, and sex before marriage. We received scientific, reproductive organ type education, sperm and egg stuff. We didn't have any discussion on free flowing, loving human relationships. But I was exposed to other information, Masters & Johnson, the *Kinsey Report*, and the *Female Eunuch*.

Describe your first exposure to sexually explicit media and its impact on you. ~ I didn't see porn magazines until I was in my 20's. Where I grew up, porn is not readily available. The only sexually explicit material was *Lady Chatterly's Lover* and other literary works. I didn't see much until I came to San Francisco. I was 19 the first time I saw a blue movie.

Were you popular in school? ~ Yes and no. It was difficult. I had friends, but I was educated in a convent by nuns. I felt a detachment from other students because I had a worldly perspective. It affected my ability to be friends with them. I was a little arrogant about my intelligence and people picked up on that. Arrogance and conceit were issues I worked with in my teenage years. I was popular enough but I wasn't, at any stage, the most popular girl in class. It was probably different than it is here, we didn't have cheerleaders' popularity. It's real different.

Describe what it was like going to school in a convent. ~ It was pretty controlled, we were strongly indoctrinated to be young Catholic ladies. We had etiquette classes, art lessons, music, and a lot of really strict rules. A very pervasive Catholic ethic in everything. A lot of heavy programming against abortion, premarital sex, and heavy programming towards marriage. I quite liked school, but I was quite rebellious against the nuns. Their hypocrisy trips really ruined it for me. We had retreats, where we went away together and communicated with Jesus, and regular religious services. Mornings everybody went to school prayer, and sometimes classroom prayer. The teachers always maintained certain moral standards.

Describe your relationships as a teen. ~ I was very active in a youth organization and had a leadership position. I was pretty outgoing, in school too, but I did have a shy aspect. I had girlfriends but my greatest problem was finding teenagers I considered my intellectual equals. I tended to hang with people who were a few years older.

Did you suffer any traumas as a teen? ~ As teenagers we're all in eternal trauma, but I didn't have one incredibly traumatic teen experience. I lived in a stable family unit, in a socially stable community with a certain amount of closet stuff. There were a certain amount of family fights and arguments. I identify with the expression "incest survivor." I didn't perceive myself as suffering, I did to some extent, but it was a very quiet kind of suffering. I don't think I admitted to myself that I was upset by any of it.

The notion of people who are not from a very rich class background, being stupid...that traumatized me. It was traumatic discovering my family's political history. I reacted strongly to my family's rightist political leanings. Awareness of World War II was traumatic. My beginnings of awareness of the world situation was really traumatic, having had this very sheltered childhood. As things from the world outside started to creep in, it was like "Wow!" Discovery of concentration camps freaked me out, the knowledge that people were – could be – so monstrous.

I was a pretty balanced, stable teenager, I didn't ever veer toward the 19th nervous breakdown kind of teenager. I was always very firmly, head on my shoulders, feet on the ground, occasionally moody, but not traumatized in the sense that Americans are.

Describe your fears and insecurities as a teen. ~ Some of my insecurities were related to being educated with children of wealthier families, who weren't as smart as I was, and having to deal with snobbery. Not understanding how class operated gave me a great deal of insecurity.

Fears...well, I was afraid that somebody was going to discover my incestuous relationship and that I was going to get blamed for it. I was afraid of my father's temper, but I became unafraid of him towards 17-18 years old. I didn't have much fear, the world was, as I knew it, pretty safe and okay. I wasn't afraid of the people around me. The world wasn't about to end any minute, I didn't know that until I got to college.

Did you have any heroines or heroes as a teen? ~ My heroes were

Huckleberry Finn and Robin Hood, Maiden Marion, David Bowie and Joan of Arc. I was really into Robin Hood because he stole from the rich and gave to the poor.

What did you plan to do after graduation from school? ~ I planned to go to college, become a career woman, and get the fuck out of my place in the society I grew up in. I planned to travel and see the world. I had a lot of hopes and dreams and when I got to college I discovered the nuclear industry and the bomb. I was a big fan of rationality until I discovered its drawbacks, and that sort of confused me. I graduated, but I didn't choose to follow a career because of my disillusionment with the system. That's something I made a very clear choice not to do, out of awareness of the contribution the system was making to the destruction of the planet. Then I started travelling the world and becoming a cosmopolitan woman. (Laughs)

Describe work you've done prior to dancing. ~ I worked a large variety of casual jobs. In factories, in bars, in restaurants, in the fields, in the gardens, in the laundries of the world. I worked with my mind, as much as with my body.

Have you had other jobs in the sex industry? ~ No.

Describe the living situations you've been in since you left home. ~ I've been in a lot of experimental, strange living situations, since I left home. I've shared houses with people, lived in apartments. I lived as an au pair with a family. I've hitchhiked around and lived in camp sites, on the street, and on the beaches of various European countries. I've travelled around France and lived like a peasant in old drafty, dungeon type places. I've lived in squatted houses with avant garde people. I've lived in lofts with artists and communes with anarchists.

Describe your current living arrangements. I live in an international, collective household. A house that has nine people, four nationalities. I share a room with two other women. It's a house of people who are all political and social activists, who have moved beyond the nuclear family. And are striving to create new forms of social organization outside of the nuclear family.

Do you still practice the religion you were raised with? ~ No. From the time I was 12 to the time I was 24 I became imbued with a strong sense of rationalism and slowly disengaged from Catholicism, to the point of reaching that fine borderline between the atheist and the agnostic. I moved on in my mid 20's to a sense that there was another force outside of the rational line. I became disillusioned with rationalism and belonged to the New Heresy, which firmly believes that a big part of the world's problem is the body-mind-spirit split, that we need to re-awaken an awareness of the existence of the spirit. I'm a practicing pagan with an interest in ritual and magic, but I also revere Mary as one of the many faces of the goddess. I am presently working towards a reintegration of my Catholic heritage with my other exploration.

Describe significant friendships and love relationships you've had since leaving home. ~ I've had long periods of celibacy. Maybe four male lovers and some skirmishes with female lovers. I haven't had deep committed relationships because I travel. I tend to be good friends with my male lovers as distinct from just being a girlfriend. Intellectual compatibility is as important to me as sexual compatibility. Most of the relationships could be described as serial monogamy. I've had long separatist times where I explored the archetype of the virgin. Some of my male relationships have ended due to sexual dissatisfaction on my part.

I have peer groups in several different countries, I travel between them. I guess they are the lunatic, dissident fringe in whatever society I live in. Most of my women friends are staunch feminists. Most of my men friends are trying. I have friends in the environmental and anti-nuclear movements, friends in the gay community, sex workers.

Describe your social life. ~ I like to party. Partying is not consuming large amounts of food and drugs and people. It's having a good time, so I have a hard time with the way people party in this country. I haven't done much lately because I'm too busy.

Do you use drugs? ~ I smoke pot. I don't smoke cigarettes or drink alcohol, occasional use of psychedelics. I don't use drugs a lot. I have used, at various points in my life, acid, mushrooms, ecstasy, speed, cocaine, TCP, Adam and Eve, and all the fun exciting drugs that are worth exploring at least once for curiosity sake. But, I'm not a regular user of anything. I'm extremely careful about mental health, physical well-being and foremost, don't abuse drugs.

Have you suffered any traumas as an adult? ~ I've had traumas around hitchhiking and being driven off the road and almost killed by the driver of the car. Traumas related to street violence against women, traumas related to the police and the State. But the ever present trauma, is living under the threat of nuclear war and beneath the domination of sick old men.

Describe your fears and insecurities as an adult. ~ I'm confident that humanity can get through our crisis, I'm not sure we will. Most of my insecurities are around what's the basis of planning for a future. Sometimes I have a high level of confidence, other times I feel an imbedded insecurity, that I can't do stuff because I'm a woman, though I fight against that. I have somewhat of a sense of powerlessness or self-doubt that I now attribute to my incest experience. That's something I'm fighting to overcome. Inferiority is something I experience in spite of my many abilities.

Do you have male inspired fears? ~ No, no God! How can anyone be afraid of loving, charming, careful, nurturing man, my God. Yes, of fucking course, rape! I don't fear rape that much, but planetary destruction, nuclear war, genetic fucking technology, reproductive engineering, environmental pressure. All these are male inspired fears, they're the end product of 5,000 years of patriarchal domination. I'm afraid I hate them pretty much, you know. I don't like to hate, I'm afraid of the hatred that I hold in, becoming controlled by my hatred of patriarchy. Men as individuals, when they don't have the uniform and the gun, I'm not afraid of them. I never met a man who was able to dominate me without using force.

What media do you consume? ~ I like film, books, and theater mostly. I never watch TV, except for a very occasional documentary. I'm highly critical of the printed media. I read certain magazines. The world press is totally controlled, I read with a jaundiced eye. I try to read as little nonsense as possible.

Do you have a favorite book ? Author? Movie? ~ My present favorite author is Deena Metzger. She's written *The Woman Who Slept With Men To Take The War Out Of Them, The Tree*, several books of poetry and short stories and other works which appeared in various magazines.

"One Flew Over The Cuckoo's Nest" is my favorite movie. It showed the way they try to get people and control them, and the way the human spirit can go around it. I think Jack Nicholson is an interesting and sexy man.

Do you read romance novels? ~ I used to, when I was a kid. (Laughs) One of my first sexual experiences was getting that hot feeling across the loins when the hero and the heroine embraced passionately and kissed in the last paragraph. I guess a lot of the time I was reading them for that hot flash. I certainly became aware of the insidious, passive programming, waiting for the hero to sweep you off your feet. Romance is a social construct used to keep women in position, waiting for men and not to take active roles in their lives.

Do you use sexually explicit media? ~ Not really. I like to read good erotic short stories but there's not much available. Collette, Anais Nin, and some of the lesbian anthologies are pretty good. I don't go to porn movies or read porn magazines as part of my private sex life.

Had you been a customer in a peep show or other sex show prior to taking this job? ~ I was in a peep show once in San Francisco before I took the job. I was with some friends and we went in for a giggle.

Which of society's values have you rejected? ~ I reject hierarchy, male control, domination of women and nature, abuse of power, power-over dynamics, exploiting the "third" world for the "first" world's benefit, I reject polluting the air, locking people up, and the excesses of capitalism (very prominent in this country). A lot of American values I reject. I reject profit before people. My values are centered around loving people, loving the planet and trying to save it. The values I reject are militaristic, imperialistic and patriarchal.

Has the media ideal of beauty affected you? ~ Surely. I've had periods where I wore makeup, when I was 13, 14, 15, then I quit. Apart from work I wear very little makeup. I don't wear a bra. I'm not as curvaceous as society's ideal of beauty but I don't diverge so much that it's been a bother. It annoys me to have to be pretty and have people treat me nice because I'm pretty, put emphasis on my face as distinct from my being. It's a very double edged thing. Beauty has a power and it also causes hassles on the street, on the subway, while you're hitchhiking, or on the road in relation to men. Men are attracted by a pretty face, it affected me greatly that they want something from me.

Many humans love the attention of others and adorn themselves to get it. Do you? ~ Sometimes I like to dress up, sometimes I like to dress down. I don't spend a lot of money on clothes. I like to look good for myself, for my self-esteem and not necessarily for onlookers.

What is your self-image? ~ It varies. I see myself as another woman wielding the labyrs double axe, in a not very obvious way to some, but in a very obvious way to myself. My image is of a woman struggling to become herself, sometimes rising to the challenge and sometimes not. Of someone whose focus is to evolve to the extent where I can make a contribution to saving the earth and demolishing the patriarchy. Sometimes I think I'm nowhere and other times I think I'm getting somewhere.

Do you trust people? ~ I've learned in this country that it is naive to trust people unless you know them. Living in the United States you learn to withhold trust until you're sure. Whereas I was brought up to trust unless a person proves untrustworthy. That's been a difficult dynamic for me to adjust to.

Have you ever been violent with people? ~ Once when I was 15 I beat up my little sister and I was extremely contrite.

Define power. ~ Power is when I feel in contact with my body, my higher self, people around me and nature. I can act to solve my problems, step over the obstacle and be myself.

Describe the variety and frequency of your current sexual activity. ~ Right now, one polarity is moving between exploring the actual and psychological state of virginity, the other is exploring an active sex life with my lover. I'm exploring virginity when he is out of town. When he's here we get down, we do a lot of stuff, more like a couple of times a night than a couple of times a week.

Working in the sex industry is a conscious exploration of part of my sexuality and a focus of my life right now. At other times I have not focused on my sexuality and been perfectly happy. My sexuality, as all women's sexuality, is very much limited by the roles offered to women in patriarchy. We are all socialized by our roles at a very early age and I can see beyond the role offered, but I'm not sure this incarnation will present me the opportunity to fully live out my sexuality.

Do you masturbate? ~ Sometimes when I'm ovulating and I don't have a lover around. I don't really find it all that fulfilling.

Describe your sexual fantasies. ~ I am bisexual and a lot of my sexual fantasies are related to women. Working in the sex industry I've been exposed to too much cock, so it doesn't lead to fantasizing sexual relationships with men, apart from my current lover. My favorite fantasy is a circle of people giving each other head and everyone cumming at the same moment and channeling that energy for the healing of the earth. The thing I find the most beautiful erotically, is women giving each other head, licking each other deliciously. Juice.

Do you act out your fantasies? As much as I can. What I act out now was fantasy years ago. I hope that I'll act out my current fantasies soon.

Are dominance and submission a part of your sexuality? ~ Yes, because women are conditioned to be submissive and part of my nature is very dominant, and I like to assert it. It's been a process for me to be able to assert my dominant sexuality, and I'm still working with that. I live out my sexuality sometimes on top and sometimes on the bottom, but like I say, my dream is a circle.

When do you get sexually involved? ~ When I feel like it. My desire is related to the phases of the moon. I get involved before I ovulate, before I menstruate, on the third day of my menstruation, on the first day of my menstruation, when I love somebody, when I'm attracted to somebody, on a hot afternoon, under the moon.

Prior to becoming a dancer had you publicly exposed your body? ~ Yes, nude bathing on beaches in Europe.

What sexual taboos besides dancing have you broken? ~ I'm unclear as to what is taboo in society right now. The circles that I'm in and those I was raised in are so radically different that I have a certain amount of confusion. A lot of stuff I do in bed, such as oral sex, is taboo in the society I was raised in. Anal intercourse is taboo in that society. I've made love to a woman, that's taboo. Anything but the missionary position was taboo, I have transcended that. The taboo on the erotic relationship between women is one that I'm still exploring. I aspire to moving through that and to freedom on the other side.

What is sexually degrading for you? ~ The occasional experiences when I haven't been able to relate to the person the next day or the person has been cold and unloving.

Do you ever use sex as a weapon? ~ Yes. All women can deny sex to someone, in that sense it's a weapon. That's a classic strategy in the patriarchy. Poor ole Gary Hart, it's possible to ruin a man's reputation by sleeping with him.

I should have mentioned Nicaraguan, Nora Astorga, in the list of heroines. She is a great political heroine of mine. The way she used sex as a weapon, against one of Somoza's General's is right on and I would do it anytime. In the context of seducing fascist leaders or the history of the French resistance women used sex as a weapon. Cabaret dancers in fascist Berlin seduced the General. These women slept with the General to take the war out of him.

Do you ever experience guilt or shame about your sexuality? ~ Yes, I've had guilt, I'm getting away from that now. Guilt was put on me as punishment for being an attractive woman and stimulating my father's desire and the desire of whoever looked on me. I personified Eve, it was thrown back at me that I'm guilty, guilty of being born female and being a seductress. I've grown beyond that, but my primary imprint does re-assert itself. It's a continuous struggle. Being a sex worker, you can't bother being burdened by guilt, so it's certainly a good way of getting beyond it.

Do you think your sexuality would be different if you lived in an egalitarian or female-dominated society? ~ It probably presents possibilities to grow and evolve that we can barely dream of under the distortion of patriarchy.

Sexuality would be more open, a channel for pleasure and love without all the dominance and aggression. In a female-dominated society, my sexuality would be a lot safer to express. There would be less repression and sexual abuse, and bisexuality and lesbianism could be more freely chosen paths. Love between men and women would be a lot different. There'd be a lot less violence.

Have birth control and medical technology affected your sexuality? ~ Yes. I grew up in a culture that was dominated by the Catholic church which maintains that women should not use artificial birth control. My early sexuality was influenced by fear of pregnancy. I'm not happy with the pill. We all know the horrors of the coil, the IUD, the Dalkon Shield, the politics of it. I use a diaphragm. The onus is still on women to take care of contraception and to carry all the consequences if it fails. His part of the so-called "sexual revolution" has been severely abused by men who get away with not having to worry about the consequences of pregnancy, reproduction and pleasure are disconnected.

I've been greatly influenced by Mary Daly's *Gyn Ecology*, and have contempt for modern western medical practice in the area of gynecology. They try to fix us at every contact with our genitalia. I know there are a great variety of enlightened gynecologists out there, but this is one of the major areas of interface with a woman's most intimate part of her being and the fucking probing stethoscope attitude of doctors is a major area of unacknowledged abuse. Doctors are the arm of the patriarchy that burned the witches and midwives. We need a lot more female gynecologists. Gynecology shouldn't be in the realm of men at all, unless they can prove themselves fit, and they haven't.

Has the women's movement affected your sexuality? ~ Yes, the women's movement has been my saving grace and thank you very much women of the world, only for you, I'd still be lying on my back being fucked over, and under. It's affected my sexuality, of course, the basic tenet of a woman's right to control her own body has been a big part of the battle for the past 30 years. Having control of my own body, at last, has affected my awareness of the potential of my sexuality and it's offered me the vision of female sexuality beyond patriarchal fixing and control. Researchers into herstory have uncovered a freer female sexuality at earlier times in human culture, with roles such as the sacred harlot.

Describe your current love relationship. ~ We got together around the time I started dancing. Currently, he's working abroad. I am involved with him, and interested in one female, both are Geminis. We experience the typical instability of a triangle with jealousy and competition. While they've been gone, I've been presented with lots of opportunity to come to terms with it. My present love life has to do with finding the compassion I need within myself as I work at my job. While my lover is not around my love life is linked to how much work I can infuse with love. Doing that is subversive to monogamy. Hopefully our relationship will evolve in the direction of freedom, openness, and mutual support.

Is your partner supportive of your decision to dance? ~ Not exactly. He sort of feels that I'm casting my pearls before swine, but he's not down on me about it.

How did you feel about your body prior to becoming a dancer? ~ I felt pretty good about my body, but I didn't feel *in* my body. Now it's really happening with this, the body/mind/spirit as whole being. That's a high.

How did you get this job? ~ I came to a theater Christmas party, met some dancers, and looked around the place. A few months later I needed a job and I remembered that it seemed so free and fun, so I walked in one day and applied. It took a few days to gather the courage to do that. I walked past the place several times before I came in.

Part of taking the job was the drive to explore an aspect of my sexuality and women's sexuality that one cannot express in the sexual roles on offer for "nice girls". Like monogamous marriage. You can deviate from that by having more than one lover, or becoming bi or lesbian. Beyond that, there is a role which is part of the female being, which is, to explore or be a "whore", what that means in its holy sense. That's why it needs to be explored.

I had a lot of trauma working through society's projections against being myself. When I started dancing I divested myself of socially acclaimed notions of woman. I have examined respectability and what it is based on. Being respectable is to be controlled, limited, and kept in a box, good middle class, nice girl, slave to the patriarchy definition of woman. Outside of that there are vast realms of female being waiting to be explored. Now I know.

Do you recognize any characteristics common to those who dance? ~ Yeah...exhibitionism, curiosity, daring, a high level of self-confidence, not necessarily self-esteem, but, you have to have a certain level of confidence to go out there and strut your stuff. It takes spunk. We have women who want to own their sexuality. They are strong women, they can withstand all this stuff that's thrown at them. Of course, there are women who sink into the morass. I really wouldn't like to make generalizations because I don't know that they really hold up. Each woman has an individual process.

When you started dancing did you fear being separated from other women? ~ Yes. Shortly afterwards I lost a close female friend and I was afraid to tell other women friends because I thought some of them would disown me. I was aware there was a potential for alienation and distance from other women due to becoming a "bad girl", and that I was setting myself up for "good girls'" target practice. I knew they would project onto me. Sure, I picked up stuff from women in the community, but I can deal with that. Some people do treat me as a bad woman. They keep a distance and I can see that they can't deal with what I do. Some women feel threatened, I guess, and others feel I'm letting women down, or that I'm degrading myself. Some people say it's daring and on the edge. It can be kind of awkward and embarrassing socially when I enter this mine field of projections that exists and when people direct negative projections towards me. A lot of women are not comfortable with sexuality, and most are disconcerted by the sex industry context of expressing one's sexuality.

Have you lost self-esteem due to dancing? ~ Well, I go back and forth on this one. In the beginning it was a rush, breaking through the old morality, I felt good about having the courage to do that. After a while, when I was constantly in touch with the low status of dancers in society, it became harder to affirm myself. I used dancing to explore the question of what I base my self-esteem upon, it's complex, really.

Does your family know you dance? ~ The family of people I live with knows, but my blood relatives don't. They would disown me. There are a lot of people I can't tell, but sometimes people can take it. That's my acid test of who's cool.

Has dancing affected your politics? ~ Oh, yeah, it takes it to the edge. You get a chance to look at the difference between theory and practice. I was and am familiar with the concern for the sexual exploitation of women as "these are the poor victims." At an earlier stage in my life I was a proponent of the poor victim theory for prostitutes. It changed my politics to be confronted with reality, to move out of the ivory tower. Quite a change of perspective. It's broadened and deepened my political respect, sharpened the edge, and made me really aware of how intricate sexuality and politics are, the sexual roles. How so much patriarchal programming is wired onto the sexual circuits of the central nervous system and so much else.

Dancing gives ample time and space to ponder how patriarchy is functioning for men. Some say, "Why bother about what happens to the enemy?" It's affected my opinion of separatism, the separatist solution can function in the short term, but it's not going to supply a solution to future life on the planet. I've gained insight on what constitutes collaboration with patriarchy, what constitutes active resistance to patriarchy, and how and where you find the power to resist.

Do you fear becoming a prostitute? ~ I have fears and fantasies. I'm doing some political liaison work in San Francisco with Coyote, the prostitutes' rights organization, and becoming sisters with the most despised section of the sex workers. I'm learning to have respect and increase my awareness around the difference between dancers and prostitutes, who traditionally have not gotten along very well. I could become one if I chose to, and to quote Priscilla Alexander, "The right to become a prostitute is as important as the right not to become one." It's a valid expression of female sexuality. In lots of cases, it means far greater autonomy than the housewife has traditionally had, which is a reason for the enmity between them. I've had fantasies, some were good and some not.

Do you identify and feel solidarity with other sex workers? ~ Yes, with the women I've been working with I've felt support and camaraderie and I can identify with women who do other kinds of sex work. I feel like they're the only people who can really understand, how it feels to have this pariah position and to be on the other side of the double standard.

Have you been discriminated against because you are a woman? ~ All women are discriminated against because they are women. Whether they are aware of it or not. Sometime in their lives the strongest, most successful, best educated, richest women are discriminated against because they are women. I haven't been refused access to education or anything, I just think that the way society is set up discriminates against women.

Are you politically active? ~ Yes, I have some involvement as an environmental activist and around Central American issues. Right now I'm trying to set up a dialogue between sex workers and other women interested in pornography and its issues.

Are you a feminist? ~ I'm a feminist, and also a critic of feminism. And being involved in work that hasn't been owned by the feminist movement as a valid contribution to humanity, I feel quite alienated from middle of the road feminism. My understanding is that feminism is a philosophy that allows me to live to my potential as a woman. And that means, reclaiming many roles, many levels of being, many aspects of femininity which have been downtrodden and lain in the dust for millennia. Feminism for me is exploring the depth and the width of the mystery of femininity. It's very broad.

Historically some women have tried to exclude other women from the women's movement based on their sexual behavior and preferences. Do you experience this exclusion? ~ A lot of sex workers are active feminists in the broad range of the women's movement. There are upper middle class prostitutes involved in the womens movement, anti-imperialist sex workers, and women who are active in all kinds of political issues who were sex workers at one time. Many don't say they were sex workers because they know their sisters would not accept them. I know an ex-prostitute who was in a feminist forum which discussed prostitution and never said she had been a prostitute because of the fear of social stigma from those women, her supposed sisters. Solidarity is clearly lacking, some of this is unconscious. And sympathy can be really hard to take. A lot of people treat me fine and a lot of people choose not to get to know me. I would say that's one of the reasons they choose not to get to know me.

What is your relationship to the women's movement? ~ I've never been involved with any official organization of the movement. I've participated in lots of fronts. I've been involved with women's groups internationally, mostly spontaneous, ad hoc, self-determining groups. Anarcho-feminist groups. I would say I am on the fringe of the women's movement. Feminism is one thread of my larger political understanding. My analysis is anti-imperialist and I see imperialism as a tool of the patriarchy. I want to maintain as much of a dialogue as possible with the women's movement. I'm happy to be interviewed, I feel the dialogue between sex workers and the movement is long overdue. I would like to have an open relationship to the women's movement, rather than being a closeted member.

What have been the most damaging and the most constructive influences in your life? ~ The most destructive has been living in the patriarchy controlled culture which devours and exploits women and nature. The most constructive has been travelling and moving around in alternative societies and encountering alternative ideologies. The friendship, love, and criticism of my friends have been very constructive.

What person or people have had the greatest influence on your life? ~ Emma Goldman, she's dead. Karen Silkwood, she's dead. Emma Goldman, rebellious, anarchistic, exponent of radical sexual politics and overthrow of the State. Karen Silkwood, willing to infiltrate, use her position in a nuclear establishment to expose Kerr McGee. Murdered. Very influential in my realizing what they do to you if they get you, what it's going to take to free the world of nuclear terror. Lolita LeBraun, Puerto Rican independence fighter, prisoner of war. She attacked the United States Congress in the fifties to expose U.S. colonialism in Puerto Rico and went to prison for 20 years. She came out and still fights for Puerto Rican independence. A strong woman, unafraid of what the big superpower can do to her in her fight for the freedom of her people and country. Louisah Teish, a powerful charismatic, still alive. Spiritual leader and healer. They all have personal power, a sense of personal power.

What are your greatest gifts and limitations? ~ My greatest gift is curiosity about everything. My greatest limitation is that I play the judge to myself and other people instead of just going with the flow.

What would you like to be doing in 10 to 15 years? ~ I would like to be living somewhere beautiful, in harmony with the earth and making a contribution to healing the planet. I'd like to be working with people, travelling, and learning. I'd like to be living collectively with people who share my goals.

Recently in San Francisco we witnessed the appearance of women dancing for women. Why do you think this is happening? ~ Because women like to watch other women dance, it's beautiful and erotic. Because we now have the freedom to do that.

Have you danced for women only? · Not yet.

If social and economic equality for women became a reality would some women still dance? Would you? ~ Yes. This is a key question. People think that money, that better pay than minimum wage is the only motivation. A lot of women would still dance to feel a part of themselves, they'll seek to see that part. Those energies are constant in the universe and will continue, even after the revolution. Personally, I would dance more.

Would commercial sex work exist in your ideal society? ~ Not in the way that it's manifested today. I can envision people who have sexual problems or are lonely going to others for healing and relationship counseling and maybe pay them for that, but it wouldn't be exploitive of either party. It would be open and respected work. Erotic dance would certainly exist but it wouldn't necessarily be in the context of work or commerce, even if it was dancing in public. Long live the dance whatever happens.

For many people it is impossible to conceive of anyone choosing to dance as you do. Why do you think that is? ~ Some people feel that we are here because we have no other choice, no free will in the matter. They can't conceive of being an erotic dancer as a free choice. Those people can't conceive of another consciousness besides victim-consciousness.

Many people paint female sex workers as among the most obvious victims of male domination and declare that if you don't see yourself as such you are suffering from "false consciousness" or "delusions of the oppressed." What is your response to that? ~ Many "social purity" feminists are white, middle class and quite happy to be part of the oppressor system in terms of being happy little capitalists. I accept their concern for the supposed "low class" women who see no other choice provided except sex work (while often suffering wounds of stigma). I refuse to accept that stigma and I believe there are no more victims in the sex industry than there are in any job. There are many victims, wives can be victims, secretaries can be victims, police officers are victims. We are all victims of the patriarchy, women and men included, if we so choose.

Women who enter the sex industry are consciously faced with this portrayal of themselves as victims and it is an excellent opportunity to examine the idea of being a victim and how you can transcend it, and a lot of women do that. They can rise above and beyond the victim status as can be seen by these interviews. These women choose otherwise.

As for "false consciousness", I would rather be a slave to the rhythm than a slave to money any day, or a slave to the respectable notion of white American women who are so fucking tied into patriarchy. There's the race issue and there are women in this work who feed six children. Feminists could pay more attention to class and race and the military prostitution complexes around U.S. bases.

There are many ways the patriarchy governs its lower class. White American women could divert their attention to confronting the economic exploitation of minority race women in the sex industry, especially in the Philippines, which has a lot to do with the privileged position of white people in this country. To those who deliver the critique, I appreciate the concern, but not the condescension and purity I feel from them. Sex work at least confronts you with a total picture of yourself as a sexual being, and you come to terms with that. There are a lot of women who've become stronger being sex workers than they could have after years of feminist consciousness raising, because you take back the power, you find the power within yourself, above and beyond the cycle of victimization.

Why do you think people use sexually explicit media? ~ I feel people use it as a supplement for the real thing, to stimulate their sexual fantasies, or to substitute for real experiences that maybe they're not able to create in their own life. Some people want to get new ideas to try out because they're bored or tired with their own life and some people are just obsessively into pleasure, pleasure, pleasure. They use sexually explicit media to pleasure themselves in a way they can't with a partner.

Has the sexually explicit media you've seen accurately portrayed humans and their sexual relations? ~ I don't think it's really an accurate portrayal. There is sort of an ideal standard of beauty and an obsession with the exotic. It's usually very put on and devoid of any emotional tone or feeling. It is possible to create erotica with different nuances as many women are doing now, but there's always the camera in between, the perception of whoever's using the camera, as well as the perception of whoever consumes the media afterward. I don't think it can ever be really accurate.

At what age do you think people should be allowed to view pictures of human genitalia? ~ People should be allowed to see living images of human genitalia while they are growing up. Parent to child nudity is the issue. If children were seeing their parents, brothers and sisters, aunts and uncles, and their great grandmother's genitalia at the bath house or the sauna, or by chance in the bathroom on a Saturday afternoon, then by the time they get older and see a picture of it, it doesn't mean anymore than a picture of a tree, or a leg. I do believe that one of the biggest reasons women are so sexually unsatisfied is that when teenage boys are programming their sexual circuits to be cumming really fast to pictures of women, it has a bad affect on their sexuality.

At the outset, the Meese Commission declared that it intended to contain the spread of pornography. At its conclusion, the Commission, like most others, could not define pornography. Yet it recommended the prosecution, fining, and jailing of people who produce, distribute, and consume it. What do you think of the Commission and its recommendations? ~ With Meese, it's hypocrisy to the extent that I can't even find enough fucking expletives to comment on it. Harmful to this society that produces a bomb, that's fucking warring in Central America? How can a naked woman dancing and someone watching and enjoying her, even if it's not in the perfect context, how can that be more harmful than all the violence on TV? As such, it's harmful to the patriarchy, it's subversive, because people continue to exist, don't get tromped into the ground and become pulp for their fucking mind control games. It's rank hypocrisy, in that we are blamed in a society run by the Pentagon, doing all this shit, to talk about sexuality being harmful. Come on you guys, you're not fooling anyone, anymore. I would be really surprised to see the State locking up all the men who look at beaver shots, all the video store owners, all the filmmakers. When have men ever locked up other bunches of men who make profit on women's bodies? I just don't believe the State would ever legislate away pornography. I don't trust them, this is the window dressing.

Why do you think the government shows virtually no concern with violence in the mainstream media? ~ For one, because people don't complain enough about it and because it's seen as representing an already existing reality rather than creating and encouraging violence. Because the link between media violence and violence in society hasn't been proven. It's only strongly suggested by studies. It shows no concern chiefly because the government supports violence, controls society by a threat of violence. The police and the army are an expression of the collective male psyche. Also, because it sells, it's an addictive diet. The Pentagon is the most powerful part of the ruling establishment. What do they represent?

How are sex work and sex workers portrayed in the mainstream media? ~ It's portrayed as a dead end or last stop on the road to ruin. It's also portrayed as risky and a little bit exciting. Women are portrayed as being exploited by pimps and club owners. There's not much negative portrayal of the customer which shows it's totally controlled by this double standard.

Some people argue that humans are born with a sex drive and after that our sexuality is socially constructed, produced through our experiences. How do you think human sexuality is shaped? ~ It's shaped by a variety of factors, the level of openness in the family, whether nudity is an issue in the family, or in society. It's controlled by the understanding of the role of sexuality in the culture. It's usually mediated by a religion, for example, here in the U.S., it's the Puritan heritage. It's constructed by taboos and customs. The circuits in our nervous system are imprinted and activated by our first sexual experience, whether its positive or negative, and the nature of that is a very big factor. It's also shaped by sexual repression and fear of sexuality, by the urge to mate and the dating culture. It's shaped by attitudes toward homosexuality and bisexuality, by how much we've been touched as children, by the number of partners that we're allowed to have, whether experimentation is encouraged or forbidden. It's shaped by the media, by the birth of children, by attitudes towards breastfeeding. To answer a question like this, you need to look at other cultures from Trobiand Islanders, to Islamic culture, to West African tribal cultures. Just answering this through U.S. culture is too narrow.

Do you think the State tries to manage sexuality? ~ Yes, and its been going on a lot longer than two hundred years. It's been going on since ancient Sumeria, or by marriage laws in ancient Greece and Rome, as long as states have existed its been going on. Certainly since the Industrial Revolution it has been more pronounced and especially since women were banned from medicine. People's energies in general have been managed so that they could be molded into a suitable industrial work force.

What do women and men have in common sexually? ~ Desire and passion. Sex organs, sex drive and the desire to love.

Is there any sexual expression that society should ban? ~ People being tied up in chains, snuffing, and pedophilia. I would not call that sexual expression, but destruction. But, with undestructive, mutually consenting, sexual expres-

sion, I don't think the government, or other people have any business in people's lives. Men cutting out a woman's clitoris so they can control them
should be banned. My position is that we cannot trust the State apparatus that
is totally imbued with patriarchal thought forms to work for the common
good.

What part does sexual pleasure play in life? ~ A large part. The role of sexual pleasure is to keep us healthy, to make life worth living, and for procreation. The role of sexual pleasure should basically be to create more and
more love energy, that role, that function, is not being fulfilled. And I don't
think it will be fulfilled, on another level, by all these people jerking-off in
magazines or to girl dancers because it's very hard to have love in these relationships.

*Some people seem to think that sexual pleasure without procreation is a
threat to society. Is it?* ~ Yes, it is. Say people could stay in bed all day
fucking, who would want to go to work in a factory? I wouldn't, would you?
And, healthy sexual relations give women a lot more power. Sexual frustrations are a means of control.

*Do you think the gratification of sexual needs diminishes anti-social
impulses?* ~ Yes, somewhat. We know a lot of people use their sexuality as
a channel for their aggression and that they would probably exercise their
aggression anyway.

*Feminism as it emerged in the early 1970's had as basic tenets sexual explo-
ration and sexual self-determination. Subsequent exploration has led to
intense debate over female sexual identity and behavior. How do you define
female sexuality?* ~ Exploration is continuing and a definition at this point
will be very limiting. Female sexuality is moving beyond the bounds of definition. It's really important that this happens.

*In the late 1940's American writer Philip Wylie saw equally strong tenden-
cies to excite and constrain the erotic drive as pervasive in this society. He
observed that they continuously reinforce each other and declared, "The
United States is technically insane on the matter of sex." Is his diagnosis
good for today?* ~ Pretty much. The constraints have lessened somewhat
and the excitement has increased somewhat, but the insanity continues. The
moral majority would still like to regain control, the ad men would like to be
able to show more and more skin to sell more products, and AIDS has
unleashed a whole new turmoil. Certainly, to try to constrain women's freedom is totally insane at this point, but then, you know, these old guys, whoever said they were sane?

In a recent decision the Supreme Court ruled that the State does have a role in regulating bedroom behavior. Do you agree? ~ I disagree with them. It's blatantly homophobic.

People in the United States are spending billions of dollars each year on sexual needs. What does this say to you? ~ That people have an intense sexual dissatisfaction. Also that sex is seen here as totally fun. People here spend millions of dollars on any kind of fun, that's part of it. No distractions, fun, fun, fun. I'm into the fun aspect of it too, but, in some ways, people are just obsessed with the problems of their sex life. They could give at least a part of their money to Ethiopia and have less fun.

Can sexual needs be met commercially in a non-sexist way? ~ They can, but it takes work and it's rare. It seems like men are sexist unless they work on it and insist that they're not really sexist.

Do you think the schools should teach about human sexuality? ~ Yes, and they should teach much more than the present biological information. They should teach about relationships, contraception, AIDS, the natural cycle of fertility, orgasm potential, the role of orgasm, about feelings, and about respect for other human beings.

How is sexuality portrayed in the mainstream media? ~ It's portrayed more and more openly. There's been sort of an obsession with sexuality since the 60's, that's tapering off. AIDS has sobered everybody up. There's a kind of panic and it's suddenly seen as risky and irresponsible to want greater sexual freedom. Deeper questions have been shoved back under the carpet. There's still a lot of Puritanism in the minds of those who control the mainstream media, but they're quite willing to use sex to sell products.

Some people argue that there is a sexual hierarchy in the United States with heterosexuals at the top and everyone else treated as second class citizens. Do you agree? ~ Heterosexuality is definitely viewed as the "norm", and any other orientation is deviant. There's still a lot of caricaturing of gays, lesbians, and bisexuals. This hierarchy was instituted and is perpetuated to serve the ends of the patriarchal ruling elite. This, of course, isn't just in the U.S., it's everywhere.

Some people also think that non-heterosexuals should not have the same rights as heterosexuals? What do you think? ~ Nonsense. Very repressed sexist isn't the word for it, it's taking away people's rights because of their sexual orientation.

How does society respond to the outspoken sensuous person? ~ Well, this society tends to be freaky. There are people like Bette Midler, who make a career of it, and yet mainstream society definitely puts it down.

What have you learned about people through sexuality? ~ Loads and loads. I've learned that we always need moments of pleasure and release. We need to give in to the joy and pleasure of being alive and in contact with another person. If we don't experience this release, this orgasm, we carry around a lot of emotional baggage. We feel separate, alone, uptight, stiff. I think that sex is our contact with the life force energy that recharges and revitalizes us, and that most people are still not getting the love and support that they need to be fully alive and evolving. I think that sex and sexuality is one of our main ways to evolve.

Do women play a part in the creation of male sexuality? ~ Men are born from woman, they suck on her breasts, and they're naked with their mother until two, and child rearing practices for women are passed on from one generation to the next. Women could train little boys to do different and they wouldn't have this whole scene going on forever and ever.

How do you think batterers and rapists are created? ~ We know that battered children often batter. There's a cycle of violence in the home, which causes the children who have suffered violence to do that to their own children. And they are created by society condoning violence, the whole macho thing, that if you can't get them to shut up and stop nagging, just slap them across the face. Violence in the media is also a factor. Men who are insecure about their masculinity rape to assert themselves – their male power.

Are there feminist men? ~ There are a few out there, I suppose less than five percent. Groups like Brother to Brother in Boston, the people who produce the Rhode Island Men's Journal, those who strive to understand gender roles and sex stereotyping and try to relate to other men in a non-competitive, non-hierarchical, caring way. Some of these men counsel others who are involved in abusive relationships with girlfriends and wives. They're trying to develop new ways for men to relate to one another.

What is their relationship to sexually explicit media? ~ The ones I know have a varied response, but most of them are not avid users of girly magazines or porn movies. They are capable of being turned on by them.

Describe the impact male dominance has had on women. ~ Dominance is backed by a threat of rape, violence, and war. It has contributed to women living in fear, poverty, and submission in the worst cases. Most women are insecure about their ability to live in a male society, and to achieve their full potential as humans because of the prejudices against women and the ban on women having real power. Also, the rational male way of perceiving the world and reality is seen as the only way. Male values are perceived as being right and correct, the only ones, to the detriment of other values. So women have been written out of history. We don't have herstory in schools. Our contributions and achievements have been rendered invisible. We've been reduced to being bearers of children only.

Do you see men working at changing themselves? ~ A minority. Many stop at the level of not making overtly sexist comments or trying not to interrupt women when they're talking. It seems more difficult for them to share their feelings and to lay aside their egos. Many are so cut off from their real feelings that this is going to take some time. They seem so unaware of exactly how they are being patriarchal and resistant to self-examination. There are men's consciousness groups, but they're not in the mainstream. I think first you have to open to the possibility that transformation can occur, and then see where we get from there.

How can women help men change? ~ Women can become involved in a process to illuminate individual men when we see them sticking in their traditional roles, but only when the men are open to it. Women have devoted a lot of energy to trying to change men. If they're not self-directed then it's just another example of devoting our energy to them instead of to our own growth and transformation.

What do you think the future holds for relations between men and women? ~ Uncertainty, forgiveness, struggle, potential, hope. The majority of men still want to perpetuate their dominance and a minority of women have an increasing awareness of how patriarchy shapes our relationships and our gender roles. A minority of men are becoming aware of this too. They are expressing some solidarity, but they are under pressure to be "real men." There is a lot of change but the momentum seems to be lost. The war between the sexes continues, but an uneasy truce holds sway from time to time.

Heterosexual relationships will change as family break-down continues and women work. Institutional power in male hands will continue to warp relations but women are getting stronger during this intermission. Meanwhile, there's little change for women in poorer countries and genetic technology threatens our reproductive roles and our choices.

If rape and sexual assault ended today how would your life change? ~ It's hard to imagine. I can only speculate that I'd feel safe out alone at night.

That'd be a big change. All the energy of fear could transform into power, once the biggest weapon of male dominance disappeared. I'd breathe freely, life would change for my sisters, too. But as we know, rape is on the increase.

What is the source of inequality between men and women? ~ The idea of divinity being male legitimizes male power. The use of physical force to maintain that power is the source of inequality.

Feminist people have long observed the system of male domination in the United States and exerted considerable effort to overturn it. What strategies do you think have been effective? What strategies do you recommend now? ~ My background is European, so, I'm not fully informed of the history of the Women's Movement here. The struggle for control of our bodies has meant a certain freedom for women, but it's very tenuous as can be seen by the attempt to overturn *Roe v. Wade*. Highlighting sexism and sex discrimination at work has raised public awareness. Women's research and scholarship play a vital role in reclaiming our herstory. Seeking equality with men on their terms has proved a limiting strategy. Separatism is a necessary intermediary strategy for some but has no long term future.

What do you consider to be the failures of the women's movement in the United States? ~ The cult of the career women is the main concern of white middle class women. There's a failure to address classicism and racism and the lack of solidarity of these career women with women of color who are trying to overcome their barriers. So, I guess, hanging onto white privilege. But now this has been identified and attempts are being made to redress it. Another problem is blindness to U.S. imperialism, there is a lack of solidarity with women in other countries. And they can't see that poor women and dancers might be feminist, too. Obsessing on porn has been very divisive, poverty is much more important. Maybe some of these career women could tithe ten percent of their salaries so women wouldn't have to be involved in porn because of economic necessity.

Anti-censorship feminists have emerged who believe that some sexually explicit media reflects and reinforces the oppression of women, but disagree with the pro-censorship feminists' view that sexually explicit media is the cause of women's oppression. They argue that the causes of women's oppression are much deeper and precede the mass production and distribution of sexually explicit media by centuries. What is your point of view? ~ Women's oppression has a variety of causes. And while porn is one of their tools, looking to the State to deliver us is naive. Looking to the people who run the military, who send soldiers on R&R to Thailand is naive. I tend towards an anti-censorship view point, except for snuff movies, because I see it as a right wing tactic. The questions of free expression and freedom from bombardment with "tit advertisement" are complex. Some sexually explicit media does reinforce our oppression but I don't think the State can deliver us. Banning violent porn might help, but it won't stop it.

I was born in a society where there's very little pornography and a lot of violence against women. Violence exists in many forms. America has all this street violence. It's endemic, because war is endemic, not because of pornography. Pornography is a very late arrival. Was pornography the cause of the witch burnings, the cause of footbinding in China, is it the cause of burning brides in India, the cause of children not eating enough? It is not.

Some men are pushed by pornography. But how can you legislate, who's going to be the judge? Is Meese going to be the judge? Judges who beat up their wives, their children, go to prostitutes, the police who sleep with prostitutes and then bust them...are they going to be the judges?

Where do you think sexually explicit media should be placed on the movement agenda? ~ Well not number one, lower down. Below the threat caused by reproductive technologies, below U.S. economic exploitation of, so called, third world women, below paid maternity leave, the right to breastfeed on the job, below wages for housework.

Do you think our constitutional guarantee of free speech includes sexual speech? ~ Yes, free speech should include sexual speech. There's been a historical battle from Lenny Bruce to The Free Speech Movement to say "fuck" on TV, it's just late Victorian stuff that's still going on.

How would you advise courts ruling on sexually explicit media? ~ I would advise the courts to wise up, sexual arousal is not harmful. Drop this blatant, paranoid fear of sexuality. The legal system is based on control, injunctions against sexuality and women. It's all testament to their Christian misogyny. I would advise them that their fucking time is up. Get off our backs. (Laughs)

Tell us what you know about AIDS and describe the impact it is having on your life and society. ~ Multiple partners increases the risk, we need safe sex, less experiments. I'm less experimental, willing to have sex only where there is genuine involvement. It certainly limits the option of bisexual exploration. Safe sex is less fun, so the fizz has gone from sexual revolution. There's sadness. There are broad implications for civil liberties because of AIDS. And it exposes the whole medical set up, the cost of the drugs, and all that. They should give out free needles like they do in Holland. It's conditioning those who might have had multiple sexual partners and gone into a whole new way of arranging family and sexuality. There's no question that AIDS was intended to push us back into the 50's.

Do you think it is possible that this society will confine those who test HIV positive in spite of the medical evidence that it is not casually transmitted?
~ It's possible but not immediately. They did lock up the Japanese in World War II. There would have to be more panic.

What future do you see for erotic theater and erotic dancers? ~ This depends on how the Bush Administration handles the issue. It's no longer a breakthrough like it was in the sixties. It doesn't need to spring on to the stage and declare its existence in a wild abandoned way. Deeper questions need to be asked about how a context can be created in which the erotic dance can thrive and what function it can fulfill. Whose needs are being met and at what cost? Clearly it needs to be removed from the murky, sordid atmosphere in which it now finds itself. This will probably happen if women dancing for women continues. I'm sure the erotic dance will end up in another place and not just be seen as servicing the needs of business men in need of a thrill on lunch breaks. Dancers themselves should decide where , if anywhere, they want to take it from here, and create some measure of autonomy by running our own premises.

PHOENIX

IF WE CAN'T FEEL GOOD ABOUT OUR BODIES, IF WE CAN'T FEEL GOOD ABOUT OUR SEXUALITY, WE'RE CRIPLED.

Part of the promotion for your show says, "Live Nude Dancing, Lovely Lusty Ladies, Naked Naughty Nasty." Is this a good description of who you are and how you perform at work? ~ Being teaseful is definitely a part of my relationship with men in that setting. I behave in ways that are normally considered taboo. When power and self-censorship are not in the way, I have ways of touching myself and playing that are ways of communicating with a customer.

What were you told was your job? ~ Dancers are often really stiff when they first come in. A dancer learns slowly through experiencing herself on stage. You're coming up against your own taboos, your own limitations, and challenging yourself. I was not told anything, nor shown anything...there definitely are no teachings!

Describe your first experience on stage. ~ The women were really warm. For me, auditioning was about giving myself permission to be my sexual self. It was conscious, alive. I felt like I went wild. I was moving all over and really into being explicit for the show directors.

When you were hired were you asked to work on certain aspects of your performance? ~ Sometimes my shows were about taking the stage, and saying "OUTTA MY FACE!" I was saying physically, I'm in charge, I'm not having a dialogue with you, you're just here to watch. They wanted me relating to the customers, having a dialogue. I've worked on it.

Describe how you dance, display, and touch your body during your performance. ~ I show and touch parts of my body that I really like. My ass is really gorgeous. (Laughs) I can start out very seductive and sultry, letting someone in by my enjoyment of my body. I gradually open up by showing and touching and coming closer to him/her. Establishing eye contact is really everything. That's where something really electric can be communicated. That's not a cliche, that's what I experience. With eye contact, we're exchanging certain kinds of understandings, or power. Sometimes I give shows where I'm not doing that, and that can also work, but it's a completely different kind of experience, it's more two-dimensional. I am being this visual, sensual machine for the customer. Sometimes customers want to connect with me, and I'm not in a space where I want to do that. For the most part, eye contact is really enjoyable, the eroticism is much more powerful. No matter how much you talk about commercializing a sex transaction, you're still talking about two people with their own agendas and needs of the moment, and that shapes the interaction.

What sexual depictions do you perform? ~ My response is what sort of images am I enacting? Through the way I move, my facial expression, and a certain character I am involved in. I am exploring inner facets of myself. I've explored all-out domination with submissive customers who just eat it up. The way that happens convincingly is through eye contact and embodying nuances of that sexual place. The way you are able to figure that out is by seeing him, by really opening your eyes.

At one time I thought by opening my eyes I was allowing a stranger to invade myself and that was really scary. That was why I gave more of a visual, visceral show. In the last several months there has been the realization that I don't have to be afraid of that person. I've come to some understandings about my fear of men, my fear of being controlled by men, which is something that is imbued in all women from day one. I've had the experience of accepting our humanness. We are doing this, and it's okay.

When I'm sexual there, it's not the way I'm sexual with my lovers, where I let down all my barriers, definitions. I have felt myself being a sexual child, and wanting to be played with sexually, and that's scary. I know clearly that I'm in a safe space, but that one takes courage.

Describe the elements of dominance and submission in your performance.
~ There's one customer who looks very much like a little boy and he really likes to be told what to do. It feels like that relieves him of something. I tell him what to do, how to do it, and when to do it. (Laughs) So much of sexual relationships is power and working with the current of power. To say that sex does not participate in those is ridiculous. I definitely demonstrate, most of the time, that I am running the show.

I am being paid to entertain but, if I don't want to dance for you, I'm not going to. In fact, you have to behave in a certain way, or you have to leave. There has to be the understanding that this is a transaction, and that it's *only a role*. You have to relate to me as a human being. If you're not, then I'm not going to participate anytime in anything with you. Period. I'm very clear about it, because there are all these conditioned victims of patriarchal society walking in and a lot of them are exhibiting all of the behavior that goes along with that, which is, "You are a woman, you are my property, I tell you what to do." You have to establish immediately that that is not the case.

I'm talking about power; dominance and submission to me is a whole different subject. I need to establish this first before I talk about roles, because that really has to be there for anything to go on. And it's not that I have power over you. It's just that there has to be an atmosphere of respect, of mutual acknowledgment. I am not there to be your slave. I might be there to play out a role of being a slave, but that has to be acknowledged by respectful, enjoying interaction for that to be established. I enjoy looking at the customer as having fun, enjoying their bodies, and enjoying showing their bodies. There is that level.

A lot of men are playing the little boy in some way, and they really like to be bossed around. That's a fairly enjoyable role. (Laughs) It does have an element of revenge. I also like to be dominated, but I have to feel safe. There has to be this feeling that the customer is appreciating me, more than just staring at my body parts. That happens through looking in my eyes.

From stage you see a lot of tongues. Describe this. ~ Lizards, slime. (Laughs) When the window goes up and the first thing I see is a man sticking out his tongue at me, I laugh. It's hysterical. I don't go up to someone I'm trying to arouse and stick out my tongue and wiggle it. I find it so absurd! I love being an animal, too, but it's something you work into.

How much of your performance is you and your sexuality and how much is persona? ~ It's both. Sometimes I'm dancing as me, a lesbian enjoying my own sexuality. Other times I'm playing a straight woman and how a straight woman is being sexual. My mood before I go on stage is how I'm going to be. If I'm in a pensive mood, I might play coy, come-and-get-me, I've got something you want. It's very subtle. Other times, I might be charging around very brazen, "Here, come on and take it!"

Why did you choose the stage name you use? ~ Moving to California was definitely starting over. When I was asked to pick a stage name, I was at a loss. And then Phoenix came at me. Phoenix rises from the ashes. I'm letting go of all these ways of being that haven't been working for me, and this is very powerful. So it's not a stage name that's separate...it's very much a part of my life.

How do you use costuming and makeup? ~ To enhance my normal magnificence! It depends on my mood. I may feel like being really cute and soft and inviting and receptive, so I'll dress in my white corset, something fluffy and froo-froo. Or I might feel like a real bitch and put on some leather and black stuff and bring out my cattail whip. I really enjoy putting on makeup. I was such a nature girl growing up, very much a tomboy. I never wore makeup until I was twenty or twenty-one. There's been joy in discovering the ways I can transform myself and look really adult and sophisticated. It's play. It makes me feel good about myself and I enjoy what I'm doing more.

Do drugs play a part in your performance? ~ No. I've come in after a drink maybe two times and I generally don't want to do that because it takes stamina to do the job. If you come in high, halfway through the shift you're going to crash, and that's work.

On stage music plays almost continuously. Describe the variety and part it plays in your performance. ~ It enhances the mood and persona aspect of doing erotic dancing. It creates and supports an atmosphere for me to act out those personae. Funky music is definitely the best for doing this kind of work. I don't like and cannot dance to heavy metal, it's totally cerebral.

The stage is covered with mirrors ceiling to floor, what role do they play in your work? ~ It's great because no matter where I am on stage I can see myself. There's the enjoyment of seeing your body, all these different people at once. That brings out the funhouse, the other reality aspect of the theater, which, to me, is in any theater. The mirrors bring up the Alice in Wonderland aspect, if you will. We're in another reality and different things go on here.

Describe the interaction and commentary among the dancers on stage. ~ That can range from "Oh, God, this guy is a jerk!", to "Oh, my God, look at the cock on this man! How does he walk around with this thing?" It's both appreciative and scathing commentary on the customers.

For me what's enjoyable is that we're in it together and that we like moving together. Almost every woman who works here just loves to dance. Talking on stage about life stuff is discouraged because that distracts from giving a good show, but there's not too much of that.

Is there competition among the dancers on stage? ~ Definitely, depending on who the dancers are. If somebody comes on who is really full of themselves and thinks they're really hot, it's very clear. That kind of energy stops interaction, the flow of good feeling. There are some dancers for whom that's habitual.

There are some women at the theater who don't think about very much, except here's my job, here's my money, my food, and my boyfriend. I really get into my creative-self and different thoughts and I get zany. Dancing with a group of people who think that's weird, who just dance and get it over with...that can be a drag. They're sending out messages of limitations.

As far as competition about physical beauty, there are dancers who are absolutely, stunningly beautiful who I don't feel a sense of competition with because they're not caught up in it. There might be some dancers who feel threatened by a dancer's beauty no matter what kind of person they are.

Is there humor on stage? ~ A lot of it. The job can be very absurd! There was a lot of uptightness about sexuality in my family, but nudity itself was not such a big deal. So to have people drop quarters furiously just to see my naked body, sometimes it just makes me laugh. It's the same with the other dancers, it makes us laugh.

Is the myth of the perfect body perpetuated here? ~ Management perpetuates that. Their current trip is to have Playboy dancers. We've been recently reminded that this is solely a business. In the past it was not only a business, but a place where people are *being*. Eroticism is an aspect of their life as workers there. There was an awareness and support of that consciousness at the theater. That has changed. The management and owner have been trying to enforce that this is a business, and peoples' personal problems should not come up. Consequently I have become more aware of the exploitation of the artists by the theater.

Do you ever become aroused by what you are doing and what's happening around you on stage? ~ Definitely. Dancing is beautiful and everyone is up close. There's lots of sexual interaction among the dancers that's enjoyed by everyone involved. Occasionally there are homophobia freak-outs, by dancers who are not participating. This isn't very explicit interaction, people aren't screwing each other. There's a lot of innuendo, light touching, dancing together, and erotic exchange. Waves. If I'm dancing for someone and playing with myself, I'm enjoying it.

Do you ever have sexual fantasies during your performance? ~ Sometimes I think about my girlfriend and go off into a full daydream while remaining semi-active physically.

Do you ever wish you could be having direct sexual contact with the customers? ~ That's happened very, very rarely.

What can you do on stage that you can't do off stage? ~ If I were in the dressing room masturbating that would definitely not be as acceptable as it is on stage. The stage is a place for me to do just about anything I want to do. I would not interact with myself even in the privacy of my own home as brazenly and as sexually crudely and gargantuously, lasciviously, as I do on stage at times. That's interesting, because at home there's the atmosphere of permissiveness. The message is loud here, it's a Siren saying, "You can do anything you want!"

Have you ever cum on stage? ~ Once. Normally I don't let myself go. I can masturbate a lot and it's enjoyable but I don't orgasm because it brings me to a more personal place that, for me, is not part of the job. When I came I was really relaxed, very self-absorbed, really enjoying it and it just happened. I was doing it for a customer, but I wasn't so connected on a real interpersonal level.

What won't you do on stage? ~ I'd love to go farther. I'd love to screw women on stage, I'd love to be screwed on stage, but that's not permitted. I'd love to fuck myself on stage, that's the big fantasy. Oh, God! I would just *love* to do that, really.

What are you prohibited from doing on stage? ~ Putting my hands and yams and whatever else is available up my cunt. Which I do anyway sometimes. Touching or fucking another dancer is not allowed. It's supposedly illegal. So whatever rules are broken it has to be discreet...unfortunately.

Do you ever do sex education on stage? ~ I consider myself more a role educator, in that I make it really clear to the men that I'm very much my own person, I enjoy myself, and I'm also open to them, *by choice*.

How does having your period affect your performance? ~ It usually doesn't affect it very much. It changes my mood. I get a lot more connected to the earth, to my channels, my sexuality. You are letting go, your body is releasing all these fluids. It's like the rain is coming down. That's an enjoyable state.

I was quite surprised when I first heard that healing occurs here, women healing themselves, each other, and customers. Describe what you know about this. ~ That's definitely true, I've personally experienced it. I'm a professional body worker with a private practice in my home. I'd be interested in talking to some of the other women who are healers to see if they dance with the intention of doing healing work. I don't approach my dancing in that way and, frankly, I don't think it's healthy for a lot of women to do that. It has been our continuous role to heal, which is a natural skill for women, and it has been subverted into serving men for hundreds and hundreds of years. I think it can be very disempowering for us to approach what we do as "Here, I'm going to help you feel better." My experience is that if I am dancing powerfully i.e., dancing with respect for myself, a kind of joy and enjoyment of my experience comes across as a powerful thing. When I'm doing that, if a man respects it and is capable of opening himself up to that, then healing, or an opening to a more authentic experience with him can occur.

Healing is about opening to a more authentic part of oneself. It's really important to make that distinction rather than actively pursuing, "Here, I'm going to help you, heal you, and make you feel better." I don't think that's really healing. That's codependency and a habit ingrained in women.

People have to be receptive to be helped. They have to be willing to be changed and experience something that they don't know. They have to be ready to go somewhere they don't know. If a customer is not in that place, I'm not going to overwhelm him with some kind of good intent that's going to transform him. That's a two-way street.

Women healing themselves happens a great deal here. Healing as re-training sexuality that has been taken away from us by this Christian guilt trip. I see this happening over and over again, in a conscious way with some dancers and unconsciously with others. Some are not too verbal, but you can see from things they say that they're feeling better about them-selves and their sexuality and enjoying that. When they first come in they might be feeling a little unsure, a little guilty and, "Oh, this isn't really good, I'm being bad." I've seen countless women work through that kind of stuff and that's profound healing. If we can't feel good about our bod-ies, if we can't feel good about our sexuality, we're crippled. We can't function, because our bodies are our vehicle.

Yesterday there was a lot of teasing on stage, in a very good way. Nevertheless, they were saying things like, "Oh, you disgusting slut." I said, "Hey, let's not do that to ourselves. Let's not call ourselves by words that have been used against us. We're participating in and perpetuating this trip of feeling bad about ourselves." They really heard that. Not that I think calling each other a slut isn't funny. It can be very funny if it's used in the right way. It's more the words like *disgusting*.

Another morning one of the women said, "I think pussies are really ugly, just the ugliest things." I was just like – Wow – but she wasn't saying it like she was totally believing it. I said to her, "Well, that's probably because you have been conditioned to think that way." She said, "You're probably right." I told her about Judy Chicago's paintings of vaginas, these colorful, streaming, stunning expressions of energy. I hadn't changed her ideas, but she was receptive to what I was saying.

So there's a dialogue going on, a consciousness of society's judgments, it can keep us down. Women perpetuate that, and it takes a few women who are working on that a little more consciously to bring it to the fore and talk about it. That happens very, very often and it's really great.

We're here for lots of different reasons but it's definitely a place where really strong things happen. You deal with yourself in an exposing, reveal-ing way. It makes a lot of people experience themselves in ways they never have before. You have to deal with your sexuality and it puts you through changes, for the most part in really positive, opening ways. When you're in a group of women...the energy that's happening is powerful. I feel as though I've been healing a lot.

Do you ever feel caged or wish you could cover up? ~ Occasionally and it could be that I'm just in a more vulnerable state. If it weren't for the fact that it's a job it would be better that I not dance on that day, because I need to be more inside myself. Occasionally I experience having something taken from me by the way the men look at me, don't deal with me on a personal level. But ultimately I am responsible for that, I don't have to be in that space. Women have been buying men's criteria for their identity. That criteria is their physical appeal, a certain size body and body parts. On the days that I feel I'm having something taken from me it's because I'm reverting to that criteria, not viewing myself through my own.

Many of the dancers who work here say they prefer this closed type of stage and see it as safe and fun because of the absence of physical contact with the customers. How do you feel? ~ The same, definitely. I don't want to have contact with customers. There's too much virus out there, too many men who are out of control. This way we can all have a good time together. That comes from feeling safe.

Topless dancers I've talked with are appalled at the thought of going bottomless as well. Is this difficult for you? ~ Having nature around me is very much a part of my life. In Vermont people go swimming, for the most part, without bathing suits, because they are living close to the earth. My parents did it, and it was no big deal. Once I lived way out in the middle of the woods and spent virtually the entire summer not wearing clothing unless I went shopping. Being bottomless is different than being topless, but for the most part I don't differentiate. But, because you've been taught your whole life naked cunts are dirty, you don't overcome that in a few days or a few years.

Describe your performance at its best and worst. ~ At my best I'm letting my body move without being self-conscious. I'm just having a good time dancing. I'm enjoying being sexual and sharing that with the customers.

At my worst I'm completely sick of them, I find them nauseating. I want to put my feet in their face, call them names, and humiliate them.

Describe the customers. ~ You have businessmen in the uniform, haircut-wise. They all seem to look the same. On the other end of the economic scale, you have street people who barely know up from down. There are a fair number of married working class men, probably in their forties, who come in after work. There's a fledgling group of 18-year-olds for whom it's all a big novelty. And there are some very cool rockers in their twenties, who tend to be not too involved. Dancing for the married men in their thirties and forties, if I can make a general statement, tends to be a little better. Young men are extremely abusive. Older men can be abusive, too, but there is a quality about married men, they've had to deal with their wives. The majority of men tend to relate to us as in a normal exchange.

About five percent of the customers are women. Some of them seem to have been coerced or forced to come in with their husbands or dates. They often avert their eyes. They seem extremely embarrassed, extremely uncomfortable. They don't know how to deal with us. There seem to be a few hookers with clients, who have a really great time, really get down and sexual in the booths. There have been some really great exchanges, total sexual being and enjoyment with some of the couples. I've never experienced dancing for a couple that has wanted to be sexual that has been anything but totally respectful and enjoying. Gay women come in too. Some are butch, some are not really any role stereotype. They really enjoy the show and we have a great time with them.

Do the customers leave their social roles and status behind when they come to see you? ~ Some do and some don't. Some jump into the booths and immediately let it all go and they're just their animalistic selves. Lots of men jack-off with fucking armor around them and refuse to relate to you the entire time. That's probably how they screw their wives, too. When I say, "Can you say hello?"...sometimes they refuse to change their expression. There is an expressionless iron barrier, and that is a very different experience. Sometimes they'll look terribly embarrassed or like they want to dissolve, or want me to dissolve. They don't want to interact. They just want to jack-off like they're statues. It's really awesome. There are businessmen who jack-off as though they're standing there talking to a client or talking on the telephone. It's incredible.

Describe your favorite type of customer? ~ Generally, my favorite customer is in his 30's or 40's – and seems to have control and an enjoyment of his sexuality. He interacts and has the freedom to let himself go. He is receptive to what I'm doing, instead of having a program for exactly what he wants.

I like guys who are able to think of new ways to stimulate and play with themselves. And I don't just mean their genitals. There was one young guy who was just dancing in the booth. He was so completely free with his body. It was wonderful. He was opening himself to me and it was just beautiful.

Another regular customer I enjoy dancing for doesn't try to have any verbal exchange. But his sexual energy is very focused and he is totally focused on me. That allows me to totally focus on him. He isn't trying to shut my expression off, and there is no aggression or put-down with how he comes across.

Do you encounter men who you think hate women? ~ Oh, yes. How do I know? Some men demand that you do this or that. They can't have very much respect for women. If you don't respect women I don't see how you can really like them, not as whole beings. You like them as a tool for your pleasure. That's not liking women.

Have you ever felt it was dangerous to arouse a customer? ~ Definitely. You get this vibe from some men like – this guy is a little out of control. I don't mean guys who come in high. You can just tell from their expressions and their body language that they are violent or coming from a really twisted and confused place. I will not dance for them. It makes me feel like I could be psychically abused.

I've experienced men being positively transformed in the theater, by being sexual and having a good exchange. I don't see why that couldn't happen with anyone. But because of the completely derogatory foundation that the patriarchy stands on in regard to women, sex is regularly connected with violence. If a man is in a violent place, getting sexual might just further the violence. I don't think sex perpetuates violence at all. Men are violent to begin with because of their frustrations and disconnection from their emotions and the earth.

Do you think you've ever danced for a rapist? ~ Nope. I am pretty selective about the customers I dance for intimately. Now as far as dancing when the rapist is in one of the booths, I don't know.

There are customers who come here with great regularity. What are they like? ~ There's more likelihood that they're going to be operating within parameters of mutual reciprocity. Generally it's more rewarding and enjoyable to dance for a regular customer.

Are there any customers who come to see you on a regular basis? ~ Yes. There are younger and older men, white men, Asian men, businessmen, and working class. They seem to be really enjoying it. There were a few in their 30's who were never sexual. They expressed that they enjoyed my body, my sexuality, my energy, but that they came back because I seemed really intelligent and they liked talking to me.

I've made two friends, both are men who weren't sexual with me in the theater. One became a lover. The other is an extremely well educated artist with position. He really likes the sex industry, for a lot of different reasons. It's an art experience, a different culture.

Describe the variety of sexual behavior customers express. ~ There are the stone faces who do their sexual thing as though they were standing on the street corner waiting to cross! It's hard to believe that they can be so uninvolved, so rigid, but they are. There are the wild folk who jump up on the bench and take every stitch of their clothing off. There are the guys who take a long time, spend a lot of money enjoying the show, maybe being sexual, maybe not. Some of them are really intense. They seem to get into playing out a feminine role. There are men who want to be dominated. They get enjoyment being watched, controlled in a way. That's valid, in a safe space with mutual consent, to have someone give up their control, which can be such an armor for us in our society. It can be a really positive thing. Some executives give it up, not a lot. They generally seem to remain uptight and removed whether they fulfill their sexual needs or just watch. There are customers who screw themselves with cucumbers and stuff. There's the guy who has tattoos all over his genitals and legs, and his penis is pierced. He likes to show us. He's totally impotent but he seems quite intelligent, lively, energetic, and a very nice guy. He's very respectful, it's like we're friends and he's just really wild.

Many customers show a great deal of interest in the dancers' genitalia. Why do you think there's such great interest? ~ I think this whole cult has been created because we've been taught that that's bad and dirty. At the same time it's fascinating, pleasureful. Many women and men make love in the dark and never see genitalia. I think that has a lot to do with the preoccupation. Also the perpetuation of the *vagina dentata* concept, that the vagina is a source of potential power over men, and at the same time it's a secret. There's a lot of mystery in there! Talking about this makes me feel better, because often it can be completely tiring and offensive to have to deal with that desire.

I think you are possibly the only or preferred sexual outlet for some customers. What do you think? ~ Absolutely. I saw this play, *The Malady of Death*, where this woman is paid by this man to let him watch her sleep for three days. Just to watch her. Just to be around her. He goes through subtle changes throughout the play, and it is revealed that he must have this malady, that he can't love, and he's trying to do something about that. He's trying to understand. The play made me realize more about the connection between men and women, and men being so divorced from their emotions. For example, I saw this father walking down the street with his little boy who said to him, "Daddy, hold my hand", and he reached up with his hand. His father slapped his hand and said, "I only hold hands with women. You don't need to have your hand held." There it was, in a capsule, the beginning of this little boy's conditioning to be what a man is. You don't hold hands. You only get your emotional needs met from a woman. You only hold hands to show affection with women, and maybe that's just a show, too. In other words, there's just so much re-routing of emotion that I think men become incapable of having an emotional exchange after this. So it's a lot easier to be sexual in a context where they don't have an on-going relationship with the woman who is dancing for them. That's not bad, it's just a sign of our society.

Is there a difference in the customers' behavior when they are alone or in a group? ~ Men in groups should be banned from the streets. (Laughs) They exhibit this animalistic behavior, boosting-of each other's ego, and try to psyche each other into believing that they actually are in control of the world. I find it truly offensive. More often than not we have them kicked out because they're behaving like little five-year-old monsters. Men in groups always, without exception, further foster their aggression. I've never seen men come in in groups and not be aggressive and derogatory towards women. It's infallibly that way. The only explanation I can come up with is that men, just like that little boy and his father, have been taught that they are constantly being examined by each other. So they are constantly trying to prove themselves when they are together, their prowess and their ability to command women, et cetera, et cetera.

When they're alone that dynamic just isn't there. I see a lot of men being really shy when they come in alone. I think when a man is alone, more often than not, he's a little unsure of how to deal with the situation. Then it's my job to make contact and bring them out of their shyness, and let them know that it's okay to communicate!

What do the customers say when they speak? ~ Some will be very involved in their fantasy, and speaking in a fantasy mode, "You are beautiful", but not addressing you. And, "Hey, let's get together when you get out." I've also held conversations for hours through the glass, that have nothing to do with sex.

What do you say when you speak? ~ I'm usually coming from a fantasy place. At a one-way window, I might just talk dirty, imagining who they are, or talk about my body in a really explicit and adjective-filled way.

Some customers experience ecstatic surprise when they first encounter the stage show. What do you think surprises them? ~ I think it's the energy, the lights, the movement, and the *nakedness*! That's different! We do not walk down the street seeing nakedness. I think they're really surprised and excited, both pleasurably and sexually, by seeing women enjoying being in their bodies. I think that is the main image the women at the theater present, an enjoyment of being naked, physical, sexual, and moving. It's a real enjoying place that we're dancing from.

Sometimes a customer will leave angry or disgusted. Do you understand

why? ~ I can only imagine, seeing how uptight a lot of the men are about their sexuality, that sometimes having it right in their face is going to bring up inner conflict about their sexuality. What they think they want is really more than they can handle.

Do you ever encourage customers to leave messages? ~ Oh yeah. For some of them it extends the fantasy about you and about having you, that is a part of their life. But if they entertain any notions about that physically coming true, that wears off quickly when there's no response. I've gotten messages from men who want to be my slaves, offering their services to clean my house.

Do you ever abuse the customers? ~ I've acted out my rage at men and their abuse at times. Anger and resentment have come up for me, but I can't maintain my job in that state, so I've had to deal with it. That's been my process of evolving and dealing with my rage and fear, and my sexuality. And taking charge of it again. And when I own it, I don't have to continue to be angry.

Do you ever feel controlled or possessed by the customers? ~ No. Controlled would only happen in a fantasy context. Whenever a customer tells me what to do, I say, "Excuse me, I give orders here, not you." (Laughs) A customer can never be in control of me.

When customers show disrespect the dancers can call security and have them removed. How often do you ask that a customer be removed? ~ If I ask twice and he still doesn't stop, I call. It happens on an average of once a shift.

How do you respond when a customer orgasms? ~ Depends on the fantasy, and their surrender to it. If they're really enjoying themselves, I can enjoy that fact, even though looking at mens' dicks is not at the top of my list of fun experiences. Though some are beautiful, it's hard to see penises as really beautiful because they have been such instruments of domination and abuse.

Do you try to get customers to spend? ~ On the business level I'm definitely there to get customers to spend, I do that by giving a good show, one that I'm enjoying.

How do you feel about dancing for customers in the three booths with one-way glass? ~ I love it. I can get more into my fantasy. So how do I feel about the other person seeing that? Well, basically, I feel that objectification is okay. Even though I don't know who that person is, it is still okay that they're involved in their fantasy. I don't feel that anything violent is being done to me. If I followed the premise that something violent was being done to

me, because I couldn't see that person, that we weren't having a "personal" interaction, I would have to subscribe to that every time I look at a picture. I would be
violating the person in the photo. I don't think that's a commonly held belief, nor
is it mine.

As the desired do you have power? ~ Being the object of desire is certainly a
powerful place. Desire, mutual desire, is a component of our reflecting each other
and when we reflect each other we help each other love ourselves. To say you
want something you have to expose yourself. And when you expose yourself
communication can happen.

Have you experienced burnout in this job? ~ Definitely. Sometimes I go
through a phase where I don't want to deal with the sexuality of men. I just want
to be with the sexuality of women. Or I'm not into being sexual, period.
Sometimes I'm just really sick of the job, sick of the trip that comes up. It's happened a few times, and I've taken a break.

*Off stage you encounter other dancers, support staff, and management.
Describe the interaction and conversation that occur.* ~ Generally it's pretty
friendly. When I'm on my break though, I basically want to be in my own space,
and not be an entertainer. For the most part, I just lie down, hang loose, and read a
magazine. But the other day I was deliciously accosted by a wonderful dancer,
who made me feel really wonderful. Delicious accostments happen at times.
(Laughs)

Sometimes it's like a party here. Describe these occasions. ~ Wild. Raucous.
Rambunctious. Orgiastic. This feeling of people coming to enjoy themselves, to
really give a good show, has great possibilities of it feeling like a party rather than
a job. It happens frequently.

*The owner and management of this theater say they want to create a safe, nur-
turing, fun, and profitable business. Have they succeeded?* ~ Yes and no.
They have certainly succeeded at being profitable. As far as being safe and nurturing, there's a lot of ambiguity there. There is generally a sex-positive attitude
promoted by management. But because it is for profit, they often fall into the
exploitive category, where they want women to put up with stuff. Sometimes
they're totally insensitive to the stress they put on dancers. They schedule them
up the wazoo, dancers start to falter from being overworked, and then they're let
go. It's unjustifiable and consistency has been a problem.
   There's a nice area for us to hang out in when we're off stage. There's a shower,
stuff to drink. The pay is inadequate for the amount of physical labor involved. It
should be more, but it's certainly above many jobs that women can have.

The owner and management also express the desire to empower people. Have you been empowered here? ~ Definitely. And their sex-positive support is definitely a part of that, a part of me breaking through certain barriers and fears about objectification, and being a woman in this society.

Is there a difference between the male support staff and the male customers? ~ Yes and no. I think some male staff come in with the idea that "Ooh, baby, I'm going to get to see all these naked women." If they continue that attitude in a way that's disturbing to the dancers, that feels like they're just thinking about their own enjoyment, they don't last. That attitude is not supported by anyone here. I've seen them get more comfortable, it's like, so what, naked, that's natural.

Describe the periodically scheduled dancers' meetings. ~ They can be tedious but there's definitely a good feeling of camaraderie in the room. There's an experience of us being unique, in that we have this experience that's definitely different from most women's. That lends a feeling of rapport, friendliness, and warmth that's really fun. Sometimes the meetings are dominated with management agenda but there's generally an openness to whatever needs to be discussed.

What do you feel passing customers in the hallway whom you have just danced for? ~ A little strange. A jarring of the fantasy-reality against the real-life-reality. I have the feeling they experience the same thing. They realize that the way they relate to me here is different, and they usually don't say anything. They might say, "Hey, I just saw you naked." I might say, "Hi", but generally I don't interact with them.

Do you ever feel in danger coming to or leaving work? ~ I've felt that a few times. I don't like leaving really late, when buses are infrequent. I've been followed a couple of times. Once I saw that I was being followed and went back to the theater and had one of the support staff walk with me. Then the guy split. I think when I first started working here I expected someone to approach me maliciously, but I haven't experienced that.

Do you change your appearance coming to or leaving work? ~ I don't really need to. I look different because I'm wearing clothes, but I might change my hair trying to not be recognized.

Do you have anger about this job? ~ Yeah, I would like the world to be different. At a deep level I have anger about women's status in the world. Having a job in the sex industry has been an empowering experience for me, but for a number of women I know, a big part of the reason they're working in the sex industry is there's nowhere else to go. It's a way for them to make money and have a certain degree of autonomy without being some peon in an office, being physically inhibited, and not paid well. My anger is at the system that at its roots has women as less powerful and with less status than men.

How does this job compare with others you've had? ~ This job is the longest I have ever had. That says a lot about the level of satisfaction. As a student it's been important because I can tailor the schedule to my needs. Because you're doing something creative, this is definitely more desirable. The freedom to make my show as I see fit is pretty desirable.

Describe your earliest memories? ~ One is my grandfather coming into the room, picking me up and throwing me into the air. I have the memory of a trip to Florida, when I was two, memories of being really physical. I remember being in a field. My early memories have to do with being alone in nature.

Describe your family and its circumstances as you remember them during your childhood. ~ I was born in New York, and moved to Vermont when I was thirteen. I was born into an upper middle-class family. My parents were schoolteachers. My mother taught at day care. My parents would come home and my mother would cook dinner and my father would drink his beer and read his paper. It was real methodical in terms of the ritual of their lives. One time I found my mother crying hysterically in the kitchen. And that never, ever happened.

My memories of my childhood – it's like this repetitious feeling interrupted by these really weird experiences. There was this feeling of something underlying going on, but it was secret. We lived in this upper middle-class neighborhood, very nice actually – older houses, surrounded by a forty acre park. Life was pretty routine.

What kind of child were you? ~ I was really disciplined, it was a way of escaping the bullshit in my family. I read, and was very disciplined as an artist, a musician, and a writer. It was very difficult for me to trust, because of the secrecy I was brought up with, and my father's continuous verbal abuse. There was always shouting and yelling going on. It was generally hard for me to be open to people. I was an excellent student. I have a half-brother.

Describe your relationship with your half-brother. ~ It was very conflictual. He was always teasing me. It had a lot to do with the fact that my father didn't like him, he wasn't his son. I think my brother had a lot of emotional problems already when he was four or five, when my parents married. My mother's first husband used to beat her up, she left when he threw a glass milk bottle at her. My brother was a few months old, so his first three or four years were with babysitters. One babysitter was locking him in the closet and feeding him peanut butter. To this day he hates peanut butter.

He couldn't open up to my father, and my father couldn't be sensitive enough to give him what he needed. As a result, they never got along. The first time he ran away he was thirteen. Later my parents shipped him to different members of the family and friends to finish high school.

I was the apple of my father's eye and naturally got drastically different treatment. That was a lot of the contention between my brother and I. When he was really ticked off about it, he'd take it out on me. I got tricks played on me all the time. Books were hung on my door jamb so when I opened the door they would fall on my head, all kinds of things like that. (Laughs) So we weren't close.

Describe your relationship with your parents in those years. ~ My mother was the perfect mom, she was cub scout den mother, went to PTA meetings, we just never talked about anything. When I think back to our relationship, all I come up with is her cooking and cleaning. I was always trying to entertain my parents. That's my relationship with them. My father was always in a bad mood and we were always trying to get him to feel better.

Reading was a way for me to escape this emotional repression that was in every aspect of my life. I started writing when I was six years old. My world was very private, one reason being that things were simply not talked about. My parents didn't talk about sexuality or money, kids were not supposed to know about that stuff. My father used to say children should be seen and not heard. He would laugh, as though it was a joke; however, it was definitely a threat.

We went to Vermont every summer for the whole summer, and once a month to what used to be my grandparents' farm. Eventually my parents bought it. My relationship with my friends was continually interrupted. I never had summers with them and that affected me in a lot of ways. Being in social groups hasn't been easy. All these factors made me feel separateness. I knew there were secrets you had to keep, things you didn't talk about, even though they were going on.

Were you raised under a particular religious tradition? ~ Being alone with my mother was doing grocery shopping and going to church every Sunday. It was Presbyterian, very boring, and made me feel really stiff. My memory of it is standing up and sitting down, reading stuff and repeating stuff after other people. It was all incredibly methodical. Halfway through the service the kids were supposed to stand up and walk out. We ran out, and down to the store screaming and yelling.

We had to go to Sunday school. It was a total joke. I hated it and always brought a book to read. I was eight when I put my foot down and said, "No way, I'm not going any more. I don't like church." My mother tried to force me but she couldn't. It was about that time that mother was trying to spank me. Father never would touch me, mother was the spanker and she could be pretty vicious. The last time she spanked me I was about nine. I really fought and hurt her.

My father is not into Christianity, he thinks it's a crock of shit. He said on his visit here last week that he couldn't understand how any woman could have anything to do with Christianity because it's oppressive to women. He doesn't talk about it too much because my mother is still into Christianity, though she's not real vocal about it. She was brought up a devout Victorian Christian. My father is really a pagan, very into nature. And even though he's very repressed I think that very deep down he believes there are spirits in the natural world. He has more of a cosmic view of things. So there was that tension in regard to religion. My father would go to church once a year on Christmas Eve. My brother eventually refused to go as well.

Describe your childhood play and friendships. ~ My best friend was a kid who lived on my block, Joan. I met her when I was two years old. We were constant companions. We were very physical and spent a lot of time in the park spying on the drug dealers and climbing trees. We developed a code language that was a series of finger movements.

For years and years and years I read a book a day. My parents' library covers the whole second floor of the house. I read a lot of black writers who were writing about the South after the Civil War. I read Howard Fast, and *Uncle Tom's Cabin*, a lot of American novels. I was studying the flute in an incredibly disciplined way from about age eight until fifteen. I practiced an hour and a half each day.

My only group time with kids was playing kick-the-can and stuff like that. I have vague memories of masturbating, but it was something that I couldn't acknowledge to myself. I did have some S&M scenes with one friend. I have no idea where this came from, but we played "Slave Girl," "Middle Eastern Harem." One person was the master and one was the slave and we whipped each other with belts. I was about eight and she was a couple years older. We were really into it but knew that we couldn't tell anyone. We had to make sure that our parents were out of the house and that the curtains were shut, then we would undress. I remember tying a robe around my groin and hers as chastity belts. After a while we decided that we couldn't do it any more and we never ever talked about it again.

Our parents were a little unhappy with the age difference between Joan and I, and we got the vibes from them. A lot of things seemed to happen...awakening of consciousness things, about age nine for me. Joan suddenly had a boyfriend who lived on the other side of the park. One time I went to meet her by the tennis courts and she was with him and they were laughing. I'll never forget that, I felt completely betrayed. I could not understand what was going on that would make Joan laugh at me. It was shattering. It changed the nature of play and the time I spent with her. Suddenly I felt like she wasn't my companion. Nothing was quite the same after that.

Describe your childhood school experience. ~ I was a really good student. I loved learning and gaining skills. I had a few wonderful teachers and a few awful, awful teachers. One teacher locked me in a bathroom because I was humming in class. That was an unforgettable experience. Throughout my childhood there was the shock of discovering that what I was doing, that I thought was totally normal and acceptable, was a terrible thing in other people's eyes. I was always asking questions about why you did math a certain way. My teacher thought I was a total dummy and was very deprecating.

Joan's father was the grade school principal and my brother used to get into trouble a lot, so there was this feeling of trying to disassociate myself from him. And yet, discovering that I was bad too. I got a little rowdy as I progressed through the grades, but I never became a *bad* student. My greatest thrill during recess was to chase boys and beat them up. (Laughs) We had a girl team and boy team, I was a ringleader and really into it. I remember getting into a fight with this little Italian kid, we literally beat the shit out of each other. We were crying and it was like this total rage purged. That was the last time I did that. I thought, "This is more than I can handle." As a kid, if someone was attacking me, I didn't have any qualms about fighting back.

Did you receive information about human sexuality in grade school? ~ We were shown a film, and I remember the teachers being really weird, like they felt uncomfortable about it and how to deal with us seeing it. We all knew that we were being shown something that was a little taboo. It was all diagrammed and talked about people like they were guppies. The way the film described sex and reproduction was very removed from real people. I must have been about seven or eight but I got the basic idea from that film. Kids should get good sex education in school.

Describe the nudity in your home. ~ I have early memories of seeing my father's dick, and seeing my mom nude, but that ended at a certain point. In my early teens my parents got into skinny dipping in our pond, they were a little uptight about it, not quite sure if it was cool.

Were you ever punished due to sexual expression? ~ They never caught me at anything so I was never punished.

Were you ever sexually abused as a child? ~ Not that I remember, but there was a lot of sexual energy between my father and I, along with constant, silent reinforcement that sex was not okay. Whenever something sexual came up, like in the news, it was tittered at or the channel was changed. I think in some way the repercussions of the sexual energy between my father and I have been reflected in me, in ways similar to the experiences of incest survivors. I felt implicitly anxious about sex, in my relationship with my father.

What were you taught about human relationships in your family? ~ That everyone had a role. Mom had a certain sphere, and Dad had a certain sphere. Mom worked all day, so did Dad. Dad came home and sat in the chair and read the paper, and Mom cooked a meal. And washed the dishes, et cetera. That a woman's role is to serve her husband. My mother played out that serving role very, very well. I learned that the only way I could not be a part of that was to laugh at her role. So I was really denigrating to her. I also learned that to get things, to have good relationships with people, you had to play a game. You had to find your role in relationship to them. And your role was created by what they needed from you in order to make them feel good.

I was taught that being attractive was really important. Mom always worried about her weight, being a visual artist she was really adept at disguising it. By going to Mom's bedroom and seeing the array of makeup and things like tweezers that would bend your eyelashes I saw that making yourself beautiful required important looking and specialized tools. I was always dressed up with my hair in curls. My mother used to brush my hair...it really hurt a lot, and yet it was this important thing that had to be done.

Were you taught to value truth? ~ (Laughs) Very funny. Given everything that I've been saying, it's pretty obvious that truth was not the object here. Creating a system of denial in which you could comfortably avoid your feelings and reality and truth was the object. You weren't supposed to know about the ways in which other people lived, in extreme repression and abuse and poverty. A little later on my mother did get involved in some civil rights stuff. She went to the Poor Peoples' March...there was this duality. There was this upper-class streak of emphasis on appearance, on things looking right physically and emotionally, that we were all together and happy and nice and good people. Real contradictions. My mother got involved in the housing authority. It was white people trying to help black people obtain housing and fight discrimination in housing.

Did your parents teach you that you could have power, choice? ~ There's this duality in what I was taught as a kid. My parents were literally straddling. My mother was straddling the fact that she was from the Victorian upper class. She was brought up with maids and servants in a wealthy doctor's family, a member of the Daughters of the American Revolution, lived in posh houses, had country houses. When the women's movement started, even though my mother was a housewife primarily at that time, she was aware of the movement and feeling the reverberations. There was this attempt to confront things and yet reinforce these old values of "Let's make everything look right."

I got a little about power and choice from my father. He was thrilled that I was academically on top of things. I got from him that the only way you could get power and choice was by becoming educated. In some ways my father treated me like a son. "Go out, get an education, and when you have a kid, give it your name, don't take your husband's name, 'cause you're the last and we want the name to continue." At the same time, "No, you cannot go out to a movie unless you wear a dress." Really confusing!

From very early on, part of me knew that power was definitely in the man's world, and was about academically achieving and getting a man's job. And definitely, going out and getting a job was separate from what being a woman was, which was looking good. So power as a woman meant becoming sort of like a man. Choice definitely had to do with having some kind of privileged information, so that you could have power over people. I learned in my family that you should fake it, put on a good appearance, put on a good face. The only way you could have choice was by manipulating people.

What effect did your body changing have on you? ~ My father stopped being my buddy. I was feeling a little bewildered by it, not really understanding it, but knowing it had something to do with my chest suddenly moving outward. I very much wanted to be a boy as a child, because being a boy was about having power. I was very clear on that. And having power was being really physical. I was incredibly strong, constantly running and moving. I was a long´distance runner later on. When I started developing I felt like that prevented me from being so physical and I really resented that.

Describe your adolescent sexuality. ~ In my adolescence one major thing happened which really changed my life. We moved to Vermont to a very, very isolated area. Suddenly my whole life changed from having been involved in this developing social scene in a cosmopolitan community outside of New York City. That's where I had my first boyfriend in junior high. He dumped me because I wouldn't make out with him the way this other girl would. That was really trying. Suddenly I had to travel twenty miles each way through a mountainous forest just to get to high school. The social relationships became much more of a trial. Just to go out and meet someone was an expedition. I was very alienated and freaked out, very traumatized by the move.

I started to see this boy who lived even further away than the high school. We saw each other mostly in school. Sometimes he would hitchhike to where I lived and we would romp around the woods together. That's when I started experimenting sexually.

At the same time, there was a guy who had a bottle shop, in this little township. He was just one of the neighbors. The closest people lived a mile from our house. I would visit him, and at some point we started talking about sex, and experimenting. We never had intercourse but we fooled around. I was precocious and very curious. Looking back on it, he was really into little girls, but I don't think he ever would have raped me. When I ran into him on the street about four years ago he was unbelievably embarrassed, he didn't want to deal with me. That said a lot to me.

When I was with the other boy I started smoking pot. We would get stoned, go into the woods and make out. We tried to fuck but we couldn't because I was still a virgin and he was extremely well hung. It was like, "Oh my God, I don't think you're going to fit in." (Laughs) One weekend when my parents went away he came over and we got it on. We made it in the bedroom next to theirs, it was sort of like neutral territory, a guest room. I was into sex, but unable to have an orgasm. I had no idea what an orgasm was.

How did you first discover and use the ability to arouse? ~ It's weird because you learn it so early on, it's not something you discover when you're a teenager. You learn it in a variety of ways, at all these stages of development. I certainly learned it with my father. I learned how to entertain and titilate him in a way that was emotional, sexual, psychological, intellectual. It all meshed. But way into my teens I was always putting down and trying to hide my ability to arouse.

When I ran away I got a taste of a whole other culture. I met hustlers in Boston and became lovers with a boy who hustled men. That's when I became more aware of being sexually explicit. When I went back to Vermont I was dressing much more provocatively in tight pants and shirts. I was extremely thin because I had been living on coffee and donuts and I had gotten very sick.

In Vermont I gained a lot of weight, and was very, very unhealthy. I had pneumonia for six months and then I met this man who taught me yoga. It totally rehabilitated me and turned me into this voluptuous sex-bomb. I continued to wear fairly tight clothing; I don't think I was consciously trying to be provocative as much as I was discovering that I *was* provocative. I was discovering that my body could literally make men stop their cars in the middle of the street. It freaked the shit out of me. It felt powerful, and yet terrifying. I felt powerful, but I couldn't handle it. I gained weight again in order to protect myself from their gaze.

Describe your discovery of how pregnancy occurs. ~ By getting pregnant. But first, I slowly figured it out from grade school bathroom graffiti. That's where I got my information! And that little film on reproduction. I lived with a man some time after I ran away and I got pregnant when we went to Europe. We were in a Catholic country so I had to come back for the abortion.

Describe your first exposure to sexually explicit media and its impact on you. ~ I saw it in stores when I was a kid, but I always avoided it, because that stuff was bad, taboo. I remember finding magazines that my brother had. My feelings were that they were dirty and awful. Even in my late teens I was really down on pornography. I felt pornography was real trash and denigrating to women.

Describe your high school years. ~ They became the reflection of this traumatic move to Vermont, and not really being very able to adjust to this entirely new culture. I wasn't very interested in school itself, then I started having sexual experiences and ran away because of my father's obsession with me, and my family's repressive lifestyle. The curriculum was much lower quality than it was in New York, so I was really turned off. I finished high school after I left my family. High school was a backdrop to a lot of big changes in my life, I wasn't with my family and I was starting to have a life of my own. My last two years were about survival, emotional and psychic, and total upheaval.

What was your first job? ~ I had an allowance for jobs around the house. My first job where I got a wage was at Dunkin' Donuts when I was thirteen. It was *awful*. I was hip enough to realize that this was really a bad place to be and I quit after two weeks.

Did you have any heroines or heroes during your teen years? ~ It's only recently that I've had heroes and heroines. As a child and an adolescent I was aware that other kids looked up to celebrities and musicians, and that I didn't. I think it had something to do with coming out of this really controlling situation, and thinking that looking up to someone was giving my power to someone else. I fell in love with a man when I was fourteen, I don't think he was a hero, but he was someone I respected.

What did you plan to do after graduation from school? ~ The kind of disruption that I experienced in my teenage years precluded any kind of thinking like that. I was involved in survival.

What did you do after high school? ~ I lived with a professional guitarist I met when I was finishing school and we started making music. I became very involved in making music and living on the land. I experienced a real emotional opening, he became someone I really trusted. He empowered me as an artist instead of treating it like it was a hobby. That had been my experience with my family. He thought that I was talented and could support myself with my art. We formed a duo and toured Europe and the Caribbean. I was a flutist and also sang in a studio. He had a lot of connections and they became a way for me to empower myself. That went on for three years. After touring we came back to the house in the country. I was really getting into meditation and spent entire summers nude. I went through tremendous spiritual and emotional evolution at that time, and experienced a lot of support from him. At the same time, he could be very imbalanced, very violent, and he beat me up. He had a real blood sugar problem, he was very moody and it was a pretty intense time.

Describe other work you've done prior to dancing. ~ I've done a lot of waitressing, which as a woman not trained in anything, was the most lucrative thing I could do. I did a lot of cocktail waitressing, which I really hated, because I had to deal with drunk men pawing me and a drug environment. It was really hard to stay out of it. There was alcohol and cocaine going on all the time.

I supported myself in my late teens by performing music and growing marijuana in Vermont. I mean big-time growing. There has always been this question of how to support myself, so that I can still have a creative life. If I don't have it, I can't function. Growing pot was one way to do that. It enabled me to travel, do therapeutic bodywork, have it done with me, and continue my studies as a dancer and musician. In my early twenties I ran a theater for two years.

Have you had other jobs in the sex industry? ~ Waitressing.

Describe living situations you've been in since you left home. ~ I lived with two gay men in Boston who ran a theater. I lived with a friend's parents who treated me very much like their daughter. I'm still very connected to them. I've lived in a commune with a large group of artists living close to the earth. I lived with my musician lover in a house where we built additions I have had my own apartment, lived on a college campus, and behind the theater I ran in Massachusetts.

Describe your current living arrangements. ~ Right now I pay a lot of money for a relatively small amount of space. For what it is, it's good, in this city. I live alone.

Describe your interests outside of work. ~ Up until now I've been completing my degree in theater. What I've always done outside of work, has been my creative life, making new work, whether that's music or theater, collaborations with other people. Another part of my life is being involved in the healing arts. I started meditation practice when I was fourteen. I've done that in the context of Hatha yoga. I've also studied with psychics, and been healed by my involvement with them. I've worked with Native American healers.

When I came to California I got a degree in body work. So now I work with people on a physical, emotional, and psychic level.

Describe your social life and current friendships. ~ I'm getting away from a predominance of one-on-one relationships. I'm now more involved in small groups. I really wanted to change that. One of the ways it's happened has been a growing involvement with a twelve-step program. I see that some of my issues and family background stuff have been alcohol-related...that's been really useful. It has been good to be involved in a group and talk about personal experience which is very, very difficult for me to do. A lot of my relationships are art related and there's often friendship and spiritual healing involved. My social relationships are also in the sex community, the leather community, the S&M community. They're crossed and intermingled, all of them, with my sexuality, my life as a healer, and as an artist.

Do you use drugs? ~ Occasionally. As a teenager I used acid, mushrooms, and pot, but it was never a regular thing. Pot was a regular thing for maybe a year or two, it wasn't a daily thing. Now I smoke pot once in a while, I'll do cocaine like once a year, and I drink alcohol. I'll go for months without having a drink, and then I'll go for a period where I drink when I go out and dance, maybe a couple times a week.

Have you suffered any traumas as an adult? ~ Coming out as a gay person and integrating that into my life. Owning that. Also living in this world with the threat of being annihilated is a traumatic experience. I have consciously spent a lot of time looking at that, not only intellectually or politically, but feeling it emotionally. In my late teens I went through a month long period of mourning for the planet. I suddenly started experiencing the pain of that, and I cried almost every day for a month. It was really scary. I didn't know why it was happening, where it had come from, but I felt enough courage to let it happen. It was very real for me. The destruction of the earth is very much a part of my daily reality, and not something that I'm politically forcing myself to be aware of. I feel it. I cannot emotionally divorce myself from feeling that something's being taken away from us.

Do you have any male inspired fears? ~ My experience of the earth being destroyed is completely a male inspired fear. Of course women are involved in this destruction, but I feel that war is from men, that the rape of the earth is from men. I have incredible fear, anger, and rage, and it has a lot to do with men. Fear of being attacked on the street is a daily experience. I'm disgusted with men except for you and a few others. I experience rage against male domination that I see as having guided the destruction and imbalance of the earth, the current reality physically, emotionally, psychicly, and spiritually.

What media do you consume? ~ Everything. Magazines, books, TV, movies. Everything from pornography, that's both straight, gay, and S&M, to art journals, to The New Yorker magazine. I see art and mainstream movies, live music...and a lot of theater. Theater is a weekly thing, more so than music since I'm performing all the time.

I really love to perform in sex shows and art shows. I would like sexuality to be more a part of art shows and I've been watching those boundaries dissolve over the past two years. Outside of this job my live strip shows are very theatrical, intellectual, and political. They evolved from a character who would talk about and act out scenes from her life.

One of my characters is Diamond Lilly. That show is based on research I did on turn of the century madames from San Francisco. I discovered this incredibly creative and different group of women. At that time your options as a woman were either to get married or to be a barmaid or prostitute. So a lot of unusual, different, or creative women became involved in the sex industry. I also discovered that some of these women were at least bisexual. Diamond Lilly had a lover she discovered at one of the soirees they used to throw. She was a cross-dresser, a woman who passed as a man. Another character I do is Maggie, a word processor and a closet case. This performance shows her breaking down being a closet case. She was really a very sexual person.

I've noticed as a singer I am allowing myself to be more sensual, not allowing my sensuality to be censored. This has been a real breakthrough that I directly attribute to being involved in the sex industry.

Do you have a favorite book, author, or movie? ~ There are so many. Everything from French feminist theorist Helene Cixous, who writes incredible treatises on women opening their voice and changing, literally, the form of their writing, instead of writing from a male point of view. I like Anne Rice, who writes about vampires. Those were really revolutionary books, expressing the carnality of creativity and sensuality. There are so many writers I admire, it's hard to know how to list them. Starhawk...

Do you read romance novels? ~ No. I'm too much of an intellectual. But I love the new lesbian romance novels, parodies of the cult novels of the fifties, the coming out. I like lesbian sex/romance writing, because its sexuality is allowed a much freer rein.

Do you use sexually explicit media? ~ I'm not much of a masturbator, so that's not a big part of my life.

Had you been a customer at a peep show or other sex show prior to dancing? ~ No.

Which of society's values have you rejected? ~ Most of them. But I've gone through such an evolution in dealing with them, that, in some ways, I've consciously integrated into the world in the past several years. Before, I lived a much more separate lifestyle, and felt the disadvantage of that to a degree. I want to be involved in a dialogue. I don't want to be separate from what's going on, even if I disagree with it. The world is definitely my theater, but not just for personal gratification, but as a way to empower. I see myself infiltrating an art organization and working from within. I see being able to bring events, or certain performers, or theatrical experience into production by my input, and still being able to deal with the straight art world, which can be incredibly narrow.

I reject conformism, yet conformism can be utilized to create a positive impact in which collectivism is experienced rather than individualism and materialism. Go for it, infiltrate that corporation if you can create positive change that goes against this incredible materialism, which is really the primary motive and ultimate aim of everything today. As much as I want to be comfortable there's a limit to that. I want to have more sharing and a balanced distribution. That's not some idealized goal, it's something I live.

Has the media ideal of beauty affected you? ~ For many years I resisted it. I wasn't really into makeup, I thought it was fake, putting on a mask, not being yourself. Now I see it as playing out roles. Currently there are a lot of androgynous images in the media, which is nice to see, but they're still mostly very fem. Playing out that role is really about touching an emotional and psychic level of myself. I don't feel attached to it, and I don't feel like that's not me. It's me, but it's not a role that can disempower me.

I am interested also in, and enjoy media images of men, and playing that out myself. It's also something to laugh at. A lot of media images are hysterically funny. So, the theme here is, use these things for personal and social empowerment, don't be used by it to reinforce this whole materialist accumulation ethic that's currently underpinning our destruction.

Many humans love the attention of others and adorn themselves to get it. Do you? ~ Definitely. But my father was attracted to me and there was a feeling of fear about it, so I really tried to play it down. Discovering that men could be really attracted to me was a scary thing. For a lot of years I really played down my appearance. I was afraid of the attention, because I was told that empowering myself was being selfish. I was supposed to serve other people. There was a push to deny personal expression and personal empowerment. I took that in and I didn't want to adorn myself to attract other people; it was not cool, not good. In my relationship with the musician I started to display my sexual self more. He was helping me to enjoy myself more and feel good about my body. Now, I'm not buying that it's bad to enjoy yourself physically. Now I'm into it. I like to go out in my leather miniskirts and strut the bars! (Laughs)

What is your self-image? ~ I'm starting to feel powerful, and not out of a need to control others, but as an experience of my energy and enjoyment of being here, meeting people, and sharing things. I'm starting to experience confidence in myself due to my success as an artist. I'm experiencing a lot of self-censorship and barriers falling down. I feel a lot of possibility, even the possibility of the world changing a little bit in a positive way...that feels a little tentative. I experience myself as pretty sharp and on the edge of making a lot of connections with different aspects of myself. And letting those selves flourish and talk to one another is enabling me to be in the world in a really beautiful manner.

Are you a tolerant person? ~ My tolerance is defined. I say, "Okay, I'll do this for you, I will do it only until three o'clock." Or, "I'll wait for you for half an hour, but no more than half an hour." Or, "You've said that three times, and if you say it again you'll have to leave." (Laughs) Being vocal about setting boundaries and having tolerance has been something I've had to develop, it definitely was not something I was taught.

Do you trust people? ~ I'm kind of trusting, but I feel like perhaps I shouldn't be quite so trusting. Setting boundaries, setting limits for people might come off as not being trustful, but that's not really what it is. I've been attacked a few times physically, while living in the city, and I'm feeling like not being quite so available to people.

Do you exploit people? ~ Sure. To get what I want. (Laughs) The word "exploit" is a real loaded one. Real loaded. It can be seen in the context of using someone to get what you want in a way that's not necessarily harmful for them, or in a way that is. I don't think that I use people in a way that's harmful to them. I'm not into people feeling hurt.

Have you ever been violent with people? ~ Yes, haven't we all. And that's very hard to accept. I have been on the receiving and the giving end of violence. In my family, all the violence was verbal. In my late teens I was beaten up by a lover a number of times. Since then I've been in a couple of relationships where verbal and physical violence was happening. It's a really devastating experience. It has made me deal in a fundamental way with a bunch of things. I allowed myself to be walked on and pushed around, emotionally and verbally, and I would suppress my reaction until I would explode. And that's a place I don't need to go to.

Define love. ~ Love is...sharing yourself with someone or with a group of people or with anything. It's really just a state of openness. Intimacy is the same.

Define power. ~ Power is loving yourself and not having to control people who are into pushing you around.

Describe the variety and frequency of your current sexual activity. ~ Most of my partners in love...intimacy-making, are women. I occasionally play with men, but I think of it more as play, than intimacy. That happens maybe a couple of times a year, and I seem to have a little more distance from it, or no need for continued connection. My connection with the men I've chosen to be with, though, is pretty positive, generally speaking. I was very dominating with the last man I played with and he loved it. He was a really very sweet, sweet boy, so it was really fun. I find men fun to play with sexually but an emotional connection with them as lovers seems to fail over this pattern of them wanting to control me. So, besides the fact that I find women very attractive, my reason for being a lesbian is also very political. But not intellectually, I mean in a total sense. I simply will not put up with men trying to manipulate and control me.

I had my first relationship with a woman when I was seventeen. I was in a two-and-a-half-year relationship as a couple, though I dated other women, and saw a few men as well. But I was very consistent in that relationship, and we were very sexual...virtually daily. It was fantastic. In that relationship I started exploring role-playing in sex, a little bondage and a lot of domination-submission stuff. And S&M.

I've started exploring my sexuality by myself, which I never really had before. Playing with toys and porn images...I'm not into vibrators particularly, yet. I'm into love. Intimacy is really very important. I can't imagine my sex life being just about sexuality, without the mind. When I was with my last girlfriend and dating others, a lot of it was about having unemotional connections with people, I was just exploring my sexuality. Maybe that was because I couldn't really give myself to those relationships and it was a way of having control.

When do you get sexually involved? ~ Any time of day and in a vast variety of places. There's no rhyme or reason to it. But I don't want to just find someone and take them to bed. I'm not close to that happening. I'm not as sexual as in the past. That's less about the AIDS crisis and more about my emotional and creative energy being used in other ways. Also I don't want to put myself in places where it's not going to be nurturing for me.

What sexual taboos besides dancing have you broken? ~ Playing male roles with a sex partner, S&M, domination and submission. I love to fuck men up the ass. I think most of my sexuality is in a taboo area. (Laughs) I'd say all of it is, as a matter of fact. (Laughs) I've gotten it on in such unusual places and it's all been ecstatic. It's a total charge for me to totally dominate someone against a car in the driveway of a Catholic school. It's really fun to be semi-public with sexuality. A taboo that I really enjoy is suddenly blurting out something really, really graphic in a public place.

A few years ago I was making love and experienced myself as literally having a penis. It's not something that's explainable, it was a psychic thing. I wasn't experiencing myself as a woman. It was very scary, totally intimidating, and at the same time it was, "Whoa, this is really a trip, this is neat." That's been really exciting because it affects your concept of gender, not just of sex. That you don't have to limit yourself to social conditioning as a woman can really open up a lot of awareness for you. It opened up a period of exploring my masculine self, for lack of a better term. I don't think that's the best term for a self who is taking space, taking charge, being directive. I explored that for a year-and-a-half or so, through my dress, and I had radically short hair. By acting out your fantasies, whether you consider them ultimately healthy or not, is beside the point. By acting them out you understand them, and then they don't have power over you.

What is sexually degrading for you? ~ I don't have any sexuality in my life which degrades me, I don't allow it. I cut off playing sexually with a man because he was so blown away by sex with me that he was obsessed with it. He was playing out *his* obsession with me, whether I was into it or not. Maybe on some level it was flattering but I find it degrading when someone's only thinking of themself.

Most men and some women have this approach of my pleasure is the top. Sure, there's sex where it's, yeah, I want it, but, if you're going to maintain that as a constant, you've got a serious problem, and it's ultimately abusive.

Do you ever use sex as a weapon? ~ I have to admit the part of me that's enraged about my oppression as a woman, as a sexual being, at times thinks of my sexuality in the sex industry as part of a mirage. I participate in the patriarchy and I'm given this very strong financial reward. I consider that using the patriarchy to my advantage. The part of me that's enraged gets a kick out of it, but you can have some really wonderful interactions.

Do you ever experience guilt or shame about your sexuality? ~ Yeah, definitely, thinking of my lesbianism. I mean, God, what a phobia it is. I don't think I was ever told explicitly, but you just knew that it wasn't okay for women to be with women. I deal with that from time to time. You deal with this movie about how being a sex worker is bad and wrong. It's a bunch'a shit. You know that intellectually, so you have to teach your mental self to communicate with your sexual self, your heart and your spirit. It's getting all the ducks in a row, so to speak. Getting everybody together, so you feel at home.

Do you think your sexuality would be different if you lived in an egalitarian or female-dominated society? ~ We wouldn't be making these differentiations.

Has birth control and medical technology affected your sexuality? ~ It sure has. The pill, the Copper-7, I've had 'em. They've created a lot of trauma in my life. Unforgettable stuff. I almost lost my fertility because of the Copper-7. I had a very serious infection. Fuck that shit! Why should women be the responsible ones? The diaphragm, the fucking Dalkon-Shield, the foam, all this shit! Most men expect the women to take care of it. Contraception really reveals male domination and women's victimization. It's been a way for women to take control of their bodies – but at what price?

How do you deal with birth control now? ~ I don't.

Has the women's movement affected your sexuality? ~ Yeah. Women becoming more powerful and realizing we have choices is incredible.

Has being a dancer affected your relationships? ~ It certainly put people in my life through stuff. They have to deal with here's this really bright, creative, woman and she's in the sex industry. If they have preconceptions, and most of us do, of how that's bad, it's disempowering. I had to tell a lot of people, "It's not disempowering, no, I'm fine, I *like* this, I *like* doing this." And they're like, "You LIKE it?" I've educated a lot of people, a lot people have changed. If they're going to be in my life, they have to deal with it.

How did you feel about your body prior to becoming a dancer? ~ I felt good about it, but I experienced more physical blocks, more tension. I wasn't really that in touch with my genitalia. I didn't masturbate much before I started the job and it really opened me up to that. That's enabled me to have a more affectionate relationship with my body.

In your experience are dancers more deprived, abused, and battered than other women? ~ All women are deprived, abused, and battered in some way in this society. There are a lot of women in the sex industry who have a history of having the normal sexual boundaries crossed in their lives. Or they've been in a position where they have, for survival reasons, used sexuality. In a way, being sexually intimate with strangers is more accessible to them because that taboo has already been broken. That's real and you can't ignore that. There are also women in the sex industry who don't come from that background at all. You can't make a rule that all women in the sex industry come from that background.

Do you recognize any characteristics common to those who dance? ~ There's an ability to let their sexual selves be illuminating.

When you started dancing did you fear being separated from other women? ~ Definitely. Fear of stigmatization, fear of people judging me harshly.

Have you lost self-esteem due to dancing? ~ Generally my self-esteem is the greatest, but I do go through periods where I feel, "What am I doing here?" "Is this managing me?" Generally speaking dancing has been empowering for me, but, in *my* ideal society, I wouldn't be sharing my sexuality in exchange for money. Because this society judges dancers, it is impossible not to lose self-esteem.

Does your family know you dance? ~ No. I left my family when I was fifteen, so they haven't been a part of my day to day existence for some time. Leading a double life has been my life, as long as I can remember. There were always secrets. That saddens me. It's a deeply taught sensibility. So, leading a double life is not incredibly stressful for me.

Has dancing affected your politics? ~ It has substantially affected my life. My life and my politics are the same thing.

Do you fear becoming a prostitute? ~ I consider what I do a form of prostitution.

Are you a feminist? ~ What kind? If feminist means running my life, creating my life so I have as many choices as possible, that I love myself, and believe in egalitarian relationships, and hope for the best for the planet – then yes, I'm a feminist.

Historically some feminists have tried to exclude some women from the women's movement based on their sexual behavior and preferences. Do you experience this exclusion? ~ Oh, God...yes. The straight women's movement is threatened by the lesbian sexual relationship. I've definitely received that kind of bigotry, as well as the idea that I'm a lesbian because there's something wrong with me. (Laughs) I'M A LOT MORE THAN ADEQUATE! Believe me.

What is your relationship to the women's movement? ~ Mixed. I've felt really oppressed by it at times. Once again, it's politicians, political "activists" as mental beings. You experience lots of discrimination and ultimately it comes down to doing what you really believe in.

What have been the most damaging and the most constructive influences in your life? ~ Some of the most damaging have been the most constructive. Running away from my family never to return was. That's a real sign that I am a person who has been for making my own choices. At 15 that was an *extremely* radical thing to do in my upper middle class structure. In leaving I was saying there's something here that's not healthy for me. My parents were depressing me and trying to status quo me. Along with that experience, a really damaging thing was that, for a long time, I lost my sense of family, a sense of group and belonging. That has been an incredible source of pain, an incredible ache in my heart. It has taken a long time to heal, to create my real family.

What person or people have had the greatest influence in your life? ~ My father had incredible influence, but in a way that has created a lot of challenges for me. He introduced me to the natural world and art. How many parents give that to their children? But he also, through his obsession with me, taught me that I couldn't have boundaries and I've had to learn how to create them – to develop a sense of self. I had to deal with those contradictions and make my own way.

I can only begin naming the twentieth century artists who have influenced me, like Laurie Anderson, Meredith Monk, and Marilyn Monroe. Marilyn was *the* sex goddess of our time. People paint Marilyn as a victim, and in some ways she was, but in other ways she was very free and celebratory about her sexuality. She was looked down on for it, but I like to see her as a powerful woman.

What are your greatest gifts and limitations? ~ One of my greatest gifts is that I'm willing to work with people and share my experience. As a performer, that's what you stand on. I think some of my limitations are *our* limitations. Living in this world can be very limiting, it teaches us to ruin our dreams, to not believe that we can really *live* our desires.

What would you like to be doing in ten to fifteen years? ~ I will have manifested my gifts as a singer, performer, actress, as a creative person. I will have realized my creative riches and know that people are enjoying that, that it's meaningful for them.

Recently in San Francisco we've witnessed the appearance of women danc-

ing for women. Why do you think this is happening? ~ Women finally woke up and said, "Hey, this is sort of strange that women only dance for men. I mean, isn't that sort of strange?" The lesbian community turned it around and created spaces for women to dance for women. That's fantastic. Almost every woman who came had never seen anything like that before. It was a revolutionary experience. It opened women's eyes and we heard over and over again how women were empowered and had their whole view of their own sexuality changed. Some women who weren't sex workers came out to strip for their own empowerment and to go, "Hey, my sexuality is good and I'm going to enjoy it in this public way, as a way of totally validating my experience." We're talking about making sex public. That's what sex work is, taking this private sector oppressive shit, and knocking it down. From time immemorial people doing things in a public way has been a vehicle for them to break through the imprisonment of their mental attitude. That is a universal process for people to empower themselves. For sex to become public can be very empowering on a personal level. You can break through all these barriers about, "I'm bad, I'm dirty, and I'm sexually inadequate." It exposes our self-bigotry.

Have you danced for women only? ~ Yes, and I find dancing for women, generally speaking, much more rewarding than dancing for men. The women are more involved in the total aesthetic of what you're doing. They don't want to just see pussy. However, some women behave very much like men and try to boss you around. That's totally disgusting to me. That's the choice. You can behave that way or not.

If social and economic equality for women became a reality would some women still dance? ~ The tradition of sacred erotic dancing has always occurred. Women for women, women for men, men for men, men for women. That's a part of life. I just graduated from college magna cum laude and I haven't found a different job that's going to pay my rent.

Would commercial sex work exist in your ideal society? ~ I consider my work prostitution and that is not a negative thing. I choose not to have body contact but I certainly respect those who do it in a way that's nourishing.

As with many women who sleep with men for money, my job is not necessarily just sex. A lot of the men are really more interested in getting an emotional experience than just getting their rocks off. That's a big part of the work, being with someone who maybe doesn't have someone in their life. They want to be intimate, not so much in a sexual way as, "Hey, can you talk to me for five minutes? And can I talk to you?" The deprivation of that in this society is appalling.

For many people it is impossible to conceive of anyone choosing to dance as you do. Why do you think that is? ~ At one time it was not something that I would consider because I was afraid that I would be used by men, that I would be a victim in some way. It's not the experience at all. Sex is really private for a lot of people, for me as well, but eroticism is not necessarily private. Sexual energy exists everywhere, at all hours of the day in all situations. To pretend that it doesn't is denial. It's a part of life just like any other state of being. I say it's fine for me to do this in a public place, because it happens everywhere.

Many people paint female sex workers as among the most obvious victims of male domination and declare that if you don't see yourself as such, you are suffering from "false consciousness" and "delusions of the oppressed." What is your response to that? ~ We're all oppressed, we're all part of the system. Men are oppressed because they are seen as the money makers. They're not supposed to be emotional, and their sexual performance is separate from their emotional experience. That's pretty oppressive. Whether I participate in the sex industry or not doesn't make the dynamic that the sex industry is part of go away. I find it very empowering to be able to make money to pay my bills. If you are in a situation where you can't, you're oppressed. It isn't just about sexuality, it's about so many things. If sex workers are the most obvious, it's because the sexual power gender relations are *undisguised*. It's going on in every aspect of society. We are not any more victims, we're all victims of this situation. Sex workers are no more victims than their customers. I don't choose to use the word victim because I don't experience myself as a victim. I experience myself as accepting the situation and being empowered as best I can.

Why do people use sexually explicit media? ~ Our society is so oppressive and sex is one arena where people know their energy can be liberated. They can do it in their own home. There's no way they can experience or show that kind of feeling and energy and interchange anywhere else in their daily lives. It's still a place where our animal selves, our feeling selves, our higher selves have a relationship, have a communication with our whole self. It's one of the last places where they can have that. The theater is another. Sexually explicit media have been going on forever, but the emphasis on it these days is because there's a greater demand.

Has the sexually explicit media you've seen accurately portrayed humans and their sexual relations? ~ Yes and no. I don't like watching straight porn, for the most part, because it's so staged. The dicks are on top for the most part. It's always filmed so you can see people's genitalia in an arranged fashion. I find that extremely false and very uninspiring. What I find more erotic is something that's more suggestive, that blends feeling, emotion, and images in ways that conjure up energy, not just sexually explicit genitalia. There is some good pornography out there.

Aesthetically some of the lesbian porn has a lot to be desired, but some of it is really wonderful. It's raw and into life, as well as just really sexual. *On Our Backs* is a good magazine and getting better. Their stories, poems, pictures, and photos are not just representing the genitalia. They're artistically done and that's exciting. It's revolutionary that we have a magazine like that. It's an incredible sign of women taking their sexuality back and saying, "Yeah, this is good. This is for me. My sexuality is not just here for men."

At what age do you think people should be allowed to view pictures of human genitalia? ~ Well, I plan on walking around nude in front of my kids from day one. That's me. That's life. And there's nothing wrong with it. What I wouldn't want my children to see is pictures of people being violent in a sexual way or pictures where women are just submissive sexually.

Do you think any sexually explicit media should be banned? ~ Snuff films are out. The very thought of it makes me ill. Child pornography. Young children are not prepared, generally speaking, to deal with their sexuality in an intense interactive way. It's not healthy. It's important to have a sense of yourself so that you can be in a position to say what you need and what you want. It's really fucked up to put children in that position.

At the outset, the Meese Commission declared that it intended to contain the spread of pornography. At its conclusion, the Commission, like most others, could not define pornography. Yet it recommended the prosecution, fining, and jailing of people who produce, distribute, and consume it. What do you think of the Commission and its recommendations? ~ I think Edwin Meese is one of the lower IQ people currently in the government. It's phenomenal that he ever got there. The Commission is ridiculous. The sex industry has been coming out of the red light district, has been more available to people. Sexuality is more acceptable and that is an unleashing of energy, of creative force in people, that is totally damaging to the precepts that our government is based on: "Keep the public and private sectors separate." Not just the public and private sectors in a business sense, but in a psychological sense. You have to behave a certain way in public, and in private there are certain things that cannot be revealed. If you're trying to keep society in an oppressive state, where people have total nonintegration of their emotional, physical, and mental selves, you want to keep sexuality inaccessible. I think that's an underlying force in our society.

Why do you think the government shows virtually no concern with violence in the mainstream media? ~ We live in a culture of war. War is constantly being promoted by the United States all over the world. Naturally we want to prime our children from an early age to see themselves as good soldiers, and teach them that the way of being in power is to accumulate as much as you can of another person's possessions. Whether that's their country, their home, or things. This culture is perpetuating that ideal. Under these circumstances, violence on TV is something they wouldn't want to remove, because it is part of our world view.

Phoenix, you, Jackie, and I were interviewed by Geraldo Rivera for his TV special, "Modern Love." Tell us about the interview, the interviewer, and the finished show. ~ I had never seen Geraldo Rivera's show. I had this idea that he was going to come to the interview having researched the things that we're talking about here. Geraldo Rivera came to our interview with the most bigoted, uneducated, thoughtless questions. He asked me how I felt about being a "dirty dancer." I laughed. I told him that I wasn't a "dirty dancer" and did he think that sex was dirty. He totally fell over himself in embarrassment, was stunned, and didn't know what to say. His approach came completely from a male-bigoted, "You are a victim as a sex worker," point of view. I was naive, I realize in retrospect. It was appalling.

I saw the finished show and, of course, he did not include our interview. It showed sex workers as victims. It showed him behaving in an almost contemptuous way about AIDS with some very incorrect information. He did make an attempt to be positive about the sex industry as a place where people could experience their sexuality and intimacy in the face of the AIDS epidemic. But, he made it sound like it was just an alternative to a greater evil rather than something that has total integrity and a natural place, which it has.

How are sex work and sex workers portrayed in the mainstream media? ~ Sex workers are still portrayed as victims and people who are likely to get killed in "Miami Vice", et cetera. It's an archetype that is still very strong. On "L.A. Law" I saw a story about a woman lawyer who was defending a prostitute who had been raped. She was portrayed as getting over emotional about the case, but ultimately the man was convicted of rape. The prostitute was portrayed as down and out, and not in control. She was weak and wasting her life. I know a lot of prostitutes who are not that way.

Some people argue that humans are born with a sex drive and after that our sexuality is socially constructed, produced through our experiences. How do you think human sexuality is shaped? ~ The social shaping forces are very strong. I did some study on this question in school. I learned that hermaphrodites who have chosen both operatively and socially to be either a boy or a girl could have gone the other way. That was really illuminating. I started seeing how gender is something that's socially occasioned. I believe that we are born with certain energies and that we make choices as to our environment, our sexual and social conditioners, as to what our gender is, and also our sexuality.

Are there a wide variety of sexualities produced. ~ If you choose a different course, that's unusual. But some of the sexuality produced is in reaction to our social conditioning and the oppression that we experience. Once again, people make choices; the State and the patriarchy don't have absolute control.

Do you think the State tries to manage sexuality? ~ People in the military are kicked out for sleeping with people of the same sex. There are codes of sexual behavior in public. The change in laws regarding interracial marriage occurred only a few years ago. These are State policies. Granted the ERA had its problems, but the fact that we don't have our equal rights acknowledged by the State in 1992 – I can barely conceive of that! So, if we're going to have our rights monitored or not monitored by the State, as the case may be, certainly our sexuality is monitored closely.

What do men and women have in common sexually? ~ We have a basic need to share and communicate with each other, and that's what's behind any kind of sexuality. We want to get close, break down our barriers, to not be isolated and alone. And we want to expand our view of our world.

Some people seem to think that sexual pleasure without procreation is a threat to society. Is it? ~ Well, once again, that's seeing sex as solely utilitarian. What about imagination? People have been conditioned to see imagination as a secondary part of life. It's not. When people experience pleasure they experience personal empowerment, and that's a threat to the State.

Do you think gratification of sexual needs diminishes anti-social impulses? ~ Being sexual opens me up, it doesn't make me anti-social.

Feminism as it emerged in the early 1970's had as basic tenets sexual exploration and sexual self-determination. Subsequent exploration has led to intense debate over female sexual identity and behavior. How do you define female sexuality? ~ It can be a myriad of experiences. I know so many women with so many different kinds of sexuality. There's no one answer for that question.

Are there any sexual behaviors you think women should not engage in? ~ My first reaction is I wouldn't want women to participate in behavior that would be degrading or violent or abusive towards them. On the other hand, I've experienced that in consensual situations for women to act out their fantasies of being degraded or on a less powerful end of the relationship, if it indeed is a true sexual *fantasy*, can be very healing for them because they see and confront that part of themselves.

In the late 1940's American writer Philip Wylie saw equally strong tendencies to incite and constrain the erotic drive as pervasive in this society. He observed that they continually reinforce each other and declared, "The United States is technically insane on the matter of sex." Is his diagnosis good for today? ~ Definitely. That's a wonderfully sane and truthful comment. This is in evidence everywhere. Pornography is pushed in everything, mainstream media ads, the whole thing. It's be sexual, be sexual, be sexual. And at the same time we're trying to curb the sex industry. We're trying to constantly hide sex. My parents never talked to me about sex. It's a totally contradictory situation. I could see people growing up feeling pretty crazy. Feeling, "Well, what am I supposed to do?"

How is sexuality portrayed in the mainstream media? ~ It's portrayed as hidden. It's very innuendo oriented. No one comes up and says, "Hey, you're attractive. Hey, you're a neat person." It's like the sexual innuendos of ad campaigns where the product being sold is presented as a sexual organ. It's like, "Let's talk to each other through codified language rather than being upfront about what we want." We can never say what we want in this society, we always have to play a game. We're scared. Everything has to be fantasy because we're too afraid of dealing with each other, real emotions, and real pain.

Some people argue that there is a sexual hierarchy in the United States, with heterosexuals at the top and everyone else treated as second class citizens. Do you agree? ~ Absolutely. The only official legitimate sexuality in this country, is heterosexuality. They're doing the correct thing, and no one else is legitimate or normal.

Some people also think that non-heterosexuals should not have the same rights as heterosexuals. What do you think? ~ Being a primarily gay person, I feel like I should have as many rights as anybody else, if not more. (Laughs) It's really scary when you deal with homophobia. When someone acts like they have the official word from some all-seeing point of view, that's wrong. It's a stance from which a lot of violence issues, and we don't need that.

Is heterosexism a serious problem in the United States? ~ Certainly. Gay people comprise a large section of the population. It's not just the Bay Area. We are everywhere. It's a form of human behavior that has been going on from the beginning of time and to not see it as normal is absurd. Heterosexism is just as old, and it's time to get over it.

Friends of mine just came back from the first Gay Pride Day in Iowa. What was really sad was the large gay population they met after the parade, who wouldn't march in their own town. They said they didn't want to experience all the flack they were going to get. Oppression is a really, really sad issue.

How does society respond to the outspoken, sensuous person? ~ In line with what Philip Wylie said. By oohing and aahing and congratulating that person, and, at the same time slapping them and saying, "Nymphomaniac."

What have you learned about people through sexuality? ~ How letting yourself experience all the parts of yourself is incredibly empowering because you're living in truth.

What would a sexually positive society look like? ~ Radiant, glowing, beaming people. Really. The Adam and Eve stuff, women are evil, keep them under control, keep sex a secret, don't tell your children, and all that, creates incredible neuroses. That neurosis is in every area of life. Guys on the job are harassing women on the street. A woman can't get hired because she's a woman. All that stuff comes down to our sexual ideas about how people should be, where they should be, what role they should take, and how it should be assured. If we didn't have any of that and people were sex-positive life would look entirely different. The difference would be awesome. Crime would change. A lot of people's violence has a relationship to their general oppression, which is related to their sexual oppression, and how they're taught to oppress other people through gender and sexuality. God, it really would be like starting over.

How can we achieve that society? ~ Start by clearing out the goddamned government. (Laughs) I don't know. The changes that would have to happen are so broad. That's a scary proposition to take up. I feel like we just have to start over again in every aspect. All we can do is raise children who don't have these ideas of separation from themselves and other people, and speak out about it. If a lot of people were doing that, and I think a lot of people are right now, that's a powerful force to be reckoned with.

Do women play a part in the creation of male sexuality? ~ A man can say, "Hey, come over here and do this." And I can go, "I'm sorry, but we don't take orders here." That's directly confronting his stance on how things should be. He has to deal with that if he wants interaction, he's got to change.

How do you think batterers and rapists are created? ~ People feel incredibly frustrated with their lives or how somebody is treating them. We're told not to talk about our fears, so things build up, build up, build up, and then people lash out. There's economic frustration in there too. Also I've read about boys having no relationship with their mother. Rapists aren't getting what they want and they don't know how to create it.

Are there feminist men? ~ Yeah, there are real feminist men. They're not men who when it comes down to it just want to get something out of it. There are men who are gentle and aware of themselves. They can be themselves and share their thoughts and feelings. They don't have to have power held over them by women. That's not being a feminist. If that's acting on a fantasy, that's fine. But if that's the way you live your life, that's a problem. So just being gentle is not what being a feminist is. It means being able to communicate your feelings and stand on equal ground.

What is their relationship to sexually explicit media? ~ Well, if I use Tim as our prime example, I'd say that he enjoys sexually explicit media as a feminist man just as much as I do as a feminist woman. The relationship to sexually explicit media can be vital and active as long as it's not degrading to the women or themselves.

What do you think the future holds for relations between men and women? ~ Continuing change. Women are not going to go back to being subservient. Hopefully we'll move toward a place where men will look at themselves a little more willingly. There will be more openness to each others' experience.

If rape and sexual assault ended today how would your life change? ~ I wouldn't be watching my butt every minute I walk down the street, which is a major component of life as a female on this planet, at this time. There would be a tremendous sense of relaxation. The fear that's generated creates a lot of tension, a lot of disharmony. That kind of relaxation is a fertile plain on which to create a whole new consciousness. That consciousness naturally evolves as a result of letting go of fear and negativity. I've experienced that.

What is the source of inequality between men and women? ~ The source is a quest to accumulate power and wealth. Somewhere along the line men got the idea that wealth and power belonged to them, and that everyone else had to serve. It goes back to a time when cultures were transformed from more egalitarian structures. Settled cultures experienced encroachment from other cultures, and had to defend themselves, defend the land. Men took this role. They took booty from people who attacked them and gained more power. From there things escalated.

Feminist people have long observed a system of male domination in the United States and exerted considerable effort to overturn it. What strategies do you think have been effective? ~ The first feminists really can't be under-estimated, the current that they started. They were effective at political lobby-ing, getting the vote. There are also political efforts by people not involved in "politics", who are trying to change things on a very personal level, like the dynamics in their relationships. That's just as important and powerful.

What do you consider to be the failures of the women's movement in the United States? ~ The lesbian separatist movement has really gone over-board. However, I can't deny that there is a powerful aspect to separatism: it creates separate space for women to heal. And that's a primary issue, for women to control their own space. But to not deal with men doesn't empower women ultimately. Men currently have a great deal of power and are half of the population!

I think of Andrea Dworkin. She's created a new arm of the fascist move-ment. The kind of prohibitions she wants put on sexuality and expression are totally outrageous. She's an anathema for the movement. She says that the only way she can be empowered is to take away her own expression, to con-fine it, to control it, and then to make it secretive. She says that sexual inter-actions with men are "wrong" and "bad". Unfortunately she's well known and gets published.

And what about housewives? I resent calling women who don't have jobs, housewives, like they're one kind of person. That's sick. There are all kinds of women whose needs are not addressed by the movement. Mainly upper-class white women's needs have been addressed. "We've got to get into the workforce and get corporate," as if that's liberation. When you have a man's role in a man's world, that's fine, but don't pretend that that's the only way to do something. To me, that's disempowering. A lot of this comes down to analyzing our approach to the materialist pressures that we're under, how we can create ways of supporting ourselves that challenge the patriarchal struc-ture which is economically focused.

What future do you see for the women's movement in the United States? ~ More communities are being addressed by the movement now. Sex workers are certainly being a hell of a lot more vocal. Here we are doing it right now! This was unheard of until a few years ago, that's powerful. Suddenly, a lot of people are learning about us.

You can't look at the future of the women's movement without looking at the state of the world. It's really scary. There is a sense of an incredible lack of security. People are so caught up in accumulating things. Let's face it, it's the world's focus. I think women are becoming more spiritual and that they are a powerful vehicle to bring spirituality back into the world. The most powerful, effective way to help is by spirituality being connected to our way of supporting ourselves. It's got to be connected to what we're doing on a daily basis. It can't be something esoteric.

Anti-censorship feminists have emerged who believe some sexually explicit media reflects and reinforces the oppression of women, but disagree with the pro-censorship feminists' view that sexually explicit media is the cause of women's oppression. They argue that the causes of women's oppression are much deeper and precede the mass production and distribution of sexually explicit media by centuries. What is your point of view? ~ I totally agree with the anti-censorship feminists.

Where do you think sexually explicit media should be placed on the movement agenda? ~ That people are totally alienated and not communicating face to face sensually, makes it important. Also the connection of sex workers to a Shamanic healing tradition is important. For it not to be addressed and not be a major component, just as the body is a major component in experience, would be a mistake. If you don't address the body as a vehicle, you're lost, as far as I can tell. If I can be totally blunt, Andrea Dworkin is physically one of the most unhealthy looking people I have seen in my life. Clearly she's not in harmony with her physical self. I think that says a lot for her politics, because our politics come out of our personal experience. That's just the way it is. We still experience things through the "I".

You told us how the women's movement affected your sexuality. Has it affected you in other ways? ~ The movement has affected my entire life. My sexuality is not separate, as I keep reiterating, from my mind, from my spirit. Living at this time and being a woman, even if you're politically unaware, you cannot overestimate how important the women's movement has been. The aspects of the movement that I agree with, and the aspects I don't agree with, have all been empowering. The fact that I can go to college and take courses in feminism is incredible. Women who are a little younger than me and many my age take that for granted. They don't have a clear perspective. My father saw a PBS special on the British suffragettes and told me, "Those women did so much for you."

Do you think our constitutional guarantee of free speech includes sexual speech? ~ Yes. And I think the jurists who rule otherwise need some serious sexual activity in their lives. They need to go down on themselves several times a day and maybe their bodies will wake up and they'll get hip to the fact that it's no big deal. Sexuality is no big deal, and it's really important. It's one of the few ways that people really communicate.

Tell us what you know about AIDS and the impact that it is having on your life and society. ~ AIDS has changed every single person who is aware of it, in a major way. I don't know if we'll ever be the same, if we'll ever find a cure. I think more than twice about sleeping with anyone. It's generating a lot of fear for people, forcing them to deal with themselves. There's a huge community of people who have to deal with their mortality, who have to heal themselves. There *are* people healing themselves of AIDS. That's real. It's happening by doing the most incredibly deep soul searching possible.

There's a book by someone, about his experience with his lover. They are in a state of remission, their T-cell counts have been normal for two years. People have to process all the denial stored in their body/mind.

Do you think that this society will confine those who test HIV positive in spite of the medical evidence that it is not casually transmitted? ~ Fuckin' A. It's possible. In California they've tried and been beaten down every time, but they're continuing to try. The whole thing just sucks.

What future do you see for erotic theater and erotic dancers? ~ I don't think it's ever going to go away. It's going to have to accommodate to the times, which are very conservative right now. We're dealing with that major force trying to put us under the rug. It's sad that society creates sexuality as something that's separate, taboo. These theaters are the only place that sex in a public way can happen in this culture at this time.

LUSTY LIPPS

*I'M GOING TO STAND UP ON A BUILDING
WITH A LOUD SPEAKER AND SAY,
PLEASE TALK ABOUT SEX!*

Part of the promotion for your show says, "Live Nude Dancing, Lovely Lusty Ladies, Naked Naughty Nasty." Is this a good description of who you are and how you perform at work? ~ It's a very good description of how I work it. (Laughs) Sometimes I'm not totally nude, but I'm exposing myself. I don't think they're looking at the nice little outfit, but maybe they are. Nasty, naughty...(laughs) yes, that's what I am. (Laughs) Nasty and naughty!

What were you told was your job? ~ I was told dancing, that's all. I learned by observing but I danced my own style. I just got up there and did it.

Were you told that the men masturbate? ~ No, I wasn't. (Laughs) I WAS NOT. (Laughs) But I had an idea about what would be going on. I was put up there, and there's a penis with a hand around it. (Laughs) Yanking it. It doesn't bother me, it's nature. I liked it just as much as he liked looking at me. It wouldn't make a difference if I was told or wasn't told, I'm still into what I'm doing.

Describe your first experience on stage. ~ It was kinda weird, all of these men looking at my naked body, but as they was lookin' and enjoying it, I got with them and said, "Yeah, they like what I'm doing." I felt *goood* about it after about...five minutes. I did what would turn them on, and what turn me on is their smile and responses. It was great.

When you were hired were you asked to work on certain aspects of your performance? ~ Yes. Stop talking too much. (Laughs) Stop being distracted. But I told them, "Hey, this is me, I'm not gonna change." (Laughs) I was told to concentrate on my customers.

Describe how you dance, display, and touch your body during your performance. ~ I wish you had a video camera! (Laughs) I dance exotic, erotic, and x-rated. Sometimes I get into the Soul Train mood. I play with my breasts, pinch my nipples, running my fingers through my pubic hair...God, I wish you had a video camera! (Laughs) I'm licking my lips, the whole works, to make me feel good as well as the person on the other side.

What sexual depictions do you perform? ~ I perform head jobs, the doggie style. They call me flat back, laying on your back with your legs open, holding your breasts together with a man's penis to go between 'em. Hey, I do it all 'cause I like it all. (Laughs) Do it in the butt, the whole works. (Laughs) Wherever there's a hole, put it there, baby. (Laughs) I'm for real. If it'll fit, put it there. (Laughs) Yeah.

Does your performance contain elements of dominance and submission? ~

I can be dominating at times, but a lot of times, we dominate together. I say bite my cheek, my butt, it turns me on. "Bite my ass", make me say "Yesss." (Laughs) I expect him to tell me somethin' to do too, because it makes me feel good. I submit and be dominating at the same time. It makes it more fun and relaxing. But, if he wants me to dominate the whole thing, yeah, I can do it. It won't be no problem, kiss my toes, suck me. (Laughs)

Do you test your power to arouse? ~ Yeah, I com'on with a little walk, bat my eyes, lick my lips and see if I still got it. (Laughs) I ask'em "Did your dick get hard?" (Snaps her finger) I test my power when I'm not appealing to myself. I don't go to my man, I go to somebody different, 'cause he think I got it anyway. (Laughs)

Eye contact with the customers is very important to some dancers. Is it for you? ~ Naw, it's not important to me. (Laughs) If they turn me on I'll look.

How much of your performance is you and your sexuality and how much is persona? ~ (Laughs) All of it's for real. The only difference is where I'm at. If one of the guys was on stage, I'd say sure, why not? (Laughs) It's nothing fake about what I do up there sexually, 'cause I'm actually showing them how I make love, it's me.

Why did you choose the stage name you use? ~ Because everybody used to talk about my lips! God, you got big lips. So I said, "Shidd, I'm gonna call myself Lusty Lipps." My Mom helped me pick out the name. Gotsta have'em lusty. (Laughs)

How do you use costuming and makeup? ~ Only thing I wear is lip gloss. Costuming...I prefer g-strings and teddys. And mini-skirts. A lot of men, in my opinion, like a woman to tease. I'm good at that. I walk around sexy and show 'em it's nice and tight, exposin' myself, teasin' them, instead of giv'em all in one shot.

Do drugs play a part in your performance? ~ Nope...I do not use drugs at all. I just came out like this. (Laughs) My drug is Now and Laters, potato chips and grape soda, that's it.

On stage music plays almost continuously. Describe the variety and part it plays in your performance. ~ The variety is heavy metal, rock, and slow music. I can dance to almost anything except heavy metal. Slow ballads, I like to do floor shows and get into it sexually. I giv'em all them moves and mak'em think, yeah, she's on top of me, or he's on top of me. Some men don't want to hear all that fast music. With the fast I do act the fool up there sometimes. With slow music I feel much better, the quiet storm. The music does have a big part in it.

The stage is covered with mirrors ceiling to floor. What role do they play in your work? ~ They play a good role. You wanna see every side of your body, you might have a flaw on your ass that don't suppose to be there. Lookin' good and lookin' in the mirror can make you feel good. Just look in the mirror and say, "Yeah." (Laughs) The customers love it 'cause they can look in all the mirrors to catch whatever move they want to see.

Describe the interaction and commentary among the dancers on stage. ~ (Laughs) Most of the dancers that I dance with, either talking about how we gon' have sex with our guys, or how big is the dicks, and we don't like 'em this big, and whose man done fucked who, and who's gonna help us fuck our man. (Laughs) I don't think it's nothin' else that we talk about, but that.

Is there competition among the dancers on stage? ~ No, because they're all dancing the way they feel. It's no competition for me, 'cause I dance how I want, regardless what anybody say. I'm gonna do whatever I wanna do. Their way of dancing, is *their* way, I'm not gonna tell them..."Hey, you should dance like me", or "Dance like this because that don't look cool." For all I know, I could be the worse dancer, whatever I think they're doin' wrong, they could be good, in other people's eyesight. I just do what I feel is making the men sexually aroused. If they feel what they are doing is making the men sexually aroused, the men love it, I love it. No competition.

Is there humor on stage? ~ (Laughs) *Yes there is*! The customers are very humorous; if they're not, I try and make 'em be with sexual jokes.

Is the myth of the perfect body perpetuated here? ~ Not in every man's eye, no. I don't think the perfect body is necessary for this type of job. A lot of women have that "sex appeal", they can just stand there and get a man hard, get him aroused by a look and how sensual they are. They say, "Fuck they body, this woman just moves nice." It's how you approach a man. He don't even look at your body, look at your face to get his dick hard and say, "Yeahhhh, that's the woman for me, yeah, she got it." Somehow it's not all about the body. Some men look at a woman with a perfect body and say, "She don't got shit, just a body. I'm not lookin' for that, I'm lookin' for somebody to get my dick hard." The managers are not really body conscious, if they were a lot of the dancers wouldn't be there. (Laughs) I like that, because they shouldn't be body conscious, 'cause a lot of the women got that "look", to make a man drip.

Do you ever become aroused by what you are doing and what is happening around you on stage? ~ Shit, yeah! (Laughs) Oh, baby...don't leave. I look at them and say, mmm, hmm. If their ass attract me, I tell'em to turn around, "Shit, let me see what you got." (Laughs) Oh, yeah. Gettin' hot, it's nature, shit, if I didn't, I think somethin' be wrong with me. (Laughs) Shit, yeah, I likes dat, men make me hot. (Laughs)

Do you ever have sexual fantasies during your performance? ~ No, I *am* their sexual fantasy. (Laughs) Givin' them their fantasy, that's my fantasy. Whatever their fantasy is, I'm there to fulfill it.

Do you ever wish you could be having direct sexual contact with the customers? ~ No, because I have a mate that I'm already sexual with. But I wouldn't say I would never do it. (Laughs)

What can you do on stage that you can't do off stage? ~ (Laughs) Look at the customers and their dicks. On stage you can take off your clothes, open your legs and say, "Look at this, look what *I* got." You can't do this out in the street because *it's the law.* If it wasn't the law I'm sure everybody'd be sittin' there with their legs open, "Hey, look at this, yeah." But that's just the way it is, somethin' that you have to accept. I would like to *change the goddamn law!* (Laughs)

What won't you do on stage? ~ I won't make love to a woman on stage, but anything else, yeah, I'd do it. If she wanna make love to me, yeah, I'd sit back, "Go ahead baby, shoot your best shot!"

What are you prohibited from doing on stage? ~ Being verbally abusive to customers. We're not allowed to touch the other dancers' private parts and verbally abuse them. But we have had accidents. (Laughs) One time *I* got caught by management. I touched a woman's breast to arouse a customer.

Do you dance for co-workers and friends? ~ I dance for friends, I haven't danced for co-workers. I danced for the guy that I'm with. Shoot, it gets me excited, and wet, and ready to roll! (Laughs) I *will* dance for co-workers, it's just that I haven't. Dance for the management, for anybody who wanna see me dance. Dance for a dog, shit, as long as he's lookin', yeah, "You like this move?" (Laughs)

Do you ever do sex education on stage? ~ Yes, but with a sense of humor. Sex education is showing all the good spots for me. I'll ask them have they ever made love to a woman chewing gum. I have with a man and lemme' tell you, I love it. For a man to chew gum and pop it in my ear, shit yeah, it just turns me on. It's givin' them hints of things you try with a woman they haven't tried, things a woman might like. Some women don't like to say what they like, it's just too kinky. But, shit, slap peanut butter on my pussy and eat it off. (Laughs) Yeah. That's sex education for you. Gonna teach you how to do it, make love to a woman.

How does having your period affect your performance? ~ When I have cramps it affects it a lot, I don't feel like doin' anything. It's just those three days that I sit in there with my legs crossed, my hand on my shoulder, lookin' at'em. Seein' your period, that'd turn some men on, but that's what you can't do on stage. If it was allowed, it would be no problem.

I was quite surprised when I first heard that healing occurs here, women healing themselves, each other, and customers. Tell us what you know about this. ~ I feel that I heal them by relaxing them. When they think they have to go out and take pussy from a woman who don't want to give it up, there is a place that they can come. We give it to'em, not physically, but mentally. I feel that it saves a lot of women out there that can get sexually abused by some of the men that come in here. I feel I'm doing a good job by making them relax and givin' them the good stuff that they feel they would have to go and hurt a women to get, which I wouldn't want to see. So, come in here and pay a quarter, babay, you can cum all you want, look at it all you want. I'm healing in that way, I'm not healing myself, I'm already healed.

Have you had any transcendent moments on stage? ~ All the customers that I dance for takes me out there.

Do you ever feel caged or wish you could cover up? ~ Naw, you have the freedom to come and go. It's not like you *have* to do something you don't want to do. Actually I wish I was caged with the men inside there, you know. (Laughs) If I wanted to cover up I'd have to go out in the street. I feel good about *uncovering* myself. I love to show my body. I like to show my lips, my pubic hair and my ass. I love it, love every minute of it. (Laughs) It's the way I came out, with nothin' on, so why should I cover up? (Laughs) Let the fresh air hit my naked body.

Many of the dancers who work here say that they prefer this closed type of stage and see it as safe and fun because of the absence of physical contact with the customers. How do you feel? ~ I like this too, because a lot of men can get really abusive. If it was open, they could grab you. With my temper, I'd done knock one of the fuckers out. (Laughs) They can touch on the window all they want, and I can touch on the window too. It's in their mind, they actually think they're touching us, so it makes them feel better.

Describe your performance at its best and worst. ~ At my best, I'm never sittin' down, I'm all around, puttin' on a hot show that a lot of men look at. Just being hot. Floor movements, close-ups, being sensual. At my worst, I'm just sittin' there lookin' at them, folding my arms up and seeing what they got to offer me. Being a total bitch, not doin' nothin'.

Describe the customers. ~ Hell, how can you describe 'em. They're all different races, colors, sizes, shapes, form and fashion. I love'em all. Some could be assholes, and you got to determine them the way you want 'em to be, which usually works. Some can be totally nice, some can be playful. I like'em all, because each one of 'em have different characters. If all of 'em came in being totally humorous at one set, and all of 'em came in bein' assholes, that would be boring to me.

The women are mostly tourists. I guess they stumbled in, they gasp, with their hand over their mouth. (Laughs) "My God!," I guess they like it, because they pop in another quarter with they mouth open. I say, "You ain't never seen a pussy before? Check in the mirror, you got the same thing I got." Most of'em be appalled at what they see another woman doin', like, "I could never do that." What the hell you come in here for, you could never do it? (Laughs) They alright, they just want to see what it's about.

Do customers leave their social roles and status behind when they come to see you? ~ The customers I dealt with never spoke to me about their social life or their job. They spoke to me about what positions they like. They left their social life out tha' way. If they thought they were better, I haven't seen it, 'cause I would tell them right off, "Get your ass off your shoulders. (Laughs) You just a man, just like this man over here that's all raggedy. Don't try to act better than nobody, 'cause you're not better than nobody. You might have a good job or somethin', but you're not better than anybody, you're still a human. So, get wit it, brother, whip your dick out, show me."

What is your favorite type of customer? ~ Erotic, exotic, and x-rated, along with me. One that can show me some motion. If he's gonna jack-off, jack-off right! (Laughs) Show me some *motion*. Someone being there with a smile on his face, happy, showin' me some response.

I won't dance for the ones that always hollerin' 'bout, "Open up your pussy lips" and all that. I don't give them nothin', the time of day, they couldn't ask me for SHIT! (Laughs) There's a certain way to ask. I make them say "Please", and then I *think* about opening my pussy for 'em. I won't dance for people who laugh at the other dancers. Why should I give them the satisfaction of dancin' for'em, when they're up here makin' smart-ass comments about the other dancers. I say, "No, go dance for yourself and look in the mirror."

Do you encounter men who you think hate women? ~ No, I haven't had any customers who hated women, at all. At least they ain't gave me no sign.

Have you ever felt it was dangerous to arouse a customer? ~ I think about it, I say, "Damn, he might want some when I get off, or he might be waitin'", but it's just a thought. I never trip on it. Cause I say, "Whatever happen, it was meant to be, whether it's night time or day time or whatever time it is."

Do you encounter violent men here? ~ No, I haven't encountered any violent men.

Do you think you've ever danced for a rapist? ~ Shit, who knows, I might have. But if I did, that's fine, too. Maybe he saw somethin' and he won't go rape a woman now, maybe he says, "I can cum better here, than goin' out raping a woman."

There are customers who come here with great regularity. What are they like? ~ (Laughs) The regulars that I have, they're *full of cum.* They know what it's about, since they've been coming here so long. They're pleasant, they're nice, they know what they want, how they want it, and they know how to ask for it. It's no problem, everybody comes out happy.

Some customers come to see certain women. Are there any who come to see you on a regular basis? ~ Yes. There's a couple that like gettin' a threesome here. They're lookin' at my ass. He's very polite, he don't even have to ask. I stick my ass to the window, they doin' their show, he's lookin' at my ass and everybody come out happy.

Single men, yes, they come and see me. Couple of 'em ask to get married, but it can't be no marriage thing. It's just for your little fantasy, to come see me arouse you. All the dancers have a male come and see them on a regular basis. I think it's good. *Real healthy.*

Do you have friends you first met as customers? ~ No.

Describe the variety of sexual behavior customers express. ~ Oh, dear. (Laughs) They bring their little tools and sexual things, such as dildos. One hand is holding his penis and the dildo is in the ass, which I think is totally their thing. It is great they can express themselves like that in front of us. It's no problem, doin' their own thing, like givin' theirselves head, and us bein' there supportin' them. "Yeah, baby that's it!" "Suck that bitch, wish it was mine you were suckin'," "You lookin' good down there." (Laughs)

I guess some of them feel the need to wear women's clothes, to feel closer. Hey, if that's yo' thing, you like it, I love it. I don't have nothin' to say about that. One man likes to smell women panties, put panties over his head. I say, "Shit, yeah baby, that's cool, I'm glad you did that." One man sucks the bananas and smash 'em against the window wit his chest, and it turns him on. He turns me on, too, when he do it. (Laughs)

So everybody has their little thang. Couples come in and make love in front of us, she'll give him head, he'll suck her...give *us* a show. I like it, I give 'em thumbs up. Shit, not too many people can express that. I think sex is a beautiful thing. I think it's great that couples are comin' in. Men get hot off'a us, and she gets off on us too, by him touchin' her. They do their little business and they get on. Everybody's happy. They leave and we sit here...NEXT!

From stage you see a lot of tongues. Describe this. ~ Most tongues that I see are usually down in the window, imaginin' suckin' somebody's penis. I'm gon' tell you, some tongues turn me on...the little waves in'em and how they wiggle. Fast tongues don't interest me at all. It's the slow, smooth ones, that go up and down and around and around. (Laughs) It's nice. It's good that they can express themselves by doin' the tongue movement. A lot of customers think stickin' out their tongue is gonna suck us over and open up our pussy, which it won't!

Describe some of the more unique encounters you've had with customers. ~ (Laughs) I've sat up there with my tampon and play with it. I'm not supposed to do that, but it turns a man on...that did turn on a customer, he said "Wow." He was gettin' into it, he had a big splash of cum. He thanked me for about two minutes. I thanked him.

There was the man givin' himself head and stickin' his penis up his butt, now that really shocked the shit out of me...(Laughs) I couldn't do nothin' but *look*! He swung it, it wasn't that hard, but, he stuck it in his asshole, and I said "Well, goddamn, baby, you don't need a woman, you can do all that by yourself."

There's the guy with the pierced dick who sticks a candle in it. I said "Shit, I'm gonna sit back and relax, I can't do shit, they doin' it for me." That was really somethin', I said, "Damn, woooooooo."

Many customers show a great deal of interest in the dancers' genitalia. Why do you think there is such great interest? ~ That's a favorite question, 'cause I don't know. They just stand there and look. In some cases, they told me they like the hair. They look at what unique things it can do. The muscles can open up and close. A lot of 'em never had the experience of lookin' in a woman's pussy to see what it's really like. If their wife won't open up for 'em, their girlfriend won't, they think we will, which, *I will*. (Laughs) It shows them all the things that's goin' on. Back to sex education.

I think you are possibly the only or preferred sexual outlet for some cus-

tomers, what do you think? ~ A lot of 'em come in and say, "This is the only way I can get release. I get the pressure off me by comin' in here and jackin'-off by the beautiful ladies."

Do customers get needs besides sexual needs met here? ~ Some of 'em don't come for sex, some of 'em come to talk about how sex can be. Some of 'em don't come there to jack-off, they just want to sit and look and relax. It's somethin' to do to pass time. Some come in to listen to the music, for all I know.

Is there a difference in the customers' behavior when they are alone or in a group? ~ Yeah. When they're alone they're much quieter and'll whip out their dick and jack-off. But when they with a group, they're tryin' to put on a front for the group they're in. If three guys came in and you get them separate they're not the assholes they pretend to be when all three of 'em are together. Together they want to put on a front to show this other guy, I'ma tell this woman to show me her pussy. They're ashamed to let their true self come out in front of their friends. I say, "Go home and think about it." Who give a shit what your friends say, your dick hard, you want to pull it out, pull it out.

What do the customers say when they speak? ~ They compliment you, ask is it alright to leave you a note. Most of 'em ask me, can I go out to dinner or somethin' like that. I say leave a note and I'm not goin' to say yes or no, because I cannot talk like this on stage. That's what they ask you, can they take you out, take you out...and *fuck* you. (Laughs) Fuck me and all that good stuff. (Laughs) I got my dick already, so I never call.

What do you say when you speak? ~ "How has your day been?" "Where'd you leave your wife?" (Laughs) I compliment them, if there is something to compliment. I ask them do they chew gum and tell them gum turns me on. I say talk dirty to me, to get 'em really goin'. They say, "Wow, what she about!" And they keep poppin' the quarters in.

Some customers experience ecstatic surprise when they first encounter the stage show. What do you think surprises them? ~ Us beautiful women and that we care. We're not there for them to get their feelins hurt. Unless they want that. That's their thing to tell us, "Hurt my feelins," and if they get off on that, it would be easy for me. Some men expect ugly women or somethin' that's totally different. Crusty feet or somethin'! Some of 'em haven't seen five pussies at one time, it shocks 'em. They go from booth to booth, and say, "Wow, I never seen this many women naked before." Well, you have now. (Laughs) So just sit back and relax.

Are you ever disturbed by the effect you have on customers? ~ (Laughs) I get disturbed if they cum when the window go down, I wanna see. (Laughs)

Sometimes a customer will leave angry or disgusted. Do you understand why? ~ No, because they haven't told me. Sometimes you can't pay much attention because you have to share yourself, and they leave before you can get to 'em. Most of mine left with a smile on their face. (Laughs)

Do you ever abuse the customers? ~ No, I don't abuse the customers at all.

Do you ever feel controlled or possessed by the customers? ~ I sure-in-the-hell don't. (Laughs) No, no, I'm controlled by me and only me. I don't share a brain with anybody but myself. So, I'm in control of myself. No, they can't control shit. The quarters don't mean shit to me. (Laughs)

When customers show disrespect the dancers can call security and have them removed. How often do you ask that a customer be removed? ~ I only had to do it once because they were botherin' the other dancers. Usually they're just young kids, who haven't seen the light yet.

Do you try to get the customers to spend? ~ When they look bored I try, so I can communicate with them. I want to see what the problem is, 'cause I'm interested. I say, "Well, come on and put some more money in, you want to see, but you look like you're scared or somethin'." Only those types of men would I try to get them to spend.

How long do you stay with a customer? ~ Sometimes me and a customer act like we're actually havin' sex, so I'm showin' the different moves before I leave. I explain to them that they're not the only one here, I have to share myself. If the windows are all covered by the girls I would stay with a customer until he reaches his needs. I'm helpin' this man reach his value. About ten or fifteen minutes is as long as it takes for a smile to be on each of our faces.

How do you feel about dancing for customers in the three booths with one-way glass? ~ Good, 'cause you can be in the window blowing kisses and they could be sticking their tongue out and you don't give a shit, because you can't see 'em. Most of 'em are shy, but that's fine. I tell 'em, "Tell me when you reach it baby." (Laughs) I say talk dirty to me. They like that, can't see each other, but yet we have this communication.

As the desired do you have power? ~ I know what I can do to get whatever I want out of a man, period. I don't consider it a power, it's just knowin' your-self. It's the same as a male.

Does this job suit you? ~ I love every minute of it. It's the best job I ever had! I was born to be a lusty lady! (Laughs)

Has doing this job affected your consciousness of your body? ~ No, it's just that I had to find a place to show it, where you wouldn't get arrested. (Laughs) I've always been aware of my body, where everything was, and what I could use it for.

Have you experienced burnout in this job? ~ Not yet.

Off stage you encounter dancers, support staff, and management. Describe the interaction and conversation that occur. ~ Some of the support staff are makin' sexual comments or sayin' "Yeah, I wish I could get that, yeah." (Laughs) Or complimentin'. Me complimentin' on one of the support staffs' ass and how good they can move their tongue. (Laughs) If the cashier is takin' his break, I'm maybe sayin' "Yeah, I wish he'd give me a little of that!" Which is really gesture, you know. It doesn't mean it has to happen. We talk about outside of work, how some people are stuck up and not lettin' their sex life go and be free. (Laughs)

Off stage it is not uncommon to hear dancers referring to each other as slut, whore, or bitch. What do these remarks mean? ~ (Laughs) Just like our regular name, to me. It just gets our attention. Somebody call me a bitch, I'll say, yeah, I'm a good bitch. I thought my name was bitch for a while, by my mother's side. Because us doin' things bad, "Bitch, this!", you know. So I don't even trip because I'm surrounded by this kind of talk. But I also respect the fact that if they don't like it, I won't say it. But I haven't come across that yet. Slut, yeah, I'm a slut, shit, why not? You tell me, why not?

Sometimes it's like a party here. Describe these occasions. ~ The people who are not high, they're havin' a good time. The people are projecting such a good feelin' and smilin', that's what makes me high. I get in the mix, she can look at my pussy and I look at her pussy. Just kickin' back and talkin' about the things we wish we could do to the support staff. (Laughs) Everybody smilin' and talkin' about who they're gonna fuck in the theater, and how good it would be, and who's the kinkiest person, yeah, I'll go for that! (Laughs) It's a good party!

Is there a difference between the male support staff and the male customers? ~ The male support staff is not behind glass. (Laughs) If the customers weren't behind glass, sure, they could touch my ass. Some of the support staff be touchin' asses. And that's not bad, it's good! (Laughs) Y'all got to let-it-all-hang-out. (Laughs)

The owner and management of this theater say they want to create a safe, nurturing, fun and profitable business. Have they succeeded? ~ They have over succeeded, if you ask me. I say, one out of ten dancers is not happy, that's good. You've still got nine that's doin' the work. It's very safe for me, but *I* nurture me, very well. It's profitable and it's fuckin' fun, yeah! (Laughs)

The owner and management also express the desire to empower people. Have you been empowered here? ~ Naw, 'cause I had it when I came. I'm self-controlled.

Describe worker/management relations. ~ I respect management's job of tryin' to support us if they see we're doin' somethin' wrong. Then again, I don't support them sayin' "Why is it wrong?, or why do you *think* it's wrong?" Fix my payroll right, and everything will be okay.

Describe the periodically scheduled dancer's meetings. ~ I tell you the main reason I go, if anybody talkin' 'bout my ass, I can defend myself. (Laughs) In the meetings they talk about the same shit. About the abuse of customers, and how you gotta take time to understand, put the shoe on the other foot. How to make the show better, bein' nice and respectful to our co-workers, bein' like a family.

Do you have job security? ~ Yes, I can go on leave and come back. It's pretty secure if you know how to keep your act together.

In response to the question "Are you exploited?" a well known dancer and erotic film star replied, "Yes and no. We don't have a union, but I like what I do." How do you answer that question? ~ I like what the fuck I'm doin'. I don't care what they think about exploitin' or not exploitin'. (Laughs) Let them give their opinions on what I'm doin'. As long as I'm happy with what I'm doin', fuck what they say.

Do you ever consider unionizing? ~ Shit, give myself a headache. I think about it, but put somebody else who knows what they would be doin' in here. I say, "Fuck it, leave me alone, I'm happy bein' this way."

Is sexism promoted or resisted in any way here? ~ I can't speak for the other women, but I don't think I'm treated as a sex object. Some of the time I think I'm treatin' the men as sex objects. The men see the most beautiful women in there, but I don't think it's sexism.

What do you feel passing customers in the hallway whom you have just danced for? ~ If they got an ass I like, I say, "Yeah, baby it looks better out here!" (Laughs) Shit, most of 'em don't even know who I am, so I fuck with them first. It don't make a difference, I'm not afraid. If I like somethin', I say "Have a nice day, I hope you enjoyed yourself." Shit, yeah, talk to me. (Laughs)

Do you ever feel in danger coming to or leaving work? ~ No, I don't even trip on that.

Do you have anger about this job? ~ I get anger if they don't let me see them cum. (Laughs)

Describe your earliest memories? ~ The earliest is when I got my yellow bike on Christmas Eve. It was great, I was six. I rode my bike and forgot about the other presents.

Describe your family and its circumstances as you remember them during your childhood. ~ I have three sisters, a brother, and Mom. My dad left early, which was good. (Laughs) I knew him for about three years. He really doesn't matter. The circumstances of my family were good, as far as I'm concerned. Mom was Mom and Dad. She worked and my oldest sister took care of me, before school. Mom worked with newspaper advertising, checking up, squaring up the newspaper. My Mom's mom was German and my grandfather is Navajo Indian. Mom's children are half black, a quarter German and a quarter Indian. I don't know where my mom and dad met, I was never too interested in askin'.

What kind of child were you? ~ Good! (Laughs) A sickly child for a while, a homebody child. I mainly kept to myself and took it easy. I was always bein' spoiled, so, I was a sweet child. I was very even minded and easy going.

Describe your relationship with your siblings. ~ I was the youngest. The closest was four years older, we're still very close. The older ones, we're close, but not as close as me and the younger one. There's eight years between us. Me, the one over me, and the one over her, played together, sometimes. Talked rather, there wasn't too much playin' because they were so many years older than me, and they went into their own thing.

Describe your relationship with your mother. ~ She's my friend, my sister. My mother is great, I can talk to her about *anything*. I mean, *anything*.

Were you raised under a particular religious tradition? ~ No.

Describe your childhood play and friendships. ~ From the age of eight, to maybe ten, we played "hide and go get it." It's like hide and seek, but when you find somebody, you get a 'little bit.' (Laughs) You dry hump, rather. (Laughs) Nothin' happened, nobody bust a nut. (Laughs) At least that I can remember. I guess we was experimentin'. We played "two square" with a ball, hittin' the ball back over the line with your hands.

I had a lot of friends, mostly male, two females. We were all good friends at our school. At lunch time we'd slip out to the store, get some little goodies. We shared things in the boys' bathroom, each other's body parts. That was great. We enjoyed it and we didn't get caught. We were all doin' good in school and we all said we were goin' to continue to do good in school. Just have our little fun during the periods of recess, which we did.

Describe your childhood school experience. ~ It was great, kindergarten through fifth grade, because I had Chinese and English class. It was plenty to do. I really enjoyed Chinese. I know how to count and write the numbers in Chinese, but all the other stuff, I kinda' lost because I didn't keep it up. (Laughs) I liked the homework, I enjoyed school, period.

Describe your teachers and classmates. ~ My first grade teacher, I hated her. (Laughs) She was mean. You couldn't do nothin', you couldn't write on your paper when she talked or she would spank your hand with a ruler, or yank your ear. My classmates were alright. I didn't have any problems with classmates, just her.

What were you taught about human sexuality by your mother? ~ Everythang...my mother never hid nothin', whatever we wanted to know, she told us. When I wanted to know how a woman got pregnant she said, "Well, a man's penis goes inside..."; she just tells the whole thing. Instead of talkin' about the birds and bees, she talk about the dick and the pussies, 'cause that's what it actually is. She tried to explain orgasms to me, but she said you have to find out by yourself. She said, "I knew it felt good to me." And I said, "Well, yeah," I was all into it. She explained how a man ejaculates, what it looks like, how big the penises can be, how small they can be, how wide, how...all this. It's great, she didn't hide anything from me.

Did you receive information about human sexuality in grade school? ~ Nope.

Was there nudity in your home? ~ Yeah...everybody walked around nude. It didn't bother me any.

Were you ever punished due to sexual expression? ~ No, Mom never caught me.

Were you sexually abused as a child? ~ Nope. I wish I was. (Laughs)

Did incest occur in your family? ~ No.

What were you taught about human relationships in your family? ~ I was taught that if you felt shit was right for you, go for it. You have to make your own decisions, whether it's right or wrong. I was taught to be careful. My mother never forced me to do anything she wanted me to do. She always gave me advice, and if I wanted to take it, fine, if I didn't, fine. I was taught to follow my feelins' in a relationship and if I thought it sucks, then it sucks.

Were you taught to look good to attract and be chosen by a man? ~ No, no, 'cause I look good anyway. (Laughs) I was just born with it!

Were you taught to value truth? ~ I was taught to speak the truth, regardless.

Did your mother teach you that you could have power, choice? ~ No, she didn't really talk about power or how much power a person has. It was just makin' that decision for yourself. She told me you can control a person, 'cause that person wants to be controlled by you, because of the feelins' they have for you. Not because you have this power over them. I was always taught, you could be whatever you wanna be, how you wanna do it, how you wanna present yourself, you can do that, because you're your own person.

What effect did your body changing have on you? ~ I went to a doctor one time because I had a lump in my tit, well, it wasn't tits yet. Mom took me and said, "She has lumps." He said, "Well, her breasts are starting to grow." (Laughs) Mom said, "Oh!" I said, "Wow." I used to look in the mirror all the time and say, "Yeah Mom, I think I need a bra." Which I didn't. (Laughs) I was happy that I was gettin' breasts, and gettin' hips, it was interesting and fun watchin' myself grow.

Describe your adolescent sexuality. ~ I wasn't too interested in boys at that time. I was into sports, doin' my homework, and havin' fun with my mom. No masturbation, no more playin' "hide and go get it," that played out. No sexual stuff was goin' on.

How did you first discover and use the ability to arouse? ~ At about fifteen or sixteen I noticed I could turn men on. I go around, tryin' to flaunt it, walkin' front of 'em and they say, "Yeah, oh, yeah." You start gettin' feelins', you start gettin' hot. You look down and say, "Damn, I have somethin' new, my pants are gettin' wet." (Laughs) It was great, I liked it, a lot.

Have you ever been pregnant? ~ I was pregnant at 17 and had a baby when I was 18 and out of school. Pregnancy was nice, it was fun. I have two children. I was pregnant three times. The second time, I had a miscarriage. It wasn't no fourth time, because I got my tubes tied.

Did you receive information about human sexuality in high school? ~ In junior high I did, but not high school. It was mainly talkin' about how you can get pregnant, but not really gettin' down into it. My mom already explained it to me, and the films were totally opposite, bein' more discreet, not really puttin' it out. You had to use your imagination and put it together. So it was really of no interest to me, 'cause I wanted to see the whole thing, a penis entering a vagina. It was just boring. I wanted to see the actual body parts moving – together – what they could do. Show me somethin'. (Laughs) Yeah.

Describe your first exposure to sexually explicit media and its impact on you. ~ The first time I saw a porno movie I was about 17. I already had sex when I was sixteen. The books didn't do anything for me, but the movies get my pants wet. (Laughs)

Describe your high school years. ~ I never dated anybody in my school, period. I didn't want a boy, I wanted a man. (Laughs) I was basically, goin' to school and comin' home, doin' my work, and playin' basketball. Never hung around female friends, 'cause they wasn't 'bout nothin', always tryin' to steal somebody boyfriend.

When I was sixteen I dated a 33-year-old man, he was my first "piece." (Laughs) It went on for a little while, I wasn't serious with him. It was just a nice friendship. I didn't want a commitment at the age of sixteen, I just wanted to experience – fuckin'. It was nice. I also dated a 32-year-old guy and I screwed him too. I had curfews and all that, but any time I could spend with him, I did.

Describe your relationship with your family during those years. ~ My mom was great. I hated history, so she did it for me, just the history, 'cause it's not goin' to help me out anywhere I'm gettin' a job. I did my own math, and we read the English together. My sisters helped me out, I didn't really have to do anything, just sit there and listen. (Laughs) My brother, he was in his own little world out there, on a "mission." If I'd call him and say I needed him, he would always come. But, as far as bein' around the house, no, he was always into what's happenin', he was in his own little field. My family was very supportive towards me. Everybody was supportive toward each other. It was great. Everybody understood where I was comin' from and I understood them, so there was no problem.

What was your first job? ~ Workin' with my English teacher in her office. Filing, answering phones, grading papers, and helping students over the phone. That was pretty cool, she paid me $3.50 an hour.

Did you suffer any traumas as a teen? ~ Not at all. The biggest trauma I had was when I couldn't go on a date one time, and that just broke my heart. I call that a trauma. (Laughs)

Describe your fears and insecurities as a teen. ~ Fears and insecurities were never in my vocabulary. I wasn't insecure about anything I did, or didn't do.

Did you have heroines or heros during those same years? ~ Naw, I'm my hero, I'm lookin' at me and sayin' "Yeah." (Laughs) There she is!

What did you plan to do after graduation from school? ~ I was goin' to take criminology, so I could become a policewoman. But I got pregnant that year, and was throwin' up for fuckin' five months, and I said "Fuck college." (Laughs) I got fed up. I stayed home pregnant, had my baby, and raised her.

Describe other work you've done prior to dancing. ~ McDonald's. That sucks.

Have you had other jobs in the sex industry? ~ The 32-year-old friend was a male stripper and we did a show together, one time. I guess I got started from there. It wasn't a love act, we did a routine, g-string and pasties, me grinding him, but no insertion.

Describe living situations you've been in since you left home. ~ God, I just recently left home. (Laughs) Actually, I didn't leave home, I'm still there, in and out. My living situation is fine, I've got three places. I'm either in Oakland with my lover, or in San Francisco with my roommate, or at my mom's, they're all my homes. I have keys to every apartment. At Mom's we watch movies and talk about what everybody is doin' and look outside the window and talk about the people walkin' by. Just enjoyin' one another's company. That's where my girls are.

One of them is 4-1/2 and the other is 2-1/2. My 2-1/2 is still in diapers, I wish she'd get out of those diapers! (Laughs) When she takes a shit, "Mommy, I shit, you gonna' hit me?" Hell, yeah, I'm gonna' hit you! (Laughs) But I don't. She has to go through it, I'm not goin' to pressure her.

That's where I see my girls, take them out, bring 'em back.

When I'm at home with my roommate, the music's on, we're always talkin' about fuckin' some man. (Laughs) We're always talkin' about who we dislike, about personal things. We always take nude pictures, I took one takin' a douche. (Laughs) At my old man's house, on weekends, we're talkin', fuckin', suckin', goin' out, talkin' about things we want to do in the future.

Describe significant friendships and love relationships you've had since you left home. ~ As far as friendships, my man, my roommate, and my mother, it's still the same. Other friendships from when I was growin' up, those are gone. I'm not really lookin' for a friendship, 'cause I have my mom, my lover, and my roommate. My roommate and I do a lot together. We act silly together. We are called "Lucy and Ethel." (Laughs) It's great, we can talk about anything, share anything. What I don't have, she gives me, what she doesn't have, I give her. Nobody has a trouble about bein' with the other's man, 'cause they can screw 'em if they want. It doesn't matter, that's how close we are. We share everything!

My friendship with Mom, is, (laughs) I can tell her, "Hey, Mom, me and my roommate screwed my guy." She said, "Yeah, that's great, you're just like your mamma. That's one thing you got off your mamma, (laughs) your sexual behavior." My friendship with Mom is *really* tight. When there is a card game, I'm always her partner.

I'm more open than my man is, but it's good. If any arguments go down, it's more me than him, but I wouldn't tell him that. He's a great man. He stood by me a lot of times when I felt depressed. And when I didn't feel like doin' nothin' he motivated me to go ahead and do it.

Describe your interests outside of work. ~ Playin' basketball, miniature golf, doin' things with my girls, goin' out to dinner, movies. Simple things like that. I'm not into partying after work, just havin' a good time with my girls, my roommate, or my man. The kids like to go to the zoo, the park, and eat. The oldest does not like to stay out long at all. The baby really don't give a shit, she's like her mamma. (Laughs) Just sittin' there talkin', they like that, so I sit there and talk to 'em or take a book and read it. That bores the hell out of me though, but I do it because it satisfies them. So that's great.

Have you suffered any traumas as an adult? ~ No.

Describe your fears and insecurities as an adult. ~ I don't have any. Whatever comes up, I handle it the best I can.

Do you have any male inspired fears? ~ Naw. The males I have are good to me.

What media do you consume? ~ I take in whatever I see. I never stay in one spot long enough to read a book. I watch "60 Minutes" sometimes, that's a pretty interesting show. Not that I care, because it don't concern me, it concerns other people. I'm not in it, I'm just lookin' at what goes around with other people. I'm really not interested, until it happens to me. (Laughs) I go to all types of movies, comedies, horrors – I like horrors, I like to see people's guts ripped out. (Laughs) I love to see eyes poppin' out, it just fascinates me. (Laughs) I like movies where they're shootin, I like to see blood.

Do you have a favorite book? Author? Movie? ~ No.

Do you read romance novels? ~ Yeah, I read one the other day. It was alright. It was about this young guy, he had such a high position givin' him stress, so he retired. He put an ad in the paper: "Needed, a woman, such and such tall, can type this many words a minute, send your resume." So, Linda, that's her name, sent a resume. She got there, and the first thing came to her mind was, "Wow, I want to fuck this guy", wasn't no make love, it was "fuck." (Laughs) I said, "Whoa," you know. Shit, she came right out and said she wanted to fuck. And he was thinkin' the same thing, sayin', "Wow, she looks good, and those nice long legs could wrap around me and I could stick my cock into her cunt," and all this. I said, "Whoa." (Laughs) It was just basically, a relationship startin' and how they fuck, and how many people they fucked together and expressions and sounds they made, like, "Oh, I'm cumin', I'm cumin', oh, Paul" – that's his name, Paul. (Laughs)

Had you been a customer in a peep show or other sex show prior to dancing? ~ No.

Which of society's values have you rejected? ~ Their belief – I don't have to believe it. I go on with what I would like to do. If they don't approve, I don't give a shit. I'm happy and I'm satisfied. Lusty is gonna do what she thinks is right for her, okay. Males not supposed to be with males, and females not supposed to be with females? It's up to them who they want to be with, not the rest of the people that's lookin' down on them. That's the main one I reject. Stop tellin' people what they can and cannot do. They're gonna do it anyway.

Has the media ideal of beauty affected you? ~ Naw. 'Cause I'm beautiful anyway. I consider myself a beautiful woman. You should have a video camera.

Many humans love the attention of others and adorn themselves to get it. Do you? ~ Naw, I don't get dressed up. I'm in jeans damn near *everyday*, that's dressed up to me. I don't get dressed up to arouse and be noticed, 'cause if a person wanna notice you, they'll notice you regardless of what you have on. Hell, you either like me like I am, or don't like me at all.

What is your self-image? ~ I see myself as a beautiful woman – with great lips. (Laughs) I think I'm an open person about relationships, and intelligent. I see myself as a pretty easy goin' person who doesn't mind listening to other people's objections, rejections or whatever. Just an easy goin' gal.

Are you a tolerant person? ~ Yes! Very! Very tolerant, because whatever people do, if they're happy, do it. It doesn't bother me a bit. I get along with damn near everybody, just about, unless I see a reaction that they don't like me. I'll tell a person if I don't like 'em.

Do you trust people? ~ I hardly ever trust anybody, shid. I don't even trust myself. (Laughs)

Do you exploit people? ~ Oh, dear, no. Use 'em for what, shit. I can't use them for their dicks, because they give it to me. They give it to me, I didn't use nothin'. No, no, I wouldn't use people. Like I said, nobody can be used unless they want to be used. I think as long as I can walk, talk, see, eat, and all that, I can do everything myself.

Have you ever been violent with people? ~ (Laughs) Yeah, I've been violent with people. Some people keep talkin' shit to me, yeah. I mean violence where I was out sockin' somebody in their nose. The reason was, she was frontin' me like, "You just think you're somethin', you old yellow woman." I said "Bitch, I'll show you yellow woman, this is what a yellow woman can do." (Laughs) Oh, yeah, I get bold at times. It's mainly with people who are talkin' shit towards me, like I'm gonna sit there and take it. I'll get up and slap the shit out 'cha. We'll see what happens. But as far as me startin' trouble, no, I don't.

Define love. ~ I can't define love, 'cause I'm still askin' the question, "What is love?"

Define power. ~ I can't define that neither. I have power over myself, because I know what I can do and I can motivate myself, because it's me.

Describe the variety and frequency of your current sexual activity. ~ I'm into my mate's ass, his butt. (Laughs) I'm into sittin' on his face, (laughs) him sittin' on my face. Into whip cream, cherries, and peaches. I'll try anything sexual with my mate. If I don't like it, I don't have to do it again. But

I'll try just about *anything*. Fuckin' upside down. (Laughs) Outside, where somebody can't see. Recently, we went in front of the bedroom mirrors and I told him that I wanted to stick my fingers up his ass while he was about to cum. He looked at me like I was crazy, but he knew he'd better do it anyway, 'cause I'll get pissed-off. (Laughs) So I did it, and he liked the feelin'.

I like to suck dick with ice inside my mouth. The ice melts and right when he's gettin' ready to cum, I put ice on his nuts. He has a good sensation out of that. We do all kind of shit. (Laughs) A threesome, he wouldn't allow that with me, him, and another guy. I told him, if you said it, I wouldn't say no. (Laughs) It doesn't bother me if another woman's involved, me and her fuckin' him. Me and my roommate fucked the shit out of 'em. I'm there makin' up my bed, she's over there knockin' him off. I don't give a shit. (Laughs) If he's happy, I'm happy. Everybody's happy. Cool. I just told him, don't do a move on her that he didn't do on me, or I'd be pissed. It worked out fine. I have sex pretty frequently, but he works at night, until four in the morning, and I'm at the theater half the time at night. If we were there during a straight week, it wouldn't be one day missed without us fuckin', or havin' sex, or makin' love, or whatever you wanna call it. (Laughs)

Are you orgasmic? ~ Yeah, I have orgasms. I'm not the kind that has them every five minutes. I have one or two, that's it. It's a feelin' that just knocks me to my knees. (Laughs)

Do you masturbate? ~ There are times that it's hard for us to see each other and I'm hot, shit, these fingers work good. (Laughs)

Describe your sexual fantasies. ~ My fantasy has always been pleasin' other people's fantasy, my mate's rather. He wanted two women, he got two women. He wanted to feel somethin' up his ass, but he wouldn't say so, I just went ahead and took advantage. (Laughs) Yeah, it works out. He hasn't had that many, but I always ask him, you have anything else? (Laughs)

Are dominance and submission a part of your sexuality? ~ Dominatin', not really, unless we both agree. Anything goes, and if one another don't like it, nobody tries to force it on the person. Both parties agree to whatever sexual behaviors are taking place.

When do you get sexually involved? ~ I like to turn 'em on first, I don't like to just jump on into it. In the morning, in the evening, basically all times of the day. (Laughs) One time we got sexually involved on the bus he drives. I wanted some and it was dark, and he wanted some, his dick was hard, my pussy was wet, so...I sat on it.

Had you publicly exposed your body prior to becoming a dancer? ~ (Laughs) I did it working in McDonald's. They'd be playin' the music, and I said shit it's borin' up in here, the people are bored. So, I started peelin' my shirt. The guys were lookin' so I flashed 'em. I guess they liked it, they kept sayin', "Ohh, yeah." This was with the employees, but I did the customers like that, too. (Laughs) I do shit like that, so what? If you don't like it, don't look at me. (Laughs)

What sexual taboos besides dancing have you broken? ~ Is that a taboo, using "love potions," "love goddess" things? I put it over his body and lick it off from head to toe. (Laughs) He does the same thing. We sit there and admire one another's body. We just sit back and relax, let his dick stay hard for a minute drippin' and let my pussy stay wet for a minute, before we actually get into it. He'll jack-off in front of me. I wanna see him jack-off, period. I've done a threesome. That's about it.

What is sexually degrading for you? ~ Nothin'. (Laughs) What would be degradin', shit..Nothing! No, no, with my mate, nothin. With anybody, if they're happy, if they want to screw ten men, or five men and five women, if they're happy, shit, that's good. But speakin' for myself, I'm happy just with my man, and there's nothin' degradin' about what me and him do sexually. I'm not into animals, I'm into humans here. If people are animal lovers, and *they* love it, fuck it, why not. (Laughs) That's their own personal kick. I'm not into it, but that doesn't mean I have to tell them don't get into that. Hey, they're happy, go for it. (Laughs) I'm not into females sexually, but I'll fuck a man any way, however you want'a fuck.

Is sex a power for you? ~ Sex is an art, for me. (Laughs) It's no power, it makes me feel good, it's an art. It's a million different things you can do.

Do you ever use sex as a weapon? ~ Naw. Fuck it.

Has living in a male-dominated society played a role in shaping your sexuality? ~ I was born like this. (Laughs) It don't affect me at all.

Do you think your sexuality would be different if you lived in an egalitarian or female-dominated society? ~ No, it wouldn't be different, I'd still be the same way. I'd still look at the bodies, and thinkin' about the dicks inside the pants. I'd still be my own person regardless of who's runnin' what or **whatever**. I'd still have my own personality, my own mind.

Has birth control and medical technology affected your sexuality? ~ It helped me out, 'cause if I didn't get my tubes tied, I'd be pregnant every fuckin' year. I'm not takin' no damn birth control pills, I wouldn't take the motherfuckers. I'm not gonna stick a diaphragm up my ass, and I'm not gonna put on no rubber, 'cause the shit kills the mood for me. I tied my tubes, and that's good. I can fuck all I want to, and I won't get pregnant. If I do get pregnant, it was meant for me to have another baby, so until then...I'm happy. Birth control, shit, yeah. It helped me to be freer, let it all hang out. After midnight, baby... (Laughs)

Has the women's movement affected your sexuality? ~ It ain't changed a damn thing for me. Like I said, I'ma be my own person. They're speakin' for theirselves and all I can do is speak for myself. I can adjust to anything, if it has to be that way. I'm not gonna try to break my damn neck, give me stress, tryin' to change somethin'. It's gon'take years, and years, and years to change, and I'll probably die. Man is goin' to be a man, period. I'm not gon' try to take nothin from a man. Fuck it, I'll join 'em. (Laughs) I'll fuck 'em all, shit. (Laughs) I appreciate what the women's movement is tryin' to do, I'm not tryin' to down 'em. They're tryin' to stick up for what they feel is right, but it hasn't changed me sexually at all.

Describe your current love relationship. ~ We got together way before I started dancin', but he said do whatever makes you feel happy. When I started he got an attitude about it. He didn't like it at all, and said I don't want my shit up there doin' that. I said, "Well honey, I'm not quittin', so you better go get you some other shit." (Laughs) I said, "Yeah baby, they wish they had the shit like you got it, you should feel proud." I was fuckin' with 'em. He learned to adjust a whole lot to what I'm doin'. He even comes in there some Saturdays and get turned on, but he's givin' all the cum to me. (Laughs)

We got together when I was sixteen. I caught his bus, he turned me on by his beard and we just started talkin'. Two years later he saw my sister and asked, "Where's your shadow?" He said, "Here's my number, give it to her to show her I'm not married." I called him up that Saturday. He said, "Who is this?" I said, "This is your future wife, future woman." He started laughin'. We got to talkin', got together, went out, everything just clicked. It's still the same. He was interested when I was sixteen, but he was thirty something. He respected that, so I respected him. We get along very good right now, because I know his crazy ass, and he know me. It's great.

How do you think your relationship will evolve? ~ I can't be sure, I just take one day at a time. I'm not goin' to say how it's gonna be because it might not happen that way. Who knows what will happen tomorrow. Who knows? He might go off and get married. I'll be his flower girl. (Laughs)

How did you get this job? ~ I wanted to dance nude, or somethin' like that, ever since I met a stripper. But not in front of a crowd where they'd be feelin' my body. My mother always said, well, you oughta' go audition. She always knew that's what I wanted to do. So, we were lookin' through the paper one day, I find this theater and go check it out. I filled out the application, the next day I auditioned, the next day work.

In your experience are dancers more deprived, abused, and battered than other women? ~ Naw, most of 'em do it for the money, 'cause the pay is good. It's non-stressful to me, although I've heard some stories. Other women could be deprived and all that, but just not tellin' anybody. You can't see through a person without them tellin' you. Speakin' for myself, I'm not deprived, nor not loved, or abused, or battered. I never been battered. You never know who's been battered whether it's a dancer or the President, until that person opens up and tell you. I always envy strippers, I never thought they were battered.

Do you recognize any characteristics common to those who dance? ~ Yeah, everybody shows their pussy. (Laughs) And, like me, like men.

When you started dancing did you fear being separated from other women? ~ No I didn't, because I don't give a shit what them other women think. My oldest sister doesn't like what I do, she says I'm doin' the devil's work. But I don't give a shit what she say. (Laughs) I told her, you need to get up here and dance and get loose. She gasped, oh boy, I just broke her heart on that one. (Laughs) But my mom and the rest of'em, totally agree with what I'm doin'. I'm happy, I'm not hurtin' nobody. My oldest sister thinks it's just degrading. I asked her, "Do you call takin' your clothes off for your husband or the few men that you did take your clothes off for degrading?" She shut up because she didn't know what to say. 'Cause she took her clothes off for these men, how many men has it been? Mine come in groups, that's all. (Laughs) I have no fear, because I really don't give a shit. 'Cause they not buyin' my clothes, payin' my rent, or nothin'.

Have people treated you as a "bad woman" since you started dancing? ~ No, nobody ever treated me as a bad woman. My sister just said I think you could find somethin' better to do. I said no I can't 'cause I like showin' my pussy. (Laughs) Naw, nobody just threw me away, it hasn't happened.

Have you lost self-esteem due to dancing? ~ No, no. Why would I lose respect for myself when I'm doin' beautiful art? (Laughs) I wouldn't lose respect for myself, nor the customers, or the dancers. I'm still the same. Respectful ole me. (Laughs)

Do you lead a double life? ~ No. Everything is out in the open, it's up to them whether they want to accept it or not. I'm not tryin' to force them to accept it. Let it all hang out. It's legal.

What have you learned due to dancing? ~ (Laughs) I haven't learned nothin'. I already knew how to arouse a man. I learned that from the men arousin' me growin' up, bein' a teenager. I already knew exactly what I was comin' into and how to work it.

Has dancing affected your politics? ~ I wasn't ever into fuckin' politics. Fuck politics! (Laughs)

Do you fear becoming a prostitute? ~ Pardon me? (Laughs) I don't fear becoming a prostitute, 'cause I'm not becomin' a prostitute. (Laughs) Personally, I wouldn't sell myself, I'm not into that. They get upset about prostitution because they can't tax the shit. If they make it legal and tax the shit then they'd be afraid they might stop. People want to sell they body, hey, that's fine with me. Go right ahead. That's they way of livin'. I don't blame 'em, they makin' money, money is a necessity. Prostitution, if they like it, I love it.

Do you identify and feel solidarity with other sex workers? ~ I feel close to some of the dancers, we've shared a lot of experiences on stage, and some of them are callin' each other sisters. It's a big family, you feel close to 'em, our bodies are up there together. We communicate with one another, see how one another feels, and try to take over when one is not feelin' well.

Have you been discriminated against because you are a woman? ~ Naw.

Are you a feminist? ~ In some areas I would voice my opinion. If women can do the work that a man can do, I say they should get paid the same. Don't discriminate against them because they're a woman. Some women can do the job better than men. Some women don't need to be doin' things that men are doin'. I know I'm not no fuckin' garbage person. I'm not liftin' shit, breakin' my damn back and hurtin' my organ. A garbage truck!?! (Laughs) It's strictly for a man, period. Their body is structured different than a woman, you couldn't get me to empty no garbage. I wish somebody would tell me to take down the garbage if a man in the house, shid! (Laughs) I am not a feminist.

Historically some feminists have tried to exclude some women from the women's movement based on their sexual behavior and preferences. Do you experience this exclusion? ~ If this is supposed to be women doin' this project, and they discriminatin' against a woman just because of her sexual behavior, or preference, or wildness, that's discrimination still, against a female, a human bein'. She's still a woman, she still probably has great ideas of helping this project go on. What I should tell 'em is practice what they preach, have their shit together first before they go on about men discriminating against women. That's just full of shit right there. I'm still a human being. I wouldn't discriminate against another woman regardless of what her sexual preference was, she still a woman, she still has a brain.

What is your relationship to the women's movement? ~ I don't have no relationship with the fuckin' women's movement. (Laughs) I don't give a shit what they do, I don't care, shit. If they reach whatever they're goin' for, God bless 'em. If they don't, still God bless 'em.

What have been the most damaging and the most constructive influences in your life? ~ A lot of people try to influence me to use drugs. Hell, I don't need it, I'm already too wild, if I did that, I'd be overboard. (Laughs) Fuck it, I don't want to try it. That's it, people tryin' to get me to do somethin' that I don't want to do.

Positive influences, I do what I feel is right for myself, to help me, my family, and my loved ones, my children. Make the decisions that you think are right for yourself and don't let nobody drag you down with what they're sayin' is right. You have to go with your own feelins.

What person or people have had the greatest influence on your life? ~ My mom, my sister, my man, my girls.

What are your greatest gifts and limitations? ~ My strength is I do whatever I need to do. I can talk to people, I don't have a hard time sayin' what I feel, whether it's good or bad. I can relax and be myself. I don't have to be a fake, tellin' you one thing and doin' another. I'm not goin' to sit up there and lie about it. I don't have any weaknesses. (Laughs) I haven't really come to that spot yet, where I can say, "This is one of my weaknesses."

Do you feel like you are growing? ~ Oh, yeah, I'm not finished growing mentally yet, physically I stopped.

What would you like to be doing in 10-15 years? ~ Hopefully, firefighter or a policewoman. But yet and still, I have skill working with children. I *know* it's going to be one of the three.

Recently in San Francisco we witnessed the appearance of women dancing for women. Why do you think this is happening? ~ (Laughs) That's a helluva good question. I don't know. Maybe they liked the other women's body, or they're attracted to women, period.

Have you danced for women only? ~ No I haven't.

If social and economic equality for women became a reality, would some women still dance? Would you? ~ Yes, they would still dance, and yes, I would still dance, because I like to dance, period. It doesn't matter whether anything became equal or not, it depends on if you like dancin' or not, period.

Would sex work exist in your ideal society? ~ Yeah, no question about it. It probably would be more than it is now. At least I'd try to make it more, 'cause it's a million dollar business. (Laughs)

For many people it is impossible to conceive of anyone choosing to dance as you do. Why do you think that is? ~ Like I said, my sister can't understand why I'm doin' this. She said it was the devil's work. She hasn't really told me her feelin's, she's just goin' by what a book says. So, actually I can't figure it out myself. Don't go by the book, sit down and think about it. Get up there and try it, you might like it.

Many people paint female sex workers as among the most obvious victims of male domination and declare that if you don't see yourself as such you are suffering from "false consciousness" and "delusions of the oppressed". What is your response to that? ~ My response is, compare their office work to what we do, less stress and more money. (Laughs) Who's to say that the male domination is not makin' them work their job, what's the difference? A job is a job, you know what I'm sayin'. We're doin' a sex job, they're doin' a computer job. Yet and still, male domination, they *have* to work. I see it as just work, okay? Me, I'm not sufferin' from nothin', because I like what I'm doin'. I'd be sufferin' workin' behind a desk, thinkin' hell, I'm doin' this. That's what I call sufferin'. As far as a head trip or somethin', I think some feminists have the delusions. They got it real bad, and need to come and audition to see what it's really like, instead of basing it upon I don't know what.

Why do you think people use sexually explicit media? ~ Shit, to get excited. (Laughs) To get wet! To see what's happenin'. Maybe to find some of the parts that they have on their bodies that they couldn't find with they hands. Some people need that. Then they really can enjoy their sexual life.

Do you use sexually explicit media? ~ I don't use it that much, but when I look at books, I look at the male parts and say, yeah, damn, baby got a big one. (Laughs) I wish he was here with me. But I really don't look at it much, because my sexual life is happy. I know all the parts of my body and I use my imagination and do whatever I damn please.

Has the sexually explicit media you've seen accurately portrayed humans and their sexual relations? ~ It looks real to me, it looks very real.

At what age do you think people should be allowed to view pictures of human genitalia? ~ When they start asking the parents, *what* does this do? How do you get pregnant? I wouldn't bring it up to my kids unless they started askin' questions. Hey, let's go watch a film, then I could point out, and they could point out, the differences between a male and a female. I would show them pictures, not influencing them to go out and try any of this shit, but just to show them the difference. When they start askin' the questions deeply of what sex is about, show'em. I really can't put an age on that, it might be six. "Mommy, what's that?" Come here. (Laughs)

Do you think any sexually explicit media should be banned? ~ Naw, it shouldn't be banned. If they've got more ideas, bring 'em on out. Some people need this to really open up, to see what it's all about. Let the people make their decision whether or not it's good or bad for them. Don't just say, "That's bad, doin' it in the butt," when the other person hasn't tried it yet, 'cause they might like it. It depends on the person.

At the outset, the Meese Commission declared that it intended to contain the spread of pornography. At its conclusion, the Commission, like most others, could not define pornography. Yet it recommended the prosecution, fining, and jailing of people who produce, distribute, and consume it. What do you think of the Commission and its recommendations? ~ This Commission needs people who are in erotic dancing or whatever, to show them things where they can have a change of mind. People like them never tried nothin', they never tried all kinds of sex to really get into it, so they're all boring. What we need to do is bring the Commission together, and I bet you if just ten on their side, eight out of that ten is gonna come on our side when we get finished with'em. Eight are gonna say, "Don't fine these people, bring it out more, yeah, let it all hang out!" The Commission is full of shit. (Laughs) I recommend me. Put ten of us erotic dancers on the Commission with the bored people, and then it would be balanced. Fuckin' ten people bored to death, they didn't have sex lives from the beginning, how do they know. Who pointed them out to recommend something that they never tried, that we already know what it's about. Put us on and we'll give them somethin' to see. They gonna recommend to keep it all 'cause these eight people came out with they minds healthy, stronger, they dicks hard, and they pussys wet. The other two gonna be sittin' over there goin' "What I miss?" For them two, I recommend they come over here and stay all night.

Why do you think the government shows virtually no concern with violence in the mainstream media? ~ They're screwed up, they have shit backwards. They should be concerned because the violence is not healthy, that shit can kill you. Sex is gonna give you good orgasms. (Laughs) What we should do is go grab the people that say they don't care, and sit 'em in front of this tape. I can't speak for them. Maybe they do prefer violence to sex, maybe that's what gives them an orgasm.

Some people argue that humans are born with a sex drive and after that our sexuality is socially constructed, produced through our experiences. How do you think human sexuality is shaped? ~ It depends on who your mate is, or who your mates are. It depends on the person, each individual how their home front is. Me bein' born with this sexual thing, and growin' up through people that have more experience than I have, has really shaped me very well, I think. I'm *good*, now. It's gonna stay shaped, and I'm ready to learn some more.

Do you believe the State tries to manage sexuality? ~ They try to manage it, but they can't manage what goes on in another's bedroom. When the public comes in here to see sexual things, they try to manage these things. In certain places, you can't insert, or touch your breasts, and this and that. It all basically runs down to the government tryin' to manage, tellin' you what you can or cannot do. But you've got a house and behind closed doors you can do whatever the fuck you want. A lot of people are doin' things they say don't do, they're doin' it and there's not shit happenin'. As time goes by, the government is just gonna join in and not say nothin'.

Are there a wide variety of sexualities produced? ~ Yes, and it's interesting to me, I love to see a lot of different sex acts goin' on, if I'm included or not included. I love it all.

Describe what men and women have in common sexually? ~ Men can have a pussy, because they got a dick, and the pussy is gonna sit on it. The same for women. Women can have all the dick they want, because they gotta pussy. (Laughs) What they have in common is that they both can orgasm real good once they're together. We both have mouths that can go down on one another and have an orgasm. We can get off many different ways, by our hands, feet, or whatever it takes. A man and a woman have a lot in common just by havin' genitals.

Is there any sexual expression that society should ban? ~ Naw, they shouldn't ban nothin'. Whatever it is people want to do, let it all out. It depends on each individual whether they wanna try it or they think it's bad for them. What's bad for them, might not be bad for twenty people out there in line ready to come up and try it.

What part does sexual pleasure play in life? ~ It plays a big part in feelin' good. People who haven't tried it yet, that do try it, will say the same thing. I like sex in the morning, it makes me get up feelin' good about myself. It plays a very big part in my world. It's half of a relationship for me.

Some people seem to think that sexual pleasure without procreation is a threat to society. Is it? ~ No. If people have sex to have kids, that's a threat. They're bringin' in kids that's not wanted, just throw 'em away, now that's the threat. That's a *big* threat. Sex should be just for fun, period. People always bitchin' about money and stuff. Bringin' more kids into the world, that's money, that's time, and that's a threat. I can't even see how they could think like that, when all these kids are here and no place to go. Somethin' wrong right there. It hasn't really came out yet that havin' sex just for fun is not a threat.

Is it ever okay to be a sex object? ~ If a person agrees with their mate or even a one night stand. It all depends on where the person's mind is. I could go for a one night stand and you can call it sex object or whatever the hell you want to call it, felt good to me. He made me climax, I made him climax. We used each other as a sex object.

Do you think gratification of sexual needs diminishes anti-social impulses? ~ People not gettin' sex, they're still social. Then, on the other hand, people who are gettin' it, that can make them more violent than they already were. Then again, it can't. It all depends on the people who you hang around with...

Feminism as it emerged in the early 1970's had as basic tenets sexual exploration and sexual self-determination. Subsequent exploration has led to intense debate over female sexual identity and behavior. How do you define female sexuality? ~ Female sexuality is whatever they might want to do. If they're explorin' their body with a vibrator, that's fine, that's their own sexual thing. If they want another woman, or a male, doin' sexual things with them, that's their sexuality, that's fine. I define it as whatever you want to do that makes you happy.

Are there any sexual behaviors you think women should not engage in? ~ Naw, they do whatever they want. Whatever makes them have a good orgasm, or happy. DO WHATEVER THEY WANNA DO, fuck what people say. You want to fuck a dog, fuck the dog, okay. Fuck the damn dog, if it's gonna make you happy.

A recent Kinsey Institute survey of western nations concluded that people in the United States feel the worst about their bodies. Have you seen evidence of this problem? ~ Not in San Francisco. People are free with their body, openly free. I think you got shit backwards. What I see on TV, I think we're the most open people there is, we let it all hang out, we don't give a shit who look or say what. Most of us are not ashamed, but we do have some that are.

In the late 1940's American writer Philip Wylie saw equally strong tendencies to excite and constrain the erotic drive as pervasive in this society. He observed that they continuously reinforce each other and declared, "The United States is technically insane on the matter of sex." Is his diagnosis good for today? ~ It's basically the same, but yet and still their minds have opened up a little more.

People in the U.S. are spending billions of dollars each year on sexual needs. What does this say to you? ~ That their minds are opening up, they've finally seen the light! (Laughs) It says to me that they finally explorin' things they want to explore, instead of listening to this other man that's tryin' to ban the shit. They finally said, I'm gonna figure it out for myself.

Can sexual needs be met commercially in a non-sexist way? ~ I think it can be met in a way that's healthy for their mind.

Do you think the schools should teach about human sexuality? ~ Yes, I do. They should teach *everything*, show everything. Let the kids decide whether or not that's good for them, okay. Don't say this is bad for you, or that's bad for you, because whoever is watchin' or viewin' this in school, doesn't know if it's bad for them or not, unless they try it. They should show where the dick can go in the holes and out the holes. What they can do with their bodies, masturbation...show actually what they can do. Not lettin' somebody else tell them, "That's bad for you to have oral sex." Also, teach safe sex, because of all the things that's happenin' now. And let them decide whether or not they want to do it safe. They are told about it, they understand it, and it's their decision.

How is sexuality portrayed in the mainstream media? ~ They cover it up. You might see the sheets movin', but you don't see their naked bodies. You might see the outside of their breast, but you don't see the nipples. Each and every day, or as years go by, they let more hang out. At one time, they wouldn't show *nothin'*. Now, they showin' bare backs and almost the buttock area. It's gettin' more into it. But they're still coverin' up on television. If you want to see somethin' go to the movies, that's where they let it all hang out. They show a lot of interesting scenes, how it can be sweet.

Some people argue that there is a sexual hierarchy in the United States with heterosexuals at the top and everyone else treated as second class citizens. Do you agree? ~ Who's to say people at the top are heterosexuals? (Laughs) People who are supposed to be heterosexual can be just as gay as anybody else. They say they're heterosexual at the top, which damn near they're not. They screw those men, you know. He can be gay in his own world and still have that masculine, man-thing about him, to hold his job, keep his livelihood goin'.

Some people believe that non-heterosexuals should not have the same rights as heterosexuals. What do you think? ~ You treat a human bein' as a human bein'. Their sexual preference is none of your business. You're still human whether you're heterosexual or not heterosexual.

Do you think heterosexism is a serious problem in the United States? ~ At one time, straight people, supposedly straight, were trippin' on the guys and the gals who slept with the same sex. As time goes by they're opening up. I'm friends with a lot of gay girls and a lot of gay guys. They always say, "Birds of a feather flock together," and I'll say, "Well, you're wrong about that." They're someone you can talk to. This fuckin' ass over here says, "Why you hangin' aroun' these gay people?" 'Cause I want to, you ain't shit to hang aroun', you always criticizin' me, you need to go criticize yourself. With me, it's not a problem to adjust to anybody, or what their sexual life is. It's just another human talkin' to another human.

How does society respond to the outspoken sensuous person? ~ Most of 'em think, "Damn, she crazy. This should be kept quiet or behind closed doors." I say, "Get on woman!" Shit, tell me somethin' that I ain't done, and you done, that I wanna do. It's two sides, some people are still in the closet keepin' it hush-hush, others are talkin' freely about themself, their sexual life. I like to hear other people's sex stories, 'cause I might be missin' somethin' that I want to try.

What have you learned about people through sexuality? ~ I learned some of the men ain't good at all. (Laughs) Some of 'em are too good, the shit scare me. (Laughs) I learned to treat a man, sometimes, how they want to be treated. Sometimes I don't give a shit. You learn what some men like to see in a woman sexually, and you learn to respect each other's bodies, if you've got the right mate. I learned a lot havin' orgasms with people.

What would a sexually positive society look like? ~ I don't think everybody would be runnin' aroun' with smiles on their face, because there's gonna be a flaw somewhere. That flaw is what makes the world go round, people arguing about shit. It won't ever be a full positive society, because too many people are gonna keep sex in the closet. Speakin' for me, I'm always gonna be positive about my sex life, regardless of people sayin' shit about it.

How can we achieve that society? ~ By bein' open about sex, speakin' to the public that's behind closed doors. These people are comin' to see us because we are outspoken about sex. Evidently they want to come out the closet. We speak about how open you can be, how much understandin' there can be if you allow yourself to be open about sex.

Do women play a part in the creation of male sexuality? ~ It's just enjoyin' one another sexual wise and bein' there when he needs somebody to talk to. The part I play for my old man is dress up sexy, cook his dinner, and serve it with a nighty on. That shit freaks me out too, I like it. I'm playin' a part for him, 'cause that's what he wants to see. "Here's your dinner, baby." I'm givin' him some fun. Playin' the role of bein' someone to talk to and bein' open about anything he wants to be open about.

How do you think batterers and rapists are created? ~ Probably stemmin' from somethin' they seen from childhood. Maybe they were little kids and they seen their father do it, or seen somebody else do it. Then again, you got some women that entice the men, makes 'em get hard, and they say, "Yeah, I got to get some of this." There was nobody there to talk to, they thought it was right and when they did it they found out it was a crime.

Are there feminist men? ~ Yeah, there are some feminist men. They're just like feminist women, they fuckin' borin'. They had a borin' sex partner and think that's the way it should be. They need somebody excitin', an outspoken person to really show them the other side. One borin' person with another borin' person, that's not goin' to get it. At least one of the persons got to be outspoken about sex.

Describe the impact male dominance has had on women. ~ It hasn't been any problem for me, this supposedly male dominated world. I got a job, I think the money is good. I handle whatever is bein' dished out.

Do you see men working at changing themselves? ~ Some of 'em are tryin' to change, but not everybody. Once a person is set in their ways, it's hard for them to change. They have to find a mate that can understand their ways and live happy ever after.

How can women help men change? ~ When I see a person is fucked up, I ain't gonna stay around. I'm gonna tell 'em you need help. (Laughs) I might not be the partner to help, but, somebody will come along and be the right one for them, in sexual ways or in the mere way of talkin'. There's somebody for everybody.

What do you think the future holds for relations between men and women? ~ I see it a lot better, because it's been good to me. (Laughs) You'll run into somebody that you think is pullin' you down, but you always run into a person that seems to pull you up.

If rape and sexual assault ended today how would your life change? ~ Not a bit. I still go out two or three o'clock in the mornin' and rape hasn't ended. I'm not fearful when I go out at night, no I'm not. Matter of fact, I like the night life better than the day. If it ended, what can I say, it just ends.

What is the source of inequality between men and women? ~ They are physically stronger than a woman.

Feminist people have long observed the system of male domination in the United States and exerted considerable effort to overturn it. What strategies do you think have been effective? What strategies do you recommend now? ~ I don't know, I came up in the middle of things. Ask me again in 20 years and I'll probably know more. If women can do the work, the same as the men, they should get paid the same. They'll keep pushin' and maybe they'll get what they're reachin' for.

Anti-censorship feminists have emerged who believe some sexually explicit media reflects and reinforces the oppression of women, but disagree with the pro-censorship feminists' view that sexually explicit media is the cause of women's oppression. They argue that the causes of women's oppression are much deeper and precede the mass production and distribution of sexually explicit media by centuries. What is your point of view? ~ Oppression comes way before the sex thing. WAY before I was even born. (Laughs) Before my mother was born. I don't think sex media has nothin' to do with it, because if it did, why were the cave people doin' it? They had their way of doin' it, by draggin' us around by the hair. I think it's way before explicit sex.

Where do you think sexually explicit media should be placed on the movement agenda? ~ Sexual things should be last, period. They might not want to do it in a porno movie or whatever, but all in all, it's still the same when they're behind those closed doors, in bed and makin' love. Worry about what's goin' on with your children, childcare, or crimes that's goin' on, murders. Why talk about the sex thing, when everybody that come in here are leavin' out happy. Why talk about somethin' like that? Talk about gettin' medicine for the ills instead of this shit.

Do you think our constitutional guarantee of free speech includes sexual speech? ~ I should think so. They say, free speech, that means anything that comes to your mind. Talk about sex, that's my speech, you know. I say, "Yeah, it was good and it was long, and its cum's white, I wish it was a little lighter." It's free speech. If people don't want to listen, turn the channel. I'll say it on TV, put me on. Free speech! Even if it has to be swear words, put it on, that's what free speech is all about.

How would you advise courts ruling on sexually explicit media? ~ First of all, is this a male court, male judge? I would ask his wife, is she doin' a crime when she gets his dick hard? Well, why is it such a crime when we are out here dancin' and these men get aroused? What is the crime? You tell me. I don't think he would have an answer, so I'd ask him, don't your dick get hard? Don't your woman's pussy get wet? I'd be frank, just put me behind bars! (Laughs) What's the big deal, I would ask'em, what's the big deal? It's not a crime, I disagree with that shit.

Tell us what you know about AIDS and describe the impact it is having on your life and society. ~ I read it's only contagious by oral sex, straight sex, using dirty needles, anal sex, saliva. I never heard anybody say if it's contagious through biting. It's not havin' nothin' on my life. I always said, if it was meant for me to have somethin', I'm gonna get it. I feel sorry for people who do have it, and hope they find a cure to help 'em out. I'm not afraid to be around it. Society done went crazy! Startin' not to want you to touch'em, and all kinds of weird stuff. They're humans too, they bleed just like we do. It's having a bad effect on society, because they don't know what to do. They think everybody's goin' to get it. It's just terrible. I'm not like some people, "No, you got AIDS, don't touch me!" I like you, I'm gonna be your friend, regardless of what you got. If I don't like you, I don't like you. My life is still the same.

Do you think it is possible that this society will confine those who test HIV positive in spite of the medical evidence that it is not casually transmitted? ~ No, I don't think they'll put 'em on an island. Before that they're going to find a cure. They didn't have a cure for the flu and they found somethin' for it. Boom, cured! They'll find a cure before trying to put somebody on another planet. I don't think that's right to ship them off.

What future do you see for erotic theater and erotic dancers? ~ The only thing I can see is where I'm going in it, okay? I'm tryin' to make some money so I can become a firefighter or somethin' like that. I'm trying to get into my own little thing and this money is helpin' me out. I can't say if it's going to progress or go down the drain.

ATTILLA THE HONEY

*I FIND THAT PEOPLE TRY TO INVALIDATE WHAT I
SAY WHEN I SAY I FEEL FINE ABOUT THIS JOB.
THEY SAY, "NO YOU DON'T!"*

Part of the promotion for your show says, "Live Nude Dancing, Lovely Lusty Ladies, Naked Naughty Nasty". Is this a good description of who you are and how you perform at work? ~ I like to have a pretty graphic sexual show and I'm definitely naked. I suppose a woman being sexual is naughty. I don't see it that way. Now it's naughty, whereas it used to be forbidden, you were a total outcast. Maybe that is appropriate. We're doing what we're not supposed to do, but, it's kind of cute, kind of funny. I certainly don't see my show as nasty. To me nastiness is dirtiness, sleaziness, there's something bad about it, and I just don't see that. I'm pretty lusty, that's absolutely true. I've always been interested in sex, I like a lot of sex.

What were you told was your job? ~ I was told nothing. It was horrible. They told me to watch the show, they didn't give me any money to watch and nobody went with me. I didn't know where I was, it was dark, confusing. A disembodied voice came over the intercom saying, "Go right, no, no, no, booth 23." I went into a booth and started digging in my pockets for money. I was feeling weird about the whole thing, and thinking maybe I shouldn't be doing this. I was having a major emotional struggle when I stuck a quarter in and the little window went up. Suddenly there was a girl there with underpants stuck up her butt. She put her arms up like a little ballerina on a jewelry box and started turning. There was a really butch looking black woman on the floor doing hip lift exercises. I could barely see somebody else's arm at the other side of the stage waving around. As I looked I was thinking about the ad in the paper, creative, energetic – I didn't see any of that and thought this is the easiest job I have ever seen. All I have to do is lie on my back.

I was told to talk with the show director to hire in. It took forever to reach her, and when we talked she told me you start at $7.00 an hour etc. etc. She gave her rap and then she said, "So, do you still want the job?", with this break in her voice as though I wouldn't want it. The other show director said the same thing and I got to thinking about the fact that the ad was always in the paper. If this was such a great place, if they're so wonderful, how come the ad's always in the paper? How come they always need dancers?

The place looked pretty filthy and run down and there were some scruffy looking guys hanging out in the lobby. I was not impressed at all. The show director was great in person, but she told me that I would audition for 40 minutes unpaid and I became suspicious again. I said wait a minute, maybe that's the deal. They get people to drop some quarters and then they get them on stage for free and this thing is a total scam. That's why they always have the ad in the paper. I was really angry that I was going on for 40 minutes unpaid but I needed a job immediately. I had blown up at the last person I worked for, I said everything that was on my mind and walked out. There was no going back, and the rent was due. So I went for it.

I went on stage and looked into a sitdown booth and there was this guy jacking-off and I went, "Whoa, I didn't know it was going to be like this." It was a big shock. I had danced topless when I was 19, but this was really different. There were mirrors everywhere and I saw my butt flapping around. I felt totally vulnerable. I looked at the other women and saw the way they were playing on the handlebars and I started doing that. That was fun and I was dancing fine. I like being naked. I'm probably more comfortable being naked. When you're naked the pretense is gone. You see it all and I like that. The show director kept coaching me, "Look at the customers more, I want to see more eye contact. Your dancing is fine." The lighting on stage is high contrast and I don't have good skin. It made me look my absolute worst. But I managed and she hired me. I got used to it in about a week.

What have you been telling the women to do to succeed at this job since becoming show director? ~ I tell them that I want them to be having fun, and if they don't like the work, or if they think there is something wrong with it, that they shouldn't be doing it. I tell them to establish lots of eye contact to establish a flirtation. We talk a lot about the pussy show. Men will watch if you spread your legs, those little windows will stay open. But people don't have to do that. A lot of women find that erotic and powerful. I tell them to use facial expressions, play with your breasts and arms, kiss at them, use your whole body. I also tell them that I want them to be responsible and reliable. People think that it's not a real job. I constantly hear that when I'm not there, people are fucking-off. I stress that people should be responsible if they want steady raises. I tell them to experiment with costumes and characters. Try new dance moves, new aspects of your personality. Experiment and explore on stage. I tell them that I want them to participate and be active in the theater but it doesn't happen that often. People tend to just check-in and check-out. I encourage them to be open with each other and communicate, especially around resentments. Be supportive, be gentle, don't be threatening, tell people how you feel about them, and if you can't tell them, tell me.

Describe your first experience on stage. ~ I was pretty excited and pretty nervous about returning to the sex industry after 10 years. When I was nineteen I started dancing topless and turning tricks. I worked in nude modeling studios and I ran a massage parlor in Arizona. I went through all that stuff and quit. I decided that it was bad. I should be a good girl, be normal. I did that for 10 years, and I have never been so bored. I was shocked that that was what people wanted to do with their lives. You know, 9 to 5, predictable stuff. Everything's very safe, everyone pays attention to the rules. I did that for 10 years and I just couldn't do it any more. But still I was wondering if I should be going back into the sex industry. Maybe there was something wrong with me, because I wanted to go back for 10 years. I would stare at massage parlors and topless dance places. I would always read the ads for dancers, escorts, and masseuses, and just long to be back in that environment, where people are really wild and open and in many ways more honest than folks in the mainstream. Especially the women. There are a lot of real strong women in the sex industry.

So anyway, I was on stage and sort of in a state of shock. Here I was, I had finally gone back. I don't get along with my family, but I had just begun a reconciliation with my sister. I knew that this was going to blow that. She would never approve, so I was sacrificing that. I had many, many friends who were so upset with me. It's a feminist issue and I was like a traitor to the cause. This was terrible, this was exploitation. I thought I was going to lose all of my friends. That didn't turn out to be true, but it put a major strain on my friendships. I felt I had to do this to be true to myself.

I was taking the San Francisco Sex Information training, and got complete support from those people. They said if you want to do it, do it. You're not hurting anybody, go for it. It was the first time I had heard that from anyone. Everybody had been telling me for years, no, don't go back. Don't explore any kind of sexual issue that I was interested in, anything that was out of the mainstream. And since I come from a family that's very dysfunctional and sexually weird – I come from an incest family – it's a big concern. It's a major concern that I'm going to turn out crazy like Mom and Dad.

So anyhow I'm on stage going through all this shit, making this major decision, and there are all these guys around me jacking-off. I always wanted to watch my boyfriends do that. They always wanted to watch me masturbate but they would never let me watch them. So suddenly I can watch all these different guys and it was really interesting. It was the first time I could just stare at a man doing that, stare at his body and his cock. I got very excited. There were definitely customers who really turned me on. It was exciting and scary, a major decision, but frankly, it was really easy.

What criteria do you use in hiring women? ~ The first thing is how attractive are they? Second, how comfortable are they on stage? Would they actually be happy working here? Do they have good rapport with the customers? Are they able to look at these guys? I look at whether they have high or low energy. They have to be pretty unattractive for me to not hire them. I think I've only told one woman that I couldn't hire her, and one over the phone because her application was unintelligible. I am certainly not one of the prettiest women here and I still have a hot show. Looks do count in the business, definitely, and I pay attention to that. I would certainly love to hire lots of pretty 19-year-old college girls. It would be real good for the show, but I don't want people to just slide on their looks. It's sexiness that counts. And I look for people who are intelligent. Women who I can talk to, women who think about things, who use their intelligence to question the world around them and do some exploring, that's important. I don't like bimbos no matter how pretty they might be. I prefer having dancers and artists, actresses. Sometimes women from the financial district really cut loose.

How do you choose the women to appear on stage together? ~ I try to get a show where everyone looks different. That doesn't always work out but as far as appearances go, I look at skin color, hair color, body type, the way their show looks, the way they move. Also I've got to go by availability. A lot of people go to school and have other jobs. I like there to be a variety age wise and size wise. I'd like to see more racial diversity. I've been trying to get Asian and Hispanic women and haven't been very successful. You can't really advertise for that. Right now we have pretty much a black and white show. We don't have enough black dancers. I like something for everyone, that's the ideal, have someone who's really fufu and frilly and feminine and somebody who's really butch and dominant. Someone who looks young and innocent and somebody who looks older and more experienced. Someone who has big boobs and some-one who has little ones.

Describe how you dance, display, and touch your body during your performance. ~ I usually step up by the windows. I used to dance a lot with my back to the windows, facing the mirrors so they could see my reflection and then I would swing around on the handlebars. I use my face more now than I used to. I always establish eye contact. I always make a point of that even if they are not looking at my face. I always watch them. I like to swing around on the handle-bars and do lots of kicking and knee bends. I always end up putting my foot up on the window ledge and doing some kind of pussy show or touching myself. I've learned not to touch myself in places where it's wet because it's not hygien-ic. I usually place my fingers on either side of my labia or clitoris, and stroke very gently, sometimes I tug my pubic hair. Sometimes I'll give myself a slap on my clit, thigh, or butt, they like that a lot. I don't do it too often because it leaves red marks and you can't have marks and bruises when you're dancing. I generally keep moving and I pose. I'll lick my knee or stroke myself. I blow on the window and kiss them. I pretend that I'm jacking them off or licking them. I play with my breasts and bring them up to the window so they can pretend they're sucking them. There's a lot of pretend going on. They like to pretend that they're touching me and going down on me.

Does your performance contain elements of dominance and submission? ~ Sometimes. If I put my foot up to the window and somebody licks my shoe, I know immediately what kind of show he wants. The dominant stuff is fun and I find it real energizing. But there's one guy who's just draining. It makes me frustrated that I can't actually get my hands on him. With most of the others I like it. I'll make them kneel down and lick my shoe. Sometimes I yell at them. I have to be careful when I get really abusive and nasty because the other dancers and guys are there; it's not a private session. I like bondage, whipping, and stuff like that, which obviously I can't do here. I'm not really into verbal abuse, which is mostly what they come here for. I can order them to strip and show me their butt.

There was one guy I used to spank myself for, he loved that and that was fine. One time I started leaving his window and he yelled, "Get over here", that was it, I never danced for him again. I don't like that shit at all. He won't look at me now when he comes in. It doesn't work out for me to be submissive so much as masochistic. I'll let someone whip me with a belt or spank me and that's fine.

Do you test your power to arouse? ~ Oh yeah. Oh yeah. That's the fun part. When you see their hands shake and they start dropping the quarters in, that's great. I get a real ego trip off of that. They start dropping quarters all over the booth. I'm 31 now and for this business I'm over the hill. I definitely test to see if I've still got it. It's wonderful validation to know that I still have that power.

Eye contact with the customers is important for you. Tell us more. ~ Eye contact is also my way of insisting that I am a complete person, that I'm not a pussy nor a pair of tits. I *am* a sexual object and I *am* creating an erotic fantasy, it's not like we have a real relationship, but by establishing eye contact I am insisting that I am fully human, that I am not, in fact, a page out of a magazine or a dolly. When you look at someone's eyes you realize that they are thinking animals. It's the same with other animals. Those people who refuse to, I won't dance for them at all. And expression is important too. They may look me in the eye and look disgusted. I'm not going to dance for somebody like that. I'll go over to the guy who's smiling, who looks happy, who looks like it's okay to be here, not the guy who's feeling guilty and smutty about being here. I don't like guys who think I'm dirty, and they're hypocritical enough to show up anyway.

How much of your performance is you and your sexuality and how much is persona? ~ It's always me and my sexuality and I don't necessarily create an image. It changes according to what my sex life is like. If I'm doing a lot of dominant play in my private life, that shows up in my show. I'll do lots more spanking and what not.

Why did you choose the stage name you use? ~ It's a nickname. It's something my last boyfriend, my last real, honest-to-God, steady-type boyfriend called me. I thought it was a real good description of who I really am. People, when they meet me, generally think that I am very sweet, very nice, and a total pushover. They always find out that, in fact, I'm very dominant. I'm real nice about it but I like having things my way, I generally insist on that. I'm pretty immovable. I'm pretty uncontrollable and people are always surprised to find that out. I thought the name was fair warning. They never believe it. People have talked to me about my innocent face, especially prostitutes. I was doing outreach for a while and they would say, "With that innocent face of yours you must make a lot of money." People really saw it when I got into management. They were shocked and upset that I would actually tell people what to do, and that I would fire them if they didn't. I knew that would happen because it has happened to me all my life.

How do you use costuming and makeup? ~ I often use a costume that's going to lift my breasts. I have a jacket I wear because sometimes it gets cold on stage but it's open in front. I wear my little corset and zebra bra, something that brings me closer to the stereotypical ideal. I've learned that makeup has to be pretty harsh to show up with the stage lighting. I use blush now to bring out my cheekbones. I don't like fussing with lots of makeup. Generally I line my eyes, put on mascara, lipstick, blush, and that's it.

Do drugs play a part in your performance? ~ No, I got tired of drugs pretty quickly in my teens, I'm not really into drugs. They're fun for recreational purposes, but on stage they don't work very well for me, I lose energy. Even doing speed, once I crash, I crash so hard that it's not really worth it. If I use anything I use caffeine. Drugs would be detrimental to my show.

On stage music plays almost continuously. Describe the variety and part it plays in your performance. ~ It plays a major part. If it's not upbeat, if there's not a good, strong, danceable beat it just kills my performance. Anything slow will wipe me out. Too much pop/soul stuff kills the energy, the romantic orchestrated music too. Sometimes the lyrics are really insipid. It helps to have a song that's appropriate, something that I can act out on stage makes a big difference. There aren't that many of them. You'd think that since most popular rock songs are about sex, we could have a bunch that would be appropriate. They tend to be male ballads about beautiful women, or cruel women, or female ballads about cruel men. There's all this heartbreak stuff out there. There's not a lot of positive hot sexual stuff where hotness is great, it's a good thing, sex is wonderful.

The stage is covered with mirrors ceiling to floor. What role do they play in your work? ~ A major role, because we're dealing with visual fantasy, what people look like, and how they appear. I'm always checking myself front and back. Sometimes when I'm tired or bored with the way I'm dancing I'll look in the mirror and sort of disassociate and pretend that I'm a puppet. I use the mirrors to check out the customers and what's going on in other areas of the stage. If I'm dancing near the windows and can't see whether they want me to dance for them, I'll check in the back mirror.

Describe the interaction and commentary between the dancers on stage. ~ It varies a lot. There are some dancers who are real sociable. We tend to talk about the customers, what we look like, or how we're dancing. When I'm on stage, there's not a lot of talk about stuff that's not on-purpose. There is a lot of teasing and joking that goes on, everybody's playing. Somebody will always make little comments to try and make somebody else laugh. People show off for each other a lot. There's a certain amount of making fun of the customers, and that's often very funny. It's not fun to have guys look grim or sad. It's not appropriate there. We'll talk about the customers like, "Boy you should have seen the one I just had," or "Look at this one, he's gorgeous," or "Look at this one, he's really weird, look what he's doing." If there's somebody really weird in a sit-down booth doing a show for us, everybody will go, "Hey, come over, you gotta see this."

We don't touch each other a whole lot, most of us. Some dancers like a lot of physical contact. A lot of times we'll dance together, back to stomach, we'll form a little line and undulate. Or we'll do fucking movements together, or rub each other's shoulders, or stroke each other's hair, or put our hands under or around the breasts without actually touching them. Sometimes dancers will pretend they're licking other dancers.

Is there competition among the dancers on stage? ~ Yeah, it gets really weird. It's very, very peculiar when you start competing for guys who basically just want to watch you so they can jack-off. We don't have a tip system here, it's an ego thing. You want to be the most desirable. Everybody wants that, but at the theater the competition is pretty benevolent.

Is the myth of the perfect body perpetuated here? ~ No. We have lots of different body types and many, many less than perfect bodies and faces. Anybody who approaches that perfection does get more attention from customers as a general rule. So I'd say it's perpetuated by the customers, not by the dancers or management.

Do you ever become aroused by what you are doing and what is happening around you on stage? ~ It used to happen a lot when I first started, I was easily aroused. I became desensitized. Now it happens once in a while and I really enjoy it.

Do you ever have sexual fantasies during your performance? ~ No, because I'm doing the fantasy. I may later.

Do you ever wish you could be having direct sexual contact with the customers? ~ Sure, when somebody really turns me on, absolutely.

What can you do on stage that you can't do off stage? ~ The fact that I can be totally blatant sexually on stage has made a change in my private life. Now I'm much more open, much more verbal, much more uninhibited, and much more in control than I used to be. I definitely take control of my sexual relationships much more than I used to. I'm also less concerned in my private life about pleasing other people and more concerned about pleasing myself. So I would say at this point, is there anything I do on stage that I wouldn't do off stage? I don't think so.

What won't you do on stage. ~ I won't be submissive or do any kind of insertion. And I don't feel responsible for staying at a window until somebody cums.

Do you dance for co-workers and friends? ~ I'm pretty sure some of them sneak in and look at me through the one-ways. It is a little bit awkward because there's a real relationship there, and especially if it's not a sexual relationship. With one guy that's how the sexual side of our relationship started. What typically happens is a guy I know wants to go to bed with me, and I won't. All of a sudden I'll see this face in a window at work. "If I can't have you one way I'll have you another – then you have to." If I feel like giving them a show or turning them on I'll do it, and if I don't, I won't. One of them told me later that he went to a one-way. I guess he felt guilty or he wanted me to know he was watching. At first it was uncomfortable, but I got used to it quickly. It doesn't bother me. I'm not ashamed and if my friends want to come see me, that's fine. I've brought girl friends to see the show, but I haven't danced for them.

How does having your period affect your performance? ~ It can make me tired the first day or two, but usually, if the music is good, I'll forget all about it. I'll take an Advil for the cramps and forget about it. I use toilet paper instead of a tampon so there's no string sticking out.

I was quite surprised when I first heard that healing occurs here, women healing themselves, each other, and customers. Describe what you know about this. ~ As far as healing myself, I feel more like my real self. I have always loved the sex industry and known that would be disapproved of, that I shouldn't. Now I'm saying, politically correct or not, this is what I want to do. I have the right to do this, and I feel real good about that. I feel like I'm finally standing up for who I really am, regardless of what other people think. Other people are no longer running my life. It's been real healing in that way. Sexually it's been healing, in that I've become less inhibited and much more in control. I realized how much control I have, and how vulnerable men really are.

As far as I'm concerned, whatever the customers want to do in the privacy of that booth is fine. I don't slam anybody. I think it's very healing for people to realize that they're okay, that their fantasy is fine, that their sexual behavior is fine. And in spite of what they've been hearing about, "You can't have a shoe fetish", "Men don't play with dildos", they can do that here. I'm always real supportive. I always tell guys in lingerie how great they look. I ask them to show me. I think that's good for them. This is a place where it's okay for people to be who they really are, away from the conventions they have been forced into.

I had a guy really thank me that I would let him look at my feet. I took my shoes off and ran my fingers around my feet and between my toes. The other dancers were laughing at him. It's very healing for people to know that who they are is okay. You hear the term "deviant", that means someone who's bad, in this culture. When, in fact, a deviant is just someone who's different, who has taken off in a different direction.

Guys come in who seem to be lonely, they just want some attention, and I think it's very healing for them to get it. I'll stroke the glass as though I'm stroking their face, and kiss at them, and talk to them. I have found, not so much at the theater, but doing prostitution, that that is very healing. It's healing for men to be held, to be caressed, to be talked to, just to be physically close to a naked body, and it doesn't really have anything to do with sex. It often has to do with loneliness, or shyness, an inability to be intimate with other people.

I don't think that anything out of the ordinary goes on there in terms of women healing each other. Women tend to be fairly nurturing with everybody, including each other. At the theater we talk to each other about our feelings the way we always do, in every other aspect of our lives, in any other job. That's always healing.

Also, at the theater there's not a lot of nasty competition, "I'm more beautiful than you are, I'm more valuable than you are." That is also very healing. It's been healing for me to be around a lot of really beautiful women. I've stopped seeing them as a threat. There was always that feeling of, "She's prettier than I am, therefore, she will take whatever it is that I want." I don't feel that way anymore. Now I am very appreciative of beautiful women. I think beautiful women have the right to be appreciated for everything they are, their beauty, their personalities, for their intelligence, for whatever they have to offer.

Have you had any transcendent moments on stage? ~ Yeah, when I first started working, because it was a major decision about who I was, as opposed to who other people wanted me to be. I managed to transcend that on stage. But recently, no. It's become like any other job.

Do you ever feel caged or wish you could cover up? ~ Never.

Many of the dancers here say they prefer this closed type of stage and see it as safe and fun because of the absence of physical contact with the customers.

How do you feel? ~ I don't see it as safer. Actually, I like to be touched a lot, I'm attracted to men. A lot of the dancers are lesbians, and don't necessarily want to be touched by them. I love to sit in people's laps, to be petted, touched, and stroked everywhere. When the customers get rowdy, then I'm glad they can't grab me. If there was customer contact I would want lots more security around but your average customer is completely harmless.

Describe your performance at its best and worst. ~ At its best I am feeling strong, flexible, able, rested, energetic, and happy. I'm laughing and joking with the dancers and customers. I'm feeling real powerful.

Describe the customers. ~ First thing in the morning we get a lot of guys who have their first name on their work shirt. We get a lot of guys in ties all through the day, both young and old. Around lunch time you get mostly financial district types. Also, throughout the day we get old Asian men often in pairs, and they don't speak English. They always make motions like, "Spread yourself open." They always want to stare at your pussy. And they often giggle and give you the okay sign or thumbs up.

At night we tend to get younger unmarried guys. They're just starting to experiment with drugs and alcohol. That's fairly apparent when they come in a little out of control. (Laughs) They often come in groups and often they're scared to death. They show off a lot and tend to be very macho, rude, and obnoxious. There's maybe an 80 percent chance that they're going to be assholes and that you're going to have to throw them out. Some of the young guys by themselves are pretty nice. A lot of them seem kind of shy.

Nights and weekends we get a lot of regulars who stay for hours and hours and hours. I don't understand it at all, and I find them a little disturbing. I guess they don't have anything better to do. The customers seem like real average guys, for the most part.

We also get guys who are exhibitionists. They put on a show for us. There are at least three regulars who give themselves blow jobs. They definitely want you to see that. There's a guy with a ruler who can retract his penis into his body. He retracts it and then he'll measure it. It'll be one inch then suddenly it's three inches, and then four. (Laughs) It's very funny the first couple of times you see it, pretty hysterical. There are a couple of guys with dildos and they want you to watch. Or they want you to tell them, "Stick it up your ass, put it in your mouth." There are a couple of very submissive older guys who really like to be made to kneel down in the filthy booth and beg for my favors. There's one guy who is heavy into pain, he's got a dragon tattooed on his dick. He pierces himself, sticks roses up his penis, and lights candles on it. I love to see it, I think he's wonderful. He has rings all the way through the underside of his dick, and he has a little lock he puts on. He tries to be very creative, it's fascinating. He's poetic about it and has a great sense of drama. Many guys are average married men with wedding rings.

We don't get very many women who go into the two-way booths where you can see them. A lot of women come in with men. Sometimes it's obvious that the guy has somehow coerced them. Older Asian guys will bring their wives and the women are totally expressionless. They don't seem offended and they don't seem interested. Some of the women are obviously bisexual and make a much bigger fuss over the dancers than the guys they're with. Once in a while you get a lesbian who comes in alone. They act similar to the guys, they'll pretend to lick you, and eat you, and kiss you, and touch you. I don't think I've ever seen a woman masturbate in the theater. I've seen women have sex with men in the booths. I see women coming out of the one-way booths who tend to look dikey, or much more butch than the bisexual women and the women with men.

Do the customers leave their social roles and status behind when they come to see you? ~ Not unless they're kinky. If they're kinky, then they're assuming another role. Your average guys come across the way they always come across. They are, for the most part, members of the dominant culture, and used to having their way, being served and getting what they pay for, et cetera, et cetera. And that's what comes across. It's not bad. There's something about their casualness, the way they seem to take everything for granted.

And as far as people in other social strata, I don't see much difference between the way they behave in the theater, and the way they behave on the street. Black guys tend to strut and act real cool, and pretend a great deal more sophistication than they have, young ones especially. Your average black businessman is kind of like your average white guy, although I sense a little more insecurity. The Hispanic guys tend to be more arrogant, more dismissive. They're the ones who tend to have the sex guilt. The Asian guys tend to be emotionless and expressionless. Not the American Asian guys but the Asian guys. The kinky ones can parade around in lingerie, and then go back to the office in their suit with their garter belt underneath, and nobody knows. (Laughs)

What is your favorite type of customer? ~ Customers who are attractive, who turn me on, who have a positive attitude, and who don't stay very long. (Laughs) I get bored and tired hanging out at one window in the same position. While they're busy jacking-off they want you to hold that pose.

Do you encounter men who you think hate women? ~ Definitely. You can tell by the sour expression on their face or the fact that they say, "Spread your lips, whore." I also encounter women who hate other women. They ridicule us and put us down. They usually come in with guys and they're usually fairly young. I encounter people who hate women, and in particular hate women acting in a way that's sexual. They come there specifically to abuse, but we have great security at the theater. Everybody has such a wonderful supportive attitude, that really, it's not allowed. It's very easy to get rid of them.

Have you ever felt it was dangerous to arouse a customer? ~ Absolutely not. I've never experienced any fear of any customer. Customers have followed me after work, I asked them not to, and they leave.

Do you encounter violent men here? ~ I think some of the guys who are real rowdy and abusive are violent. I feel some verbal violence, but they're in the minority.

Do you think you've ever danced for a rapist? ~ It's hard to identify a rapist because it's so acceptable. I imagine your average guy probably has committed date rape. He told himself, "Oh, it wasn't really rape." He got her drunk and she didn't want to, or she was too tired to fight it. That's still rape, that's still forcing a woman to have sex. So yeah, probably I dance for your average, ordinary social rapist. But I don't think I've ever danced for anybody who was a complete psycho. It's hard to tell just looking at people.

Do you have friends you first met as customers? ~ There is one customer with whom I think I am going to be friends. We just started seeing each other. My sexual attraction to him is not very strong, but I like talking to him. So we'll see. I don't generally go out with customers. Once you see the real person you've got all this other stuff to deal with, and vice-versa. I am no longer in my corset or G-string, I'm a real person with a full set of clothes, ideas, and a full life. It complicates things. This place is set up for fantasy, not for forming relationships.

From stage you see a lot of tongues. Describe this. ~ It's kind of weird, this pantomime of wanting to eat the dancers out. Most of them look like they have really lousy technique, frankly. (Laughs) A pantomime is not very impressive in this town. Once in a while you can tell that if he was actually doing it, it would feel really wonderful. Most of the time it's like having a dog around. (Laughs)

Describe some of the more unique encounters you've had with customers. ~ The unique encounters are the ones where I get real turned on and end up going home and having fantasies about the guy. The kinky stuff is fun, but it's becoming less unique as I get more kinky encounters in my personal life. I'm getting real interested in S&M, and I'm meeting a lot of guys who cross-dress. All these behaviors that were so interesting at first are becoming very ordinary. The unique encounters are the ones where there's some kind of weird rapport. I don't know what it is. Something clicks and suddenly I get sucked into the fantasy. It's not just his fantasy, we're both having a sexual fantasy experience.

Many customers show a great deal of interest in the dancers' genitalia. Why do you think there is such great interest? ~ The only thing I can think of is that it's so forbidden, that their wives, their girlfriends, won't allow them to examine it. They're real curious. I also think that men grow up looking at pictures of female genitalia and jacking-off. They associate a woman's breasts or genitalia with orgasm.

Sometimes I feel like an ant farm. They have these serious looks on their faces and they say, "Yeah, open it up a little more so I can see inside." The look on their face is, "I have never seen anything like this before. This is amazing. This is wonderful." They like to see women touch their own genitalia, so you often have to do that. That kind of behavior is not sanctioned by the culture. Wives and girlfriends won't masturbate, won't touch themselves, won't spread their legs, won't let them examine them. Or maybe they feel shy about it with wives and girlfriends. Maybe they feel they can't ask, that there's something wrong with that.

What do the customers want you to do? ~ Consistently, most of them – not all of them -- want me to show them my genitals. It's spread open and turn over so they can see my ass and genitals. Those are the requests most dancers seem to get. Sometimes they'd rather see me play with my breasts or just see my face. Sometimes they come in real depressed and just want some pretend contact. They'll put their hands up to the window and want me to put my hand up so we touch fingertips. Often I get requests from young guys to do some kind of insertion, which we don't do here. "Stick your fingers in," or "Don't you have a dildo?"

The other night this little short guy with a baseball cap and thick glasses, who looked like something out of a Gary Larson cartoon, said, "So, how much for the back room?" Some guys hold twenties or fifties or hundred dollar bills up to the window. Most of the guys know that doesn't happen here, but there are requests for sex. "How much for a blow job?" "How much to fuck you?" They love to see me get wet, sometimes I'll fake that. I'll lick my fingers and touch my genitals. "Oh, she's getting excited." They never seem to catch on. They think, "I've still got it." I turned her on, this hardened woman.

I think you are possibly the only or preferred sexual outlet for some customers. What do you think? ~ I'd say preferred. We're so safe. God, you can't get any safer. There's no contact and everybody has a lot of control. You're not going to catch anything, it doesn't cost a lot of money, and it's very anonymous.

Do you think customers get needs besides sexual needs met here? ~ I do, but there are so many needs tied in to sexual needs. The married men get sexual variety and it doesn't threaten their marriage, because there are no relationships. The customers' need for an outlet for kinky behavior gets met. Sometimes their need for nurturing is met. Also I think there's this big ego trip connected with having access to lots of bodies. I often fantasize that I'm the one in the booth and that I'm watching a stage full of men. In that situation I would feel very powerful, being able to pick and choose from this harem. So I think certain needs for power are met. It's a fantasy but an enjoyable fantasy.

Some customers experience ecstatic surprise when they first encounter the stage show. What do you think surprises them? ~ I think what surprises them is that most of us feel pretty positive about what we're doing, and that we're happy with ourselves. They often find out that we are artists or students, or whatever, and they like that. They're surprised that they're not getting hustled, that we're not cold and hard-hearted, that we don't hate them. Sometimes there's this immediate unexpected attraction. They'll come in bored and something will click with somebody. Suddenly they're really excited, turned-on, and there's rapport. I think they expect things to be cold, ordinary, sleazy, and unhappy. It's not like that, it's very warm.

Sometimes a customer will leave angry or disgusted. Do you understand why? ~ They've been abusive and we've thrown them out. There are some dancers who are abusive to customers though. That happens a lot when dancers get bored. Abusing the customers becomes entertainment. I can see them walking out on something like that. Especially if they've done nothing. When I first started working here, there was definitely a tradition of abusing the customers, and, "The customers are garbage." In fact, it was considered bad form to do a good show, really catering to the enemy. But that's changed completely.

Do you ever abuse the customers? ~ The ones who want it. As far as abusing other customers, I don't think I've ever gotten real abusive. I can get pretty snotty with these young guys in groups. I will definitely make some kind of snide, nasty remark, something sarcastic, if they start being abusive. I've never made the first move to be abusive.

Do you ever feel controlled or possessed by the customers? ~ No.

How do you respond when a customer orgasms? ~ Sometimes it turns me on. Sometimes it's like, "Oh, thank God, he's finally done." Sometimes there's a certain feeling of power attached, like I instigated this, I am responsible for this somehow. Mostly I'm just glad, like, "Okay, this one's finished." It's like finishing any job, there's a feeling of completion.

Do you feel good when the customer feels good? ~ Yeah, I think superficial, recreational sex is just fine.

Do you try to get the customers to spend? ~ I do that more now that I'm management than I did as a dancer.

How do you feel about dancing for customers in the three booths with one-way glass? ~ I got used to it. At first it was really difficult. If I'm in a real playful mood I'll ask them why they're hiding. I'll ask, are they fucking a Siamese cat, what are they doing in there? There's one customer who injured his eye, and he looks ugly. He goes into the one-way booths. I assume when someone is in a one-way booth that they're very shy, disfigured, or that it's a woman. It's someone who for whatever reason is not comfortable with being seen. I feel sort of nurturing about that.

As the desired do you have power? ~ People who are desired always have power.

Have you experienced burnout on this job? ~ I did when I was getting lots of eight-hour shifts back to back. That was terrible. I actually injured my leg and couldn't get it to heal because I kept dancing.

Off stage you encounter other dancers, support staff, and management. Describe the interaction and conversation that occurs. ~ It's nice. It's like being anywhere, except you can be naked. What's really great about the theater is I can sprawl out on the couch, no clothes, legs open, completely relaxed, everything exposed, and have a normal conversation with just about anybody. I'll hang out on the couch naked and talk to Alan about his latest teaching project. It feels wonderful to have nakedness not be an issue anymore.

Off stage it's not uncommon to hear dancers referring to each other as slut, whore, or bitch. What do these remarks mean? ~ Number one, you don't hear it as often as you used to. What I think they mean is that women who are working in the trade don't feel good about what they're doing. Sometimes it's a joke. Sometimes it's a way of being rebellious, and saying, "Yes, I am a slut, and I like it. Try to do something about it." But for the most part the women who I hear call each other those names are the women who seem unhappy with what they do.

Sometimes it's like a party here. Describe these occasions. ~ It's just fun. People are playing and dancing. There's always music. Sometimes people bring food and leave it out for everybody. There's a lot of joking, talking, and wildness. And sometimes there's a certain amount of sexual excitement going on that intensifies that feeling of party. Often there's more feeling, especially on stage, that we're very much together. Sometimes it gets silly. People play with each other, tickle each other, trade costumes, somebody will get whacked on the butt, or people will show each other dance steps. If everybody's got high energy, or a couple of very charismatic people have high energy, then it gets to be a party.

The owner and management of this theater say they want to create a safe, nurturing, fun, and profitable business. Have they succeeded? ~ For the most part they have. It's certainly safe, we have wonderful security. The support staff is chosen very carefully to make sure that these guys are not just here to hit on girls. They tend to be real supportive people. They're very protective and have a very open and positive attitude. When a woman leaves the theater if she wants an escort to her car or someone to wait at the bus stop, that's provided.

There's always a conflict between nurturing people and making money off them. Nobody except the owner has any idea just how profitable the business really is.

I'm trying to make it as fun as possible for people. It's not hard for people to get raises out of me. This theater is the best place for a woman to work in the sex industry that I know of in terms of being protected and taken care of. It's not the best place for making money at all, but it could be.

The owner has a good attitude toward sexuality, real positive. That counts for a lot. Most people in the sex industry have a negative attitude toward what they're doing. The men project that negative attitude onto the women. It's okay to exploit them because they're just whores, it's okay to mistreat them because they're no good anyway. That attitude doesn't exist here. It's just not here. In fact, the dancers are probably treated with more respect and consideration than anybody.

The owner and management also express the desire to empower people. Have you been empowered here? ~ Yeah. They let me do just about anything I want. I always call for advice when I want to do something new, I always discuss it, but God, they've been great. I spent a lot of money on Fairy Tale Week. They've allowed that. They've spent a lot of money on redecorating and fixing the place up, getting new carpeting, getting the place painted, because we asked for it. That's empowering.

As far as being on stage, we are empowered to have the customers treat us the way we want to be treated. We can throw them out, if we find them unacceptable. That's very empowering. Working here has made a big difference in the rest of my life. I'm becoming more and more straightforward. I've had a chance to see that not being straightforward in order to save people's feelings doesn't work.

I talk to the general manager at least twice a week on the phone and I can tell her anything. I told her at one point, that I was having a great time at the theater, but I felt there was no place for me to go from here. I told her I was ready for something else. I told her that I'd heard rumors that she was going to leave. I said, "Are they true, and if you leave do I have a shot at your job?" She said, "Yes, it's possible, I'm either going to leave or I'm going to expand the company, either way there will be a place for you to grow into." Who else could you say that to? "I want your job – do I have a shot at it?"

Describe worker/management relations. ~ They vary a lot. I find that people don't talk to me as much as I want them to, because I'm the show director. I tend to hear things second-hand, or months later. It's obvious that I have become "them", as far as being "us and them." I don't like that too much. I am now demanding that people do things that they don't always want to do. They don't necessarily want to put on a good show for the customers, and I insist on that. They want to just hang out on stage, talk, and collect their paychecks. I won't put up with that. I would say that the relationship is fairly cordial, but I don't think the dancers trust me, because I'm management. Frankly, my motivation is real different from theirs. They're being paid an hourly wage; I'm on salary and I get a bonus when we go over a certain weekly amount. I'm motivated to make the show good. They are not, at this point, very well-motivated to make the show good. I think most of them like me, considering I'm management.

Do dancers have job security? ~ Boy, that's kind of iffy. Exceptional dancers have plenty; mediocre dancers don't have as much. It's not good for the show for people to stay for years and years and years unless they are exceptionally beautiful and give a consistently great show. The customers get bored, they want to see new women. They want to have this harem fantasy. Most dancers don't have a lot of job security, because it's just not meant to be a permanent position. It's an ideal job for students, for people doing other things with their lives, moving in other directions. I have not fired anybody just because I thought they're mediocre. I've never done that. I have cut back hours because of that and since they get paid an hourly wage, that counts for a lot. I can fire them at will, I don't have to give them any reasons. I don't even have to fire them, I can just not schedule them.

In response to the question "Are you exploited?", a well known dancer and erotic film star replied, "Yes and no. We don't have a union, but I like what I do." How do you answer that question? ~ That's a good answer. I definitely volunteer, I think it's fun, but I would like to see less emphasis on the pussy show. I feel okay about doing that, but the heavy emphasis is on *that part* of the anatomy. You're almost forced to do that kind of show just by the way the stage is designed. When you step up to the windows that's pussy level. There are lights on the floor that light up your pussy. Which is the idea. That is kind of exploitive.

I think dancers and support staff should make a lot more money. In that way everyone in the theater is somewhat exploited. But, I don't think we're any more exploited than workers in any other kind of job. Everybody I know has to do something at their job that they don't like, so they can pay the rent and buy groceries. Everybody volunteers to do the job and you can quit. I don't have to be a dancer. The customers aren't allowed to tell us what to do, so in that way we're not exploited. The exploitation is typical of any kind of worker exploitation.

Do you ever think about unionizing? ~ Constantly. I even wrote to the labor board and got the information on how to do it. When we were talking about a strike I called to see if there was a union we could join. There's no union. The porn people can join the film actors' union, but there's no union for strippers. I would love to see a union. It's really hard to get sex workers to organize. They're transient and competing against each other. My experiences with COYOTE have shown me how difficult it is to get sex workers to organize. The women don't feel good about what they're doing, because there's a stigma, and they don't want to go public. It's like my landlady, if she found out where I really worked, even though I'm not doing anything illegal, she would lock me out of the apartment. And she probably could throw me out legally, because I lied on the application about my job. There is definitely a danger in coming out of the closet in order to unionize. People are leading double lives. They don't want their families to know; the husbands and boyfriends, the neighbors, the landlady. There are very few people in the industry who are real open about it. The stigma's just monstrous, it's very, very powerful.

Women's sexuality is very tightly controlled. For us to unionize and say, "This is legitimate work, sex work is real work, this is legitimate employment" – that's a hell of a statement to make, in this culture. To say that we can do sex for money, even when there's no contact, it's still women being openly and blatantly sexual, which is a big taboo.

The more I work in the sex industry the more I notice how uptight the straight women are. They're very careful about holding those legs together, and hiding their breasts, and sitting a certain way. You have to look good, but you can't show off! (Laughs) This tremendous double standard, this tremendous oppression makes it very very difficult for people. There's also the heavy drug use in the industry, which I think goes right back to the stigma. A lot of people feel bad about what they're doing, but the money's really good, so they spend the money on drugs so that they'll feel good. And drug addiction is just not conducive to organizing a politically active group, it's just not. (Laughs) It's not a problem at this theater. There's just your ordinary recreational drug and alcohol use here, it's no different from anywhere else.

Is sexism promoted or resisted in any way here? ~ Sexism is definitely promoted by the customer. And to some extent, it is promoted in the look of the show. Most of the customers want someone who looks like they just stepped out of Playboy or Penthouse. Big, firm breasts, long legs, very young, long hair. That look is good for the show and is basically a sexist look. In order to make money it's promoted, but we have lots of women who are kind of punky-looking. We don't demand that people grow long hair, that people have perfect bodies, but the dancers the customers like the best get the most hours, the desired shifts. They get their way more often than somebody who is considered less desirable. So in a way, we are reinforcing that rigid standard of feminine perfection. It's expedient to do that.

As management I'm treated very well. I'm treated with complete respect and consideration. I feel great about the way you treat me. There's not a problem with my being a woman. I have occasional problems with the male end of the management team.

The dancers try to resist sexism, as far as catering to a certain look. It's certainly resisted in that the customers are not allowed to tell the dancers what to do. In that way, it's absolutely resisted. The women are in control of the show.

What do you feel passing customers in the hallway whom you have just danced for? ~ It depends on how they treated me. There are a few regular customers that I just hate, I just do not want to be near 'em at all. There are a couple that I really like a lot, and I say "Hi" to them.

Do you change your appearance when you leave work? ~ Coming in I don't wear much makeup generally. When I go on stage I put on a lot because it washes out in the lights. I don't usually bother to wash it off before I leave, so I look different coming in than I do coming out. I have tried to disguise myself.

Do you have anger about this job? ~ I would say some annoyance, not any real anger. I'm annoyed at the way the stage is designed, the lighting, and the way it sort of forces a pussy show. The light is about as unflattering as you can get. Now that I think about it, that really pisses me off. I'm angry that we don't have insurance. Health care is appallingly expensive and everybody needs it. I'm angry that the owner is so secretive about how much money he is making. It makes me very suspicious, it makes me think that maybe I should be making more money. I'm angry about things like that, but I love my job, both the management and the dancing. I love it.

How does this job compare with others you've had? ~ I have much more freedom in this job than I've ever had in a straight job. There's no one looking over my shoulder all day long, telling me what to do. Most of the straight jobs I've had I didn't enjoy. Dancing is physically very demanding and that feels great. I like doing physical work, as opposed to just mental work. Especially when you're doing mental work that's not particularly creative. It's torture to use my brain for something that's non-creative, that's anti-creative. Or to use my intelligence to support a system I think is ridiculous. The computer company I worked for in Virginia was doing a lot of defense work. I hated that. We were designing a security system for Saudi Arabia. They were going to keep tabs on everybody in the country, so that the House of Saud would not fall like the Shah of Iran did. I hated putting my talents and energy into that kind of work.

Describe your earliest memories? ~ My very earliest memory is of getting stuck at the top of the stairs at our apartment. This was before I could walk. The memory starts when I am reaching for the third to the last step. I suddenly realize that I have done this before, and when I get to the top I'm going to be stuck. So, I decide to go back down. First I try going backwards, but I can't see where I'm going. I try turning around and going head downward, now I *really* feel like I'm going to fall. My arms are buckling, and I'm feeling this horrible lurching in my stomach, you know, that jolt you get when you're really scared. I know that's not going to work. I remember crawling back up to the top, sitting on the landing, feeling absolutely fine and throwing my head back and just screaming. I knew that if I did that someone would come and get me, I was not feeling upset. I can see these white legs flying down the hallway, this dress opening up and billowing out.

Describe your family and its circumstances during your early years. ~ My father was a doctor, a gastroenterologist, and my mother was a nurse before she married him. She stopped working after they got married. We lived in Albuquerque. I have a sister and two brothers, in that order. I'm the oldest. We're all about a year apart. We were a middle class Jewish family and my father hated being a Jew. I didn't know we were Jewish until I was about eight. Every year we had a Christmas tree, it was silver and popped open like an umbrella – BOOM, instant Christmas tree! (Laughs) "Okay, we're one of them, now." It would go up in the front window and nobody knew. My dad hated religion and any talk about God at all. He was a man of science, right? I didn't get any kind of religious education until I was eight.

I had a good friend whose family was Irish Catholic and his mother decided to save my soul. (Laughs) One day she started reading me stories about Jesus. Jesus was so wonderful and so handsome. I had this big crush on him, right? He was so kind and so beautiful. I remember walking through the front door and saying, "Mom, why didn't you tell me about Jesus?" She hit the ceiling! It's the only time I'd ever seen my mother stand up to my dad, the only time.

She screamed and yelled at me and sent me to my room. So, I'm in my room sobbing my heart out because I'm not going to be allowed to believe in this wonderful guy Jesus. My dad comes home and she's yelling at him. I couldn't believe it, she's screaming, "You want her to grow up to be a goy? You better do something!" She was furious.

So he came into my room and said, "Look, you want to believe in sweet Jesus go ahead, but don't tell your mother." We talked a little bit and soon I started going to Sunday school, but it was completely confusing. I just didn't get it. All of a sudden I was a Jew and Jesus was a great man, but he wasn't the savior. We didn't believe in heaven, but I would read old Jewish tales, and people would talk about heaven, it was *so* confusing. All these holidays with weird names. I started learning Hebrew and it never took. Religion never took with me. I started reading a lot about religion in sixth grade to see if I could find something that made sense to me, and none of it did. I am a deeply spiritual person, I just can't find any particular religion that appeals to the way I feel.

My folks split up when I was nine and my mother took us to California. She went back to work as a nurse, which is like being a professional toilet slave, and was making very little money. My father punished her for taking us away by cutting back on child support, alimony. They were both pretty awful parents, pretty mean to us. After they split up Mom got pretty crazy. She experienced the hardship of having to support four kids who were having all kinds of emotional problems.

We'd spend a month in the summer with my dad, and all of a sudden there's money everywhere. There'd be this big pot of money in the kitchen and we could go shopping. We'd buy steaks every night. The fridge was always full of sodas and we could eat anything we wanted. He was real indulgent. He would rent an apartment for us, next door to him. He had lots of girlfriends and clearly didn't want us interfering with his sex life. He would brag about it, and we used to brag about it, you know, "Dad's got all these girlfriends, he's a stud." (Laughs)

What kind of child were you? ~ I started off being an extremely bright, fearless, inquisitive, and aggressive child. By the time I was seven I just basically withdrew. I became silent. I stopped having friends. Up to seven I had a lot of friends, most of them were boys. I was a tomboy, I liked active rough-housing type games. I used to play that stuff with my brothers. My sister didn't like it, but we would play "horses and walls" and just kick the shit out of each other. (Laughs) I loved those games, I loved to kick my little brother across the room! (Laughs) He'd come back and bite me in the arm. I liked climbing trees. I still like to climb. I liked playing cowboys and Indians, shooting arrows at each other, throwing stuff at each other. I was a pretty rowdy little girl.

We used to do terrible things. We would set traps for cars in the middle of the street. We'd put broken glass under a bunch of leaves, hide, and watch the cars go by, hoping somebody would get a flat tire. I was your average wicked hell-raising little kid for a while.

I was also a real sexual little kid. I liked masturbating from the age of 3 or 4. I didn't have fantasies at that time, it just felt good. I always got big crushes on people, like my big crush on Jesus. I had crushes on my teachers, and these big, heavy duty sexual crushes on adults. I remember that vividly. That started at around 5 or 6. I started having crushes on my baby-sitters, and I had a major crush on the Beatles. I'd pick out these sex objects and just devote myself to them. I was really curious about my body and real interested in the way it would twitch and jump around. I remember thinking – "God, this is neat!" (Laughs)

Describe your relationship with your siblings. ~ I was very close to my brothers for a long time. I never got along with my sister. We were competitors and opposites. I was the bad girl and she was the good girl. She was real domestic, real "good." Real obedient. She was always doing housework, learning to cook or sew. She got good grades and played the cello. I was out raising hell, had psychological problems, and I wouldn't wear a dress. I was interested in sex, I was messy, and I didn't always get good grades. I got good grades for a long time and then I started flaking out. I was never obedient. If I couldn't openly, actively, and angrily rebel, I would just withdraw and do nothing, and be inaccessible. My body would be there, but that would be it, the rest of me was pretty closed-off. My sister wasn't like that. She would do anything to please. She was a snitch, which always made the boys nervous. So for a long time it was me and my brothers, this little gang of three.

Describe your relationship with your parents. ~ My relationship with my parents was appalling. It was hideous. They should never have had children. My father started molesting me, my sister and brothers as far back as I can remember. I can remember just hideous, hideous behavior from my dad. And my mother would pretend it wasn't happening. For a long time she was very sweet, affectionate, and supportive. We loved each other, but she would not or could not protect me from my father. She was terrified of him and couldn't deal with reality. It was easy for her to pretend that it wasn't really happening, that she'd married a doctor and was going to be taken care of forever. She was really a childlike person herself. She was probably the most incompetent person I've ever met in my life. She couldn't do anything right. She could not take care of herself, so my dad was supposed to do that, and he did a pretty lousy job. It was a terrible relationship.

I really had this love-hate relationship with them. I led a very schizophrenic existence with them because all this weird shit would go on and then they would both say, "That didn't happen." I learned at a fairly young age that I didn't know the difference between what was real and what was not real. And there were certain things that I was never to tell anybody. Otherwise they were going to give me away, throw me in the garbage, whatever they had threatened. So there was this fake side of myself, the fake relationship: We were a happy family and we loved each other. And then there was this undercurrent, this vicious, exploitive, violent undercurrent to everything. It was a split existence, and I had a split relationship with them.

My parents were capable of acting like normal parents, perfectly capable of being affectionate, supportive, and informative. My dad was extremely bright, he was always encouraging me to learn new words, and helping me look things up in the dictionary and the encyclopedia. He taught me all kinds of medical terms. I would look at his slides with him at night. He would talk to me about his cases. Sometimes he would be a normal dad and we would have fun. I remember he liked to tickle me. That was great. He liked to scratch my back. I would lie there for hours and he would just scratch my back. It was wonderful. I felt really loved and taken care of. And then he'd force me to have sex with him, and I just hated the son-of-a-bitch. I just *hated* him.

I remember our landlady and landlord at the age of about four. They were these old people who just liked us, we were cute little kids and they would give us candy and stuff. Once we were all at their house, and I turned to my father and I just started screaming, "I hate you, I hate you, I hope you die," and stamping my little feet. Mom was scared and embarrassed. They were waiting for me to spill the beans. Dad just picked me up and took me home. And then he got me. He picked me up by one arm and threw me on the bed and jumped on top of me. He never actually busted me open but he would get on my chest and rub against me. I couldn't breathe, it hurt. That was the last time I openly stood up against him. The last time I ever screamed really hard, fought back. 'Cause I didn't want that to happen again. And it was bad. It was just fuckin' horrible.

My mother finally decided that my father was not the problem, that I was. All the problems the family was having were because I was a bad child, there was something inherently evil about me. So I became her target of abuse for awhile. Verbal abuse, and a certain amount of physical abuse. The physical abuse was not really serious. But she would scream at me all the time and tell me what a piece of shit I was. As a matter of fact, she nicknamed me *caca*. She used to call me that. I didn't know what it meant. She put it on my scissors and I remember one of my little schoolmates telling me what it meant. I tried desperately to get the tape off, she wrote it on Dad's surgical tape and I couldn't get it off. That was a fucking nightmare, I would have done anything to keep anybody from seeing that name on my scissors. Something clicked when they told me what that meant. I remember thinking something along the lines of, "Oh, *that's* why she wants to treat me that way. *That's* what she thinks I am, that I'm shit." It was horrible! What can I say, it was just horrible. It was just a nightmare.

Describe the sexual abuse you experienced as a child. ~ It was constant. My father would force me to have oral and anal sex with him. It started as far back as I can remember. At one point he was abusing all of us. I remember we were in this apartment, my mother was pregnant with my brother Sam. Paul was in a crib, Sarah was in a crib, and I was in bed, my first bed. We were sleeping in this room together, and all of a sudden the lights came on. I remember waking up and being very confused. My parents had been having a party, and all of a sudden all these adults were in the room, leaning against the walls. You know how people smell when they've been drinking a lot of wine? That smell just filled the room. There were all these drunk guys, my mother and father, and this very beautiful young girl, who was a prostitute, apparently. My father came in saying, "They love it, you'll see, the kids love it." And they started in on us, this girl and my father. I assume it started when I was just a baby, based on the fact that he was willing to molest my brother Paul and my sister when they were still babies and I was 3 or 4.

He'd dig his fingers into my genital area, so that it would hurt. He would jump on top of me and rub his penis where the rib cage comes together. He liked to fix me so I couldn't move. I remember having things tied around my wrists. When I was real little he could put his entire hand around both wrists and ankles, stretch me out, and do pretty much what he wanted. It was just awful. He'd make me give him hand jobs. He would put his hand over mine, just grab it so I couldn't get away. Afterwards he would always look confused and ashamed. If I put up a fight he would look confused.

I remember one time being in the bathtub, he was supposed to be washing me, and he started digging his fingers into my genitals. I told him that hurt, that I didn't want him to do that. He got angry and scared me, and told me that I was a bad girl and that he was very disappointed in me. I remember that, God, I thought, "I'm very disappointed in you, very disappointed." I'm in the bathtub and everything is hurting. Everything is hurting, and I'm furious, I'm angry, I'm backed up against the tub. But I could see the confusion in his face. The fear, and the guilt, and the weirdness. I knew that he knew he was doing something wrong. I knew that from the look on his face. And that was constant. I think he felt horrible every time he did it. But he was also addicted to downers. I'm sure that a lot of times when he did it he was high. I found out years later that has an amnesiac effect. Some of those times when he told me nothing happened he may not have remembered. This went on forever and ever. Sometimes I would withdraw, I would go to this place in my head where I would curl up and wait for it to be over. Sometimes I would fight, sometimes I would just bear it. I wanted not to fight very much. I learned that no one was going to defend me, that I didn't have any allies. That I was completely alone. As a child, I knew I was helpless, that I could not support myself, that I could not provide myself with food or shelter. And that if my parents were going to be treating me this badly, strangers would probably treat me worse. And I did *not* want to leave home. I wanted to leave home and go someplace safe, but I didn't think there was any place that was safe. Later when my parents were separated every time I was with my dad I ended up getting raped. Every time. He did it to all of us, and I'm the only one that's really been willing to deal with it. If you ask my brothers, to this day they will tell you that nothing happened, that I made it all up. Paul is starting to come around. My sister started coming around after he died. It was finally safe for her to say, okay, this happened. We were under threat of death. My dad was psycho enough to actually do that. He was a doctor and he used to talk about how you could make a death look natural, when in fact it was suicide or murder. So, everybody was afraid of him. He didn't know where to draw the line. As far as he was concerned there were no limits, there were no rules, as long as you didn't get caught.

I was twenty-one when I finally, permanently, said goodbye.

Tell us more about your childhood. ~ I loved swinging by my knees on the jungle gym, going on the swing, especially at the school playground. I'd swing as high as I could and then jump out. I loved to sing while I was swinging. Especially Beatles' songs. I had one close girlfriend who was also a tomboy. She was real rowdy, really a budding criminal. She tried to teach me how to shoplift, which I was not very good at. I always felt guilty. I did the usual kid things, try to get money out of my parents so I could buy waxed lips and candy. I would play house.

In New Mexico, the playgrounds are mostly sand, which meant that during a dust storm it was really awful. The rest of the time it was like a giant sandbox. We would make little houses, draw lines in the sand and build up little rooms.

I would make things for my dolls and drew all the time. That was one of the things I loved to do. My mother would buy me rolls of butcher paper, so I could just keep tearing off sheet after sheet. I drew incessantly and created little stories. They were like little comic strips – this is before I even knew what a comic strip was. I would create little fantasy lands, either draw them, or build them out of wax that I would get off cheese. Or clay, or cardboard, or whatever I could think up. I was always making things. I had a craft book and science kit. I liked bugs, I would catch bugs and watch them. I used to play monopoly all the time. I didn't like playing with dolls, unless I was going to make something for them. I liked my Barbies because I could make them clothes, and little houses and things.

One time I built a little village out of mud in the back yard. I planted gardens with the tiniest little flowers I could find. I created this little culture. If I was going to have a doll, I would make it out of a flower. I'd get a piece of clover and stick it through an ischia or something, so it would have a dress. If it was a boy, I would make something out of a leaf. I would make these little people and act out these little dramas. A lot of times they were sexual dramas. I would enact this little drama where this beautiful girl would be in love with this beautiful guy, and she would get kidnapped by an evil older man, who would sexually abuse her. Finally the beautiful guy would rescue her, they would escape together and the evil older man would be killed. I would enact that over and over and over. One of the stories I would draw over and over and over again was about a beautiful, creative girl and a wicked princess. They would fight over a prince. The wicked princess would steal the prince away, and then the beautiful girl would get him back. I played a lot by myself.

Describe your childhood school experience. ~ School was kind of weird. In Albuquerque the school's are pretty terrible, pretty lax. I was extremely bright and really good at reading and writing. I was generally five steps ahead of everybody else. I was great at art work. I got sent home from kindergarten with a note pinned to me because I had drawn a picture of an Indian and a horse and a cactus with the shadows in perspective. My teacher thought this kid's going to be an artist. Of course, I'm not. After kindergarten, it was kind of over. I was mostly bored in school and began to withdraw when I was seven.

Pretty early on in my school career I stopped relating to other children. And to teachers. After my parents split up my mother didn't take very good care of me. I had ugly hand-me-down clothes and my hair was not clean. She would make me look as ugly as possible. I was oblivious – I was living in a fantasy world by that time. I was sleeping a lot, reading a lot, and daydreaming a lot. I was fairly disconnected from the world around me. In California I was completely disoriented and Mom had complete control over my life. It got into some pretty heavy abuse, and I just withdrew.

My mother got put away when I was six, and when she came out of the hospital she was a different person. She hated me. Before that she loved me, and was very sweet to me. Although she wouldn't defend me against my father, she was still really good to me. Before she went to the hospital she was crying all the time and sleeping a lot. When she came back from the hospital she was a fucking bitch, a raging maniac. I used to have dreams that she wasn't my real mother, that it was an imposter. I knew it was an imposter, because she'd always spell my name with a C instead of a K. The very last dream I had like that, she came back and she wasn't mean any more, she was retarded, which was even worse. I think that's what did it. I no longer had my mom. I no longer had anybody. I started coming out of my shell by the time I was thirteen.

Describe your teachers and classmates. ~ I had some real good teachers, some really bad teachers, people who were abusive. My classmates were usually not as smart as I was. And it's possible the teachers were not as smart as I was a lot of the time. I had a second grade teacher who was wonderful, really sweet and funny. She was the one who found out that I needed glasses. She really paid attention. I had a lot of teachers who didn't want to get involved. I know it was obvious that something was wrong with me after a certain point in my life. I was the weird kid in class.

I had a fifth grade teacher who was a monster, he treated all the kids like shit. Once a little Japanese boy, this was when there were a lot of demonstrations against the government, during a discussion about the flag, he said, "burn it" under his breath and started giggling. The teacher just went off – told the kid he should be shot for saying that.

I had a wonderful fourth grade teacher. Gosh, she was just the sweetest. She was real young, fresh and new.

I had a high school social science teacher who was exceptional. Real creative. Really went out of his way to make it alive for us. To make us look at culture he did this "nacirema" exercise. This weird culture is described to you, and you learn all about their strange rituals. It turns out that "nacirema" is "american" spelled backward, right? Your entire culture has just been described in anthropological terms, and it sounds weird. You get to see how screwy some aspects of our culture are. It was great. By that time I was in ninth grade and coming out of my shell, thanks to drugs. Drug use did help me out for a while.

At an early age humans exhibit a wide range of erotic behaviors. Describe what you were up to as a child. ~ Well, I liked masturbation. I remember one experience with a little friend of mine, I was probably six. We were playing monopoly at his house, and he told me about this neat thing he knew that grownups did. He learned the word fuck and was telling me what it meant. He said, "Want to try it?" I said, "Sure." So we jumped into his closet, right? He said, "Okay, pull your pants down." So I pulled my pants down and he pulled his pants down. He goes, "And I put my penis in between your legs." It wasn't even hard, right? We're standing there and I have his penis between my legs, and we're hugging each other. I'm standing there thinking "God, this is really boring. Is this *it*? Is this what they do?" So I said, "Is that it?" He goes, "Yeah, that's it!" We jumped out of the closet and started playing monopoly again.

There was a neighbor boy who wanted to rub butts with me. So we rubbed butts and it was no big deal. I told my mom and, of course, she flipped out and called the neighbors: "Your son has been molesting my daughter!" He was older, like seven or eight.

I used to talk in sexual terms with my girlfriend, we would talk about all the sexy things we were going to wear. We didn't actually have any sexual experiences together.

What were you taught about human sexuality by your parents? ~ Oh, God. I was taught verbally by my father that everything is okay as long as you don't get caught. I was taught verbally by my mother that sex is bad, sex is dirty, sex is wrong. And that I was a bad person, specifically around sexual issues. That I was defiled, ruined, no good, I was never going to be any good, because of all the sexual stuff that was going on. And that I was a seductress. It was my fault that I had this innate capacity to force people to rape me. I was taught by experience that there's a big difference between sex and rape. I realized pretty early on that consent made all the difference.

I learned I could give myself lots of pleasure masturbating. As soon as I started to read, I started looking at pornography. Dad had a big collection of pornography, so I found this wide, wide range of sexual behaviors. I learned through reading my father's pornography that women could be in control of their sexuality, that there were women who liked having sex, who would actively seek purely sexual relationships, which they had total control over. He had a lot of S&M stuff, that's basically what I was going through. My Dad would pin me down and make sure that it hurt, always. I learned that there were lots of different sexual behaviors and sexualized behaviors. And that what I was going through with my dad was not the way it had to be, at all. On some level I realized that he was using sex to hurt me, and that sex was not really the issue at all.

Did you receive information about human sexuality in grade school? ~ No.

Was there nudity in your home? ~ There was never much nudity.

Were you ever punished due to sexual expression? ~ Oh yeah. My mom didn't want me to trust myself sexually at all. She could get pretty nasty about it. I remember telling her about masturbating. I told her, "I found this great thing that's really wonderful and I really like it." She said, "No, that's dirty, don't do that. Don't ever do that." But she didn't actually punish me. I was definitely punished for the thing with my dad. *I* was punished for it. Consistently.

What effect did that punishment have on you? ~ Well, it left me feeling pretty confused. I consider the denial part of the punishment, having it happen and then saying, "No, that didn't happen," that's a mindfuck, that's a mind rape. It left me not trusting myself for a long time, not trusting my ability to perceive reality. It left me not trusting other people at all and mostly, unable to be emotionally intimate with people.

I never had a problem being sexually intimate. I always liked sex as long as I felt like I was the one initiating it, that I had some control over it. As long as I gave my consent it was great, I loved it. When it came to love and trust, I was completely crippled for a long time, and unable to relate to people in any way other than sexually. I could not relate to people emotionally. I consider that a punishment. It was sex used as punishment and punishment for getting raped.

What were you taught about human relationships in your family? ~ I was taught that things are not what they appear. That loving people is not a good idea. That you can't trust anybody. That human beings are dangerous to each other. That we're not nice to each other. And that blood ties don't mean a thing.

Were you taught to look good to attract and be chosen by a man? ~ I was taught by my father to look as slutty as possible to attract men. I was taught by my mother to dress so that I wouldn't be raped. I had to teach myself to fall somewhere in between.

Were you taught to value truth? ~ No, I was not taught to value truth. I was taught, verbally, to value being honest. I was taught by my father to – "be realistic, be cynical."

I was taught that truth didn't exist, that truth is relative, that human beings are dishonest by nature, that we deceive each other, that we deceive ourselves, that it's really tough to get a good grip on reality. It's hard to grasp the truth. It's hard to find the truth.

Did your parents teach you that you could have power, choice? ~ They taught me that I had no power and no choice.

What effect did your body changing have on you? ~ It had a major effect. I could no longer have boys as friends. I was no longer one of the boys. I could no longer run around without a shirt on, no matter what, because I was developing breasts. It rekindled my dad's interest in me. That was a drag. All of a sudden I had other men interested in me, too. Grown men were pursuing me, coming on to me, staring at my tits, staring at my butt, making suggestive comments when I walked down the street. It was horrible. And I couldn't be an equal to boys anymore, once I was obviously female. They treated me differently. I couldn't roughhouse with them. I couldn't have physical contact with people anymore, except for little kids, because physical contact is always attributed as sexual.

Describe your adolescent sexuality. ~ I remember being incredibly horny all the time. I became the high school slut. I liked sleeping around and I didn't like being punished for it. That was real traumatic for me. The boys were free to sleep around as much as they wanted, and I wasn't. I had big problems when I first started sleeping with guys. I wanted to sleep with a lot of different guys, and they would get hurt over that. I would try to explain, "It doesn't mean I don't care about you. It just means that I care about somebody else also." Ultimately I found out that they didn't care about me. If I was going to sleep around, nobody was going to care about me. They were going to fuck me and drop me. But I liked it. I remember feeling like if I didn't get laid at least once a week I would just go crazy.

When I was sixteen I had my first real lover. He was a 27-year-old law student and we had great sex together. But he was not honest with me. He was always telling me that I was his only girl and that he really loved me. Then he would disappear once in a while. I finally ended up with the clap, and didn't suspect. He told me he was faithful. I was faithful. I figured I had a bladder infection or something. I ended up with the Vietnamese clap. It's really hard to treat and he never admitted it. It was awful. He was so sure that I wasn't faithful to him.

How did you first discover and use the ability to arouse? ~ I used to pick up guys. I'd go to a party and pick out somebody I wanted to sleep with. I'd just go for it. As far as my ability to arouse, I would dress very, very provocatively. I would always have my breasts exposed or really jutting out, I'd wear a real short skirt or shorts. I would make a beeline and just radiate, "I want you, I want to go to bed with you." It worked great as far as getting people to go to bed with me. It didn't work great for forming relationships.

I had the ability to arouse because of my father. I was taught that was my fault, that it was me. I would get him excited just by existing. He would lose control. I was taught that I had that kind of power over people. As far as using my ability to arouse someone that I actually wanted, I don't remember when I first did that. When I decided that I wanted to be sexually active, I started using that power. It was a real instinctive thing.

Describe your discovery of how pregnancy occurs. ~ I had some kind of understanding from home that if a man's penis gets in your vagina you can get pregnant. I don't remember how I learned that. In junior high they talk about the sperm and the ova, they don't tell you how the two things get together. But I already knew that. I remember getting very embarrassed talks by physical education teachers who hated having to do this. I suspect my P.E. teachers were dykes who didn't enjoy teaching about heterosexuality.

The thing about Pop was you could talk to him about anything. I could ask him any question about sex and he would answer, boom. It was right out there. There was no censorship at all. He put me on the pill when I was 16, when I first started going out with this law student. I found pills on the kitchen counter with a note.

I was always very, very careful not to get pregnant. I did not want to have children. I was terrified that I would be a parent like my mother and father. I was afraid that if I had a child I would become crazy. Somewhere along the line I decided that having children had driven my mother crazy. I was convinced also that I would get involved with the wrong man, a man who would rape my children, abuse them. I would not have sex under circumstances in which I thought I would get pregnant. It was never a matter of some guy pressuring me. It couldn't be done. I've never been pregnant.

Did you receive information about human sexuality in high school? ~ It was mostly about sperms and ova. And, "Your body is changing now, and these are normal body types, and normal changes." They also talked about, "boys and girls are trying to relate to each other," the different ways we try to relate and the misunderstandings that can happen. There wasn't a whole lot of talk about sex, there was no talk about sex as recreation, zero. It was sex as reproduction in a marriage. There was no talk about pleasure. Certainly no talk about technique, except among those of us who were doing it.

I had one year of high school in California before I went back to Albuquerque and that was wonderful. People were pretty open about their sexuality. Girlfriends would talk about technique, how to handle the guys and what to do. In school they showed horrible movies about VD. God, people with syphilis of the eye. Big open sores all over your body, and you will go insane. Lots of scary messages about "Don't do it."

Describe your high school years. ~ I started doing a lot of drugs, and it really brought me out of my shell. I started being able to talk to people. And I started rebelling against my mother and the way she dressed me. I started dressing in a way that was acceptable to my peers. I started taking better care of myself and grooming myself better. But, I wasn't doing my work and my grades started going down. I started cutting classes. Then I went back to Albuquerque to live with my dad, because my mom was going off the deep end.

My mother started molesting me my first year in high school and she also became more and more physically abusive, to the point where I was afraid I was going to be actually mutilated. I decided to live with my dad. I figured I could be molested, mutilated, and verbally abused by my mother, or I could be raped by my dad. It looked like a better deal in Albuquerque.

In this high school all the rules were different. I was considered very shocking, my drug use, the way I dressed, the fact that I was a hippie from San Francisco. People were shocked and interested in me. That year was really good, probably the best of my entire childhood. I felt wonderful.

Then there was a huge custody battle when Dad tried to change custody. We had gone to visit him for the summer as usual when the boys and I decided not to go back to Mom. I had been planning this for a while. The boys didn't want to go back without me, because I was the one who caught the most abuse. If I wasn't there, they were next in line. So they decided not to go back. My sister went back because she had not previously been abused. Suddenly she was severely abused, and it was just horrible for her because she wasn't used to it. She didn't expect it.

My dad didn't like that I was dressing like a hippie in very baggy, colorful clothes with lots of beads and stuff. He didn't think that was very sexy and he started putting a lot of pressure on me. And I was getting the old sexual abuse routine again. He had a lot of girlfriends though, that took a lot of pressure off me. He was pressuring me to be this slut ideal that he had, wearing these really tight, revealing clothes and all this stuff. So I started dressing more the way he wanted me to. I was doing very well in school, great at math. He sent me to a hypnotherapist to get rid of this math block I had. It was great. My grades were great and I was making a lot of friends. I was really feeling pretty good, but it gradually started to erode.

I guess becoming sexually active in high school finished me off, because people decided that I was a slut. I lost my friends and I was badly treated by the boys I went to bed with. I was ostracized by a lot of people. People liked me a lot, but they thought I was a slut. I remember starting to round a corner in my apartment complex, hearing somebody say, "Yeah, she's kind of a slut but I really like her." That started to wear on me, and this whole thing with my dad started to wear on me.

I lost my interest in drugs. I had been using them mostly to maintain while I was with my mother, trying to hang on. I was smoking a lot of pot and doing psychedelics. Actually my dad was keeping me pretty well medicated. I had hay fever. He gave me these real powerful antihistamines that would knock me out. Any emotional problem, my father would give me a pill. There were always mood elevators, and a lot of barbiturates. He gave me a quaalude once in a while. I guess I was pretty high. I didn't need the other drugs, I was on this pharmacy shit.

When I was 15 I stopped growing. I used to eat constantly, and at 15 I found that I couldn't do that anymore, that I would get fat. So I stopped and that's when my blood sugar problem cropped up. I didn't know what was going on. I just knew that I would have these tremendous drops in my energy level and I would crave sugar. My father said, "Well, it sounds like you've got a little hypoglycemia." End of story. He didn't do anything to help me. So between the hypoglycemia and the drugs that he was feeding me, I was pretty out there. And the depression – just plain, ordinary depression and despair. It was a bad time. I withdrew again, gradually, and stopped being with other people.

This affair with the guy who gave me the clap really destroyed my faith in guys. But I was having an affair with another guy who lived in California, and he kept coming to see me. He was really sweet and wonderful, then he got addicted to coke and kept getting girls pregnant in California. He had several marriages behind him. It was just a fucking disaster and I was getting more and more turned off to men as people. I just couldn't relate. I couldn't relate to anybody about anything other than the sexual. It was awful. High school ended up being really hideous. And I lost my ability to do math.

In my last year of high school I got a lot of out of my women's history class. I was really into feminism. I read all the trendy feminist books and I was getting pretty hard core about it. But I liked sex and having sex with men. Somehow that was always in conflict with my feminist ideas. And, of course, I couldn't seem to get along with men, couldn't get them to treat me as an equal, or as though I was okay.

When I went back to live with my dad I became completely cut off from my sister, and soon became estranged from my brothers. My brother Sam was becoming more and more a macho asshole. Both brothers were constantly saying things like, "that dumb bitch," referring to me. There was a lot of hostility against women. My father would make my brothers do housework and cooking. Everybody had to take two days out of the week to do house chores, and Sam really resisted that.

I remember one incident when this guy came to my door and asked me to go get my girlfriend Laurie who lived just a few doors from me. I said, "You go get her, you want to see her." And he said, "I said, go get her." And I did it. I've never forgiven myself for doing that. I've always wondered why I obeyed him, you know, like how dare he. But I did it. I did it. I've always regretted that. I started thinking a lot about why I was so obedient to men. Why was I afraid of them? I think I became aware that I was afraid of men at that point, and I started fighting with my brothers. I'd been real close to them, but not anymore.

Describe the sexual abuse you received from your mother. ~ It didn't last long and it wasn't heavy duty, like my dad. It was fondling. I found that I could not bend over with my back to her and not get goosed. She would walk in on me in the bathroom and fondle my breasts and kiss me. She looked like she was in some kind of trance when she would do that stuff. A couple of times she called me Rose, which is my grandmother's name. Her mind was blown, she was not there. She never hurt me, it was very easy to make her stop. It was not the same kind of thing, as with my dad. Still, I didn't like it, I didn't want it.

What was your first job? ~ My first job was working for my dad. He got fired from the clinic he was working at and went into private practice, so I kept his books for a couple of years.

Did you have any heroines or heros during your high school years? ~ Buckminster Fuller and Germaine Greer are the two that stand out.

What did you plan to do after graduation from school? ~ I wanted to go to art school. I wanted to draw and paint and make a career as an artist. I had very vague ideas about how I was going to do that. My father was determined that I was going to be an architect, so I started thinking along those lines. So, I had a double image of what I was going to do after high school. I was trying desperately to find something I wanted to do that would actually make me some money.

After graduation I went right to college and studied architecture. It was really fascinating for a while, but I was cracking up. I had suppressed my entire childhood. I couldn't remember things. I couldn't concentrate on anything. I had no social life. I was working for my father and I was completely under his thumb. I was beginning to wonder whether the thoughts in my head were mine or his. I really didn't know. I felt like I had been brainwashed, which essentially I had. I tried to do my schoolwork, but ended up completely freaking out and flunking out in a year-and-a-half.

Describe other work you've done prior to dancing. ~ After I flunked out of college I started streetwalking and I became a topless dancer in a bar on an Indian reservation. I was 19 and you had to be 21. I was dancing and turning tricks out of the bar. Then I worked in a nude modeling studio for a while and the owners decided that I should run a massage parlor in Arizona. I did that for eight months and then gave it all up. I realized that I was seriously ill mentally, that I had worked myself into something of a trap, and that I had better find out what the hell was going on. I felt that I didn't have any control over what I was doing, that I didn't know who I was, and that what I was doing was bad. Everybody around me was saying, "It's bad, it's bad, it's bad."

So, I went into therapy and decided to go straight. I got a job in a department store as a sales clerk. Next I got a job at a computer corporation, first as a receptionist, then as a documentation clerk, where I was keeping files and entering data. These papers...these endless papers they were writing. I wanted to go back to art school. My boss said, "Don't do that. You'll regret it. You won't make any money. Stay with the company, I will create a graphics department for you." And he did . I ended up doing computer layouts, diagrams, flow charts, forms. We used clip art. I didn't do any illustration.

It was a computer firm that would do anything for money. Computer whores. They were talking about teaching me computer graphics, and two of these guys showed me this system they designed. On the computer screen in these giant blocky pixels they had this woman with huge tits, right. They're giggling and saying, "Look what we can do, and you're going to be our artist, we're going to break off from the company and make a million dollars." I waited for them to come to me and say, "Okay, now we're leaving, you can be a computer artist." One day I said, "What's going on? This is taking a long time. Are you guys going to go, or what?" They went, "What? We don't know what you're talking about." They had forgotten in a big way. I finally left and went to art school for a couple of years and did childcare. I lived with a boyfriend for one year, he supported me while I went to art school.

I was a live-in childcare person after that for a couple of years. I did about a year-and-a-half in Virginia taking care of a little boy and a house. I was incredibly poor and exploited. Now there is an exploitive job – childcare. Especially live-in childcare, that's serious fucking exploitation. These enormous fat people would not feed me. They had me give all the leftovers to the two dogs. (Laughs) I would sit on the kitchen floor with the dogs and say, "One for you, and one for me, and one for you, and one for me." (Laughs) It was fucking horrible. Just nuts. They were really affluent people working at good jobs in D.C. I was fucking starving, and they're huge, fat people, right. And they're always commenting about, "How do you keep your figure so slim?" I'm fucking starving to death, there's nothing in the refrigerator but cottage cheese.

Then I came out here and did more childcare for a while. Also I worked in a residence club as a waitress and a switchboard operator. I took care of twins in Lafayette. That was an education. A girl and a boy. It was fascinating because they were exactly the same age and so different. Their growth rates and developmental rates were completely different. I loved the twins but their parents were just shitheads. They were also fairly exploitive, tried to cheat me out of taxes. They were taking deductions out of my checks for taxes, but I hadn't signed a tax form, and I wasn't getting any pay stubs. I found out from a girl who had worked for them that they just kept the money. These are phony white liberal types who are involved in all kinds of civil rights and feminist causes. Complete hypocrites.

I did childcare specifically to see if I could do it. The first time that I thought I even might become abusive I was going to kill myself. I had been watching mothers and fathers with their kids for years and years to see what works and what doesn't. I was great. God, it was such a relief – you have no idea – to find out that not only am I not abusive, but I did an exceptionally great job. I am wonderful with children. It took a huge load off my shoulders.

Then I got my inheritance, and I was looking for a business. I went back to school and studied film and video. I was going to buy video equipment and start a business and the video teacher said, "No, no, no. You're an artist. I just got this brochure in the mail. Check this out." It was a computer graphics system. I ended up buying it and had my little business for a couple of years. I was not successful and I got a job as a part time reader for a stenography school.

Later I got a job doing computer graphics for someone who had been a client of mine. That was the last time. I just blew up. I just couldn't do it anymore. I couldn't put up with any more crap. And I couldn't stand computer graphics anymore. It was not the fun, creative field that I thought it would be. My last job was putting blinking red dots on a map of China. I'm sitting in front of this goddamn map of China, with blinking lights thinking, "I cannot do this anymore. I never, never want to do this again." I quit.

I had been looking at the ad for this theater for years. I cruised around looking longingly at all those places. I had wanted to go back into the sex industry for years. I always told myself, "No, you can't. That's bad. You want to go back into the sex industry because you were sexually abused, and this is sick." I went into therapy and I got this great therapist who has this real open attitude towards sexuality. She told me to take the San Francisco Sex Information training. I really wanted to go back into the sex industry and to explore different areas of sexuality.

I became interested in S&M, it was no longer scary. The fact that my dad was a rapist has nothing to do with it. Or if it does have anything to do with it, it doesn't matter. I want to check this out. All my friends from video and computer graphics were saying "No, no, no." And all the people at SFSI said, "Yeah, go ahead. Check it out. You want information." They gave me information and my therapist would either give me information, the name of a book, or someone I could talk to. There was no censorship and no judgment. Anything I wanted to do, as long as it was consensual, was okay. The key for me has always been consent. So I went for it, I went for my job here.

Describe other experiences you've had in the sex industry. ~ The bar I was turning tricks out of and dancing at was Mafia run, which is not the big deal people think it is. I had a Mafia pimp and it was no big deal. I always thought he was taking more than his share of the money but we couldn't come to an agreement about it. When I decided that I was going to leave I was scared, because I knew he was Mafia and I'd seen him chase people with guns before. With my suitcases under my arm, I said, "I think I'm going to go into town for a few days." He said, "No, you won't be coming back." I said "Well, no, I just want to think about it." He goes, "No, sweetheart. I know you won't be coming back." He gave me a hug and a kiss and said, "Good luck." That was it, my big bad Mafia pimp. Didn't try to stop me, never beat me, never did any of that shit.

One night he sat me in the back seat of the limo, shook me and said, "What are you doing to yourself? You don't need money that bad." He said, "I'm going to teach you how to make money without giving them anything. You promise them the moon, but don't give them anything." He taught me how to scam these guys. He trained me in a nude modeling studio. You charge these outrageous amounts for a massage or for a photo session and you don't give them anything. They get a massage but they don't get a hand job or a blow job. They don't get sex of any kind and you charge them eighty bucks.

I was his mainstay working at the nude modeling studio in this little migrant town outside of Phoenix. I was isolated and living in the parlor. He wanted me to stay isolated, to stay there 24 hours a day, seven days a week, working for him He was going to take all the money and I was going to be a good girl, not complain, and be really sweet to him all the time.

On about my third night there, and without phones in, we were open for business. I was all by myself and nobody had told me that once a month the neighborhood goes crazy. This is in the middle of a million cotton and watermelon fields and the migrant workers go crazy. These boys range in age from about eight to twenty. They form gangs and go around raping, robbing, and pillaging. So I got gang raped and robbed. It was a really bad scene.

This other pimp Phil said, "Go ahead and prosecute." The police made me take a lie detector test but I wouldn't give them my legal name. They said, "We know you're lying about the whole thing. You know you invited those guys in."

It was just a fucking disaster. Actually only one cop was really an asshole about it. The other two were really nice and used to come by to check up on me after that.

Anyway, after this whole ordeal Phil picked me up at the police station and took me back to the parlor. I said, "What are you doing? We're going to be open?" He said, "I don't believe in spoiling nobody." I said, "You've got to stay with me." I made him stay and we ended up falling asleep together in bed. I didn't work that night, but his attitude that I was going to keep working – that shook me up.

Later I became involved with Phil. He wouldn't sleep with me for a long time and that impressed me. I knew he wanted to. I had never met a man who wanted to go to bed with me who wouldn't. It made me trust him. I had never met a man who tried to control his sexual impulses before. Never. And of course it builds up the anticipation and the desire. He was always teasing me and getting me excited but there was no fulfillment. It was actually a pretty good mindfuck, a pretty good way to get control over me.

Soon I had a bodyguard, this enormous, giant, fat guy who would sleep in the back of the parlor like a big dog and wait for something to happen. One day when there were no other girls working this really attractive young country looking guy comes in. We started to talk and he said, "I noticed you were reading *Helter Skelter*." He said he knew some people in the Manson Family, "Don't ever get involved with those people. They're really dangerous, they're crazy." We talked for a little while, and then he just got up and left. It had been real pleasant, right, and then he came back. I go, "Did you forget something?", and all of a sudden there's a knife at my throat. It was that fast and I screamed. He thought that I was alone because there were no other girls, and he said, "Cork it. Get up." I started getting up and thank God, my bodyguard showed up at the door. He was enormous and he didn't shave. (Laughs) He just looked like trouble. He obviously just woke up from a nap. The guy heads out the door and I'm going, "Get him. Get the license number. Get something." Ben didn't know what was going on, it just didn't click. Didn't get on it. I was terrified, shaking all over. I was frozen in place and hanging onto my neck. (Laughs) The guy actually cut me and I was bleeding a little bit. I said, "How bad did he cut me?" Ben goes, "Cut?" "Yeah. He had a knife." Ben goes, "Knife? What knife?" Anyway we ended up going to the other massage parlors to warn everybody about this guy. We didn't call the cops.

We went to the El Matador, it was a dungeon. I had never been to a place like that before. This enormous, real tall and fat, red-haired woman, hair all the way down her back, came to the door. She was real jolly and laughing. Her husband, this little wimpy guy, in thick glasses and a baseball cap was sitting in the kitchen area playing cards with his buddies. He had brought her some candy and she said something about, "If you eat my maple walnuts I'm going to spank your butt." He's wiggling around giggling and smiling. Then she says, "Would you like to see the place?" I said sure. I had no idea what I was walking into. None.

We went downstairs and she showed me her dungeon. She says, "This is where we turn the guys over and paddle them," and "I'm building a track in the ceiling." She showed me this track with cuffs hanging from it, where you can hang them up and swing them around the corners. The girls bash them as they go by. (Laughs) It was great. It was the first time that it had ever clicked for me that women could be that powerful, that they could completely turn the tables and abuse men sexually. It made a huge impression on me. We went back upstairs and it was like we re-entered the world of guys. She had a pretty profound influence on me. I'll never forget her. I started fighting with Phil more and I left shortly after that.

Do you see current connections with the abuse you suffered growing up? ~ I see a constant effort by myself to somehow turn the tables and claim my power, to get my power back. And to get some revenge. There's certainly an element of revenge to it. To some extent my interest in S&M has something to do with reclaiming my male side. Everything I associate with men I decided I didn't want to be or do. I pretty much threw out the baby with the bath. That was a mistaken decision. The things that I associate with men are actually traits inside me, and I have a right to them. They're not bad, and they're not destructive. But it's one thing to understand that intellectually, and another thing to actually change your behaviors and your feelings around that. So I have lots of issues over control. Particularly around sex and sexual issues.

Describe living situations you've been in since you left home. ~ I lived by myself for a short while in New Mexico, in a little studio, and became totally isolated from the world. I lived with crazy people in Arizona, and behind the bar on the Indian reservation, in this big house with people who worked at the bar. I lived in the massage parlor in Arizona. Then I went to Virginia and started living a straight life, and did regular roommate things like anybody else. I lived with roommates who I didn't get along with for a long, long time. I did live-in childcare, house-slave kind of stuff, where you get the shittiest room in the house, where you have no money and no clothing. I've lived with boyfriends, which was okay if we were both working. If I wasn't working it was a bad situation, because I was dependent and pretty much afraid to stand up for myself, for fear of getting thrown out. If they weren't working I felt that burden because until I went into the sex industry I made very, very little money. Now I'm living alone, at last, for the first time in about ten years.

I have my own large, downtown studio apartment. I spend most of the time in the bathtub reading. All my books are warped. (Laughs) It's my favorite place to hang out. I have floating cushions and everything. That's the room that I have worked on. When I get the time I paint, which feels wonderful. I just tack the canvas right up to the wall and go. There's no furniture in the living room, just a set of bookshelves. It's too noisy and it's hard for me to sleep there, which I need a lot, but it's mine.

The unfortunate thing about this place is that I had to lie to get it. I'm living in the closet. A friend has a small moving company, so I told the landlady that I worked for a moving company. She made it very clear to me that they only want "nice girls" in that building. Sexually active and sexually outspoken women do not qualify as nice girls.

I found when I was looking for apartments that saying I worked at the theater, and that I was doing AIDS outreach 20 hours a week for the California Prostitutes Education Project was a bad idea. People would hear those job references and say, "Go away. Not a chance." Whore, prostitute. I'm sure that's what went through their minds. Nobody said it, but nobody called me back to get the apartment. So I lied, and I don't like that, I hate that. This is my home and I would like to be out of the closet.

I'm getting real involved with S&M now, and I have this huge walk-in closet that I would love to turn into a dungeon. It could be a problem. There are some very nosy old people in my building. They're not going to be happy with my little activities. (Laughs) Screams. I'm going to have to do something about the acoustics in there.

Describe significant friendships and love relationships you've had since you left home? ~ It took me a long time to understand friendship and love. My relationships after I left home were primarily sexual, financial relationships. I don't think I really learned anything about love until five or six years ago when I met Adam at the residence club where I was living. We were both waiting tables in the dining room. He is the first person in my life who just loved me, exactly the way I was, thought I was wonderful. And he's the person in my life that I trusted enough to love back.

Most of my relationships after I left home were superficial. There wasn't a lot of closeness. It was after I met Adam that I started forming closer friendships. And only since I moved to San Francisco that I started understanding friendship and how those relationships take time to develop. It's pretty recently that I've learned to relate to people normally and easily. I always felt like such an alien. I was carrying this tremendous burden of secrets with me. I was watching myself every minute, afraid that something was going to slip out, about my home life, or the sex industry, or whatever. I was always in the closet.

It's only since I moved to San Francisco that I started feeling like part of the human race. I still tend to be mostly a loner, but I do have these great long term friendships. I like them to be open and honest. I have risked friendships since going back to the sex industry. They've stood up to it, but, it's made things a little rocky. Especially with the women I knew in the video and graphics industries. Let's say I have some strained close friendships and some real supportive ones.

My love relationships have not been very successful. Adam was about as close as I got. We really loved each other and it still didn't work. I started growing in a different direction and he wasn't growing at all. In spite of the love we had for each other, I left him.

After that I tried to get into some monogamous, in-love romantic type relationships. And they didn't work out. I finally decided to bag it, that's not really what I want right now. What I want now are friendships, sexual and otherwise, and that's happening. I'm meeting people I can date and sleep with but we're mostly friends. I've started going out with women. I've been thinking about it for a few years. It's great. I'd say my relationships now are more between equals, they're more friendships, with sex added in. I don't have a sense of dependency or any kind of inequality, like in the past with more romantic type relationships. There have been a couple of times where I almost went in that direction, and I've backed out. It was the right thing to do. I don't think I was made to be a wife, companion. I'm not even sure I was meant to be a mother. I like kids a lot but I don't think it's me. I think I'm always going to stay pretty independent, somewhat a loner. And I've finally made my peace with it.

Describe your interests outside of work. ~ My major interest is art. I like to go to galleries and I like to paint. I would love to do ceramics. I like doing ceramic sculpture. I'm interested in making things but it's something that takes a lot of time and energy, which I don't have very much of right now. But I am painting.

I'm interested in S&M. I'm interested somewhat in politics and the position of women in the sex industry as far as the feminist movement goes. We have been isolated and outcasts from the women's movement. I am interested in getting women in the sex industry, or women who are interested in being sexy, involved in the feminist movement so that we are represented. That's another thing I don't have a lot of time for. I am still connected to Coyote and the California Prostitutes' Education Project. I just got a call from them to work on a fundraiser soon and I'll be involved with that.

One of my favorite things to do is curl up with a book. I love going to the movies, I would love to make movies. I write little scenes. I'd love to do something about the sex industry. I think it's real important for people to know what really goes on. They have a lot of misconceptions. They're always shocked to find out that I'm intelligent. Some of the dancers we hire are shocked to find out that the women around them in the industry are intelligent, that they're not the only ones, that in fact, that is the norm.

Do you use drugs? ~ Not usually. Actually I like mushrooms a lot and I have been experimenting a little with using real low dosages and hypnosis to try to bust up some of my old behavior patterns. I'm trying to use hypnosis to get the euphoria and the energy I tended, in the past, to get from drugs. I have nothing against drugs, but I find that they wear me out and I can't afford to get that tired. I like psychedelics. Once in a while I have a drink. I'm addicted to caffeine and that's a drug even though it's sanctioned by the culture. I don't get a lot of sleep so I use it to keep me going.

Have you suffered any traumas as an adult? ~ I'd say getting gang raped when I was 20 was pretty traumatic. But it fit in with what I was used to. Getting gang raped for me was probably not as traumatic as it might have been for somebody who wasn't used to being sexually abused. For me it was, "Oh, this again."

What's been traumatic in adulthood is constantly experimenting with new behavior patterns, constantly moving in new directions. I don't think that's bad trauma, but still, it's upheavals. It's traumatic but it's in the interests of growth.

Describe your fears and insecurities. ~ I am terrified of becoming destitute and living on the street. I don't have any kind of financial support system. If I fuck up, I'm out. I'm afraid that I'll reach 40, 50, 60, or 70, and suddenly be destitute. I am fairly insecure about my looks and my ability to compete with other women on that level. I have a habit of expecting to be physically over-powered and I am constantly sizing people up who I don't know, particularly men – but not just men – to see if there was trouble, if there was a fight, how would I do it. That's an old, old habit. That goes back to my dad, and it keeps getting brought home, like getting gang raped. I would love to go back to prostitution, but I find the idea of having to fight the vice cops all the time unacceptable.

Describe your male inspired fears. ~ I find them pretty consistently insensitive, disconnected, and that's scary. I find males consistently stronger than I am. That always frightens me, even if it's someone who I know loves me. I've met 13-year-old boys my size who were much stronger than I was. That's my major fear around males.

What media do you consume? ~ Books and movies. I watch very little television. The news business is pretty ludicrous. I try to keep on top of what's happening in the world, but I'm also absolutely certain that it's all being biased and censored, that I'm not getting the real picture, that I'm only going to know what's being fed to me. The media that consumes me is either escapist or expresses my thoughts and feelings about the culture in a way that I couldn't do by myself.

Do you read romance novels? ~ No. There's an element of phoniness and exploitation about them that irritates me. They're real manipulative emotionally, and I don't need that. I don't need something artificial to make me cry or feel wonderful. I want something real. I think romance novels are destructive. They increase the alienation between men and women because men don't read them and women end up with all kinds of expectations that men know nothing about. Women are reading romance novels and men are looking at *Playboy*. It's no wonder we don't see eye to eye. (Laughs)

Do you use sexually explicit media? ~ Not so much, because it's hard to find anything that I like. Porn for the most part is pretty ludicrous. It's kind of stupid and boring. The last porno I saw that interested me had a hermaphrodite in it and it was fascinating because it was a hermaphrodite. But the video itself was pretty stupid and contrived. The acting was not so hot. I like things to be sexually explicit but still graceful and beautifully done. There's very little that's being done that way.

Which of society's values have you rejected? ~ All the nice girl values. I see no value in hanging onto virginity or sexual monogamy. I see no value in being law-abiding. Laws are stupid. I see no value in blind acceptance of authority. I see no particular value in organized religion. I see no value in maintaining a pretense. I'd really prefer more honesty, more connection with who people are, what we really are, instead of trying to maintain these ridiculous contrived ideas, "ideals", all this pretend stuff that's popular in the culture. Pretend so that you don't offend people. Pretend so that you won't upset people. Pretend so that you hang onto your job. I hate the bullshit in this culture. I hate the dishonesty. There's a high level of deception and dishonesty that's acceptable in the culture. And to me it's not acceptable. I hate the conformity. That's not acceptable to me. Talking about people being different, if we're all that different on the outside, it's certain we're all that different and diverse on the inside. There should be room for people to be who we really are, say what we really think, feel the way we really feel, and our culture should make that operate smoothly instead of trying to deny that we are the way we are. I reject racism, sexism, ageism, all those "isms." Anything that doesn't leave room for people to be who we are, that doesn't make it okay for people to be exactly who they are, I reject.

Has the media ideal of beauty affected you? ~ Definitely. I'm finding that the closer I get to the ideal, the more money I can make and the easier it is to manipulate your average white guy. Those are the guys with the money. For instance I am growing my hair out, and I'd really prefer to cut it off. I am experimenting with makeup, and I'd really prefer to walk out the door without it. And I'm considering breast surgery. So I'm trying to live up to this media ideal so that I can make money. I'm also aware that I don't have that much time left because part of that ideal is for women to be perpetually 20 years old. And there's no way. (Laughs) If I'm going to make big bucks in the sex industry as an object of sexual fantasy, I've got to do it soon. It has influenced me definitely, because it works.

Many humans love the attention of others and adorn themselves to get it. Do you? ~ I have to remind myself to do that. It's real conscious with me. If I'm going to a party and I want to get laid, I'll adorn myself. (Laughs) I adorn myself at work, to make more money. If I'm adorning myself for other people, it's because I want to manipulate them into either giving me sex or money. I never adorn myself to get someone's approval, love, or affection because it doesn't work. That's not how you get love and affection.

What is your self-image? ~ I'm currently in a state of major transformation. My image of myself, at this point, is that I am not entirely myself. There are major portions of my personality that have been suppressed for a long, long time, and they're starting to emerge now. My image of myself is that I don't appear to be the way I really am. I appear to be much nicer and much easier – much wimpier than I really am. I know I'm attractive, but that's not my image of myself. People are attracted to me and I see that. When I look in the mirror, I don't see it – I don't know what the deal is. I'm extremely bright, and as a general rule I'm smarter than the people around me, but I'm not terribly well educated. I feel a lack there. I feel I got stuck in the wrong body, I should have been bigger. (Laughs) This little tiny body does not really fit who I am.

Are you a tolerant person? ~ I'm extremely tolerant of different lifestyles and such. I am not especially tolerant of bigotry or sexism. I'm not tolerant of intolerance at all. I'm pretty tolerant as long as nobody gets in my way.

Do you trust people? ~ No, but I trust my ability to take care of myself. So I find it very easy to open myself up to people. I figure if they hurt me I'm going to bounce back. So it doesn't matter.

Do you exploit people? ~ Yeah. Yeah. Occasionally I do that. Especially anybody who pisses me off. I get a certain amount of sadistic pleasure out of fucking with them. Yeah. I'm thinking of somebody specific right now. (Laughs) Somebody who got in my way. I used him and abused him and he's still coming back for more. (Laughs) I don't get it.

I don't know if exploit is the right word in terms of my relationship with the dancers because I'm management. I definitely push people a little further than they want to go sometimes. So there is some – I would say, mild exploitation. If I know somebody is a pushover and I want them to do something that they don't want to do, I'll push them around. If I need a dancer to be on stage and she doesn't want to be there, I'll push her. I don't know if that's exploitation.

Yeah, it is. She doesn't want to be there and I know it. I need her there but she gets paid, so it's not total cold-blooded exploitation.

Have you ever been violent with people? ~ I used to fight a lot when I was a kid. I loved it. I'm getting involved with S&M now, and I like it. I'm thinking of joining the San Francisco Women's Wrestling Association to have an outlet for that side of myself. I like violence. I like watching violent movies as long as there's not a whole lot of blood and gore, I like fight scenes a lot. I like car crashes. I like to see things blow up. I like the energy in male violence. I'd love to go to the fights if I could get someone to go with me. I wouldn't want to go by myself because the crowd gets violent.

I'm constantly trying to control myself. I like violent play. I'm constantly fighting these little impulses. I was in a hot tub one time with two people on my lap and I had this really strong impulse to suddenly stand up and and throw them both face down in the water, just for fun. (Laughs) I was in a bunk bed with a guy at a sex party and I had this sudden impulse to just kick him off the bed, just for fun. (Laughs) I'm definitely violent, but I didn't do it. I need more outlets for that violence because I feel like I'm in a state of constant self-restraint. It's just this weird, sadistic impulse.

People need adequate, safe outlets for their violence, instead of denying it, instead of saying, "No, we just won't be violent, we won't feel those things any-more." That's bullshit. We're a very violent species. It's obvious, and every-body keeps saying, "No, that's not happening. No, that's not true." (Laughs)

Define love. ~ Love is a feeling of being connected to another human being, to any living being, to an idea, to anything. It's a feeling of being at one and at peace with someone or something. It's a desire to protect and nurture and give to that someone or something. And it's an acceptance of who that person is or what that situation is. Real love is an ability to be very realistic and supportive.

Define power. ~ Power is the ability to affect oneself or others, to make things happen, or to prevent things from happening.

Describe the variety and frequency of your current sexual activities. ~ Currently I'm experimenting with S&M and group sex parties and trying to stick with safe sex. It is not easy. Even as a safe sex educator who knows the risks and what's safe and what's not, in a situation with a new lover I find this a constant struggle. Everybody wants to be the exception. I hate latex, but I'm getting used to it. It's becoming part of my sex life.

I'm experimenting a lot right now, playing a lot. I'm heading towards an ideal goal of having many lovers who are friends, people who I don't feel jealous or possessive about, people who could actually sleep with each other and I wouldn't care. I'm trying to get lots of sex in my life, lots of sexual satisfaction.

I don't want monogamy right now. I want lots of fuck-buddies.

There was an attempt to destroy my real self through rape, using sex as a tool to beat me into a pulp. Most of my sexual explorations are completely tied in with re-emerging as my real self, bringing up all the stuff that was beaten down and repressed. For me, – it's healing. It's directly related to the fact that I was sexually abused and that that was a damaging process, a destructive process. I'm turning that around now. I'm using the thing that was used to beat me down to bring myself back up.

Are you orgasmic? ~ It's really easy for me to be orgasmic. I prefer vaginal orgasm, which I've been told by a lot of guys is unusual. I've never gotten to the point where I just couldn't cum anymore.

Do you masturbate? ~ If I'm alone, before I go to sleep at night I'll masturbate. Sometimes I do it in the bathtub. I do it all by hand. With masturbation I get into a lot of fantasy, that's the most important part of it. It's one of the few times that I like a lot of clitoral stimulation. I get involved in lots of wild fantasies, all the stuff that I probably wouldn't do. I have a lot of fantasies about kidnapping guys and keeping them my sexual prisoner. That's one of my favorites.

Do you ever act out your fantasies? ~ Sometimes. But fantasies are to explore areas that you're not going to explore in your life. I am starting to act out S&M fantasies.

Describe the dominance and submission aspects of your sexuality? ~ I'm exploring formal S&M, where people say, "I will be dominant," "I will be submissive," and you work things out. I tend to be mostly dominant. I like a lot of control. I don't seek to serve in sexual relationships. I seek more to be served and satisfied myself. As far as formal role playing, I'm much more interested in the exploration of pain and the limits of sensation, than I am in getting into slave-mistress relationships, although that interests me, too. I definitely get a kick out of that. There are times when I want to be passive and taken care of, although that doesn't happen nearly as often as the times when I want to be active and in charge. I like to feel free to do both.

When do you get sexually involved? ~ (Laughs) It's usually an immediate physical attraction, and I will get sexually involved, without knowing who I'm with. We'll have a brief conversation, but it's pretty much a chemical thing if I'm into it.

Do you appreciate admiration of your body? ~ Oh, yeah. But I tend to be a little bit skeptical. I don't want to get attached to it because the women in my family live so long. When I'm 80 years old there isn't a plastic surgeon in the world who's going to make me look 20.

Prior to becoming a dancer had you publicly exposed your body? ~ No.

What sexual taboos besides dancing have you broken? ~ Being female submissive as far as getting into S&M. That's politically incorrect. Having group sex. Being bisexual. Nobody approves of that. (Laughs) Straight people don't like it. Gay people don't like it. The only people who understand are the other bisexuals. That's the funny thing about taboos. Every single group has got them, no matter how out on the fringe they are. There are certain things you just don't do. So I'm doing them. (Laughs) Just working in the sex industry is breaking a sexual taboo. I'm out there displaying my pussy for all these guys to jack-off to. That's a major taboo. Having lots of casual anonymous sex, with anybody I feel like having it with, for whatever reason, whether it's money or attraction or whatever.

What is sexually degrading for you? ~ For anyone to do something to me without my consent. If I consent for someone to be violent with me, that's okay. Anybody who thinks less of me for being sexually active, who tries to put their sexual guilt on me – that's degrading.

Do you ever use sex as a weapon? ~ If I'm pissed off at someone I'll tease them, I'll frustrate them. I'll seduce them and then maybe drop them. (Laughs) I've never raped anybody. Not consciously. I've had complaints occasionally from boyfriends that I should get my hands off them, they're tired of having all these demands made on them. They feel like they're being forced.

Do you ever experience guilt or shame about your sexuality? ~ No. What I experience is fear that I'll be punished for it.

Has living in a male-dominated society played a role in shaping your sexuality? ~ Oh, yeah. I certainly dress differently sometimes than I would like to. I like to be comfortable and that's not always perceived as being sexy. If I were not living in a male-dominated society, particularly one that's as superficial and materialistic and narrow as this one is, I wouldn't be considering plastic surgery. I like being sexually active and I know that I can be punished for it. There are plenty of guys who would kick my butt for it. I'm constantly having to reassert that I am a whole person, that I am not just a sex toy, that I'm not stupid, that I have feelings that are to be valued and respected. I'm in a state of constant struggle, in asserting myself as a sexual being, and as a whole being in a male-dominated society. I'm constantly thinking about what men think of me and how I'm going to behave in order to get what I want. I'm either hiding my body and my sexuality, in order to protect myself from abuse, or I am displaying it in a way that will get me money, or sex, or some kind of attention. I'm displaying in ways that your average guy will find exciting, which are not necessarily the ways which, say, lesbians, or unusual guys, or people interested in S&M would find exciting. I'm catering to the mainstream and that doesn't feel natural to me.

Do you think your sexuality would be different if you lived in an egalitarian or female -dominated society? ~ Definitely. It would be so much easier to take care of birth control, get health care examinations and make sure I was protected from STD's and pregnancy. I'd be able to have as much sex as I wanted without somebody jumping down my throat. In an egalitarian society I don't think there would be as much money in the sex industry. It would be okay for women to make a living in the sex industry, but since it would no longer be taboo for women to have sex, there wouldn't be the high price placed on it that there is now. And since there would be an insistence on women as real people, there wouldn't be the kind of idealization and objectification that goes on now. There would also be more acceptance of what female sexuality is and how it differs from male sexuality.

Has birth control and medical technology affected your sexuality? ~ It's had a major impact. I don't have to worry about getting pregnant every time I have sex. It's great to know that I can go in for regular checkups. I'm trying to schedule that into my life right now because I'm so sexually active.

How do you deal with birth control now? ~ Most of my partners, most of the time, use rubbers. I'm trying to make that consistent, but I've always got a sponge in.

Has the women's movement affected your sexuality? ~ Absolutely. It has reinforced my attitude that it's okay for me to have sex. It's made me want to stand up for myself and demand that I be sexually satisfied. The objection I've had to the women's movement is that it has been sort of an anti-sex movement. The emphasis has been on economic equality, and the terrible sexual repression of women in this culture has not been addressed at all. In fact, it has sometimes been intensified by the feminist movement. Let's be anti-sexy, let's really dress down and be ugly. That will show men what we think of them. Let's just make big bucks and wear ties and suits. That's a problem.

Describe your most recent love relationship. How did you get together? ~ One of my computer graphics clients told me about this guy who needed a live-in housekeeper. I took the job to get away from my ex-boyfriend and to save money on rent. He came across as being very, very sweet, very lonely, very vulnerable, very eccentric and extraordinarily bright. I just fell for him, and within a week we were sleeping together. I got hooked on him. But he was a major game player, emotionally very abusive. He found the one way he could get at me was by making me jealous, so he was constantly paying attention to other women. Then suddenly he would turn really sweet. I don't know that I was in love with him so much as obsessed. I was bored at the time and all of a sudden I was on this roller coaster ride. It was painful but very exciting.

He was a doctor and my girlfriends were saying, "Oh, stick with him. Hang onto this one." They had dollar signs in their eyes. Within five weeks I had moved out of the house. I said, "I can't work for you." He was unbelievably demanding. People laughed, and said, "Didn't anyone tell you what he was like?"

I kept seeing him and we had a pretty interesting sex life. He was the one who awakened my interest in S&M. He would pin my arms behind me when we made love or pin my arms over my head. He had me tie him up once. Once he got really high and told me it would be really fun if I took control. So we played a little that way. But he wouldn't really give up control. I would have had to hurt him. I think maybe that's what he wanted, why he was constantly making me angry. He read *Variations* magazine and hinted that there were stories in there that he really liked. But he didn't want me to find out what they were because then I'd get too much control over him. And of course, I found out what they were. They were heavy duty S&M stuff, electrodes and everything. The whole bit. He wanted me to just do it, and force him to accept it, and I didn't want a rape relationship. I wanted it to be play.

So I was beginning to get the picture. But whenever I tried to instigate any kind of play he wouldn't go for it. It was a total confusing mindfuck to say one thing and do another, or say one thing and then say the opposite. He was extraordinarily bright and he used his intelligence to fuck with people's heads. He did his best to make people around him feel stupid. He played tricks on people. He was never successful at making me feel stupid, but he could make me feel jealous and insecure about my looks. He really pushed that hard. It took about three months but I finally dumped him.

Tell us more about how being a dancer has affected your relationships? ~ It's made me realize how much I like having very superficial, uncommitted sexual relationships. It's made that okay and safe. And it's made me realize that there is always somebody else around the corner, that I don't have to worry about being left alone. I have thought about what happens when I get older and become progressively less attractive. The general manager told me that she wondered when men were no longer going to be attracted to her. It still hasn't happened and she is clearly an older woman. I remember my grandma Blanche, who was in her eighties and still dating. She looked like a grandmother, but she was a hot woman and it came across. I'd say it's enhanced my sex life, made me feel much less inhibited, much more in control, much more adventurous. My relationships have become much more egalitarian.

How did you feel about your body prior to becoming a dancer? ~ I've never liked my breasts. Other than that I felt my body was okay. I feel a lot more connected to my body now. I feel better about it. Everything feels real integrated in a way that it didn't before.

In your experience are dancers more deprived, abused, and battered than other women? ~ No way. Not at all. Women always get harassed, shit on, pushed around, cheated, and gypped. Dancers are no exception, certainly, but we don't get treated any worse. And a lot of dancers make so much more money than other women and have so much more fun. In a lot of ways it's a real healthy job. Physically it's very healthy. It's like you're exercising and getting paid for it. At the moment we don't make that much money, but it's still a good, high hourly wage, considering a lot of people in the financial district, or the retail and restaurant business are making, five, six, seven bucks an hour. Here it's real easy to get ten. In a lot of ways we get treated better, but we have to deal with the sexual stigma.

Since I was 15, stepping out the door, walking down the street and being harassed by a group of men has been consistently a traumatic experience. I'm always loudly evaluated and aggressively pursued. That's how women get treated in this culture. I am certainly no more likely to experience violence than any other woman. That can happen to anybody anytime within a marriage, a family, a workplace, just walking into a bar. It's not women in the sex industry who get singled out for that kind of abuse; all women are. As far as sexual harassment on the job, clearly it's no worse in the sex industry than anywhere else. Even though you'd think it would be, it's not. One time the computer company I worked for hired a secretary who was an exotic dancer. She had her little dictation pad and would go in for a meeting with ten guys and they would lock the door. When she got out her dictation pad was blank. This shit goes on all over. The boss and his secretary, it's so common it's become a joke.

Do you recognize any characteristics common to those who dance? ~ A lot of the women are very bright and very rebellious. They tend to be artists, musicians, actresses, or just oddball people who have no desire to fit into the mainstream. The other type of women I've found tend to be not particularly bright. They tend to be drug addicts and people who don't want to work for a living. And for some reason they don't want to get into a committed relationship.

Have people treated you as a "bad woman" since you started dancing? ~ Some people have. But most of the people I have told – I don't tell everybody – have found it pretty exciting, pretty intriguing. It's like knowing a bank robber.

(Laughs) So, being a bad woman isn't always so bad. My sister, surprisingly enough, is not treating me as a bad woman. But, I think we've resumed our old roles of her being the good girl and me being the bad girl. I think she's much happier now that I've dropped the computer graphics and straightening out, and gone back to being my evil self.

Have you lost self-esteem due to dancing? ~ No, I have absolutely gained it. I feel like I'm being myself now. Before, I had this terrible feeling that I was an imposter, a fake, that I was acting out this part, a recovered incest victim who is striving to make a better life. That I will have a monogamous, good relationship, children, a marriage and a house in the suburbs and all that shit. It's something I never really wanted. I guess I felt like I had to prove that my family situation did not, in fact, destroy me, that I could be normal, that I could be like everyone else. (Laughs) But I don't want to be like anyone else. I think everyone else is kind of boring, I mean those normal types out there. I love eccentric people because I am eccentric. I'm feeling more and more free to be who I am. I'd say that dancing has really liberated me.

Does anyone in your family besides your sister know you dance? ~ I don't know, because I don't speak to anyone else in the family. She has probably told them by now. It's like, "Oh, God. Guess what she's doing now? She's relapsed. She's at it again." (Laughs)

Has dancing affected your politics? ~ No. I'm feeling pretty helpless around politics right now and I don't think it has anything to do with dancing or not dancing. It has to do with the incredible corruption and deception that goes on within the whole political arena. I'm feeling fed up with it right now, completely fed up. It's not something I want to think about. But a little voice in the back of my head says, "You have to. This is going to affect you." Other little voices say, "No way. Don't be part of the system. Live on the underside in the black market zone, be part of the subculture, the counterculture." I guess I've always felt that way, and it's become intensified.

The one thing that has changed about my politics is that I am more concerned about women in the sex industry being politically active and politically represented. I see a real need for our voice to be heard and that's why I think this book is such a great idea.

Do you identify and feel solidarity with other sex workers? ~ Definitely, and I wish there was more solidarity in the industry in general. My experiences with the California Prostitutes Education Project really point out that it's hard to get a group of women in the sex world together.

Are you a feminist? ~ I'm a feminist. I think women should have as many choices as they can have. We should be free to do as we please. We should have economic independence and we should be treated with respect and consideration. It should be okay to be female. We are different from men and that should be appreciated and not maligned the way it is now.

Historically some feminists have tried to exclude some women from the women's movement based on their sexual behavior and preferences. Do you experience this exclusion? ~ Oh, yeah. The arguments that I've had with my friends from the video and computer graphics industry are perfect. All of a sudden I'm not a feminist because I've gone into the sex industry. I am no longer officially a feminist. My actions are not sanctioned by the movement. So, even though I identify as a feminist, even though I believe in economic parity and freedom for women, I am no longer a feminist.

What is your relationship to the women's movement? ~ I'd say I don't have one right now, although I certainly follow women's issues closely. At this point I'd say it's a fantasy relationship in which I am actually a part of the women's movement. I'm not very active except on a personal level, and I think there's a lot to be said for that. I consider contributing to this book feminist activism, an effort to get feminists to recognize those of us they have disowned.

What have been the most damaging and the most constructive influences in your life? ~ The most damaging was clearly my father. He was a real destroyer. And my mother, too. They worked real hard to destroy my confidence, my capacity to live and enjoy life.

There were people throughout my life who were very kind to me. I always hung onto those moments. The feminist movement probably saved my life. It's been a very constructive influence, even though they took this sort of anti-sex stand. There was also a "sexual revolution," that was a constructive influence. Suddenly people were saying sex is okay, sex is great. I'd say the whole cultural revolution, such as it was, during the sixties, was a very wonderful, constructive influence on me. And the movement against the war in Vietnam. It taught me that people can get together on the side of good and have influence. I have to be willing to put in the work to take the risks and abuse that people who have tried to change the way things are have always been subjected to, but change is possible.

I also think being a Jew has been a constructive influence, in that we tend to believe that mental illness is an illness that can be cured by doctors. That concept, from the time I was just a little girl, kept me going because I believed that I could heal myself. I always believed there was nothing wrong with me that was permanent and incurable.

What are your greatest gifts and limitations? ~ My greatest gift is my ability to survive and bounce back from emotional injury. I'm actually astonished that I'm able to bounce back the way I have. When I was fourteen I thought I would never be happy, but someday I would have less pain. I found plenty of happiness. I never thought I'd be able to relate to other people, or that anyone would love me. I found, that in fact, people do love me. I never thought I would love anybody, and I have loved other people, and I have a lot of affection for people in general.

Intelligence has been a great gift. Sometimes you think yourself into a corner, but in general it makes a difference to be able to analyze, process, and evaluate. Also I'm lucky to be creative. I've met a lot of people who are very bright and not particularly creative.

I'd say my ability to enjoy the sensual world has been a great gift, my ability to take tremendous pleasure out of the way things look and feel and taste and smell. A lot of times that's been all I've had in terms of pleasure, and that was enough to keep me going. I've got some minor health problems, but in general I'm very, very healthy and very sturdy. There are some imposed limitations because I'm female, but in terms of inner limitations, it's real hard to think of any. (Laughs)

What would you like to be doing in ten to fifteen years? ~ (Laughs) Oh, God...what do I think I'd like to be doing *now*...I'd like to have my own successful business, probably in the sex industry, but not necessarily. I'd like to be showing my paintings and making films. I would like to be much more politically active and out of the closet. I'd certainly like to see prostitution decriminalized, so that I can be involved without having to worry about the law. I'd like to feel very secure financially.

Recently in San Francisco we witnessed the appearance of women dancing for women. Why do you think this is happening? ~ We have a pretty strong lesbian community in San Francisco, and they want to see women. There are so many lesbians in the sex industry, it must be great for them to dance for someone they can relate to sexually. One of the problems lesbians in the sex industry have is that they've got to fake the whole thing.

Have you danced for women only? ~ At the theater. It doesn't happen very often, and it's usually not as blatantly erotic. Women tend not to masturbate the way the men do, they just watch the show. They may pantomime licking or touching you. When I was working on a safe sex video with a group of women, we danced with each other and it was very definitely erotic, very sexual.

If social and economic equality for women became a reality, would some women still dance? Would you? ~ I'd still dance. It feels wonderful and I like the attention, I like to flirt. I think a lot of women would. It's a fun job, and that's kind of unusual in this country, to have a job that's actually fun, light-hearted, and playful. I feel like I'm getting paid to play.

Would commercial sex work exist in your ideal society? ~ It'd be perfectly acceptable, integrated with everything else. Commercial food preparation, commercial health care, commercial babysitting, it would all be just part of living. There would definitely be people who were professionals providing that kind of care, instruction, companionship.

For many people it is impossible to conceive of anyone choosing to dance as you do. Why do you think that is? ~ I think the perception is that because it's sex, I'm being used and degraded, and I couldn't possibly be getting anything out of it. People don't understand because I'm not supposed to like it. The conventional wisdom is that women don't like sex, that women certainly don't like anonymous, casual sex, and that being paid for sex is degrading. I find that people try to invalidate what I say when I say I feel fine about this job. They say, "No you don't!"

Many people paint female sex workers as among the most obvious victims of male domination, and declare that if you don't see yourself as such, you are suffering from "false consciousness" and "delusions of the oppressed." What is your response to that? ~ They don't know what they're talking about. Sex workers have tremendous independence and control. It's a very arrogant position to take. It's a white man's burden attitude: "We're trying to help you, why aren't you grateful?" (Laughs) "Why don't you listen to us?" These are people who are not in the sex industry, and they are speaking for us because they have declared themselves enlightened. It's bullshit. They never consulted us. I don't understand how they can do that, how they can treat us as non-people, as unintelligent beings, as people who do not have the right to think for ourselves. They are being very dehumanizing in their attitude and very controlling. There's a strong element of that old patriarchal control over other people's lives, that rigid definition of what's right, what's moral, and there are no deviations allowed from that.

Why do you think people use sexually explicit media? ~ People like to feel sexually excited, and have strong orgasms. (Laughs) Sexually explicit media is a way of promoting that. (Laughs)

Has the sexually explicit media you've seen accurately portrayed humans and their sexual relations? ~ Not necessarily (laughs) ...that's the problem. The stuff that's really explicit tends to come off as really phoney. You get all the mechanics, that's about it. You don't get the emotional and sensual complexity of a sexual experience. I don't think I've ever seen that portrayed very well. It's going to take a lot more time, care, and lots more money to produce material like that. Also there has to be an acceptance that this is good...that this is in fact a valid part of human life, and can be expressed as an art form.

At what age do you think people should be allowed to view pictures of human genitalia? ~ At any age. It's a part of life, this forbidden zone. We're not Ken and Barbie dolls, where the area's just a blur! (Laughs) I think it's awful. When you see young children, they're so at one with their bodies. They stick their finger down their pants, they stick it up their nose, it's the same thing. No law should make it taboo, that these parts of the body should be unseen.

Do you think any sexually explicit media should be banned? ~ Kiddie-porn. That's where I draw the line. I don't think that kids should have sex with adults, it goes back to the issue of consent. Children are too vulnerable. I don't think they can really give consent to an adult. They're too easily coerced or threatened. Everything between consenting adults I think is fine.

At the outset, the Meese Commission declared that it intended to contain the spread of pornography. At its conclusion, the Commission, like most others, could not define pornography, yet it recommended the prosecution, fining, and jailing of people who produce, distribute, and consume it. What do you think of the Commission and its recommendations? ~ They should mind their own business and leave us alone. People's sexuality should not be regulated by the government. Pornography meant something that had no redeeming social or artistic value, they couldn't define that because it's too subjective. The range of sexual behaviors people are capable of is too wide, it's too diverse. It was a ridiculous commission, worthless, and a waste of taxpayers' money. I hope they had a good time watching all that pornography. I hope it enhanced their sex lives. (Laughs)

Why do you think the government shows virtually no concern with violence in the mainstream media? ~ Because it's a violent government, very violent. They're committing murder all over the world, sometimes great mass murders, supportive of violent regimes. There's something real macho about violence. Although we say it's a terrible thing, in fact we don't believe that. For men violence is a way of proving one's manhood, of gaining power over another. The ultimate act of power is to force someone against their will.

This is a country obsessed with power. I lived in D.C. for awhile, and I'm telling you, the whole city is psychotic around the issue of power. All the way down to the clerk in the mailroom. They are all like sharks fighting for power. Power there translates into making everybody do what you want them to do, and taking from other people. It's too much a part of the culture, it's too much a part of the way we do things, for there to be any criticism of it. No matter what kind of lip service people pay to nonviolence, the fact is that it's supported, enjoyed, and condoned by the entire culture.

How are sex work and sex workers portrayed in the mainstream media? ~ Sex work is portrayed as dangerous and degrading, and sex workers are portrayed as bimbos and helpless victims who are being forced to do this by some evil man or men. It's a pretty unrealistic picture. Sex workers are generally portrayed as easily manipulated, easily frightened and coerced. Or as drug addicts. They're never portrayed as choosing rationally to become sex workers. Except maybe Jane Fonda. She was about the most rational, realistic prostitute I've seen. It's portrayed as being completely negative and completely ridiculous. The portrayals of pimps and prostitutes, they look ridiculous, they look outlandish.

Some people argue that humans are born with a sex drive and after that our sexuality is socially constructed, produced through our experiences. How do you think human sexuality is shaped? ~ Well, it's basically repressed, in this culture. You're taught immediately not to touch your sex organs, not to display yourself sexually. Little kids know that that's bad, that's naughty. In this culture children don't see their parents having sex together. On the New Mexico Indian reservations often people live in one room and the children know exactly what's going on. In this culture everything's hidden, secret, and that has a big effect. Something that should be a natural, normal part of human life is separated and made into something very mysterious and more powerful than it really is, and more important than it really is, because it's taboo. People are torn in this culture between being taught that it's bad and forbidden and knowing how good it feels. And it's a natural drive. Trying to suppress a natural drive is pretty ridiculous, it can't really be done. It's going to leak out somehow.

People are shaped in school. You never found out how the sperm and the egg got together. And the movies about syphilis and the eye, my God, ...(laughs) it's like, "this is *bad*." Mysterious and strange and bad. It's not talked about openly, it's not looked at openly. It's shaped by every part of the culture and the culture is dedicated to repressing and controlling our sexuality.

Do you think the State tries to manage sexuality? ~ Unfortunately I'm very poorly educated, particularly in history. I would say that now it's certainly true. Look at their inability to cope with the AIDS crisis. They don't want any sexually explicit material around a disease that's transmitted sexually! I'm not sure what the motivation is, but it's pretty obvious that it's true.

What do men and women have in common sexually? ~ We like it. (Laughs) We like having orgasms, touching each other, being physically close to another human being. And I think both men and women like feeling free to have a lot of sexual variety.

Is there any sexual expression that society should ban? ~ Banning is pretty dangerous. The one area that's a problem, is sex between adults and children. Even saying you must not do it drives it underground, that makes it a secret, and that's dangerous for children. I don't think it should be made such a horrible crime that it increases the victimization of children. If it's so terrible that no one can find out about it, it leaves children vulnerable to violence and violent threats, and living a double life, which is horrible. Living a life in fear of sex, that's just horrible. Or living a life of guilt. I know a woman who as a child was molested by a neighbor and loved it, and went back for more, and to this day feels guilty about it, thinks there was something wrong with her.

I don't think anything should be banned, but I think that this particular area should not be encouraged and should be dealt with in a humane and reasonable way. I don't think children are capable of giving consent to adults, and they have problems with non-consensual sexual behavior, even if they like it. Children should be encouraged to have sex with their peers, not with adults, because it's an unequal relationship. The adult has all the control, all the power. Most of them will do anything to please the adults they love. And they will certainly do almost anything to please the adults they are dependent on.

Children are easily influenced, if you tell them something, especially very young children, they'll believe you. They'll believe anything! So rather than banning this particular type of behavior, it should be dealt with out in the open. Then children are going to feel that they have more control and more say. If they don't want to engage in this behavior, they'll feel much more free to say no. A lot of very young children are capable of understanding that a sexual relationship is ideally a relationship between equals, and that as much as they would like to be grownups, they're not grownups. That really it's more fun for them to play with their peers, and that they can get hurt, because of the size difference. It should be talked about openly. Children should be free to express their opinions. We don't allow children to have sexuality, and they certainly have sexual feelings and behaviors. It's even worse than the situation with women.

What part does sexual pleasure play in life? ~ Having an orgasm is absolutely the best feeling that I know. It is the best physical sensation I've ever had and it changes the way I feel afterwards. I feel better, in general, when I'm having a lot of sex. I'm more relaxed, more energetic, more affectionate, more tolerant. I feel more nurtured and more confident. It plays a major role in my life. And judging by the way the media uses it to manipulate people, it probably plays a major role in everybody's life. It's certainly a strong drive. When you're free to express it in the way you want, it does wonderful things for your life, your emotional state.

Some people seem to think that sexual pleasure without procreation is a threat to society. Is it? ~ No, there are too many children already. There's a need for much less procreation. Everybody wants to be affluent, and there's only so much to go around. Fewer people means more for everybody. Fewer children means more for those children already here.

Do you think gratification of sexual needs diminishes anti-social impulses? ~ It does for me and I suspect it would for everyone else. It depends on what one's sexual needs are. I'm thinking once again of the issue of children. In that case I would say no, those needs should not be met. But anything consensual, sure.

Feminism as it emerged in the early 1970's had as basic tenets sexual exploration and sexual self-determination. Subsequent exploration has led to intense debate over female sexual identity and behavior. How do you define female sexuality? ~ How could you possibly define it? Female sexuality is what any female wants to do sexually and that covers a very wide range of behaviors.

Are there any sexual behaviors you think women should not engage in? ~ Sex with children. That's it.

A recent Kinsey Institute survey of Western nations concluded that people in the United States feel the worst about their bodies. Have you seen evidence of this problem? ~ (Laughs) Ads for plastic surgery are everywhere. We've set up an impossible standard for women to live up to, in the ads, in the fashion magazines. It's impossible for anybody to always look that good. The plastic surgeons in this country are making a fortune. And the fashion and diet industries. There's a new diet and a new exercise plan in every single women's magazine every single month. Also it's becoming more and more important for men also to look good and youthful.

In the late 1940's the American writer Philip Wylie saw equally strong tendencies to excite and constrain the erotic drive as pervasive in this society. He observed they continuously reinforce each other and declared, "The United States is technically insane on the matter of sex." Is his diagnosis good for today? ~ Absolutely. Yes, it's true, we're insane. (Laughs)

In a recent decision the Supreme Court ruled that the State does have a role in regulating bedroom behavior. Do you agree? ~ No.

People in the United States are spending billions of dollars each year on sexual needs. What does this say to you? ~ That people like sex, that you cannot regulate people's enjoyment of sex out of existence, and you cannot teach it out of existence. It's primal behavior and people will seek sexual gratification. It's time for it all to come out of the closet.

Can sexual needs be met commercially in a non-sexist way? ~ Sure they can. 'Cause the commercial sector of society just reflects the culture. In a non-sexist culture you're gonna have non-sexist commercial sex. I for one would *love*, at three in the morning when I can't sleep, to be able to call up a massage or escort service and get some absolutely gorgeous person to come over and massage me, have sex with me, and then leave. That would be *great*.

Do you think the schools should teach about human sexuality? ~ Absolutely. Not only should they teach about it, there should be discussions. Children should be allowed to discuss their sexuality, to voice their opinions and views. We don't know how children feel about sex because we don't want them to talk about it. They have the right to talk about it. They have the right to ask any question to get any information they want. I would love to see human sexuality taught in a way that is not authoritarian.

How is sexuality portrayed in the mainstream media? ~ It's a pretty confused portrayal. It's never portrayed as an entirely good thing. Even when it's portrayed romantically there tends to be an element of tragedy in there for somebody. Or there's an element of complete unreality, an inability to deal with the basic human issues of getting along with each other, that's glossed over. For women it's heavily repressed, for children non-existent. For males it's not repressed, but it's become separated from everything else. It's become very much a genital orgasmic experience, disconnected from emotions and communication with the other human beings involved.

I think it's resulted in alienation from our bodies and unrealistic expectations about and how "the others" are supposed to be like sexually. It's used to sell people things that they don't really need. That's been very destructive. The idea is if you buy this, if you own that, you will get lots of sex with the culturally defined desirable sex objects. Sexuality in this culture has been perverted. And limited! It's become terribly limited.

Some people argue that there is a sexual hierarchy in the United States with heterosexuals at the top and everyone else treated as second class citizens. Do you agree? ~ Definitely. It's not just heterosexuals, it's heterosexuals who are either married or in a monogamous relationship, they're at the top. We still haven't gotten away from the husband and wife and kids agreement as being the ultimate in sexual relationships. Even a monogamous couple or a married couple who don't have kids – somehow they're suspect, they're not quite as good, they're not as normal. There's something wrong with them.

There are all kinds of hierarchies all the way down. I find as a bisexual woman that I get trashed by the lesbian community. I've had lesbians tell me that I couldn't possibly be bisexual, that all I need is the right woman to make me realize that, in fact, I don't enjoy having sex with men. But it's very clear to me that I do! (Laughs) And I've found that men don't take my sexual attraction to women very seriously. They don't understand that there certainly is the possibility of having a strong, loving relationship that's completely on a par with any relationship I could have with a man. There are plenty of hierarchies. There are plenty of gay men who hate women, plenty of gay women who hate men, to the point where they won't even own male animals, to the point where they are abusive to the male children of other lesbians.

Some people also think that non-heterosexuals should not have the same rights as heterosexuals. How do you feel about that? ~ I don't feel too good about that! And that's not too unexpected. I've said this all the way through, people's sexuality is their business. It's nobody else's business to regulate their sexuality, as long as they're engaged in consensual behavior. There should be no stigma or prejudice or whatever attached. It's personal. It's not public property, it's not in the public domain, until it becomes destructive. And like I said before, as far as I'm concerned it only becomes destructive when you involve children.

Do you think heterosexism is a serious problem in the United States? ~ Absolutely. I'm really lucky to be living in San Francisco. I remember walking down the street my first day and seeing gay and lesbian couples walking hand in hand, and lots of children of mixed race. I thought, my God, this is the place. *This* is where I want to live. I've never seen anything like this anywhere else.

A friend of mine was telling me recently how she wants to move back to Texas where her family is. In Texas she can't hold hands with her girlfriend when they're walking down the street, and that's a consideration. Even here there's plenty of fag-bashing. People get killed for having a different sexual orientation! I receive all kinds of wild reactions about my interest in S&M. Sometimes straight women get upset about my sexual interest in other women. They immediately assume that I'm going to put the make on them, that I'm going to force them into something. It's just ridiculous, the hysteria around any deviation. People are denied jobs for it, denied housing, and health care. In many parts of the country people have to live a lie if they deviate. That's a terrible way for anyone to live. People have the right to be who they really are.

How does society respond to the outspoken sensuous person? ~ Society in general is not very good to the outspoken sensuous woman. Now a man who is a lady-killer, that's fine. He can talk about his conquests and his exploits all he wants. For women to be sexually outspoken, it's like women being sexually active, it's not nice, it's not acceptable. To be sexually outspoken for some people means the loss of family.

What have you learned about people through sexuality? ~ I've learned that we're all pretty vulnerable. That we all have a need for human contact of some kind, on a real primal, physical level. That we all have a need for sexual satisfaction, and that everybody is different. Everybody's different, even in terms of their ability to feel sensation. When I'm with a new sex partner I never assume anything. I find that people are consistently inconsistent about what they like and what they don't like. That's nice, that diversity was kind of unexpected.

What would a sex-positive society look like? ~ We'd all go naked whenever we wanted. We'd be comfortable with our bodies. You'd see many, many more women in positions of authority. And many more gays. Many more people who deviate from the norm would be out of the closet, and suddenly you would see them. Or maybe you wouldn't, because there'd be no need to wear these badges of, "I am lesbian", or "I am gay." Nobody would need to be strident about that. I think you'd see a lot more bisexual behavior. The educational system would be completely different. Sexuality would be a part of it. Human relationships, in general, would be more a part of what we teach and what we talk about. It would become an art form that everybody would try to be more proficient at. There'd be a whole lot less tension. People would be less obsessed with power and money. People would be more relaxed and open, more satisfied, at peace. Everything would change.

How can we achieve that society? ~ This book will help. And people gotta come out of the closet, as dangerous as it is. We can expect a hysterical reaction, but fortunately it's such a strong primal need that maybe once people start realizing that some people can cut loose, maybe everybody else can cut loose. I think more and more rational, sexually open, sexually healthy people have got to come out of the closet. And it's happening. Look at Doctor Ruth! (Laughs)

Do women play a part in the creation of male sexuality? ~ We have accepted this role of being the guardians of sexual morality. And we oughta knock it off. We have allowed men to be sexually irresponsible, by not insisting that men use birth control, by not insisting that we be sexually satisfied. We have allowed men to get away with all kinds of irresponsible shit. We've allowed men to turn sex into a playground exclusively for men. We have given away our own sexual power. This is typically what women do. It's shaped male sexuality, and it's a mistake.

How do you think batterers and rapists are created? ~ I suspect that they've been victims of extreme violence themselves. Although, who knows how much body chemistry and genetic makeup play in it. I just saw a TV show that indicates that it's a mystery. I'd say it's a combination of factors: environmental, physical.

Are there feminist men? ~ Yeah. They try real hard to treat women as equals. I've never met a man who didn't once in awhile slip back into the authoritarian posture that men tend to take. But I've met a lot of men who try real hard not to. They stay conscious. They are conscious of the culture and they're fighting it.

What is their relationship to sexually explicit media? ~ Mixed. I've met men who in their efforts to be correct, have bought the party line about sexually explicit material. And there are those who think that sex is great and sexually explicit material is alright.

Describe the impact male dominance has had on women. ~ We constantly have to reassert ourselves as human beings. It's a constant fight, every single day, in any interaction with a male. It's a constant struggle to insist, "I am important, I am intelligent, I have value." It's exhausting.

How can women help men change? ~ We've got to become economically independent. It's vital. And we've got to stop being emotionally dependent. We've got to stop treating men as money objects or success objects, and start becoming our own money and success objects. We've got to start insisting that men be sexually responsible. We have to start communicating with each other sexually about what's okay and what's not okay. Women should concentrate real hard on what we want and who we are, and stop concentrating so hard on what men want and don't want.

What do you think the future holds for relations between men and women? ~ What I hope the future holds for relations between men and women is a near equality, an acceptance of who we really are, an appreciation of both our similarities and our differences. As far as what I think is going to happen – it's going to be an uphill struggle. It's hard for people to give up power and wealth.

If rape and sexual assault ended today, how would your life change? ~ Oh boy, it'd be great. I could go outside any time, any place...it'd make a major change in the way I live. I wouldn't take a cab home from work at three in the morning. I'd walk. I wouldn't be afraid to be alone with a man that I didn't know. Now I never assume that somebody is not a rapist when I first meet them. I wouldn't be so concerned about noises at night in my apartment. I wouldn't have a lot of the fear and tension that I have, that readiness to fight and defend myself.

What is the source of inequality between women and men? ~ I think it has a lot to do with pregnancy and the toll that takes. I don't know how things changed around to the point where property began to be inherited by male children, but the inequality is certainly closely connected to the idea of hereditary ownership and special problems around pregnancy. Also I think menstruation may take a toll on our energy level.

Taking care of the twins I got a chance to see how much faster girls grow than boys. What I found watching these kids in nursery school, is that the little girls turn into blazing bitches and kick the little boys all over the play ground. Who knows whether little boys wait until their teens to finally get revenge. I think the current source of inequality between men and women is economic. Women are denied access to economic independence. We're forced into a dependent position in which we have to cater to the needs of men

Feminist people have long observed the system of male domination in the United States and exerted considerable effort to overturn it. What strategies do you think have been effective? ~ Any strategy that involves women making more money, that gets women politically active and out there voting has been effective.

Which strategies do you recommend now? ~ Women should stop having children until they have established economic independence, until they can support themselves without a man. Women should be more politically active.

What do you consider to be the failures of the women's movement in the United States? ~ They've had a very rigid definition of what is okay for women to be. Exactly as males have had for centuries. They have taken a few traits and said, these are okay, but the rest are not. They have ignored those special concerns of women of color. They have ignored all kinds of cultural and religious concerns. They have ostracized women in the sex industry. They decided that they were going to save us without ever asking us whether we wanted to be saved. They have really trashed homemakers and people who want to stay home and bear children. They've alienated them and other large, important groups of women. They have adopted pretty much a male, patriarchal view of what is okay. They are very concerned with education and upper middle class, white *male* values being transferred.

What future do you see for the women's movement in the United States? ~ I hope that it will have a rebirth, that it will become a movement that's concerned with gaining much more freedom for women, in terms of behavior. For me the women's movement was about women having more choices about who you were and what you could do. I would hope that the movement really becomes supportive of that diversity, instead of taking a hard, punishing, party line about what is correct and what is not correct.

Anti-censorship feminists have emerged who believe that some sexually explicit media reflects and reinforces the oppression of women, but disagree with the pro-censorship feminists' view that sexually explicit media is the cause of women's oppression. They argue that the causes of women's oppression are much deeper and precede the mass production and distribution of sexually explicit media by centuries. What is your point of view? ~ It's not sexually explicit media that's the problem. The way sexually explicit media looks is the result of the repression and exploitation of women. A lot of feminists have put the cart before the horse.

Where do you think sexually explicit media should be placed on the movement agenda? ~ Nowhere. I think the whole issue could be dropped. As women become more independent and free in this society, sexually explicit media will change. We're going to start demanding, as consumers, a different type of sexually explicit media. The market will respond to the demands of the consumers, so the goal should be to change the demands of the consumers.

You told us how the women's movement affected your sexuality. Has it affected you in other ways? ~ It taught me to look for economic independence. It's made it okay for me to not have children. It's made me rethink the romantic relationships that have been encouraged for the past few centuries. I'm looking for alternatives to romance because I think it's basically a relationship of inequality and obsession with an object, rather than a relationship with a real person. It's made me feel okay about my sexuality, in spite of the conflicts within the movement around human sexuality. It's made it okay for me to sleep with other women. It's made it okay for me to not sleep with men, to have friends who are men without having a sexual relationship. It's made it okay for me to have my own business, to try to run things, to try to take control, to be powerful. It's made it okay for me to dress the way I want. It's made it okay for me to fight back when I feel I've been abused. It's allowed me to explore my relationship with my father, and fight against all the negative influences involved in that relationship. It's allowed me to leave my totally ineffective would-be-mother behind. I have plenty of other role models. Very strong, powerful, independent women who are quite capable of taking care of themselves.

Do you think our constitutional guarantee of free speech includes sexual speech? ~ I do, and I think it includes sexual behavior also. I think that the laws regulating our sexuality are unconstitutional. What can you *do* with people like that, people who think of sex as bad? All I can say is, sex is good, it's fine, leave us alone. It's none of your business. You don't like it, don't do it. But don't tell me that I can't.

Tell us what you know about AIDS and describe the impact it is having on your life and society. ~ It's primarily transmitted through semen and blood. I keep track of new information about what's safe and what's not, and recently I read an article about a woman with AIDS whose only risk factor was having oral sex with multiple lesbian partners. It's made me use a lot of latex. I use rubbers and rubber gloves. I use sex toys, dildos and vibrators. I've given up oral sex. I think rubber dams are worthless. I'm not crazy about this, but as wonderful as sex is, it's not worth dying for.

AIDS is not easy to get, I'm not afraid to hug anybody. I take baths with my girlfriends and I don't have any fears around that. But when it comes to sexual contact, it could be easy to get. If you're fisting someone and you have a little cut on your hand, you can get AIDS. It's made me frustrated and angry that I have to go through all this technical rigmarole to have sex with people. It's certainly not as spontaneous as it used to be. I use a lot of nonoxynol and I find that sometimes that's irritating.

On the one hand it's protected me from other STDs and from getting pregnant. In that way it's been great. I don't have the worry I used to have when I would go through a promiscuous phase. AIDS has definitely changed my behavior, but it hasn't made me monogamous. I have no desire to do that right now. It's made me more careful, but I find myself struggling with people. Everybody wants to be the exception, the one person who doesn't have to wear the rubber, right? That's been aggravating, but I am learning to insist on it.

AIDS is having a delayed impact. Most of society thinks it's a disease of gays and drug addicts, and that they are not vulnerable. Eventually it's gonna start showing up in the mainstream because they're not taking it seriously. It's going to show up in young adults who are doing lots of experimenting with sex and IV drugs. They're not going to protect themselves, because they're not being well educated. They're not allowed to talk about their sexuality.

There's already some talk about quarantining prostitutes. As far as I know a bill was passed that makes testing mandatory for prostitutes. For me, that's just the beginning of rounding up large numbers of people targeted as high-risk: gays, I.V. drug users, sex workers. If it gets widespread there could be disaster. We could see camps, people incarcerated and losing everything they own.

What future do you see for erotic theater and erotic dancers? ~ It depends on what happens with the level of oppression in the country. People have really gone off the deep end over the AIDS crisis and they are looking for scapegoats. They've scapegoated gays and the sex industry. The country is becoming more and more conservative, and those with a liberal view point don't feel that they have any control, or have given up and don't want to be terribly involved anymore. So it would be easy for that conservative element to take over and have the sex industry go completely underground. Another possibility – what I would like to see happen – is women who've been working in the sex industry opening up places of their own. Take it out of Mafia hands and the hands of men who simply haven't been workers in the sex industry. They've always been management, owners, and customers, who really don't understand what it's like for the women.

I would like to see erotic theater become, "Erotic Theater"; I don't think you can slide any longer on nudity. I would like to see more real talent put into the shows and still have them be erotic and exciting. It's very important that it be seen as recreation, treated in a way that's playful, and not in a way that's heavy handed, sleazy, and sad. As far as what's going to happen – I don't know. It depends on whether this repressive, fundamentalist element gets control of the laws or not. If they do, then it's going to go underground and I think *it is* going to be oppressive, sleazy, and sad.

JACKIE

WHEN YOU'RE IN THE EXPERIENCE OF BEING AN
EROTIC DANCER IT FEELS FINE...IT'S A RELIEF, IT
FEELS LIKE BEING A HUMAN BEING.

Part of the promotion for your show says, "Live Nude Dancing, Lovely Lusty Ladies, Naked Naughty Nasty." Is this a good description of what you do and how you perform at work? ~ Yes. It's sexy, hot, and exciting to watch. If the dancer lives that, she is that, it doesn't *really* matter what she looks like. I'm embarrassed just thinking about what I do that's naughty and nasty. I show men my pee-pee. (Laughs)

What were you told was your job? ~ I was told that I needed to be sexy, and I was determined to prove that I could do that. But as I rode the bus in I was trembling, very afraid and worried that I was getting in over my head again. I love to challenge myself, *compelled* is probably more accurate. Watching the show told me more than anything. When I got on stage something really positive drew me to the customers. I hadn't been with a man in five years and I was curious about what they looked like. I hadn't seen too many erect penises up close and they responded to me immediately and I was like, wow! They smiled at me and encouraged me, so I kept doing whatever I was doing.

As show director, what do you tell the women to do to succeed at this job? ~ I tell them to look at the customers eyes, smile, play, "strut your stuff." I tell them that what I'm looking for is a willingness to interact with the customers, and that if I see that, then we can work from there. When they ask me how to make top money, I tell them that we look at are how well they maintain the job standards, like showing up to work on time, being responsible for their shifts, how hot their show is, and how well they play as a team.

When you were hired were you asked to work on certain aspects of your performance? ~ I was told that I would probably have to slow down or I would be exhausted.

As show director how do you choose the women who appear on stage together? ~ There's an ideal way and the real way. (Laughs) Right now, it is, I definitely don't want those two on stage together, or, I definitely think that would be a hot show, and how can I get the shifts covered. If I had the freedom I would choose dependable dancers who like to work together, who are committed to the show being on-purpose and will keep that standard as an example. We are always able to get a mix of races and colors of hair, but we don't always get the mix of high-energy/low-energy, great customer contact/more shy, that we like
.

Describe how you dance, display, and touch your body during your performance. ~ I like to give a mini striptease, but I don't do it all the time. I'll find a customer who's watching me and I'll start farther away so he can see my whole body. I do the poses that I look really good doing; side view, leg up. Sometimes I tease them by raising my leg to the side so they can almost see my pussy. It's a real tease to show them just a peek of pubic hair. Often I go up to the window and kneel on the ledge so that he can see my face and breasts. I'll tease him with my breasts and caress my nipples. I like to shake my breasts holding my nipples (laughs) – it's a trademark of mine.

I think dancers get into a pattern where they think they should just spread their legs, or bend over and spread their cheeks, and that's it. There's so much more possibility. We're allowed to touch ourselves anywhere, but we can't insert our fingers. Sometimes we masturbate or do what we would do if we were alone. I like to think of that as educational. (Laughs)

What sexual depictions do you perform? ~ There are times when I feel like I'm actually making love with a customer. That's particularly when we're both turned on and masturbating. I learned a great technique from this really hot little number who breezed in and out once in a while. She would pretend to lick the customer's cock and then look up into his eyes with these big, soft, submissive brown eyes, and he would go nuts! When I am tired of dancing for a customer I pretend to give him head and he gets off quick and goes away. (Laughs) I think most dancers know that, but we don't really talk about it. What she did looked submissive at first, which I was a little uncomfortable with, but now I see it as a whole other way to be incredibly accepting, erotic, and loving. There are times when I'm pretending that the customer is a voyeur and I don't know he's there.

Does your performance contain elements of dominance and submission? ~ Absolutely. There are customers who are very submissive, we tell them they have to lick the windows. One guy we called "Slug" loved to lick those windows!

Then there are the customers who really want to be in control of the show. They motion and say "turn around", "come here." I have a real hard time as soon as someone tells me what they want. Even when I'm willing to do it, there's still initial resistance. We always tell each other, "You don't have to do anything you don't want to. It's your show, you're in control." Sometimes we'll tell the customers, "This isn't Burger King, you can't have it your way." It becomes not fun, not ours, doing what somebody tells you to do. It's like being a waitress. It's really stressful to have a shift where that's all you get.

I've recently had a tremendous breakthrough in this area. I read *Slave Girl of Gor* (laughs) and I was exploring my submissive fantasies, being totally submissive. A lot of my fantasies when I masturbate are that I have absolutely no choice about it, I'm tightly bound. It's pretty clear to me that I don't want to let go unless I'm forced to. I don't want to take responsibility for letting go.

So anyway, I thought I'd be a Slave Girl of Gor on stage, and it was so hot.

The customers were so drawn to me. I had four of them for about an hour, non-stop. There was absolutely no room for them to tell me what to do, they just wanted to see what I was doing! I was making love to myself, really going for it. I was acting like I was totally theirs, that my whole purpose in life was to satisfy them. I had total control of them. It was really interesting to actually experience it, not just know that it's true.

From stage you see a lot of tongues. Describe this. ~ It's a way for them to be submissive, to say, "I would love to lick your pussy," "Your pussy is delicious-looking," "I would love to return this, to arouse *you*." It's a way of communicating, especially for the guys in the stand-up booths. We can't see the rest of their bodies so they can't gesture with their cocks. Our pussies are right at their face level. Some men just *love* to lick pussy! I have fantasies that their wife or girlfriend doesn't like it, or they're not in a relationship and they just need their fix. For some men it's shorthand for, "You're doing a nice job." Some are trying to get you to their bedroom, and they're demonstrating their technique! (Laughs)

Eye contact with customers is very important to some dancers. Is it for you? ~ Yes, but sometimes it's hard to do, especially in the early morning. I don't feel sexy, and I don't want to be there, so no eye contact is a way I avoid being there. It can be really nourishing to get that contact. It's frustrating when a customer won't look us in the eyes. Either they are ashamed or they don't want to give you personhood. They would rather see you as your body, and that's really insulting. Eye contact is used to determine who to dance for, to acknowledge the customers, to say "hi." With eye contact I include other customers without having the customer I'm mostly working for feel rejected. No eye contact is the way the customers communicate that they don't want you to dance for them.

How much of your performance is you and your sexuality and how much is persona? ~ Over the years I have become more and more identified with my persona, and more comfortable being sexy on stage than in my private life. I went through an identity crisis where I didn't know if I was Jackie or Eileen. I liked being Jackie, but it didn't seem okay in some environments. Now it's resolved, I've integrated Jackie and Eileen and that's really exciting.

In the freedom and safety of being on stage my persona blossomed. I look innocent and young, but I act really sexy. I'm a smiling dancer, I'm not real good at the serious, unapproachable bitch.

How do you use costuming and makeup? ~ Mostly for myself rather than the customers. If I'm doing a good show it doesn't matter what I'm wearing. I use them because there are mirrors all around and I have a lot of insecurity around how droopy my breasts are and how old my face looks. I use them to project the image that *I* want to see. I change costumes a lot to keep me going, because I get bored. I'm Jackie when I have makeup on. I don't wear makeup outside of the theater.

Do drugs play a part in your performance? ~ I've used alcohol, marijuana, nicotine, and caffeine. I usually crash in about two hours if I've had a drink or smoked a joint before I go on stage. The rest of the shift is very difficult so I don't use them on purpose. I use nicotine and caffeine to keep me going, especially late at night.

On stage the music plays almost continuously. Describe the variety and part it plays in your performance? ~ If it's a song I really love I have a hard time doing my job. I just want to dance, not having anything to do with sex, just dance. The music has always been a huge issue for the dancers, the source of a lot of dissatisfaction. The management doesn't have anything to do with it. The rule is, if you have a complaint buy some records, the theater pays.

The stage is covered with mirrors ceiling to floor. What role do they play in your work? ~ They are my partners. They give me and the customers feedback constantly. I've become a mirror-junkie from working here. I was fat in high school and then I got into my butch, lesbian thing. I never identified with pretty girls, I avoided mirrors. They've taught me how to move and I see what my body looks like constantly.

Describe the interaction and commentary among the dancers on stage. ~ I've heard everything imaginable on stage. There's on-purpose commentary and off-purpose commentary. There's gossiping about life, and what's new, girl talk. Dancers talk about how much they're in love with each other and how they want to fuck each other. They don't use those words, but that's the context. They acknowledge each other's sexiness. A lot of, oh baby, a lot of stuff that if a man said it to me on the street, I'd be really pissed off. Sometimes a guy will have either a huge cock or a great physique, or maybe a pair of red undies, nylons and high heels on, or he's doing something really kinky. We'll all start squealing and take turns looking, and telling him we appreciate it. There's a lot of trying to manage the customers, "Smile", or "Please don't do that," or "Isn't she hot?"

At its most fun, the dancers are constantly enrolling each other in activities, and it can get really wild. An old Motown song comes on, we'll start doing a Supremes routine. The barriers go down and we're "us" instead of "me and her". Dancers get into pretending to make love with each other. There's a lot about who's dancing for whom and are you interrupting them, or "Can I take a break from this guy, will you please go dance for him, I'm tired," or "I just can't dance for this guy, he looks like my father."

Is there competition among the dancers on stage? ~ Yeah, there is. I was a dancer who got a lot of attention for a long time, and the manager would tell people, "Dance like Jackie." There was a tremendous amount of resentment that built up. Some dancers don't necessarily recognize that what's going on with them is jealousy. There's one dancer who, if there's another black dancer on stage with her and she's not getting all the attention, she just pouts. So we don't schedule certain people together.

Is the myth of the perfect body perpetuated here? ~ Yes and no. Most of the customers still want to see the mythic female, and those women get the most attention. Quite often they make the most money. In this job, if you're beautiful you can go far. You don't have to be a particularly good dancer, you don't have to work as hard. But the truth is, there are some hot women who wouldn't fit the myth, and they get validated as well. What's more accurate, every customer has their own myth and there is really, literally, a man for every woman's body on this planet! (Laughs) I know from listening to the customers' comments. Things that the woman concentrates on as being the icky parts, the customers couldn't care less. They see the beautiful breast, the shapely ass, the incredible puss, or whatever. They're drawn to what they like, rather than being stopped by what the dancer thinks is not perfect, her stretch marks or her little roll.

There's not very much forgiveness for fat dancers at all, she has to have something perfect on her body, some redeeming quality. Our culture's just anti-fat. Our standard shifted to include heavier and heavier women. At one point we hired a woman who was between 250 and 300 pounds. She lasted about a day. We were really clear with her that it may not work, but we were willing to give it a shot. The owner was here for her first shift and said, "There is a woman big as a house on stage! But I'm just giving you feedback!" And the customers really didn't like her. The least forgiving in general are younger men. It was frustrating because I know there are men who L-O-V-E big women! Those chunky ass magazines say it. The *Big Beautiful Woman* magazine and *Fat As A Feminist Issue* are real breakthroughs. But it's not integrated into our culture, yet.

Do you ever become aroused by what you are doing or what is happening around you on stage? ~ I couldn't believe how aroused I got by the width of this one man's cock. He's got the hugest, widest cock I've ever seen. I felt my body reacting like, just, aaahhhh, yes, please. I was astounded, I had no idea I was a size queen! It was very interesting to recognize that on some levels I have no choice about my arousal. It's programmed and I just go along for the ride.

My fantasy is to be able to actually have an orgasm on stage. I have to move around a lot to have an orgasm, so I'd be too embarrassed, not in front of the customers, but in front of the other dancers. I think they would judge. It's a shame. One day Crystal said, "My god, I just had an orgasm. I have to go and wash off." I was so envious. It was like, right on for you!

It can be extremely arousing, exhaustingly arousing. It can ruin your sex life, because when you come home, you want to have some intellectual conversation, you want to go see a Woody Allen movie, you don't want to have sex! The lesbian dancers seem to be more comfortable exposing themselves as aroused to other women. It's harder to arouse me now, I've sort of reached a saturation point, but I am aroused by another dancer getting aroused, for sure. I'm very cyclical, there are times in my month where it doesn't matter what, I'm just horny, and times when I'm just not. When I'm ovulating or right before my period it doesn't take much (laughs), I just get aroused. So it's fun to be there. When I'm not horny it's kind of frustrating.

Do you ever have sexual fantasies during your performance? ~ Not as much as I would have thought. Not as much as I think most people imagine. I have sexual fantasies about dancing when I'm not on stage. There are times when I'll indulge in, well, what if I actually went out with this customer? Sometimes when I'm feeling in love with someone I fantasize about him, but it's so real that it's hard to bring fantasy into it. It's like you're living the fantasy. Sometimes when I'm on stage I can't wait for my break so I can go jerk-off in the bathroom, and it's sort of a fantasy! (Laughs) Sometimes I fantasize about having vibrators on stage, so I could just get off. Sometimes I go, okay, I'm going to try to get as aroused as I can, and it's part of the fantasy that I can't have an orgasm until my break. It just keeps building and building and building.

Do you ever wish you could be having direct sexual contact with the customers? ~ I wished it a few times when the customer was particularly good with his tongue, but that's pretty rare. One young man came in and it was like a scene I had imagined many times, love at first sight. He acted out my fantasy unknowingly. He put his hand on the glass and was just with me, like "You're the most beautiful creature I've seen in my life. Let's get married!"

In the beginning there were times when I just wanted to...(pant, pant)... There are one or two customers who are real favorites of mine because they so honestly enjoy my dancing. We'd be as close to each other as we could be, probably at those moments if the wall wasn't there we would be going for it!

What can you do on stage that you can't do off stage? ~ I get to be worshipped! (Laughs) I get to be totally in control of men. I get to be the center of attention, the sex kitten. The fact that I don't have to deal with these men in any other regard gives me so much freedom, it's like the zipless fuck. Sex without strings!

What won't you do on stage? ~ I won't often follow directions from the customer.

What are you prohibited from doing on stage? ~ We're not allowed to touch another dancer in areas that normally would be clothed by a bathing suit. We're also not allowed to insert anything into our vaginas, dildos or cucumbers. Or our assholes. You're not allowed to make dates with the customers or friends through the glass.

Do you ever do sex education on stage? ~ Tongue in cheek. It's part of a fantasy that I'm creating with a customer. We probably emphasize our clitorises more than most fantasy books and most of us are naturally more direct in presenting what we like about our bodies than a male writer would fantasize.

The other area of education is letting the customers know that we're whole people, not just girls who don't count and that you can order around because we're naked. Or who belong to men because we're naked. At least ten percent of the customers come in with the apparent attitude that just because we're naked they can tell us exactly what to do, and that our needs are nonexistent. They usually get a rude awakening, (laughs) particularly if they're persistent. We won't dance for them. One day I told a customer, "I'm not dancing for you because you ordered me around. I don't like it." He came back the next day, and he didn't do any of that, he watched.

How does having your period affect your performance? ~ If I've eaten real well, and if I don't have sugar right before my period, I won't get very bad cramps. If I'm not taking care of myself I'm real crabby when I'm pre-menstrual. I don't want to be managing sometimes, let alone dancing. I get fatter, which I don't like. My breasts get fuller, I like that. I imagine the customers like it.

There are times when a dancer will be bleeding and not realize it. We watch out for each other. It's not really as humiliating as I thought it would be when it happens. The customers notice sometimes and they're fascinated because they never get to see that. It's such a taboo. Some of them are probably excited by it.

I was quite surprised when I first heard that healing occurs here, women healing themselves, each other, and the customers. Describe what you know about this. ~ I noticed when I was dancing the other day that even though I wasn't particularly sexually active in the rest of my life, I could still create that for myself just by being on stage. It's like there's a door to my sexuality that I can open any time. It's always there and almost always in full bloom. The thing that's healing about that is that I know I'm in control of it, that I don't have to be dependent on my lover. I don't have to be awakened like Sleeping Beauty by an external force. That allows me to be more responsive in my relationships, more powerful, less dependent. I've gotten the key back that I've always had the right to. In our culture women are told that men have the key to our sexuality. That we don't know what it is or how to use it or where to find it. I do, I've got my own set!

I've seen women blossom over and over again, find their own vamp, find quite a few personae, love them and accept them, revel in them and play them out. I think the healing could be taken further if we could do that outside of this particular environment, but we're just not there yet. But at least we have a place to explore who we can be, who we can play.

I think it's healing for the customers to see women free. Men are more comfortable with their sexual needs, more casual and affirmative of their sexual drive. It's very healthy for them to see women who are that way, too, even if it's just temporary fantasy.

There are two types of women, those who've been in the sex industry and those who haven't. Women who have may be healed in relating with their co-workers and when they find it's possible to do this work and not have it be damaging. Many women say this is the best place they've ever worked, that they never want to leave. Women who haven't been in this industry and have the expectation that it would be an unhealthy industry to work in, get to see here that that's not always the case. A new perspective is healing.

On another level, we encourage each other's sexual exploration and sexual growth. We are very vulnerable with each other, naked in front of each other. I think it's very healing to be exposed in that way and to discover that those stretch marks, or that flab, or that cellulite, or those zits, or that scar doesn't change other people's...acceptance. Those things quickly fade into the background and other personality traits are valued. Especially teamwork.

The women get the experience of what it's like to work intimately with other people in a fairly non-competitive atmosphere. It's healing that we get real with each other. Social conventions fall apart when you're naked, so we get to play with a new social contract. There are a lot of friendships that grow, a lot of validation for who we are, for our bodies, for our sexuality, that we may not have gotten anywhere else. For being sexy women who validate each other for that, instead of competing with each other or feeling inadequate. That happens, but we're definitely more comfortable and open about it than anywhere else I've ever been.

We're in a position of validating the customer's sexuality as well, by simply saying, "Hey, right on, go for it!" I'm really committed to validating men's sexuality! Some of the men who come in aren't incredibly handsome. I wonder sometimes how many of them actually have girlfriends. How often do they get laid? That must be a source of stress and anxiety. They can come here and be accepted for who they are without playing the games either. They can get validation by using their smile instead of their wallet and their flashy car or their great physique. That's probably really healing.

That brings to mind the argument for prostitution and the stories of the way society was in ancient times. Men returning from war couldn't reenter society until they'd gone to the temple and screwed the temple prostitutes. It was part of their socialization to be in a relationship with a woman, to be vulnerable. These businessmen who come in, can't be vulnerable during their day like they are with us. Perhaps even when they go home. It's a chance for them to let it down and be vulnerable, accepted and acknowledged. Human beings need to fuck! (Laughs) We hardly ever say those words, but we're looking into each other's eyes and saying, yeah, you need it, so do I. Too bad we have to do it this way, but at least we've got this outlet.

Have you had any transcendent moments on stage? ~ There have been moments of just...the joy of the dance and the joy of the relationships. For a long time I took on the practice of not judging the customers at all, just being with them, and that practice put me in a totally different space than I usually am with people. My attention stopped being on what I was thinking about and shifted to them. I was much more intimate, more present. That supported my transcendental moments. The times when we're practically having sex together I can be put in another space.

Do you ever feel caged or wish you could cover up? ~ Mostly when a customer starts to tell me what to do, that's when I feel dirty. For some reason that brings that up. I usually don't feel caged, maybe when it's a gorgeous day out.

Many of the dancers say they prefer this closed type of stage and see it as safe and fun because of the absence of physical contact with customers. How do you feel? ~ I like that a lot, but my ultimate would be to make this a stage where I could create my own strip set, and have the stage to myself. I've seen intimate theater where the dancers are incredibly close to the customers, but the customers don't touch them. It's incredible to watch. It's possible to have no walls and still have that context of safety. I would like an open stage because I'm a ham and I like all the attention. (Laughs) I love it – it's a rush that I don't get as often working this way.

Describe your performance at its best and worst. ~ I have a lot of expression in my face, and I use my eyes a lot. I work hard on my presentation, to be pretty, standard Playboy bunny. I'll dress all in one color that makes a real strong statement. I know what angles I look good at, so I use those angles over and over again. I dance well. I'm also pressing myself to be more blatantly sexual. I'm an exhibitionist. My fantasy is making love while someone is watching. I've started fantasizing about being made love to by all the customers, while the rest of them watch! (Laughs) So, what it looks like from the customer's point of view is this pretty girl they just want to jump on, who's really willing to surrender to that sexual feeling with them. I give them a great orgasm. (Laughs) At it's worst, I'm still in my head, I hardly even know what I look like. I'll be pretty bitchy and there'll be barely concealed resentment about them. It'll be very impersonal and cold. I'll show them my body and do the moves but it looks mechanical. Sometimes I won't give them what they want, just to annoy them.

Describe the customers. ~ They really let themselves play for the most part, even the stiffest ones. They let themselves watch, they have total permission to girl-watch. They look at all those parts they're not allowed to and they let the dancers take the lead for the most part. Some come in with a hard-on. I don't know if they've been thinking about us on the way over, or they went to a video booth and got really hard. They'll be masturbating when the window goes up. Some will let you know they're getting a hard-on, they'll stroke their pants, tease you, want you to ask them to take it out. Five percent, maybe less, don't masturbate. The older men are less likely to masturbate, that's just not okay with them. The men are clearly fantasizing that they're having sex. Some have very specific fantasies and most of us don't have a problem with it, except that they come in every day, and it's kind of demanding if you're not in the mood. I'd say seventy-five percent continue to drop quarters after they've cum, to acknowledge that they've enjoyed your show, to let you know that you're more than just an orgasm to them. (Laughs) But there are quite a few who are embarrassed, they don't want any more eye contact, they just made a mess and they want to get out before anyone finds out! (Laughs)

The demographics have changed. Fifty percent of our clients, for the live show, were Chinese, and it's down to twenty percent. Sometimes there will be two generations in a booth, sometimes three. I've never seen that in any other race. The rest are mostly businessmen and blue-collar workers. Some bus drivers have a route that stops in front. (Laughs) They come in. There are tourists, especially in the summer. When the boats are in the Navy boys come in. They're so horny it's – frightening. (Laughs) Younger men come in the evening, ready to party.

331

We hardly ever have women come in on their own. There are a few loyal women and that's really great. Most of the women are dragged in by their boyfriends, and stand there giggling and hiding their eyes and making rude comments about us. They're the worst customers. We feel the most degraded in front of them, because they've got to be separate from you. They can't acknowledge any kind of identification or give you any kind of human-ness. You've got to be an "other." I want to smack them. Occasionally we'll get ones who are like, "Wow," women who are comfortable with their own bisexuality and whose husbands know that. They drag them in because they know they'll enjoy it. A few will do a show for you. That's such a blessing to get that kind of customer, it's a lot of fun. We have a suspicion that, in general, men who have wives who are bisexual like to be able to control that phenomena. They take them to do stuff like this so they won't go off and have affairs. But, that's another story. They'll display their breasts and play with themselves. Sometimes they'll have sex with their partners. That's really fun, we get to be on the receiving end.

Do the customers leave their social roles and status behind when they come to see you? ~ Not as much as we'd like. You can see the ones that aren't letting that go, the tension of them hanging on to it. I suspect that the less secure someone is the more dominant they'll be.

What is your favorite type of customer? ~ The ones with big dicks! (Laughs) There's not too many of them! I mean, B-I-G! I've seen so many of them that they have to be really outstanding. I like them just because of my physical reactions. The thrill, cheap thrills. Barring that, my favorite customers are ones who are expressive with their appreciation and their own level of arousal. With one guy who's real oral, you can tell he's imagining eating all the parts of your body, and he makes you feel real delicious. I like the more traditionally attractive and younger ones, more my age. But I've noticed over the years that who the attractive customer is has gotten less and less narrow.

Do you encounter men who you think hate women? ~ I don't take it too seriously, even when teenagers call us names. I don't feel qualified to say. We certainly encounter men who have problems with women, their sexuality, and womens' sexuality.

Have you ever felt it was dangerous to arouse a customer? ~ I've had a lot of thoughts about arousing customers, but never that. (Laughs)

Do you encounter violent men here? ~ Usually it's youth, alcohol, and drugs that are involved. Violence, for the most part, never escalates. There's one instance where a dancer was attacked by some customers. They were banging on the window and calling her bitch, and she got into an argument with them. They followed her home, beat her up, and tried to rape her. That was years ago. And there was Louisa, a janitor who got attacked in a booth. It doesn't change your odds to work in this business.

Do you think you've ever danced for a rapist? ~ I've probably had that thought about a customer once or twice. I have a fantasy that dancing prevents some customers from raping. I have no idea if that's true!

There are customers who come here with great regularity. What are they like? ~ The regulars cover the gamut. The thing that distinguishes them is their routine. You know exactly what they're going to do and how long it's going to take them to cum. Often they'll have a dancer they prefer to play with. For the most part they are extremely respectful of the dancers. We're an important part of their lives, their primary relationship possibly. So they're real protective of the dancers vis-a-vis the other customers.

Usually they are comfortable with saying, "Thank you," at the end of an encounter. They've worked through any shame they may have had about being there. They're really clear about what they're there for. A lot of times when customers are done you can see the guilt hitting them, practically knocking them over. It's painful to watch. The regular customers tend not to have that.

Sometimes I think the value customers get out of coming here are those moments when they're most threatened and we make it safer for them to confront whatever they're confronting, and then get rid of it. It's not an easy thing! Sometimes I want to say to those guys in the booth, "It's okay. You're not a bad person."

Are there any customers that come to see you on a regular basis? ~ An older Chinese gentleman has been coming for years. He wants to get extremely passionate with me, like we're having this really passionate, torrid love affair with all the sound and fury. When I see him on the street or in the lobby he'll usually say, "Hi." I never feel threatened by him because he's really clear that that's the closest he's going to get to me. It's great to have regular customers! I think almost every dancer has at least one, and it's really important to your self-esteem to feel special that way.

Do you have friends you first met as customers? ~ There are a few I became friendly with. One support staff member would go into the booth after working with me and jerk-off. I felt like I'd accomplished breaking down that barrier.

Describe the variety of sexual behavior the customers express. ~ One extreme is standing there and not doing anything. With one guy you feel like he's appreciating fine art. I'm getting goosebumps thinking of it!

There are customers who try to mesh their fantasy with what's actually happening. One guy has a fantasy, as far as I can tell, where he's being forced to do humuliating tasks, like licking someone's asshole or their shoes. He tries to get me to boss him around. He looks into your eyes like you're making him do it. Sometimes I'll put my clit up to the window, point, and wait for him to do it. Just going aaaahhhh, when he does it! But it's hard, I'm not comfortable playing that role, it's emotionally tiring for me.

Some customers will do a strip tease. They really make love to themselves. They want you to watch them cum, you focus on their penis when they're ejaculating. That get's kind of old, unpleasant after a point. The ones who do a show for you are especially common.

Some pretend they're making love to you, with their hands all over the window and their lips and tongue and they're just like "ooooh." So you pretend like they're making exquisite love to you and you go "aaaah." Some want you to pretend that you're making love to them. You use your hands, your lips, your tongue.

Describe some of the more unique encounters you've had with customers. ~ One of the craziest encounters was with the guy who fucked a toilet brush. That was pretty wild. I never saw but I heard about the guy who stuck needles and candles up his urethra. Quite a few men are into fucking themselves in the asshole, with their fingers or dildos. Every day you see that. Then there are the cross-dressers, the guys who take off their shirt and there's this beautiful teddy. We'll all go, "Oooh, I'm jealous!" A lot of guys have really sensitive nipples and they'll pinch themselves.

What do the customers want you to do? ~ They really want eye contact, they want you to be interested and involved. They want to see everything. Some have a preference for a certain position that you're in. Some just want to see your face. They want you to come to their window right away, always. There're more windows than dancers so that's never satisfied. They really get excited if you spread your pussy and contract your cunt. Boy, that's like the end! (Laughs) Dancers know all those things and the order of preference. Men ask us to turn around, that's the most common request. They want you to put your ass in the window and spread your cheeks. The doggie style must be a **big** fantasy.

Is there a difference in the customers' behavior when they are alone or in a group? ~ When the customers are alone they are more willing to show a sweeter side. In a group they're more likely to posture and be macho and objectify the dancer. That's not always the case though, sometimes a group is really appreciative and you actually get more acknowledgment. Usually they don't jerk-off in a group. Once in a while they'll take their dicks out and wave them at you.

What do the customers say when they speak? ~ "What time do you get off?" I say, "Anytime I like," or "A few minutes after I start." They'll say, "What's your number?" or "Can I leave you my number?" Some are really direct, "I want to fuck you." (Laughs)

Some customers experience ecstatic surprise when they first encounter the stage show. What do you think surprises them? ~ How much fun the dancers are apparently having. That they're actually naked and very close. That there's more than one. It's a real fantasy land, a magazine coming to life.

Are you ever disturbed by the affect you have on customers? ~ Yeah. How come they need me so much?

Do you ever encourage customers to leave messages? ~ I did until I found out that management really didn't want us to. They're fun to get. At the end of the day you have a couple of messages saying how beautiful, desirable, and fuckable you are. I've thought about calling to tell them that I liked them and appreciated their note, but I never have. Sometimes I'm frustrated because I really want to validate them. I think some of them don't have very good self-esteem.

Do you ever feel controlled or possessed by the customers? ~ Sometimes, and it really bothers me. I used to stay with a customer even though I didn't want to. Recently I've become totally comfortable with simply walking away. It's less emotionally wearing and it gets the message across without putting them down.

When customers show disrespect dancers can call security and have them removed. How often do you ask that a customer be removed? ~ Rarely. Lately I have when someone has drugs in a booth.

How do you respond when a customer orgasms? ~ At that point I'll be at my most intimate because that's when the customer is most open. I usually make a point of looking him in the eye and smiling, trying to get across validation. Oh, good, you came. (Laughs) You got what you came for. You did a good job. I feel like I contributed something to another human being.

Do you try to get the customers to spend? ~ Yeah. But I don't focus on let's milk him for another quarter. Do a good show and they spend.

How do you feel about dancing for customers in the three booths with one-way glass? ~ I like it, I feel less inhibited. I don't have to worry about, do they like the show? I think a lot of customers go into those booths because they are free to look wherever they want. It really bugs a lot of dancers. They think the customers are ashamed, hiding. I don't think they realize there are many reasons for going in there.

As the desired do you have power? ~ I have power in this setting and I take it with me into the real world. I also have obligation because, literally, some of the customers won't leave until I give them what they want.

Have you experienced burnout on this job? ~ I have. As manager it got to the point where I had to leave or else I was going to damage myself or someone else. As far as being a dancer, even when you're not in the theater, you're aware that right now the show is going on, and there are four of your friends on stage. It's like you never leave. Makeup never really comes off, you never really get dressed (laughs), you're always physically tired, your joints hurt, your feet are tender sometimes. You don't even want to walk anywhere. And, the last thing you want to do is have sex! Sometimes you get really hostile and bitchy and no one can do anything right.

Off stage you encounter other dancers, support staff, and management. Describe the interaction that occurs. ~ We always interact but if someone doesn't want to, we'll give them their space. We rely a lot on those interactions to release the tension. We do a lot of playing with each other, a lot of sexual teasing. We share everything and we are really nosey about each others' lives. When I was managing I tried to give dancers feedback about their show. I haven't seen much of that since I quit managing.

I hear workers say they can be themselves here. Can you? ~ Absolutely! It's a perfect job for me in many ways, and I just have to come out of the closet to myself about that. When I started looking for another job it became so clear that it was more difficult in other settings. With this job I can be *all* of myself. I don't have to worry about, "Oh, we don't talk about that in the office." There's permission to be totally honest and straight in communication.

We have significantly broken down the taboos around sex and being public about it. This is the amazing thing about it. There's nothing weird about it. When you're in the experience of being an erotic dancer it feels fine. It doesn't feel like you're doing something wrong. It's a relief, it feels like being a human being. It's the opposite of what the public thinks it is, you've got a gun at your head to do this. That comes, I presume, from fear of our own sexuality. You discover that what you were so afraid of is not so scary.

Sometimes it's like a party here. Describe these occasions. ~ (Laughs) When the dancers are into dancing, it's really a discotheque on stage. We try to support that whenever it's happening. We're committed to it being fun, no matter what. We'll start acting like it's a party just to get that atmosphere happening. We'll bring in balloons or have a cake or find excuses to celebrate. We'll make a big deal about the holidays. When it's really authentic on stage we're enrolling each other in making dances up.

The owner and management of the theater say they want to create a safe, fun, nurturing, and profitable business. Have they succeeded? ~ I would say so. It's been extremely safe. There are exceptions that are responded to quickly. It's a lot more fun than a lot of other jobs I've had. We're getting better at hiring people who are willing to have fun. We considered it part of our job, part of our love for the dancers to be there and to listen. That's one of the reasons I broke down as a manager. I kind of lost my ability to focus and concentrate on what needed to get done in the office. There's a real strong push from the general manager for us not to get emotionally involved, not to get caught up in the drama, not to even hear the story. I don't know how to reconcile that and that's another reason I left management. They've succeeded in becoming profitable by providing a fun, nurturing, safe job.

The owner and management has also expressed a desire to empower people. Have you been empowered here? ~ Yeah.

Describe worker/management relations. ~ I was a dancer, then management, and now I'm a dancer again. Now people are comfortable to fuck-up in front of me again. I wouldn't break confidences that would get them tired, so I am privy to complaints against management. The general complaint lately, and this is from a small sampling, is that there's less compassion. I read into that, that that was one of the things I supplied. Relations are rocky sometimes. The managers make mistakes but are usually willing to clean it up.

Do you have job security? ~ We are definitely in an "at will" environment. I have a lot of job security because I have a track record and I haven't alienated the management. I can take a leave of absence whenever I want to kick back. A dancer's value to the company tends to decrease after she's worked for a while. If a dancer is cute or gets the customers' attention she's secure.

In response to the question, "Are you exploited?", a well known dancer and erotic film star replied, *"Yes and no. We don't have a union, but I like what I do." How do you answer that question?* ~ I would say, "No." I don't feel particularly exploited in this job relative to any other job. I feel exploited by the culture I live in.

Do you ever think about unionizing? ~ I never thought about it, but I've heard other dancers talk about it. I have a strong sense the theater would go out of business rather than unionize. They definitely want control and one of the main ways they control it is to limit the payroll, there's no overtime. It's hard on the dancers because they've got to fill all the shifts, work harder, and not get paid any more. If we changed the balance of power at the theater through a union, if we had a choice, it would be great! If we were paid higher, we'd work less hours, become less burned out, we'd probably make the theater more money. They want us to make the theater more money before we get the raise.

Is sexism promoted or resisted in any way here? ~ The general manager has admitted she's favored women. The men are the janitors, the women are the dancers. The cashiers are either sex. We had a woman technician once and my impression is that the general manager doesn't trust their technical experience.

What do you feel passing customers in the hallway whom you've just danced for? ~ It's real important for us to keep a wall up as we're walking through. They're trying to engage us so it's always a little sticky.

Do you ever feel in danger coming to or leaving work? ~ Sometimes late Friday or Saturday night when I'm going to my car I feel a lot better when a security person is with me. But the violence on the street doesn't have anything to do with where I'm working. I'm not really worried about any crazed dancer killer, like you see on TV. Dancers getting wasted is a real sexy draw for screenplay writers, but it's not anything like reality.

Off stage it is not uncommon to hear dancers referring to each other as slut, whore or bitch. What do these remarks mean? ~ Another thing we say is, "Uuuggghh, you're here. Uuuggghh, I'm leaving!" There's a whole game that we play. It somehow seems really important to do that. I'm familiar with the theory that we're taking the charge out of the words. These are *my* words, these words don't hurt me. They're terms of endearment. We're accusing each other of being that way, and yet there's love when it's spoken. I guess it's a way of totally accepting it. I have a reputation of being one of the sluttiest dancers. (Laughs) I take it as a compliment and say, "Yeah, that's right." It's a powerful thing to be a slut, in the face of our programming that it's not okay.

Describe your earliest memories. ~ My very first memory is from when I was about eighteen months old. It was a hot day, Mom was pregnant with my brother, and I was out on the lawn naked.

Describe your family as you remember them during childhood. ~ I had a pretty happy childhood. Mom was home with us and Dad worked. My brother and I hung out together. Mom and Dad were both pretty much working class. My brother was retarded and from a pretty early age I perceived of myself as a babysitter. We were very much loved and somewhat spoiled. A lot of my memories are of Freddie and I bouncing on the couch excitedly waiting for Dad to come home from work. Or going to pick him up and being with adults.

Dad worked as a chemist and sales manager, Mom was an artist. They both went to college and both kids arrived early in their marriage. Looking at old photographs of Mom, I want to drool. She was so sexy, but she became a matron as soon as I was born. Her hair was cut shorter, she wore these silly looking suits and always crossed her legs at the ankles. I talked to her about it, I said, "I can't believe how you changed", and she said, "Absolutely, I was a mother now."

I remember Mom being mad at me, and Dad not being around. He went on business trips and to conventions a couple of times a year. Mom and I watched TV, it was important in our family. It ordered our lives. She made us lunch and we watched "Let's Make a Deal." My brother loved records and listened to them over and over and over again. The whole family knew them by heart!

My father was extremely loving towards me and one of my favorite memories is him introducing me to Beethoven when I was six. We'd act out the "Pastorale", I'd pretend to get scared and he'd protect me. When I had to go to bed, he'd pick me up in his arms and pretend that he was fighting a big wind to get me to bed. I'd be laughing hysterically an hour later. There was so much love there.

What kind of child were you? ~ I was very happy, always laughing, easily amused, very giggly. Very fidgety, always dancing around. I was really bright, with a voracious mind. I went to the library once a week and got stacks of books. I was reading adult books in the third grade. I was popular and people looked to me. I always had leadership qualities and got good grades. Creative. Artistic. My favorite activities were reading, drawing, and playing with dolls. As I got a bit older I would act out fantasies with friends. I liked to dress up. I really wanted acknowledgment and attention. I pretty much demanded it and knew how to get it. My life was forged by it, and still is. I always walked to school. My room was always a mess (laughs), I had clothes everywhere. It's still that way.

I always had big projects I wanted to do. For a while, my cousin and I really got into this running away fantasy. We read all the Oz books and decided we wanted to go to Oz. For a while we amused ourselves by creating amusement parks for each other's dolls. We also pretended we were cowboys from the TV show "Alias Smith and Jones." When one of the actors committed suicide my cousin and I were really shook up, it was a big intrusion on our fantasy. We decided to go to L.A. and find the other actor. We got as far as Fresno on a bus, while my dad was driving through the fog at 90 miles an hour, trying to catch us before we got to Hollywood.

My parents played therapist and asked me all these questions, I kind of liked that, I guess, because we decided to do it again, but this time we didn't try going to L.A. In the middle of the night we went to this church where we played a lot in the afternoons. Dad came to get me again and he was very upset. "Who the hell do you think you are?" I was just terrified of his anger. They totally lost their trust in me and didn't let me out of their sight for a couple of days. Dad slept in a sleeping bag at the foot of the stairs and they nailed my windows shut (laughs) – that was smart thinking. At that point I was living in this world where I was scared to talk to my mom and dad, and it was hell. Sometime later it was fine.

I also ran into problems at school because I wasn't fitting the roles that girls were supposed to take, at all. I was ostracized for being aggressive with the boys. At some point my friends rebelled against me because they were tired of me being their leader. I got into fights and spent time in the principal's office. (Laughs) It was pretty nasty.

At twelve my dad was attracted to me sexually, I looked sixteen. I had tits out to here and this beautiful face. We certainly didn't talk about it in my family, it was way too hot an issue. Dad was so afraid he would be inappropriate with me, that he totally repelled himself.

I always felt guilty and worried about my brother, I was very protective. My parents wanted him to be as independent as possible, and I thought they were exposing him to danger. I always had in the back of my mind that they aren't going to be around forever, I'm going to have to be his parent sooner or later. That's still there. Through our relationship I learned how to communicate with people who are not considered normal, I got an ability for nonverbal communication. He has Downe's syndrome. I always wanted him to stand up for himself, so I wouldn't have to feel guilty about that. And then when he did, I was pissed off! I think we had a lot of sibling rivalry, but I certainly have a deep sense of compassion for the underdog now. My attention has always been on the responsibility we have for each other, the way the nuclear family is structured, and who does the burden of taking care of people, who can't take care of themselves, fall on.

Under what religious tradition were you raised? ~ My parents were Lutheran. Later my dad was an atheist, and now he's really Christian. When they got married they were both really into the church. When I was real young I didn't know what it meant, other than you were dressed up and running around with the Bible class. Christmas and Easter were a huge deal. I went to church every Sunday when I was very young, but I don't remember very much except sneaking away from it. (Laughs) Mom became extremely disenchanted and just pulled out. Her feminist consciousness had emerged, she was in some of the first women's groups in the country. She was looking at the church, like, "They're arguing about whether Eve was really from Adam's rib?" My dad had similar absences of faith. So, the emphasis shifted from the religious aspects on holidays . We didn't have anything religious like Christ in the house at all.

At an early age humans exhibit a wide range of erotic behavior. What you were up to as a child? ~ My first sexual encounter was with a friend of mine. We acted out really sexual scenes where a woman was dancing naked for a man. One day she was real interested in finding out what fucking was like. We wrapped our thumbs in tissue paper and played with each others pussies under the covers. (Laughs) That was first grade. We were always exploring each others pussies with flash lights. One of our exciting adventures was the bondage scene. This was probably second grade, maybe third. She had me spread eagle on the bed with pillows on my hands and feet and said, "Now pretend you're tied up, and can't move." And I'd say, "Okay, okay." Then she'd put a little blanket over my crotch so that we were never actually touching. She would take my stuffed animals and rub them all over my body. Yeah! (Laughs) It was great!

I had a reputation at an early age of fooling around with my girl friends. In sixth grade I had a slumber party for my eleventh birthday. We stayed up all night telling each other about how we liked to masturbate. My friend and I found ourselves with a sheet between us humping wildly, while our friends were horrified. We kept explaining, "There's a sheet between us!" (Laughs) We would masturbate together and one at a time.

I discovered masturbation in second or third grade and got into it hot and heavy. I was reading all these adult books, *Natural Childbirth* and Masters and Johnson. I read everything in the house. I didn't understand insertion, but I found out about my clitoris. I called it my little bird and sometimes it would come out of its house, that was always what I was hoping for. I was always discovering ways to jerk myself off. My parents were hip to what was happening, but they didn't let me know.

Soon I got to studying about vibrators 'cause Becky told me that her mom had one, and her face was always happy in the morning. I wanted to try it, but she was too embarrassed to let me. I could just see the possibilities...I really wanted my own. (Laughs) I was scouring the house for a vibrator and found a possiblity. There was a little pillow that vibrated for your back. I took the padding off but the mechanism inside was too hot to play with down there. Ow! Ow!

Finally, I discovered a shaver. It had these little teeth I took out and a mechanism inside that went really fast! I played with it for five years! Mom figured out pretty soon that I was buzzing-off in my room! It was kind of noisy and I was buzzing-off all over the house! I could go on for hours, and usually did! (Laughs) I was totally addicted, just shameless. I would have my vibrator in the living room when I was watching TV and someone would come in. I'd suddenly get up, and be all sweaty and catty. I was clear that I shouldn't be public about it. My parents teased me some, but they left me pretty much alone.

Were you sexually abused as a child? ~ No.

What did your parents teach you about human relationships? ~ I was taught that men were not going to be fulfilled and being a woman was a bum rap. And that the only thing to do about it was to bitch. I was taught that men weren't quite adults. That withholding love was a good manipulation. I was taught that marriage is the most important relationship. I was taught that you couldn't say everything. I was taught to make sure that people got along, that discord was not acceptable.

Did your parents teach you that you could have power, choice? ~ They really went out of their way to do that. Recently my dad told me just how much I became his son because my brother was retarded. He really wanted me to be successful and independent. My parents were constantly emphasizing that I could do anything, that I had the skills, the brain, the looks, the emotional support. It was sort of a mixed message because my dad was certainly not comfortable with any kind of artistic career. His mother was a crazy, a writer. Members of her family who went in that direction committed suicide. His sister was an actress and psychotic as hell! He was a scientist. I wanted to be in the creative arts. My mom didn't want me to do that either because she had tried and didn't make enough money. It was, "You can do anything you want and you're choosing *that*?" (Laughs)

Were you taught to look good to attract and be chosen by a man? ~ My mom taught art history at a finishing school. She taught how to look at a piece of furniture and say, "Oh yes, that's from that century." She took me through how to do makeup, walking, all that stuff and I just loved it! She wanted me to have the social skills to go anywhere and be comfortable. There were some attempts at making me lady-like. There wasn't much advice on how to catch a man but I seem to do fine! (Laughs)

What effect did your body changing have on you? ~ It was extremely traumatic, partly because of how young I was. I remember running to catch a bus one day and this man saw my friend and I and he was totally taken in. He was talking to me and giving me his phone number, finally I said, "I'm only twelve." He looked at me again and said, "You *are* rather young, aren't you?" He was totally embarrassed and got off the bus. (Laughs) It was just as hard being with my girlfriends, we would harass each other, too. The black girls would say, "Do you have hair on your cat?" The white girls would say, "None of your business." And they'd say, "Well, we'll find out after school." All my role models for how to deal with that were in my books, or books that my mother had as a kid. They did not fit my social milieu at all! There was no safety, no chaperone. At school physical education was traumatic because we had to play "chase" with the boys, which meant they would run after us and try to grab us and molest us, basically.

Describe your adolescent sexuality. ~ I didn't actually have physical sex until two weeks before my seventeenth birthday, but romantic relationships were a big part of my earlier life. You never really went one-on-one at this point. I think it was one way it was kept safe and manageable.

How did you first discover and use the ability to arouse? ~ I discovered it very early, and did not have much sense of control over it. Men would just respond to me, older men. From the age of twelve I looked sixteen and at sixteen I looked ripe for the picking. When I finally had my own sense of arousal it was an amazing discovery. Making out and actually feeling that tingling down there and knowing what it meant, and what I wanted to do about it, I suddenly recognized, oh, *this* is what they're talking about! I knew I was ready to have sex, I mean, I was *ready*. I knew my boyfriend was practically a virgin, that he was waiting for me to make the first move. That was really a sense of power, a great adventure. (Laughs)

Describe your discovery of how pregnancy occurs. ~ My parents shared with me about that whole process from a real young age. They had a book with pictures that left it a little unclear, but I didn't quite want to ask, you know? It had pictures of the penis in the vagina...but I couldn't figure out what that had to do with the bodies and how they fit together. I knew that you couldn't get the penis next to the uterus without something in the way...or you'd get pregnant. I became clear that I wanted to protect myself and my boyfriend from any unwanted pregnancy.

When my boyfriend and I decided we were going to have sex, we told everyone in our group, and went to our local planned parenthood office. They were just blown-to-fuck-away by us having not done it and deciding we were going to and coming there first. These young black girls, thirteen and four-teen and on the pill, they were like, "Wow, hang on to him! My boyfriend would never come in here!" I got a diaphragm. A lot of my friends didn't protect themselves at all. Some were lucky, some got pregnant. I was one of the few who hadn't had an abortion by that time.

Did you receive information about human sexuality in high school? ~ We had a social living class in junior high and had the beginnings of it. The big news then was Becky fainted when we had to watch the movie about the baby being born. We were all terrified of that movie, but we weren't going to be a silly as she was. (Laughs) I vividly remember that film. I don't know if we were quite ready, but there were girls pregnant at that age, so I guess we were.

Describe your first exposure to sexually explicit media and its impact on you. ~ The very first was, it must have been first or second grade – finding my girlfriend's older brother's stash of Playboys. I couldn't figure out what the attraction was, big deal, a bunch of naked women. It didn't do a thing for me. I thought the jokes were pretty gross! (Laughs) That was where it really lived for me, trying to fathom the adult mind. It taught me that sex was dirty, something to laugh at and make jokes about.

Describe your high school years. ~ A lot of depression, compulsive drug use, eating, a lot of isolation, a lot of fights with my parents. I ran away twice in high school. I had a lot of bitterness about the world, and learned more about the world while discovering some of the more radical writers. I discov-ered that there were adults who also had that bitterness. That was who I iden-tified with. Also, I identified heavily with Berkeley and what I thought of as the hippie movement.

School was something to obsess about. I had a real hard time getting any-thing done on time and nearly flunked out. I was in therapy and it didn't seem to have much of an impact. It was adults against the kids, for the most part. I didn't have any adult confidants, though I knew of people my age who did. Lines were drawn around who used drugs and who didn't, and basically, the in-thing was to not care. It was really painful for me because I needed a tremendous amount of love and compassion. I desired to be creative and real-ly didn't feel that I could ever express it. I'm still struggling with that issue. Berkeley High had a tremendous arts program that was pretty much run by the clique, and I didn't feel comfortable enrolling for those classes. I did isolate myself and there was no one to break through that isolation. It's not some-thing I'd wish on anybody. I'm really grateful that I didn't kill myself, and that I've healed as much as I have.

Did you date in high school? ~ Hardly. The very few dates I went on were stereotypically uncomfortable, or totally oriented around drugs.

Describe your relationship with your family during those years. ~ I was really hard to live with. I did not want to participate in the family. They had to beat down the door to get me to participate. I was always retreating into books or drugs. I did have pretty good dialogue with my parents around some important issues, but they were healing their own childhoods and didn't have the tools to deal with my problems. They had a tremendous desire for things to work out for me.

Did you have any heroines or heroes during those years? ~ By the time I reached eighteen it was David Bowie. Also the cast of the *Rocky Horror Picture Show.* Bowie was androgynous, skinny, and a good musician. He gave me a goal to be creative. The *Rocky Horror Picture Show* was a real audience participatory type of thing. I could *be Rocky Horror Picture Show* right then and there, it was great. Every Saturday night Candy and I had a chance to put on all this outrageous makeup and ridiculous clothes, and be really sexy. (Laughs) And show off, be a star.

What did you plan to do after graduation from school? ~ I really wanted to be in the film industry, the performing arts, but I didn't have the self-confidence to follow that route directly. So I went into the production aspect of it. I pursued that through the film core at San Francisco State, learned about film production and gave it up. I decided that I was going to pursue a spiritual path...and get married.

Describe your college years. ~ At the end of high school I began to identify myself as a lesbian, or at least as a bisexual. One of my best friends, who I had an on-and-off relationship with since fourth grade, was also identifying herself that way. Somehow that gave me permission to explore that. I got the book *Lesbian Woman* and read that sucker right through. I was freed and enlightened about what was going on with me all these years, all my traumatic friendships. I was so happy I immediately tried to hook up with under-21 lesbian groups. I started going to groups that my friend was in, and discovered to my horror that I was the topic of a lot of her conversations in these groups! (Laughs) She was really angry with me, for many years of struggle in our relationship.

I found a woman and lived with her for twenty-two months. She was a year-and-a-half younger than me, and had a nervous breakdown while we were together. It was a hard time, but also a time of exhilaration, finding a career that I could identify with, the women's movement, the lesbian movement, the gay movement in San Francisco. We were young, really growing and we had a lot of media attention. I was on public television doing inter-views. It fit my bill, being an outcast, being angry, being famous...it was great. We were involved in the riots at City Hall. I got to live out being in the sixties again, but with a little more wisdom. When the tear gas came, I took my friends and said, "We're leaving, it's going to get hairy." It got hairy, we got calls all night...people in the hospital, concussions, broken bones, the cops were really nasty.

We were really experimental at that time, three-way relationships, five-way relationships. When my girlfriend went back east to get support from her family, I kind of abandoned myself to the rest of our friends in that experi-mentation. We tried to have sex but we didn't enjoy it. It was not a healthy thing. When she came back they were pretty scared of her anger, and dropped me like a hot potato.

I was going to school again, at U.C. Berkeley, and there was a pretty good community of women there. I hooked in as best I could, and fell in love with a really wonderful woman. She was from the Northeast and studying conser-vation and natural resources. Talk about personal responsibility for the envi-ronment, she was deadly serious. It didn't come out of dogma, but out of her love for nature and living close to it. It was really beautiful being with her, but she was in love with someone back east. When her lover moved here it was the end of the line for me. I immediately found someone else.

At about this time the opportunity to go to Lesbos to recreate the school Sappho established came up. There were eighty of us, about half were les-bians. We had scholars from all over the world lead courses on writing, ancient history, and religions. We didn't just study them, we lived them. We re-enacted the Elysian mysteries. It was so magical, powerful, and spiritual. The island is the most beautiful of all the Greek islands.

When we came the people were very warm and friendly, but sometimes we acted really badly. They'd never seen anything like us. A bunch of dykes? Are you kidding? You know, blatantly homosexual? We disrupted a lot of things, and did it with a total ethnocentricity, with the total arrogance of Americans travelling. I'm not proud of that. We didn't realize, like the night seven of us came to my house to have an orgy, that all the water we used made a difference to the owners. The economy was really depressed.

We became aware that we were a microcosm of the feminist movement in general, and that there was a vast schism in expectations between the lesbian women and the straight women. The founder and director of our program, who was responsible to the patriarchy, was a straight woman. She was talking to the mayor and getting interviewed on the networks. She wanted us to look good, she was really committed to working for the patriarchy. We felt absolutely no allegiance to the Greek patriarchy. We were interested in con-necting with women there.

At that time they had the very first Take Back the Night march in Athens.

This was unheard of in Greece. It's hard for me to understand, even though I was there, how different the women's lives are there. Two of the women on our trip were raped while we were there, for example. It's just not safe to be a woman out at night, period. So Taking Back the Night is a real personal safety issue, not a middle class, bourgeois stand. They can't go out at night.

When we heard about this march, many of us saw this as our opportunity to connect with the Greek women, the feminists. The director and the local travel agent did their best to discourage us, to the point of lying, saying it wasn't happening. I was one who didn't go and the group that did, left knowing this was not acceptable, as far as the Aegean Studies Program was concerned. They were told very clearly to not represent the program. They went on the march and it had a tremendous effect. It was organized by some lesbian feminist Greeks, but most of the men were sure that it was us. The march had people listening. It was the birth of a movement, a really high experience for the women who went.

The director was really angry and I ended up receiving a lot of that anger, because I was willing to speak up and confront. We had these heavy meetings trying to explain that we didn't feel any allegiance to the patriarchy. What do you think we're here for? We made it really clear that the lesbians were here for play, and she hadn't included that in the program. She didn't and that was her statement, she was really clear. It was so disheartening, so depressing to find that even among these women we could not come to any kind of agreement. The rejection was really hard to deal with. One by one we all left that meeting, and I finally said to her, "Fuck the patriarchy! I said if you don't want me to say that in the program then you have to kick me out." She said, "Okay, you're out."

But the goddess was so good to us, it was a miraculous experience. I was getting in touch with my own spiritual and psychic powers, and I became one of the group...shamans, if you will. I was singing, I was on the soundtrack for a film, I fell in love with a musician, and we created songs. This was life. That night we danced on the beach in our little U.N., women from all over the world were there, talking and cheering and translating. It was such a healing thing to discover these women from all over the world who loved and accepted me, who shared my view, and had the same bottom line experiences about being a woman no matter what country they were from.

That night I had one of my most powerful spiritual experiences. The moon was full and I found myself drawn to the water. That night I consecrated myself to Aphrodite, you see, this does fit with the story! (Laughs) It was the turning point to the theater! I slipped off my clothes and ran around, I wanted everyone to see me naked. I imagined that I had this huge labyris, big double axe, in my hand. I dove into the water, and it was lunacy, just the moon and the sea. I gave myself over to the goddess and she gave me so many gifts. The gift of the sea. I brought home rocks and sea horses and it's like every day is another gift from Aphrodite. The ocean was mother and I'm still hers. Venus is my star.

There's a thread in my life of women's sexuality, which, when it's healed and untamed is one of the most powerful creative forces, and most generous, and abundant. That's what those guys were worshipping back then. It was very clear to us because it was still there. I came back a different person. (Laughs)

Describe other work you've done prior to dancing. ~ I worked in food service at the dorms, when I lived in L.A.

Have you had other jobs in the sex industry? ~ I've worked in porn films, done photo shoots for adult magazines, and danced at bachelor parties. An agent saw me in the theater. That was not okay with management, but I didn't know it at the time. All these jobs came through connections I made at the theater.

The first bachelor party I did was with seven or eight other dancers. It was for a friend of a friend. I was terrified. We drove a long way to his house and got as drunk as we could. Once it was my turn I just had a ball. (Laughs) The dancer right before me was very explicit. The other girls were really scared, "Oh no, they're going to expect more, they're going to try and get us, it's a rape situation, we're asking for it, help." It wasn't that way. The men were pretty drunk, and I learned strategies from the dancers who seemed to be comfortable and having a real good time. The guys wanted to put their arm around me and talk, and it was like, "No, no, you can't, don't touch." Afterwards, I was like, "Hey, this is fun, no problem!" Some of the women stayed, and I think they had an orgy, but I didn't want to. That was fine.

The photo shoot came about after photographers from a magazine did a couple of group shots here and decided I was the most likely material. They invited me to work with Valerie, which was just fine with me! She was beautiful. (Laughs) We went into this big costume store and got some of the most ridiculous costumes you can imagine, and then went to this loft where artists were working and exhibiting their stuff. We had professional makeup and hair people, they totally fed my ego. Valerie was a pro, she knew how to pose, unfortunately, I didn't. They did their best coaching me, but it was frustrating.

They were talking about how much more money they'd get for a cover shot, so I tried to get more information: "Well, if you guys are going to get a little more money, does that mean that we're going to get a little more money too?" "No, that isn't what that means." They didn't want to give me any more information. I started to get pissed-off and realized that this was where the exploitation takes place, lack of information. How much are they getting paid versus what am I getting paid. And they don't have the stigma for the rest of their lives. These questions became very real for me. I think it was pretty unusual for anyone to question this. They like their women very pliable, and they were kind of pissed-off. Signing my release and getting my check, was the hardest part. I got three hundred or so and kept trying to negotiate a little more.

We did a love story between the two of us, it was really fun working with her. I kept looking for the spread, but as far as I know it's never come out. It was shortly thereafter that Miss America, Vanessa Williams, got dethroned. I felt a lot of empathy with her. A lot of women have done this, it's something that we need to get into the open, just like any other thing that's got a stigma. I figure I've burned all my bridges. (Laughs) That's been my attitude: "Oh, fuck it, it's too late now!"

The other job was porn video, which I did twice, against my better judgment. This guy was not professional. He had a lot of videos die in production and he never looked at his own work. I'm a filmmaker, I knew what you do, and he wasn't doing it. We made up the script and I did the lighting. I created that film, because I wanted it to be something worth watching. I was working with a woman who used to work at the theater who was really fucked up. She was literally almost a virgin, and they kept trying to devirginize her in these films. It was really painful for her, she could hardly take it. She had run away from home, and I think drugs were involved. Since then I think she's done a little better.

In the second film I was humiliated, pretty much the whole time. The producer called saying that he needed me because he was still working on the same film. And I bought that line. It was not true, it was totally different. In the first film I played a woman passing as a man who's in love with the co-star, who has caught this wild woman, and we get to tame her. The film is pretty hysterical, it really appeals to my sense of irony. In the second film there were two men, the previous co-star and his buddy who had never done this before, but was really a hunk, and horny. And there was this gorgeous black woman who had done a lot of films, she looked like Donna Summers, better than Donna Summers. I was like, "Oh, God."

I wasn't supposed to tell anybody I was on my period because these guys would get freaked out. We were given little douches...it was just crazy. These guys were all fucking and sucking and I was watching. They didn't want to fuck me because they knew I had my period. I was just going to give head, that was my role. However, at the point where my partner was supposed to ejaculate, the director wasn't paying attention, and he told the guy, "Don't, don't yet." The guy tried to hold back and he got blue-balls, which is a really painful condition, apparently. He couldn't get a hard-on any more, so they wanted me to pretend to give him a blow job. They made a mixture of egg white and ice cream that was supposed to represent cum. I was supposed to fake him cumming in my mouth with a limp dick. (Laughs) I'm struggling and gagging, and they're yelling at me because I'm not doing it right. It was just horrible. I was nearly in tears, and it was like...this is abuse, I don't care, this is a bad scene. That was the end of that career.

I was so disappointed, because when the agent was taking me around to all the producers I got excited and thought "Ooh, this might be the chance for me to really live out my fantasies." Actually, now, I don't feel too scarred or damaged by it all. I have almost a sense of amusement about it, but also a sense of sadness for that vulnerable part of me being taken advantage of. I have a real strong desire to go public with it. I'm sure that these kinds of experiences are not unique, this is the area of sex education that isn't talked about. What about women who want to work in this industry? What's okay with this, what kind of power do we have, is there any way for it to work for women? It's a question for women in the sex industry, and one we need to address to the pornography-buying public. What is the myth and what's the reality?

Describe living situations you've been in since you left home. ~ I've lived alone just once, when I was in L.A., and that was really fun. The households were usually a bunch of young people, some of them students. We split the bills, maybe not all the food, but at least the staples. We had rice and beans, fighting about money, miscommunications, fighting about cleaning up. I'm pretty comfortable now, that's just part of living together. I've had some really great situations, and learned a lot from my roommates. My fantasy is communal living. I'd like to live in an extended family that's communicating and getting help when we can't resolve issues ourselves.

Describe significant friendships and love relationships you've had since you left home. ~ When I came back from Lesbos I was in love with a woman I met on that trip. It shifted my relationship with my girlfriend, of course, and I bounced back and forth between those two for a short while. When she told me she wanted to break up, it was devastating, but I worked quickly to heal.

I began to explore the kinkier aspects of my sexuality and found myself really drawn to S&M. I was excited and scared. But it was a strong fantasy and it really got me off. Dierdra showed up and it was part of her fantasies too, and our sexual relationship blossomed. Dierdra is a black woman from the old school in New York, she was butch. In the old school one's the butch, one's the fem, one's passive, one's aggressive. We had the most incredible sex. I didn't have to compromise, I could be passive sexually, and she could fantasize that she was a man. That was pretty much what our relationship was based on.

I asked her to stop drinking, and she did. She was using a lot of drugs and it was a problem for her. We lived together in various households. She ran on what could be characterized as masculine ethics, you know, working to support me. I ran into that with a lot of women. She'd have to buy the drinks, she was about as opposite from me as you can get. We were in couple counseling and learned about our different class backgrounds and how that affected our communication. She stopped but I continued counseling individually, and my counselor suggested I do a workshop. That was my introduction to my husband and the beginning of the end for Dierdra and I. She could see that I was relating to men in a different way. She started to drink again, that was her way of saying, "Fine, you said you would leave if I started to drink, leave!" So I did. My lesbian friends were outraged at my behavior, felt rejected, abandoned, angry, and hurt. It was devastating for me. I was suddenly cast adrift again.

So, here was this spiritual young man, full of love and courage. That turned me on. It took people a long time to accept our relationship, but we didn't notice, we were in love. The first night we were together, I told him that if there was someplace that we could do it I'd fuck him right then. I don't think that was a really authentic sentiment, but rather a manipulation. The longest I've been without loving is six weeks. It runs me. Got to have it. I was over the deadline.

He was looking for someone who was sexy, who had a little more experience than him. He hadn't had that much experience at all. Plus, my dancing was kind of a tease for him. I was experienced and open about my sexuality. The thing he was really concerned about was that I was a lesbian. I was shocked when I found out he was worried about AIDS because I was a lesbian. Four years ago that's where our culture was.

Describe your current living arrangements. ~ Right now I'm in an unhappy, dysfunctional household where we don't talk to each other or express our resentments until they're so bad that we're asking each other to leave. My husband and I share one room in a fairly big flat. There are two other people. One doesn't like us very much, and the other is really angry with us for bouncing rent checks. It got to the point where we were actively warring for awhile. The female got her *own* toilet paper, and a cat for our other roommate knowing my husband is allergic to cats. It's really tense, but I need to stay here. It's close to my job, and it's low rent.

Describe your social life and your current friendships. ~ My social life revolves around the people at work and a few friends from earlier days. I let my husband take the initiative with our social calendar but right now we're both working seven days a week. I talk with my parents a lot, though we don't see each other that much.

Do you use drugs? ~ I use cigarettes and caffeine. My body's detoxed enough from the marijuana that I really get high on the sugar. (Laughs)

Have you suffered any traumas as an adult? ~ Getting kicked out of my house, leaving the theater, the growth workshops, confronting myself and my drug addiction, my grandmothers' death, and getting married.

What affect have these traumas had on you? ~ They've matured me. I'm much more confident of my ability to handle traumas.

Describe your fears and insecurities. ~ Not being liked and not having what it takes to make it in the world. Fear that I'm gonna be out in the street and crazy. (Laughs)

Do you have any male inspired fears? ~ Yeah, but they're not a big part of my life any more. In the past I was just terrified of young black men. I had four incidents of sexual assault that didn't culminate in rape, but they were just too much for me to handle. I haven't had anything like that happen to me in about five years, and time has given me confidence. I've also studied martial arts. (Laughs)

What media do you consume? ~ The written word, mostly. Right now I'm reading eleven books. (Laughs) And I watch "Star Trek" on Saturday nights at a friend's. I don't have a TV and I don't plan on getting one. I see movies, not nearly as many as I'd like to. I read some of the free papers. I like the *East Bay Express* a lot, they're kind of radical. I read headlines, "Dear Abby", and the comics.

Do you have a favorite book, author, or movie? ~ My spiritual books are really my favorites. *The Right Use of Will* and *Original Class* are really the books that I live my life out of. I like A.A. Milne; childrens' books are my current favorites.

Do you use sexually explicit media? ~ I don't go out of my way to get it, but if somebody hands it to me, I'll read it. The books for my research are pretty fucking explicit, and they're a turn-on.

Had you been a customer in a peep show or other sex show prior to dancing? ~ No, never.

Which of society's values have you rejected? ~ I'm definitely pro-choice, that one is black and white. Another one that's hard to characterize as a value is the denial and repression of the emotional body. We're not free to express whatever we need to, whenever we need to. I'm talking about crying, screaming, yelling...just letting it out. That drives me crazy and I try to design my life so that there are places where I can. That's a healing process. We're so beaten up, really abused. I have little patience for those who are bought by the validation we get for repressing ourselves successfully.

Has the media ideal of beauty affected you? ~ Tremendously. I'm so obsessed with getting a face lift. (Laughs) Sometimes I don't think I'm attractive. It's ridiculous...because I know I am. (Laughs) I can't stand it, I want to be a teen. It's amazing (Laughs)

Many humans love the attention of others and adorn themselves to get it. Do you? ~ It's such a hassle I don't do it very often. When I do, I luxuriate in the attention I give to myself. I think it reflects on my well-being.

Are you a tolerant person? ~ I would say I'm more tolerant than the average. The reason being, I've looked enough at the phenomenon of judgments and discovered that they keep me fenced in, even more than they keep the people I judge fenced in.

Do you trust people? ~ Less and less. (Laughs)

Do you exploit people? ~ I really exploited people when I was using drugs. I hung out with people I didn't like, to get high. Fortunately, the people I'm surrounding myself with are starting to get healthy too, and they're not willing to do it for me.

Have you ever been violent with people? ~ Two incidents come to mind. My first female lover and I were having an argument about rape. She was anti-feminist in some way and it pissed me off that she wouldn't acknowledge what rape was. I attacked her, I tried to rape her, just to prove my point. (Laughs) It was really ugly. Good lord! The other incident was with my husband before we were married. I felt like he wouldn't listen to me and I threw a dish on the floor. He picked me up and threw *me* on the floor. I was really pissed that he had gone past my limits, and I let him know in no uncertain terms that that was the line he'd better not cross.

Define love. ~ Love is the harmonizing element in the universe. It's the force that keeps all the little atoms from flying apart. Its color is pink, and its greatest teacher is Jesus. It is the first step we need to take before anything else happens. I've discovered that I don't generate it, that it's available to me at any time, if I open myself to it. I have to release whatever's blocking it, and forgive myself, or someone else, to really feel it flowing.

Describe the variety and frequency of your current sexual activity. ~ Right now my husband and I are both fairly stressed, and very busy. So, it's not as satisfying in terms of frequency as we would like. Our regular pattern is every other day, and four days is the most he'll go without, it's about the same for me. I've been frustrated with my sexual response, not satisfied with how much I physically respond. So, we're working on that. We're spending a little more time with foreplay. We're trying to generate passion. It's more loving.

Describe your sexual fantasies. ~ In my sexual fantasies I'm usually playing a masochist. Usually they involve bondage, where I'm totally passive. I have a lot of fantasies about being watched that I didn't have before I danced. They really get me off. Usually after I cum, this is when I'm alone, I'll be really embarrassed. I'll react to the fantasy like it was bad or it means that I'm sick. It's been a long process for me to give myself permission to have the fantasies. I believe I'm learning something from them. Sometimes I have this vague hope that I won't have to have those fantasies when I masturbate, because there's such a strong judgment against them. When I came out as someone who's interested in S&M, it was a vast relief to discover that other people had those fantasies, and that they were actually acting them out. I got a lot of support, but it's been the hardest closet for me to come out of in some ways.

When do you get sexually involved? ~ One of the benefits of being married is having a ready, willing, able, constant sex partner. The when is any time.

Define intimacy. ~ Quality time with friends is intimacy. There's trust and when it's fully expressed it's total honesty and no judgments...and an ability to laugh at ourselves.

Do you appreciate admiration of your body? ~ It's really important to me. It's important that the person you're with like your body. I think most women assume that there's something wrong with their bodies and that they have to make it different for their partner. It's a big relief to know that my husband likes big tits. That's never going to change. (Laughs)

What sexual taboos besides dancing have you broken? ~ Premarital sex, promiscuity, lesbian sex, group sex, more bondage than discipline, S&M, and interracial sex.

What is sexually degrading for you? ~ When my husband's distracted and using sex to deal with something that's going on with him, instead of to relate with me. Then there's being at work, or on the street, or maybe in a bar where the context is sexuality, but I'm not respected as a person. I get really upset when I watch young men and women relate to each other that way, 'cause it seems like the sexual revolution so-to-speak, has failed.

Is sex a power for you? ~ Yes, very much. It's the right of every human being, it's like the core of the human heart, and if we're not completely expressed then we're cut off from our power.

Has living in a male-dominated society played a role in shaping your sexuality? ~ Of course. The main force which starts early, and that's why it has such a strong effect, is that women don't have control over their sexuality. The men want it and they have to guard it. It's the most precious thing but also the most vulnerable. For a woman, her virginity is her honor. That is such a huge responsibility. Little girls are not able to cope with that. There are all these rules. What the fuck are they? It was just devastating. It took so much emotional and physical energy to protect myself and nurture that. It's almost impossible. I'm counting on us being able to heal that wound, I'm committed to it.

Do you think your sexuality would be different if you lived in an egalitarian or female-dominated society? ~ Yeah, I do. Being a lesbian is an expression of it's got to be different, there's got to be another way to do this.

Have birth control and medical technology affected your sexuality? ~ Yeah. I have big resentment about the cervical cap being taken off the market two weeks before I went to get fitted at the Oakland Feminist Women's Health Center. Cervical caps are the least expensive method of birth control, period. Making birth control a problem has had a big affect on my life. Using the pill, I gained weight, and I was constantly on the rag. My body didn't feel good. My periods didn't feel good. I smoke and I have a murmur. I was a high heart attack risk. I decided to hell with that. Then the diaphragm I got was not fitted properly. I had tremendous problems with cystitis. I used the sponge for a while, and got pregnant twice. I got a lot of vaginal infections and I'd stink. So now I'm using condoms and I know that can't go on forever.

Has the women's movement affected your sexuality? ~ The women's movement made it possible for an unmarried woman to get birth control. That wasn't a possibility not too long ago. Abortions also became available. The main impact was that it gave me the idea that it was okay for me to have great sex. That was my right. Then, of course, it had a big influence in my lesbian years. Now it's not so much the women's movement as the new age spiritual movements.

Is your partner supportive of your decision to dance? ~ No, he's not. He always had very nice feelings about it, but now I don't have permission from him to dance. The only thing I can say is, he is an elitist. Overall in our relationship he's given me tremendous support. My dancing has affected our relationship to my husband's father. His father says, "You let your woman do this?" His relationships with his friends have been affected also. That's a heavy burden. It's unfair! It's unfair! Judgment and morals. Get off it. Take a look for yourselves. (Laughs)

How do you think your relationship will evolve? ~ I'm starting to realize that it's actually possible to have the financial freedom to pursue our dreams to heal and teach. I'm starting to see what it's going to take to get there. It's work, don't surrender to despair and resentment, just keep going, don't stop. It's an exciting place to be. Last night I couldn't go to sleep, I was so excited about our interview and my class. It's hard to let go at night. Long days is how I see it evolving.

How did you feel about your body prior to becoming a dancer? ~ I thought it was a lot fatter than it was. Part of the validation I get is from the customers, and seeing all the dancers' bodies, seeing that mine is not that bad. Now I enjoy looking at myself, I've let go of that whole question.

How did you get this job? ~ I ran into a dancer I had connected with as sisters a couple of years before. We were powerful, really exploring sisterhood. She had evolved and was at such a different end of the spectrum, I couldn't believe it. She told me she was working at the theater and gave me an article she wrote about it. I read it and wanted to do a film about it! I checked it out, and saw if she could do it, I could do it.

In your experience are dancers more deprived, abused, and battered than other women? ~ No. There wasn't a higher incidence of abuse because they were dancers, at least at this theater. The main correlation was everybody there needed money. I did know some dancers who were in abusive relationships, and dancing was one of the ways they were making money to get out. A lot of the dancers were married and had kids. That was the biggest factor in who was happy and who wasn't.

Do you recognize any characteristics common to those who dance? ~ My fantasy is that dancers are more competent about projecting their sexuality when they want to. There's the power of stepping beyond the limit, seeing what's on the other side and surviving it. They have depth.

When you started dancing did you fear being separated from other women?

~ Yeah. It was more because I was coming from the gay community and going in a straight direction. It was really hard to let go of those connections, and I did have to. Some of my friends hung in.

Have people treated you as a "bad woman" since you started dancing? ~ It's hard to take the judgment of my grandfather and my husband's dad. It's hard to take their disappointment in me and their sense of, "You could do better for yourself." Being treated as a bad woman is probably a function of identifying myself as a bad woman. Mostly I've projected that part of me as an interesting woman. When I first started dancing I told people what I was doing, and I would immediately go into my rap about what working there was really like, so they wouldn't judge me. I'd let them know very thoroughly and very directly that I didn't want to hear it. In a lot of ways, for me dancing represents the most responsible I've been, it's been the opposite of the bad woman.

Have you lost self-esteem due to dancing? ~ There is a loss of self-esteem in the sense of not having much energy left over to be creative.

Does your family know you dance? ~ I told them it was topless only, and then they picked me up at the theater one day. You can't hide that it's nude – given what the front of the theater looks like. (Laughs) I think it's sad when people can't tell their parents, it disturbs me. Anytime we're in the closet about anything it takes away from relationships. Sometimes it's all we can do given where the other person is at. Sometimes it's healthier and safer. But still, it's a loss.

Has dancing affected your politics? ~ Quite a lot. At one time I assumed that pornography was anti-woman, anti-growth, anti-sex, and that as a politically correct feminist my stance should be that pornography should not exist. I believed that it was a function of our fucked up patriarchal society, and that when everything is worked out in the end, pornography wouldn't need to exist. I don't now. I do believe that sexual expression will change a lot as we heal ourselves, that pornography may look totally different.

My actions come from a strong commitment to healing the planet, male and female relationships. Because I've danced nude for men doesn't mean that I don't have those beliefs. In fact, dancing for men has strengthened those beliefs, my dancing has been healing. I believe the feminist and conservative reaction against pornography is an emotional reaction. It is a reaction that we need to pay attention to, there's something going on there that we need to address, but it's a knee-jerk reaction. It comes from ignorance, both about what pornography is, and what the possibility is for the people participating in it. We need to take a closer look, mostly at our own reactions.

Do you fear becoming a prostitute? ~ Not at all. Every woman has the opportunity, but I've really had the opportunity. I've been in an environment where there were prostitutes and people were hoping I would turn tricks. I ran into pimps before I ever danced and I was very clear that it wasn't what I wanted to do and that I could say no.

Do you identify and feel solidarity with other sex workers? ~ Yes. But there are definitely differences between us and it's really dangerous to assume that we have the same politics. The tendency in feeling solidarity is making vast assumptions and being extremely disappointed when certain expectations aren't met. So I feel solidarity in the sense that I think people who aren't in the sex industry lump us together. I know I have a lot more choices than many prostitutes do. I'm white. Currently my parents are upper middle-class and I have their support. I identify with a good friend who was a prostitute. I understand that she chose to do that because she needed the money and it was something she was good at. She liked having money, a lot. She liked men a lot. She liked the kind of dates she had. In some cases, she was their mistress. She was independent. I guess my solidarity comes from a sense of understanding, to some degree, what other sex workers go through.

Have you been discriminated against because you are a woman? ~ The main area where it has shown up is in the real masculine arenas, like martial arts.

Are you politically active? ~ I consider the healings and meditations I do as having an impact on other people. It's been a long process to recognize that that's valid. I'm strongly influenced by the belief that the personal is the political. My lover who was an environmentalist, used the same sandwich baggie for the entire school year. I think doing this interview is an extremely strong political statement.

Are you a feminist? ~ Yes, I'm a feminist. And I think the bottom line is the feminist believes that women have the right to experience themselves fully and make choices about their lives. I believe in equal pay for equal work, reproductive rights, and childcare. We're not going to get anywhere until we deal with that one. The feminist movement has changed and evolved so much in my lifetime, it's almost ridiculous to use that word. Feminism is more mainstream now than it has ever been and the danger is that we forget about the fringes, forget to help other sisters, and give them the room to empower themselves.

Historically some feminists have tried to exclude some women from the women's movement based on their sexual behavior and preferences. Do

you experience this exclusion? ~ Yes, in a lot of ways. It's made me recognize that I have to be careful when I expect that other women feel solidarity with me or have the same agenda that I do. I have been excluded for being a lesbian among straight feminists, being a separatist among lesbians, being straight among lesbian women, being into kinky sex, sex roles, S&M, or bondage among feminists of any orientation, being a sex worker among everybody, and being a spiritual worker among political workers. I've experienced rejection, anger, loss of friends and connections. That's where it's been the hardest, and the sad thing is that I just accepted it. I didn't fight it. It was such a given that there would be these divisive judgments. It's sad that that's where we were, where we are. There seems to be a strong movement in our culture towards specialization, and smaller and smaller constituencies. Jesse Jackson was not able to bridge that. There really isn't a rainbow coalition, as far as I can tell.

What is your relationship to the women's movement? ~ It's a sad one. I'm not acknowledged as a resource for the women's movement. What I have to offer is a little bit too radical for the majority of movement women. Being radical is not valued in the way it used to be. It used to be the source of power and clearly the groundbreaking movement. There was a tremendous amount of respect for the women who did things that were way out. I feel that I'm to be closeted, that I'm a shameful example of the errors of the movement. (Laughs) I feel like it's up to the women who judge me to take the responsibility to learn about me.

What have been the most damaging and the most constructive influences in your life? ~ A lot of self-help new age movements have been extremely constructive. They're so pissed on by the press, it's sad. They have given me a sense that I am responsible for my own destiny and healing.

The most damaging influence has been denial. When I deny my feelings because I'm scared of rejection or when I deny my anger or rage at the culture because I'm scared of being jailed, that's damaging. When everybody does that, that's really bad. The denial of our rights and our right to growth by people with guns affects us more than we realize.

What person or people have had the greatest influence on your life? ~ My parents have been a very strong influence and I'm starting to relate to them in an up-to-date way, when we talk about the effects we've had on each other. My husband has been there through thick and thin. And I've had teachers, Peter Ralston, Werner Erhardt and Associates, and James Thomas. I feel very strongly that I owe a personal debt to the suffragettes, the midwives, and the witches. They kept alive a way of healing, a way of being, a way of committing themselves and putting themselves on the line that enables me to continue that. I've been influenced by a lot of writers and filmmakers who put out their vision and encouraged me to have my own.

What are your greatest gifts and limitations? ~ My greatest gifts are in the area of communication and being empathic, being intelligent enough to grasp a lot more than I can even speak about. That sometimes leads to limitations because I try to speak about it. I love playing with the energy between us and trying to speak for the relationship, instead of just for my ego or my fears.

My limitations are in my self-doubt and self-hate. That's really an expression of anger that I have been unwilling or too afraid to express. That's a big limitation. I've been limited by the fact that I abused drugs for ten, fifteen years. I feel like in some areas I'm just beginning to catch up. I need to accept the terms of the world, especially the financial responsibility that goes along with how the world operates.

What would you like to be doing in 10 to 15 years? ~ My fantasy is to have a center for the arts and healing. Maybe it's even accredited as a school or a master's program. It has a coffee house, a stage, a film studio, a recording studio, maybe even a theater. There would be an integration of the spiritual with the artistic way beyond what's happening now, where people directly experience healing. I believe many of us devolved from beings who were committed to healing the world through song and dance, or acting, writing, expression. Those were fractured and fragmented and as we become whole, our art will just explode. I want to be in the thick of that. I want to be a teacher and director sending work into the world, healing with it and opening up dialogue.

I think that's pretty close to what I will be doing in ten or fifteen years. I am anticipating a tremendous change on the planet. My sense is that we're on the brink of going into the Dark Ages or evolving. We're at a crisis point and our survival depends on what we do the next ten, fifteen years. I'm committed to go through whatever it takes to heal myself. I'm praying for wisdom.

Recently in San Francisco we witnessed the appearance of women dancing for women. Why do you think this is happening? ~ There are some very courageous women who decided that it was about time. It happened in the thirties or forties when the San Francisco underground gay culture was alive and well. It was modeled on the heterosexual relationship, women stripping for men.

The only reason we are able to have this is because the lesbian community got a little looser about sex. That came from a lot of fronts. It came from Samois putting out their book of sexually explicit stories with S&M themes, that just blew away the community. It was like, "Lesbian pornography! Aaargh!" We had lesbians coming out of the closet who were sex workers, the realization that a lot of sex workers were lesbian. They thought, "Maybe all the women could get off on this." The time was right. Why should the men have all the fun? The question was how can we create this and have it be empowering for the dancers and the women?

Have you danced for women only? ~ I feel very privileged to say I was involved in the very first three shows. It was such an exciting experience for me because I am bisexual. My first impression was, "This is going to be fun." I was going to do what I love to do in a totally safe environment, where I didn't feel the threat of men's power along with their sexuality. The first time I danced I was not very heavy on the real sensuous, sleazy, nasty side. I was very much the nice girl taking off her clothes. I dressed as a secretary. It was joyful.

After the show a few women came up to me and said, "I liked your show the best, the energy was so good." I had reached the heart. It was a blast. Afterwards we had a dance and the energy was so high. People were so released and so turned on. It was so much fun to just strut your stuff, to be around women and to be blatant, blatant, blatant.

If social and economic equality for women became a reality, would some women still dance? Would you? ~ Yeah, I think so – I would. Hopefully I'd make a lot of money. I would like to see it be less exclusively male and such that women could appreciate other women without questioning their own sexuality. I intend to keep dancing in some format or another. Currently I am teaching an erotic dance class. Right now if I could pick whatever job I could have, I would do this. There's a big power here, perhaps it's male-controlled because it's so powerful. It's way more powerful than anybody wants to acknowledge.

Would commercial sex work exist in your ideal society? ~ I think so, because commercial sex work fills a need, it is a gesture towards healing. Some people will need that sexual attention from someone.

For many people it is impossible to conceive of anyone choosing to dance as you do. Why do you think that is? ~ I think their reaction is based on the teachings we've been given about the "fallen woman." There's an assumption that, of course, women don't want to do this, because it's degrading. That comes from history, that each woman probably can identify with, of being degraded sexually, and that this would just be the ultimate, the extreme end of that. They can't see the other side, that perhaps it's empowering. There's just so much pressure about sexuality. It's a very powerful force and it's been so abused that it's hard for us to separate the power from the abuse. As we start to separate them, perhaps people will be a little more understanding and a little less fearful. I guess the bottom line is fear.

Many people paint female sex workers as among the most obvious victims of male domination and declare that if you don't see yourself as such you are suffering from "false consciousness" and "delusions of the oppressed." What is your response to that? ~ That's really scary. It's a really powerful accusation and it really worms its way into my heart. I've been forced to look at it for a long time. My gut reaction is, "How dare you define my consciousness?" My other gut reaction is, "Oh, my God, maybe they're right. Maybe I've sold my soul and I'm damned forever." That's a strong one. I don't think there's any sex worker who hasn't looked at that question. I honestly don't. And I think a lot of us have built a defense to that question, because it seems to be a standing question. Perhaps because of the charge on both sides, we haven't been able to really look at what's true about that and what's not true about that.

There's a lot to the assertion that men control the sex industry, our wages, that the reason the sex industry exists is because men are in control, and because men have a strong investment in separating women, the Madonna and the Whore. On the other hand, you could say that we are exploiting men, getting over on them in a big way, that we are in control of the situation, we're extremely powerful, and we recognize that.

Maybe there's a feeling among feminists that it's not fair, that we should withhold sex from men until they give us our equal due, that we are sabotaging the movement because we're giving them sex. We have to be solid and nobody can give men sex because they're fuckers. (Laughs) Well, the problem is that women need sex, too. And money. And women like being powerful over men in terms of their sexuality. That can be very empowering, or it can be fucked-up. There are women at the theater who hate men, at this point in their lives, who are very abusive, and very clear about their power. They know exactly what they're doing, they feel like they're torturing men, and they enjoy it.

If feminists, the ones who are polarized in that area, want us to stop what we're doing, they're going to have to appeal to us in some other way than saying we're deluded. (Laughs) They've got a lot more homework to do. Maybe read this book, be a sex worker for a day.

Why do you think people use sexually explicit media? ~ It turns them on. People who use it have a strong physiological response that enhances their sexual response. When we look at the question, "Why do they use it?" it's like, "Why do they have that response?" Why a particular thing turns us on is a really much deeper question, and it can't be answered except for case by case. My sense is that it's way healthier to know what you like than not.

Has the sexually explicit media you've seen accurately portrayed humans and their sexual relations? ~ I don't think it's an accurate representation of our experience, but it's a reflection of something that we're experiencing. The way those two pictures are going to match is if we explore what the reflection is telling us. We're going to have to look deeper into what our feelings are about sex. My philosophy is that what we're denying is going to come up on the screen. What we're unwilling to feel is going to be reflected back to us somehow. If I don't like what I see, that indicates that maybe I've got to look and see what it is that I'm not willing to see, inside of me. That's the way I would approach feminists or anybody anti-pornography. Why does this upset you so much? Really. Why does it upset *you* so much? (Laughs) Forget about all the rationale. What's the emotional reaction? What does that mean to you? What do you need to look at? That's just a start. Then there's healing that, if it's not okay.

At what age do you think people should be allowed to view pictures of human genitalia? ~ Zero. My feeling is that our relationship with children and sex is based on our own relationship with sex. Children should not be excluded from the sexual process. That's a very old division, but it doesn't necessarily promote survival or anything. I think we can grant children the ability to know when they're ready. There's absolutely no reason why they can't be exposed to that early on. Then, perhaps, it will be less charged for them, less confusing. It seems like it could only help. The best case scenario is it will be available to them and when they're ready they'll feel comfortable talking to their parents about it. And their parents will be comfortable with them. Sexual undertones in family life will be brought to the surface and dealt with. Our perspective on what the ideal family life should be is really just a slice of the continuum of the evolution in human consciousness. It's much more wide-open as to what a healthy family is than what we think right now. We have to broaden our horizons. And that's one of the ways we'll have to do it.

Do you think any sexually explicit media should be banned? ~ Maybe if it was poisonous to the environment. (Laughs) The ozone layer. There are certainly things that I don't want to exist, like snuff films. And they're banned. I don't think banning is a really effective means of controlling. It's probably more destructive than constructive.

At the outset, the Meese Commission declared that it intended to contain the spread of pornography. At its conclusion, the Commission, like most others, could not define pornography. Yet it recommended the prosecution, fining, and jailing of people who produce, distribute, and consume it. What do you think of the Commission and its recommendations? ~ When all of that was coming to a head it was really frightening to realize that there were people in power who had those beliefs and that intention. It made me feel really vulnerable and extremely judged. I think they made fools of themselves. I trust that open minded people, if they're going to have any sympathy for me talking, they'll be able to see through the Meese Commission's judgments, into what the Meese Commission discovered, and recognize that they're going to have to make their own decisions. That they would not be willing to let the Meese Commission make their decisions for them. Who the hell is making that distinction between erotic and pornographic? Where do distinctions like that really lie? Can you say they're external? Or are they only internal interpretations? Does someone have the right to say to a woman, "That's pornography. You were oppressed. You were fucked?" Who has the right to judge, is what it comes down to. Not the Meese Commission.

Why do you think the government shows virtually no concern with violence in the mainstream media? The mainstream media is more powerful than the average person recognizes. The original idea was that the media would be a balance to the powers of government. That's not the case anymore. Perhaps the government can't do anything about it. Perhaps they're not as powerful as the media.

Second is the question of how much money there is to be made from violence. When there's lots of money to be made from violence, whose fault is that? How do you decide? It's the consumers? The people who are making it? They have no integrity, they just want money? It's a complex question.

It's astounding how many acts of violence go on in a few moments of film nowadays. Sometimes I come out of theaters feeling battered. I don't have a TV; it's too upsetting for me. That's how I've responded to the violence: I don't watch it. The worst case, perhaps, is that the government wants a nation of people who watch a lot of violence. That they understand the impact it has on us more than we do, and that they're perfectly fine with the result. It serves their interests.

Jackie, you, I, and Phoenix were recently interviewed by Geraldo Rivera for his TV special, "Modern Love." Tell us about the interview, the interviewer, and the finished show. ~ I went into the interview very excited. I felt like it was my opportunity to go public, nationally, with my experience at the theater. Tell how it was a positive, nurturing experience, and how I felt powerful there. I think I expressed that fairly well.

I chose to wear regular clothing for two reasons. First, my face was shown and I decided I didn't want my Jackie image to be that public. Second, I wanted people to recognize that I was a sex worker with my clothes on or off. I wanted to make myself someone who the audience could identify with.

Geraldo was obviously running the show. He was directing and interviewing. It wasn't extremely organized, but he seemed to have a high expectation that everyone would be professional and that it was going to go like clockwork. His interview was very directed, and we had our agenda. It seemed like the intent of his communication and mine were in opposite directions. He asked me about being a prostitute, or was I afraid of becoming one. Heavily implicit in that question was: "All sex workers are alike. All dancers are prostitutes." And I said "No." He asked me what I wanted to do in the future, and I said, "Heal the planet." He said, "Good luck." At the interview I didn't feel good considering what he wanted. Later I thought, "Well, we said what we wanted to say." What I tried to express was that I am a human being first. I wanted people to understand that their judgments about sex workers were inaccurate, that there's more to being a sex worker than being oppressed. Mostly I wanted to communicate that I am a powerful person and a sex worker. And, that shouldn't fuck you up to hear that. (Laughs) It seemed to fuck him up to hear that.

We were quite excited about what we got on tape and really hoping to make an impact on the American public. We and our point of view were totally excluded from the show. Apparently it was that powerful that he had no choice but to cut the entire thing out. We were actually called part of the problem. If I remember correctly, he said dancers, prostitutes, and drug addicts are the reason for AIDS. That was the basic communication. I was outraged. Absolutely outraged. It was very clear to me that he cut us out because what we had to say was not what he wanted to say. He was not doing a documentary, he was doing a very inflammatory show using people's fears about AIDS. It had very little positive information. He looked like a jerk on the show. A drug addict, who was probably infected with AIDS, tried to attack him with a needle, because he was so judgmental and condescending. I don't think he served anybody in that show, not even himself.

How are sex work and sex workers portrayed in the mainstream media? ~ Victims of murder is the way we're portrayed. Watch any spy, police, medical show, and it's always the girl in Vegas who got murdered. Personally I don't know any sex workers who were murdered. The audience has to think, "Well, they probably deserved it." They went across the line. They're bad girls. A little distancing for the audience. "I'm not a sex worker. I'm not at risk." Bullshit. (Laughs) People are at risk who are living with handguns in their homes. Statistically they're the ones at risk.

Then there's the hooker with the heart of gold, who's willing to help out the good guy. That's really what defines them as having a heart of gold. In terms of the media, that's pretending to document this, there are few exceptions to the rule. Geraldo Rivera is maybe the extreme, but not that extreme. I guess I'll stop. It's a depressing topic.

Some people argue that humans are born with a sex drive and after that our sexuality is socially constructed, produced through our experiences. How do you think human sexuality is shaped? ~ I agree with that. I think healthy people are the products of orgasm. (Laughs) The rest of us, something else. I believe that we're a reflection of our parents' health at the time of conception. In the worst case, there's rape. In the best case, simultaneous orgasm. And then we're bombarded by society.

Are there a wide variety of sexualities produced? ~ Yeah. But there are problems. The force of repression possibly stimulates some really strange sexual behavior. On the other hand, perhaps there would be an even wider range or only one way to have sex if there wasn't any repression.

Do you think the State tries to manage sexuality? ~ Yes, I do. And my evidence would be the laws about abortion, prostitution, age limits, and sodomy.

Describe what men and women have in common sexually. ~ Sex and orgasms are real important. It's important for both men and women to feel confident sexually. A lot of their problems deal with confidence. There are a lot of traits that aren't universal but that are common to both men and women. The generalizations of style, like people who really like to be expressive, loud, and passionate. Or very passive, quiet and restricted, subdued. I think we focus on the difference and forget how common our interests and needs are.

Is there any sexual expression society should ban? ~ It's my belief that society can't ban anything. There are certainly taboos, laws, moral codes, and heavy judgments, but they don't work. I don't really trust society to make those kinds of decisions. (Laughs)

What part does sexual pleasure play in life? ~ It serves the function of uniting us with our own hearts and relaxing us physically and emotionally, allowing us to totally express ourselves with another human being or human beings. It's socially very important. It keeps us off the streets. (Laughs)

Some people think that sexuality without procreation is a threat to society. Is it? ~ No. But people understand on a very deep, unconscious, intuitive level that sex is a creative act and there's a lot of fear about it. Some do think we should only have sex when we're going to make babies, and then we won't have to worry about creating darkness or empowering our denied emotions.

You believe that sometimes it is okay to be a sex object. Tell us more. ~ The difficulty with being a sex object is that implied in being a sex object is that the person objectified has no choice about it. But yet, it's okay when they want to be. I don't really have a sense of, "Okay, given this situation, then it's okay," or, "Given that situation, you shouldn't be a sex object." I just have the sense that sometimes it's probably exactly the perfect thing to be and that implicit in that is that you want to be that. There's a whole realm of playing a role that I use, that makes me feel sexy when I dress up like a tramp or on purpose display my sexual characteristics. You could interpret that as I'm being a sex object, especially if you take the feminist perspective that any woman who does anything besides just being hairy, is objectifying herself or is objectified by men.

Do you think gratification of sexual needs diminishes anti-social impulses? ~ Yes, but I don't think it's as simple as that in general, because usually people's sexual needs are a function of who they are as a whole person. And if they're anti-social, their sexual needs may come out in an anti-social fashion. So, in some cases it may be too late, that route won't work. But I think being committed to having a great sex life and being willing to work through everything that is in the way of that will heal as well as increase the chances of being more socially acceptable. (Laughs) I'm laughing at myself because I know how far out my beliefs are.

Feminism as it emerged in the early 1970's had as basic tenets sexual exploration and sexual self-determination. Subsequent exploration has led to intense debate over female sexual identity and behavior. How do you define female sexuality? ~ In general, I would say that pure female sexuality is actually very receptive, responsive, and intense. That it calls forth the male active principle, and that receptive doesn't mean passive. It means open, even encompassing or enfolding. My personal experience is that to be satisfied, I need to be extremely receptive. But I can't do that unless I trust my partner. There has to be some acceptance from the male principle. As a matter of fact, my impression is that the men have to be willing to acknowledge the effect that they have on women, and see women's sexual behavior, in part, as a function of how they are putting themselves out. Women can trust if they know their response is totally accepted, and that the man will make adjustment if it's not okay for either party.

The other aspect is that in reality, we have both those typical "male" or "female" characteristics. That goes on internally as well as between people, and people can switch their roles around.

Are there any sexual behaviors you think women should not engage in? ~ I don't think they should stay in a relationship that's abusive.

A recent Kinsey Institute survey of western nations concluded that people in the U.S. feel the worst about their bodies. Have you seen evidence of this problem? ~ That doesn't surprise me. I haven't travelled extensively, but my impression in talking to people of other cultures is, "What's the big deal? What's with you white people?" (Laughs) In our culture, most of the people I know personally have a real problem with their "flaws". There's such a strict standard. I presume it has a lot to do with the media. I'm starting to get wrinkles and it just drives me crazy, because on one hand, I don't want to present myself as anything other than who I am. I don't want to get a facelift and fuck with my body that way, but I don't like the wrinkles. I go back and forth. The main evidence I have is myself and I figure I'm a pretty healthy specimen. So the rest of our culture must really be suffering.

In the late 1940's American writer Philip Wylie saw equally strong tendencies to excite and constrain the erotic drive as pervasive in this society. He observed that they continuously reinforce each other and declared, "The United States is technically insane on the matter of sex." Is his diagnosis good for today? ~ I think so, but we've made some progress. The evidence is a literal loosening up – well, I would say that women can show more skin and it's not as dangerous. The excitement has gotten higher and perhaps because of that, repression also. We still don't have permission to have bacchanals, but perhaps more people do act out their fantasies.

I saw a poster the other day that has a picture of all these women without their shirts on, and it says, "Girlie, keep your shirt on." It gives a brief analysis of how once men weren't able to expose their breasts or nipples. That was against the law. They said, "Forget that," and started taking off their shirts at the beaches. The law changed because they were unwilling to have that rule. We could take our shirts off too.

Think about the investment, particularly of the advertising culture, to prevent us from desexualizing the breast. The breast is a powerful tool in advertising.

The poster's point is that our breast is a secondary sexual characteristic, just like theirs; that the male torso is no less inherently erotic than the female torso; that women are oppressed because they can't take their shirts off and men can; that the breast is a symbol of femaleness, of motherhood, of nurturing, not just of sexuality, and that women are separated from their own bodies because they're not allowed to expose them; that exposing yourself does not incite rape; that covering yourself does not protect you from rape. I think that's what Wylie was talking about. It's pretty fucking insane.

Wow, if everyone were to take their shirts off, maybe I couldn't make as much money dancing. (Laughs) Maybe there would be top dancing, not topless. I would be willing to take the risk of looking for a job to have everyone be able to take her shirt off.

In a recent decision the Supreme Court ruled that the State does have a role in regulating bedroom behavior. Do you agree? ~ Good heavens, no. That's not the State's function. God can't even handle it. Our sexual behavior does not belong to the State. It's a powerful spiritual force and the State has no right to take that away. It's like freedom of religion. It should be covered by the First Amendment.

People in the United States are spending billions of dollars each year on sexual needs. What does this say to you? ~ It's my opinion that it's perhaps the most important part of being human and that says they're having to spend money to get it. That's the problem. (Laughs) We should not have to spend money to handle that. We shouldn't have to spend money to get health care and food. I guess it's par for the course.

Can sexual needs be met commercially in a non-sexist way? ~ As long as we've got money in this culture, and imbalances of power, that will come into play. The main problem is men, in general, have the money and the power.

Do you think the schools should teach about human sexuality? ~ Yes, but it's a very touchy field. By the time I got to junior high we had social living, and received quite a bit of sex education. Our teachers really handled it well. That was only a positive experience for me. My teacher mostly demystified and took the charge out of talking about it. That was the main benefit of what she said. She said, "If you asked everyone in the world if they masturbate, 90 percent would say yes and 10 percent would be lying." We all went, "Ooh," and all the boys went, "Oh, yeah? Do you? Hmmm? Hmmm?" She'd already answered that.

We got the physical function stuff and talked about other issues that were crucial to us. Am I normal? It's real important for teenagers to know, "Yeah, there's at least one other person on the planet like you, probably, no matter how far out you get." Young people, especially teenagers, are real curious and vulnerable to sexual information, especially if they're not very experienced. So the more positive information you can give them, the better. Give them a dose of good, healthy conversation. Another thing, we should allow them to lead the discussion. Not every child develops at the same age and rate, but people protect themselves from information they don't want to know, so you probably can't err in going too young. We can trust the younger people to know what they want to know. They'll tell us if we really listen.

How is sexuality portrayed in the mainstream media? ~ Through the presentation of how people are groomed and madeup, what they're wearing, what their postures are, what shape their bodies are in. The message is that what's sexy for women is, someone who's slender but busty, with lots of curves that are muscular, very little body hair, done hair on their heads, makeup, full lips, beautiful eyes...blonds are always preferable...white, of course.

The men have intense expressions. They don't obviously have makeup on. Bushy eyebrows, hair's done short but with a tousled look. The clothing is simple and shows their bodies off, they're very built. The sexual attributes of each sex are very much played up. The women and men don't look much alike, for the most part, although some advertising agencies play up androgyny. I'm focusing mostly on ads and billboards, still photographs. I don't watch TV, except for Star Trek.

There's no one in a relationship on that show. Everyone has sacrificed their love life for this greater cause, the Federation. Anyone who gets into a relationship is there only for that week. I think there's kind of a negative message in there, you can't mix commitment to the human race with sex. (Laughs) It's a shame.

Sexuality is everywhere in the media. There's a new trend of women being rather cool, the Garbo cool, unapproachable sex goddesses...no, ice princesses. Extremely desirable, really attractive, but not soft or receptive, totally in the role of demanding pursuit from the male. The other place that sex is heavily used is in the beer commercials. The emphasis is not on romance, but on fun with the opposite sex, flirting, drinking the right beer to do that.

Some people argue that there is a sexual hierarchy in the United States with heterosexuals at the top and everyone else treated as second class citizens. Do you agree? ~ Absolutely. I had personal experience of this when I made the shift from being exclusively gay to being exclusively straight. The response I got from people when I'd walk down the street with my boyfriend was so different from the response I got when I walked with my girlfriend, it really was unnerving. It was a real part of my identity crisis at the time. People smile, they approve.

I was trained from being with women to be very careful of how I expressed my sexuality. Straight, I was still in the mode of, it's somewhat dangerous, and I have to protect myself. Being with my woman I had to portray myself as being invulnerable and tough, you couldn't mess with me. For protection there was this attitude of "Fuck you."

Being with my boyfriend...that's when heterosexual privilege hit me full in the face. It was very subtle but very real. Then there are even more subgroups...the fact that gay marriages aren't legal. This is changing in San Francisco, but you know, couples can't get health care or a job because their partner is not their legal spouse. There are those kind of problems, multiplied by every privilege that heterosexual married couples get. It's in the legal system, our attitudes, it's on the street. In public there's no place when you're gay, except being with other gay people or in a predominantly gay environment, where it's safe to be sexual with your partner, or affectionate.

How does society respond to the outspoken sensuous person? ~ Mixed messages. On one level, the sensual, outspoken sensuous person is completely squelched. Many people don't feel the permission to be that. I can't go out and fuck anywhere I want. Why is that? Why is it always in the bed? Why is it private, what is that dynamic, what are we so afraid of, what's going on? People who are sensuous either didn't get that programming in the first place or worked through it and got validation somewhere along the line.

People are excited about sensuous people, that's the other half of it. Secretly we're all really turned on by that aliveness. It's an expression, for many people, of self-love and, yeah, I have sex and I like it.

What have you learned about people through sexuality? ~ Now that I have this commitment to supporting other women in the expression of their sexuality, I'm noticing that most people are not free around their sexuality, but that most are willing to work with it. In '72, when Nancy Friday came out with *My Secret Garden*, women were afraid to talk with each other in such a free way about their sex lives. That's not the case anymore, there's been a definite change. It's really valuable to see how other people deal with the same problems, to see that our problems are not unique, that there are some universal ones. A chance to express them and have other people not judge us as weird is invaluable. People are willing to be more vulnerable than I originally thought. I thought it was just me and everyone else was being an asshole. Now I feel more connected to the rest of humanity.

What would a sexually positive society look like? ~ There would be a hundred times more dialogue about sexual issues, that's the first step. Sex would be perceived as a joyous event, free from the power struggles that go on between people. It couldn't be manipulated by people in power.

Do women play a part in the creation of male sexuality? ~ Women do a lot in that area and it's not conscious and it should be.

How do you think batterers and rapists are created? ~ I think we all have been battered and raped, in one form or another. That problem is much bigger than each individual. We tend to focus on, "What's wrong with him, or her, what's wrong with you?", rather than us. It's not, "What's wrong with the culture, why does this exist, why is there a tolerance for it, why aren't batterers and rapists taken into a safe environment and healed, so that they don't do any more damage?" We can point our fingers all we want and say, you're responsible, but that doesn't get us anywhere. Putting people in prison doesn't solve the problem, it seems to make it worse. That's what I'm angry about, that we don't deal with it effectively, at all. How can we put a man on the moon and not cure a rapist? What is going on here, what is the message we're giving to them and they're giving to us? Neither side is getting across. It's war. So, I think that question has not been answered.

Are there feminist men? ~ Yes. There are men who have listened to the messages of feminist women in the last several centuries, and incorporated them into their lives. Men who have been willing to look at the questions, who see the benefits of changing rules they have internalized. Men who are willing to take risks and sacrifice their privileges. It takes a lot of courage to do that.

What is their relationship to sexually explicit media? ~ I think it's quite varied. Some are perhaps disturbed that they're turned on, they know they shouldn't be, because it's politically incorrect. I suspect that a lot of them take their cues from women. They would want to know how the woman in the media they're viewing was feeling, or the woman they're viewing with. They'd ask, "What do you think of this?" They are probably able to recognize media that is sex-positive for women, and probably like that. Boy, it's really dangerous to generalize, (laughs) there are so many feminist men out there.

Describe the impact male dominance has had on women. ~ It's caused women to doubt themselves, their feelings, their response to what's happening. When we're constantly told that our feelings are worthless, our responses inappropriate, that there's no point to them; that's damaging. The effect of that self-doubt is that a person loses their integrity, their power, and their freedom to make appropriate choices. Out of that comes a sense of dissatisfaction, depression, anger, and rage, a lot of it unexpressed, and fear. There's a whole population that is not functioning, and that's not good for society as a whole. That in turn affects men.

The answer is for women to recognize that we don't need to identify or describe ourselves in relationship to what men value in women. We can choose our own values to strive for and judge ourselves against. That's a very difficult process, but one that has been initiated in this culture, and in Europe as well. That's the radical feminist job, to give women some space to go, "Wait, wait a minute, do I really want this, I never really looked at this, I never had a choice about it. Maybe I need to get away from that and be with some women and talk things through."

Do you see men working at changing themselves? ~ I wish more of them were doing it faster, but I certainly see it happening. Because of the difference in power between men and women, women have much more invested in looking into these issues, reading lots of books, going to rap groups, all the manifestations of feminist art. I wish more men had the same sense of urgency around it. I'm sure that if they apply themselves they could do the research. I'm speaking generally, but I'm really talking about my marriage. (Laughs) My husband is open, but I wish that he was freer to really delve into these issues instead of me having to take the lead. I am clear that he's working as fast as he can on as many issues as he can, and that he's fairly healthy. My fantasy society would have more opportunities for men to look into that, starting at a very early age.

How can women help men change? ~ The most direct, the most powerful thing we can do, is nurture ourselves and be clear about what we need. We must recognize that helping men change is not necessarily our goal in life, but that everything that we do to nurture and grow is going to have an impact. It's probably a more authentic way to approach the problem than saying, "I'm going to fix you," or "I'm going to put my needs, again, secondary and work on our relationship." Women have to start from the inside out, in whatever way feels right for them, and they have to be willing to rock the boat. Compassion helps a lot, as well. We need to recognize that if we're speaking in an accusatory way, and we can't help but do that, that the response that we'll get will probably not be the one that we really want.

What do you think the future holds for relations between men and women? ~ Trouble. I think it's gonna get worse before it gets better, for most people. Literally, for the planet to survive, we've got to start working out these issues of imbalance of power. We've been blind to ourselves and the lessons that life is giving us. Life has to come back and hit us with a harder and harder lesson until we get it. So, for most of the population, it's going to get nasty. It's going to look like the end of the world to a lot of people. But the outcome will hopefully be much more satisfying, a lot more orgasms! (Laughs)

If rape and sexual assault ended today how would your life change? ~ I would wear a lot less clothes. (Laughs) I think I would be a nudist, I think a lot of people would be nudists. I would be much more willing to interact with people I don't know. I'd probably be more responsive to men...and go out at night alone a lot. I probably would have a lot more of the energy that is channeled into fear and protection available to me, so I might be a lot more creative, and supportive too.

Feminist people have long observed the system of male domination in the United States and exerted considerable effort to overturn it. What strategies do you think have been effective? ~ Consciousness raising, women talking to each other, sharing information, opening up, coming out of the closet, recognizing that their individual situations are not unique to them but the function of a system, and a system wide problem. Women can take that back to their lives and really do something about it. It works. I think the movement and the progress we've made is based on individuals taking control of their own destinies and being willing to be in communication with their friends, their families, their husbands, and make the changes from the inside out.

What do you consider to be the failures of the women's movement in the United States? ~ The hardest lesson is the fragmentation and loss of the political power base. Apparently, that has happened. It's important that we recognize that we're evolving as a movement, that we be willing to admit mistakes, and acknowledge that our perspectives change. The things we used to exclude we want to include, things we used to include we want to exclude. It's important that we be real honest about where we've been, what we've learned, what we don't like, what we like. And that we be comfortable with the fact that it hasn't been a smooth road.

I think there's a drive toward perfection that comes out of our fear of powerlessness, our fear of revealing to outsiders, or those in power, that there's any weakness. That prevents us from learning from our weaknesses and healing them. I feel like a lot of us, as feminists, have gone back into the closet, and just don't want to deal with the pain that looking at that issue brings up. But the truth is, it's not resolved. We need to accept the pain and do our best to heal it – that usually means honestly communicating it and then hopefully that will be reflected in a widespread movement.

What strategies do you recommend now? ~ It's important that we don't stop and rest on our laurels, or give up in the face of the backlash of recent years. We must educate our young women concerning the history of the battle between the sexes, so that they don't take for granted the freedom that they have. So they can acknowledge their foresisters and hopefully carry the torch. There's a lot of fragmentation in the feminist movement. In the early '70's or so, there was a real sense of unity, it's important that we continue to work towards that goal.

I've observed in the San Francisco lesbian community that the bar scene is real different now. The women are all femmed out with their haircuts, their nice outfits, their makeup. Looking good seems to be the main criteria. I have a friend who's recently come out and she really has a negative attitude towards dykey-looking women. I don't think she recognizes that these dykes took a lot of risks, put up with an awful lot of abuse, and stood their ground. And that in San Francisco we're in an extremely specialized environment. We're at the far end of freedom here, and for us to be worrying about our nails...and, "Oh, look at her, she's not in style", is just plain dangerous. We can't afford that, we can't afford to lose sight of the big picture, or forget that women around the world literally look to American women as role models, as groundbreakers. They look to us as teachers. They want to know how we dealt with the problems that they're now dealing with. They need our support and inspiration. We've got to go further into ourselves, *and* we've got to connect outward. We can do that now. We've spent the time, we can learn from our history, there's a wealth of information. There's absolutely no reason why we can't change the world.

What future do you see for the women's movement in the United States? ~
I see us reforming with respect to our differences, gaining a much broader constituency, hopefully with a very clear platform. I personally feel that the issues of childcare and the changing demographics of the American family are key.

Not too long ago I was listening to a Republican legislator make a very disparaging comment about Jesse Jackson's inclusion of child care in his platform. He was like, "Where do these people get off thinking they have a right to childcare?" I just about crashed my car. I saw that we've got to continue a rational dialogue with the people who feel that they can brush our concerns aside. We've got to say, no, these concerns are not minor, they're not an aside. Foreign policy is not any more important than domestic policy. Everything is related, there's a connection between what's happening in our foreign policy and what's happening in our families, absolutely!

We need to keep speaking rationally in a way that people can understand, and give people a framework in which to think about these issues. We need to acknowledge the emotional aspects of the issues, but look deeper into *why* these issues are so emotional.

I see a lot of the humanist, the personal growth, new age, and the family therapy movements we're going to be able to draw from and recognize the dysfunction in our own society. We'll see that we're creating a society, as dysfunctional people, people not whole, not able to use all of their capacities. I see a definite evolution, and a deeper understanding of the human condition, of what makes us human.

Anti-censorship feminists have emerged who believe that some sexually explicit media reflect and reinforce the oppression of women, but disagree with the pro-censorship feminists' view that sexually explicit media is the cause of women's oppression. They argue that the causes of women's oppression are much deeper, and precede the mass production and distribution of sexually explicit media by centuries. What is your point of view? ~
Speaking as someone in the sex industry, I can't say, oh, fuck those pro-censorship people, they want to take away my job, or, they don't understand, they're right-wing, they want to take away my freedom of speech. We have to

look at that whole issue, including how women and men are portrayed in sexually explicit material. We have to take responsibility for the message.

Where do you think sexually explicit media should be placed on the movement agenda? ~ I wouldn't say it should be the top. I feel like that's almost a waste of time. I'm someone who wants to see a change in the culture, and I don't think that's the route to take. I don't think, even if that was the cause of oppression, we'd get very far with it. It's very difficult to fight the media with its power base. We can simply choose not to have it in our lives, choose not to be with people who have it in their lives. I really don't think it's the cause of oppression, and I would say it would come after concerns for our environment and family life. Issues of war and peace, feeding and nurturing people, seem to be the central things to work with. How people avoid their pain by media will come after the central issues are resolved.

You told us how the women's movement affected your sexuality. Has it affected you in other ways? It's affected the choices I've made around being a parent, being married, being a heterosexual, the kind of relationship I want with my husband, and that I expect. About how I'm going to make a living. The feminist movement, especially with the advent of birth control and the availability of abortion gave women a lot more choice. That has probably had the most impact on my life. Knowing that I have a right, if I assert myself, to the kind of relationship that I want, that's certainly given me a lot of freedom. It's given me the relationship that I want. I deserve to make as much as any man, and any field should be open to me. I was never encouraged to find a rich man to marry, that's certainly a function of feminism.

Do you think our constitutional guarantee of free speech includes sexual speech? ~ I suspect that the framers of the Constitution didn't include that in their own minds. (Laughs) However, I feel that they left a lot of room, especially if you consider sexuality spiritual, which I do. Therefore it falls under freedom of religion. I think freedom of religion speaks to the God-given right that each of us has to live to our fullest, to really flourish. That's what their intention was. At that time, maybe they couldn't see that that would include sexual issues, but in our time, we can say, "Absolutely, it includes sexual issues."

How would you advise courts ruling on sexually explicit media? ~ Providing for sexual arousal goes on all the time, it's just veiled. That's more of a manipulation than straight-out close-ups of the cock and the pussy and the juices and the sweat. My job doesn't have anything to do with 7-Up Michelob, new skis, or a hairdo! (Laughs) So I think they want to contro this. I don't know what they are afraid could happen if we became sexual free? That's the real question, what *are* they afraid of, what *is* that sense of breakdown, what *is* that fear? Who *are* they protecting with those kind of laws? (Laughs) I would tell them to come to the theater and just relax.

Tell us what you know about AIDS and describe the impact that it's having on your life and society. ~ Because I was involved in the gay community I was educated about AIDS at a fairly early point in the outbreak. Every day demonstrates to me our unwillingness to be rational about issues of sex, particularly sexuality that's not considered mainstream, and also the issue of drugs. There's this force that really does not want to deal with it, wants to put it away, wants to disown it, wants to deny it, wants to make it go away by locking it up...*it* actually being people with a terrible disease. And...that's really frightening.

The main thing I know about AIDS is that it can be prevented, and that prevention is a combination of specific actions protecting oneself biologically, and also dealing with things on a spiritual level. I come from the belief that all disease is a function of breakdown, not just the physical, that's when it's really getting bad. In terms of the impact on society, it points out the drastic breakdown that we are having. We've shit on gay people, we've shit on drug abusers, and the message we're giving them is, "Sorry, die. You deserve to die. You don't deserve to be informed, you don't deserve health care, you don't deserve to get hugged."

I left the gay community right when it became a big problem, so I didn't have much contact with friends. I know a lot of them are dead, and I grieve. Reading the *Names Quilt* book was a moving experience. Everyone should read it. It talks about the individuals, the sons and fathers and lovers who have died. It's a memorial and a statement that these are people.

Do you think it is possible that this society will confine those who test HIV positive in spite of the medical evidence that it is not casually transmitted? ~ It's possible. We're a crazy society. We've done outrageous things, and we need to acknowledge that possibility and face it head-on. It's no good to say, come on, nothing will happen. Look at the holocaust. We have to be committed to continue to be rational, to bring that topic up no matter how sick people are of hearing it, and ask them to state their commitment at the polls. That's what it's going to come down to, register and vote. People's fears motivate them to vote for those kind of proposals. They think that's going to protect their lives, and it won't.

What future do you see for erotic theater and erotic dancers? ~ I see it diversifying. I see dancers starting their own companies as they recognize that it's a profitable industry and that they are very in touch with what the customers want. One of the reasons it has declined is because sexually explicit media became more available to more people. It became less the studs' night out kind of thing. There's a definite niche that we fill that is irreplaceable.

The women will be educating the public about what their standards are, what they will provide, what they won't provide, and make a clear distinction about, "I am a prostitute," "I'm not a prostitute," "You can touch me," "You can't touch me." The stigma of being a dancer will be reduced, partly because it won't be women out of control of their lives. They'll be coming from choice. I am thinking specifically of the stigma that some feminists have laid on us.

Erotic dancers will be coming out of the closet. It's not that uncommon an experience. It's certainly not that uncommon a fantasy. As women begin to control the industry, women who would like to work there but are unwilling to work in a male dominated industry will be more comfortable.

I see politicizing and spiritualizing the whole process of erotic dance. I think every woman is an erotic dancer. That's a role we need to take back for our own, recognize the power of, and realize we have the choice of playing it or not. Recognize that it's a gift and healing for everybody involved. We need to recognize that dancing is erotic, and that having our clothes on or off is a false distinction. Someone can be very erotic with their clothes on, and somebody can not be very exciting even though they're naked. Hopefully we'll achieve a lot more freedom. And more orgasms!

ABOUT THE INTERVIEWER

Tim Keefe has worked as a chauffeur, hotel auditor, iron foundry furnace tender, lathe repairman, autoworker, college student, construction laborer, union organizer, baseball coach, book-store manager, deliveryman, community organizer, photojournalist, baker, cabbie, mental health therapist, public school teacher, foundation researcher, juvenile detention center teacher, county administrator, publisher, darkroom manager and peep show operator. He has co-authored two American histories and has begun work on a new book with his sons.